APPLYING LINGUISTICS IN THE CLASSROOM

Making linguistics accessible and relevant to all teachers, this text looks at language issues in the classroom through an applied sociocultural perspective focused on how language functions in society and in schools—how it is used, for what purposes, and how teachers can understand their students' language practices. While touching on the key structural aspects of language (phonetics, phonology, morphology, and syntax), it does not simply give an overview, but rather provides a way to study and talk about language.

Each chapter includes practical steps and suggests tools for applying different kinds of linguistic knowledge in classrooms. The activities and exercises are adaptable to elementary or high school settings. Many examples focus on the intersection of math, science, and language. Teacher case studies show how real teachers have used these concepts to inform teaching practices. Given the increasing use of multimedia resources in today's schools, multiple mediums are integrated to engage educators in learning about language. The Companion Website provides a multitude of relevant resources that illustrate the diversity of language functions and debates about language in society.

Engaging, practical, and informative, *Applying Linguistics in the Classroom* is an ideal foundational text for courses such as Linguistics for Teachers and Educational Linguistics, and for bilingual and ESL education courses and others addressing language, culture, and learning.

Aria Razfar is Associate Professor of Literacy, Language, Culture, Learning Sciences, Linguistics and Director of Bilingual/ESL Education at the University of Illinois at Chicago.

Joseph C. Rumenapp is a doctoral student in Language, Literacy, and Culture at the University of Illinois at Chicago.

APPLYING LINGUISTICS IN THE CLASSROOM

A Sociocultural Approach

By
Aria Razfar and
Joseph C. Rumenapp

Routledge
Taylor & Francis Group

NEW YORK AND LONDON

First published 2014
by Routledge
711 Third Avenue, New York, NY 10017

Simultaneously published in the UK
by Routledge
2 Park Square, Milton Park, Abingdon, Oxon OX14 4RN

Routledge is an imprint of the Taylor & Francis Group, an informa business

© 2014 Taylor & Francis

The right of Aria Razfar and Joseph C. Rumenapp to be identified as author of this work has been asserted by them in accordance with sections 77 and 78 of the Copyright, Designs and Patents Act 1988.

Library of Congress Cataloging-in-Publication Data

Razfar, Aria.
Applying linguistics in the classroom : a sociocultural approach / By Aria Razfar and Joseph C. Rumenapp.
    pages cm
  Includes bibliographical references and index.
    ISBN 978-0-415-63315-4 (hardback : alk. paper)—
ISBN 978-0-415-63316-1 (pbk. : alk. paper)—
ISBN 978-0-203-09519-5 (ebook) 1. Language and languages—
Study and teaching—Social aspects. 2. Language and culture—Social
aspects. 3. Applied linguistics. 4. Sociolinguistics. I. Rumenapp, Joseph
C., 1985– author. II. Title.

ISBN: 978-0-415-63315-4 (hbk)
ISBN: 978-0-415-63316-1 (pbk)
ISBN: 978-0-203-09519-5 (ebk)

Typeset in Bembo
by Apex CoVantage, LLC

Printed and bound in the United States of America by Sheridan Books, Inc. (a Sheridan Group Company).

CONTENTS

This book is dedicated to ALL the Teachers in our lives
Whose sacrifice is a beacon, that enlightens and thrives
From the cradle to the grave
Our Hearts they did save
To Our mothers and our fathers
Our Sisters and our Brothers
Our Uncles and Aunts
Who HEAR ALL our rants
Through thick and thin
And the predicaments we're in
To Our Children, through the bliss and the bother
To ALL of our significant OTHERS
Our Sisters and Brothers from OTHER Mothers
Special Shout out to the FLESH who departed
Struck down by the blindness of the hard hearted
Never forgotten, in ALL the words we write
Guided by HEART, and honed by sight
To Michael Elliott Lewis II "Noonaboone"
To Jeannie Rumenapp
Who gave us vision and light

PREFACE

This book is a foundational text for applying linguistics in school and non-school learning environments. While many of the examples come from the diverse linguistic and cultural landscape of the United States, the concepts, activities, and case studies are relevant to teachers who must engage "other people's" children everywhere. From phonology to ideology we consider how language mediates our lives, our learning, and our struggles to give coherence to the multiplicity of voices that surrounds us.

Our analysis of language answers critical questions that encompasses all of our language practices, including the code, what is said, performance, how it is said, semiotics, how people mean and how they make sense, and ideology, the values and worldviews indexed by language. These four questions carry us to a deep and thick understanding of language that goes beyond its FLESH and into its HEART. These questions lead us to a critical consciousness about an even more fundamental question: What is the nature, function, and purpose of language? It serves to show how the "linguistic," "cultural," and "ideological" are inextricably linked through practice across multiple timescales and across the life-span, in vertical and horizontal learning spaces.

In each chapter we develop the sociocultural and the critical approach to language and learning. We provide multiple tools and perspectives for teachers to reflect upon their practice and identities of their students. Beginning with phonology, we show how to do basic linguistic analyses to learn about second language learning. Later, we provide tools for larger social analyses of classrooms, homes, and neighborhoods to understand how they play a role in learning. Finally, we present ways to analyze social and cultural issues and how they are evident in classroom practices. To do this, we provide not only content, but rich examples, activities, and case studies of teachers we studied who applied these tools within their own classrooms.

This book empowers teachers to reclaim "linguistics" as their own. It enables them to consider linguistic function not only in terms of structure, form, and "flesh," but also in terms of relational meaning, function, and "heart." This meta-linguistic journey moves us through the embodied experience of language and into inspirited and inspired cognition. "Linguistics for Teachers" courses every-where will benefit from our practical methods to foster greater understanding of identity, affect, and relational functions of language and how it mediates learning for everybody. Our primary objective is to give prominence to the study of lan-guage in the lives of educators and to turn the linguistic stranger into a critical friend. As we engage other people's children and other people, we hope that the insights generated by this book will lead to embodied and inspired lives filled with life-long and life-wide learning built through semiotic struggles of solidarity.

ACKNOWLEDGMENTS

First, we would like to acknowledge all the reviewers for their excellent comments that helped shape this text. We would like to thank ALL of our tireless mentors, whose names are few, but beyond the reach of this page, who challenged us to think about language and learning in ways that matter for non-dominant populations everywhere. I (Aria) would like to thank all of my life-long and life-wide mentors at UCLA, USC, and beyond. I especially want to thank my doctoral advisor Kris D. Gutierrez for modeling rigorous, interdisciplinary, and resilient scholarship. I would like to thank Professor Robert Rueda for first introducing me to sociocultural approaches to language and learning. I would like to thank Pam Munro for helping me see the power of linguistics as a meandering undergraduate and directing me to the "Who's Who" of language study that makes a difference. First on this list is Paul V. Kroskrity who knocked the experimental linguistics out of me by showing me the way of language ideologies. Also, I (Joe) would like to thank my linguistics advisor Steven Clark for his dedication and continued mentorship.

We are greatly indebted to all our colleagues in the University of Illinois at Chicago (past and present). A heartfelt thank you to the past fellows and colleagues of CEMELA, who are indeed mi familia: your legacy is etched throughout this book. Another heartfelt thank you to my LSciMAct and now ELMSA who struggle 24/7 to bring real transformation through struggle and sacrifice to never quit making third spaces of learning: Dr. Beverly Troiano, Dr. Eunah Yang, and soon to be doctors Ambareen Nasir and Joe Rumenapp. Last but not least, we thank our families, my children (Aria), and ALL our communities, whose unwavering and unconditional support makes it all possible. We love you ALL!

1

LANGUAGE AS SOCIAL PRACTICE

Sociocultural Foundations of Discourse and Learning

LEARNING GOALS

1. Overview of the history of linguistics.
2. Understand the "social turn" and shift to sociocultural views of language.
3. Learn the seven-step hierarchy of language studies.
4. Learn the four guiding questions for discourse analysis.
5. Apply discourse analysis.
6. Connect discourse analysis to learning.
7. Understand learning as shifts in discursive identities and primary to secondary discourses.

KEY TERMS/IDEAS: autonomous/ideological models, code, discursive identity, language ideologies, IRE discourse, mediation, performance, primary/secondary discourse, prosody, semiotics, social turn, sociocultural learning

Introduction

> The heart has its own language. The heart knows a hundred thousand ways to speak.
>
> (Rumi)

A group of blind men, or "unenlightened men," walk into a dark room and touch an elephant. Each one feeling a different part not knowing that it was part of an elephant. One of them touches the leg, another touches the tusk, another touches the tail, and when they come out of the room and begin to describe what each of them felt, they fall into dispute as to what the "truth" is. Each firmly committed to his discrete part but also blinded by his subjectivity and egocentric perspective. As a consequence, each of them fails to see the whole, the "elephant" in the room. To see the elephant one must be enlightened by the language of the heart. To see the elephant the men should compare notes and HEAR the "other." When we rely only on the perspective of what is accessible by our senses—"the flesh"—then we can expect to experience a "failure to communicate." This ancient Persian folk tale from Jalaludin Rumi captures the essence of the journey of language we are about to embark on together.

Throughout this book we present a sociocultural and ideological view of language. We move from formal linguistics' emphasis on form and move into how language is shaped, and indeed, shapes our lived narratives. By examining the variation inherent in classrooms and beyond, our approach to language, cognition, and learning moves from embodied functions of a physical brain to inspired and inspirited functions of meaning, values, and "the heart." Language evokes deep-seated emotions, not in the ephemeral, chemically induced sense, but historic bonds of affinity, affiliation, and solidarity. This book presents the foundations of linguistics, *from phonology to ideology*, from embodied brain to inspirited mind/heart, in short this is a journey of language as flesh to language as heart. This journey is only possible through the lived narratives of educators struggling to make sense of their students, their communities, and their lives.

As a tool for teachers in classrooms, the book provides practical applications of linguistics in formal spaces of learning and instruction. While "linguistics" as a formal discipline sometimes feels beyond reach and bound by ivory tower brains, this book brings linguistics to the ground, using the sociocultural contexts of schools and society. We present ways to study language in classrooms and therefore provide opportunities for teachers to become "linguistic" professionals in their own right. This book serves as an opportunity to reclaim language for educators and the diverse populations they serve. Teaching, more than any other profession perhaps, demands a linguistics that doesn't get lost in the forest of tree diagrams since teachers and students, in any given moment, are concerned with language on multiple levels.

Sometimes, as teachers, we may wonder why a student is "mispronouncing" a word or re-inventing syntactic structures. Sometimes we may wonder why a student talks in a different or "non-standard" way. We may even judge these "incorrect" forms as less or more. Its meanings are strange, so how do we make the strange familiar? In order to answer this question we may have reconsider that which is familiar, and make it strange. This will allow us to see ourselves in the OTHER and begin the walk of solidarity. It will allow us to critically reflect on sociocultural and ideological points of coordination as well as points of contestation. These questions help us to better understand our students, ourselves, and as a consequence become better teachers. These questions will help us re-examine our ideas of "language" not simply as form, but sociocultural "discourse" organized by human activities that are goal directed, rule governed, and socially mediated.

Beginning with this chapter, we will kick off the broad ideas we seek to cover in this book. Then we will look at different views of linguistics as we study the relationship between the brain and language (Chapter 2). Next we will look at the structures of language and how they relate to classrooms, students, and curricula

(Chapters 3, 4, 5, and 6). In Chapter 7 we will begin to look at how language "means" by looking at semiotics, literacy (Chapter 8), language learning (Chapters 9 and 10), functions of language (Chapter 11), and narratives (Chapter 12). Finally, to return to this current chapter, in Chapters 13 and 14 we will present how language is related to wider values. Each of these chapters provides new ways to study language and approach learning in the classroom. So, without further delay, we begin with situating language as a social practice.

Learning the "Discourse"

Imagine you are at a casual get-together and overhear two people having a conversation that seems like it is in a completely different language. As you move closer, you realize it is indeed English, but you don't understand what they are talking about. It is almost as if that discussion is completely foreign. You try a little harder to follow along, knowing you understand the words they say, but you still know something more is being talked about that you are not grasping.

We attempted to simulate this experience in a teacher education class before. The class was split into groups based on their expertise in baseball. If they thought they were experts they were placed in one group and labeled "experts." Everyone else was a "BLL," or baseball language learner.

The professor (Aria Razfar) said, "now I am going to teach you the language of baseball," and proceeded to write down a list of terms and definitions on the board including: ball, bat, base, inning, at-bat, RBI, run, and several others. The professor and the experts began to talk about baseball, and occasionally a BLL would even chime in during the classroom conversation. A lot of names and politics and details were tossed around that essentially meant nothing to the BLLs. In fact, the BLLs in the class were quite bored, very quickly wondering, "what does this have to do with linguistics, teaching, or the ELLs in our classrooms?" The first group enjoyed the five minutes of discussion, counting it as an escape from the heavy academic day, but the BLLs just sat (mind you the TA in the class was in this group as well).

Finally, the professor stopped the conversation and offered an activity requiring a few basic math calculations. The class split off into small groups based on expertise in baseball and began working on the following math problem: "Barry Bonds, one of the most prolific home run hitters of the modern era, slugged over eight-hundred in one season. If he had six hundred at bats, how many total bases did he get?" (Razfar, 2012a, p. 55).

For the experts in the class, the question was completed very quickly (and they began to talk amongst themselves about baseball again). The other groups struggled much more. Some didn't even attempt to answer and just gave up while other groups had a variety of attempts including: $4*800 = 3200$ bases; $800/4 = 200$ bases. After the assignment was complete, the professor asked the expert group to perform the problem: $600*0.8 = 480$ bases.

Following this correct answer, the class was baffled, so the experts attempted to explain that the 800 was actually 800/1000, or 0.8. To find out how many bases

Bonds ran, they had to multiply this by 600 chances at bat, yielding 480 bases. The experts had trouble, however, explaining this to the BLLs. The teacher connected this experience to their ELL students in their classrooms, saying the following:

> Expert: It was so hard to explain to BLLs how this problem is solved without using baseball language. I think it is the same way when teaching math to ELLs, we need to be conscious of the language we are using. Also, it is very easy to give them the formula and assume they understand the problem because they can solve it using the formula. But that doesn't mean they know baseball or understand the language used in baseball.
>
> BLL: So, for example, just because I can solve this problem now it doesn't mean I really understand. Like if you give me the same exact problem with different numbers, sure I can solve it but if it is worded differently or if there is another baseball math problem I would be lost. So it's the same way with math. We can't assume that because our students solve something because they memorized a formula that they really understand it.
>
> Expert: Also, it was even harder to explain it to those BLLs that don't know anything about baseball so I can see how important it is for ELLs to be familiar with the context when working on a math problem and how they can learn the language of math in that context easier than in another context they are not familiar with.
>
> (Razfar, 2012a)

Surely we have all had an experience like this. We all have been lost in the conversation as people are talking past us and we have all had difficulties explaining certain concepts to others, even when they speak the same "language" we do. It may have been walking in on a conversation between two stock brokers or maybe you overheard your junior high daughter talking with a friend and had no idea what they were saying, but we have all been there. You understood the words, perhaps, but you could not follow the discussion. If you are honest, you probably thought that coming to a linguistics class would be the same.

In this next chapter we will attempt to give an overview of how the field of linguistics has developed over the years and how linguistics can be used in your classrooms. So, if you are an LLL (linguistics language learner), we urge you to keep learning the language used to talk about language. Chances are, you have students in your classrooms that feel very much the way you will on this journey.

A Brief History of Linguistics

Language: It's all in the Head

In response to psychologist B.F. Skinner's behaviorist model of thought, Noam Chomsky championed a cognitive approach to language. His views toward language revolutionalized the way in which it was studied and the working assumptions about the nature of language and the human mind. Prior to Chomsky's study of language, the discipline of linguistics largely looked at languages contrastively. Behaviorists talked about language learning the same way they described other aspects of human development. They viewed language as a set of learned behaviors that are the product of rote repetition, imitation, and a system of rewards and punishments. Linguists during this period did not talk about language in terms of its role in learning and development. They emphasized the differences in languages through contrastive analysis of grammatical forms and studied the historical evolution of written texts. They studied how languages change and how words relate to meaning.

Chomsky, however, took a much different approach to the study of language and introduced linguistics as a scientific study of language. This approach entailed the pursuit of universals, emphasized generalizations, and led to the study of how all languages were similar. He also tried to understand the nature of language; what it was; how it worked; why humans so naturally used it. His book *Syntactic structures* (1957) showed how a pure structural analysis of human syntax revealed that language cannot be adequately explained as learned behavior. He assumed that if language was so complex, there had to be some biological predisposition for children to acquire language.

According to Chomsky, the world's languages were so similar that a Martian visiting from outer space would quickly assume that there was only one language, the human language. He talked about language as "natural" and "innate." It was created in the mind by some type of "Language Acquisition Device." The theory that Chomsky spearheaded is known as *generative grammar*, indicating that grammar is generated by the child's brain. Grammar is actually created in the brain, or as Chomsky said, it "grows in the mind." Therefore, as grammar is discussed in linguistics, it takes on a much different meaning than when it is discussed in traditional English classes. Grammar in the context of linguistics is "descriptive," as it describes how people speak. Because the grammar is generated, linguists could map out the way language was used by speakers of a language to determine rules that could be used to describe the structure of the language. These rules were generated by the child's mind as he or she encountered language. As the brain picked up on the patterns in language, the part of the brain assumed to be responsible for language generated the rules. So, language is innate, or with the child, but the specific languages spoken by humans were generated based on what was spoken in one's childhood environment. Every child recreates or generates the language according to those rules that were acquired (Pinker, 1994).

Further evidence Chomsky and his followers, most notably Steven Pinker, put forth was that children learn language at an astonishing rate. No one has to teach the child how to speak in a correct sentence, she/her just seemed to know. It was as natural as the child learning to walk. The supporters of generative grammar conclude that because children learn language so fast, they must be programmed to speak language. It must be a biological and evolutionary trait that is unique to humans. An obvious observation to anyone who is around children is that children are not like parrots or a recording device. Children do not simply repeat what they hear (although we do have to be careful what we say around children!) but constantly come up with new and innovative sentences. They are capable of saying words that have never been said before, and words they certainly have not heard before. Since grammar has been built in the brain, all humans are able to generate an infinite set of new sentences. There is no limit to the number of sentences that can be spoken because every sentence is new, and every sentence follows the rules generated in the mind.

Talking Takes a Social Turn

As Chomsky and his Language Acquisition Device continued to win over dedicated followers, some scholars began to question his theory and fundamental assumptions about language. In the 1960s and 1970s, scholars began to view language as a culturally embedded practice, rather than an object in and of itself. Dell Hymes (1964) focused on the social aspects of language and is often credited as one of the major leaders of the "social turn" in linguistics. Sociolinguists and linguistic anthropologists took on a distinct focus of equity and social justice (Gumperz, 1972; Hymes, 1964; Labov, 1972; Smitherman, 1977).

   While the fields of linguistic anthropology and sociolinguistics began to flourish and inspire more authentic accounts of language, culture, and learning (especially in language arts and literacy). Many of these early scholars studied African American Vernacular English (AAVE) and the social implications of dialect (Smitherman, 1977; Wolfram, 1969). William Labov (1972) also studied the social implication of language varieties, specifically AAVE, more recently referred to as Ebonics, or African American English (AAE). These scholars were interested not so much how language worked as a system in and of itself, but rather how it was used as a cultural tool and social marker indicating the inequities between African-Americans and Caucasians.

   Another prominent area of research that arose from this social turn is the active pursuit of language preservation and revitalization (Skutnabb-Kangas, 2008). With the extinction of a language comes the loss of very specific knowledge. Certain ways of thinking or ways of knowing are lost when a language dies. The study of language contact, of language's place in the social world, is of central concern to many scholars who employ ethnographic and critical lenses to see how this change contributes to equity issues in the world (Holm & Michaelis, 2008). Revitalization programs sought to resurrect dead languages or preserve dying ones. Bernard Spolsky (1970), for example, studied how bilingual education was being used to maintain the Navajo language. Over time, the Navajo language was falling out of common use, especially amongst younger Navajo people. However, through bilingual education, it became possible to preserve the language and maintain its use in everyday tasks. Other notable languages with wide support of revitalization efforts include Hawaiian, Hebrew, and Gaelic. The *Ethnologue* (Lewis, 2009) catalogues all of the languages in the world, again, bringing the issue of linguistic and social groups to light. Later in this book we will look at language contact more explicitly since the very concept of language as a social practice has great implications for equity and justice issues.

The social turn also brought about a focus in the symbolic nature of language. Language, as we traditionally think of it, is one system of symbols out of many systems of symbols. Thus, linguistics took on an interdisciplinary approach to the study of language (Bundgaard & Stjernfelt, 2010). Scholars realized that the methodologies needed to study language could no longer be limited to observing the structure of language alone, but must include how humans make sense of the world by using language. This book will look at both the structural forms of language, but will also go beyond that. We will provide you with tools from different times in the history of linguistics to study the language use in your classrooms.

It is in this sociocultural tradition that we now find ourselves. Having learned from Chomsky and Pinker some important lessons for language study, we also find that those explanations do not sufficiently account for the contextual dependence of language or meaning. Their work does, however, provide helpful insight into analyzing the formal characteristic of language. The social turn provided numerous methods from many different fields to delve into how language is used and how people think about language. The notion of language was expanded to encompass systems of signs that are dynamic social and cultural practices. As we study language as a social practice, we will begin to see how language mediates learning in our classrooms. We will be able to study and think about how our students use language and how they think about language so that we can better understand how learning takes place in our classrooms.

Hierarchy of Language: From Linguistics to Applied Linguistics

Linguistics is usually studied in a progression of the structure of language, called code, beginning with the smallest units of language to the largest. Think about the term "decoding" used in reading, and this is a very similar concept. In addition to four different levels of structure, there are also three levels which consider the way language is used and what it means. The first four levels were of primary interest before the social turn described above. After the social turn, however, the top three levels became the primary interest. The transition from emphasis on scientific descriptions of language to language use in context is widely understood as a shift toward applied linguistics and its derivatives. Figure 1.1 shows the levels of linguistics as it is traditionally studied. In the following chapters we will dive into each of these levels to discuss how they are studied, what we can glean from studying them, and how studying these aspects of language can be useful in educational contexts. The gray area represents "applied" approaches to language where the focus is on use/ meaning.

Code, Performance, Semiotics, and Ideologies: Four Fundamental Questions

Before we begin our study of the structure, or form, of language, we first want to look at four fundamental questions that will be asked throughout the book. Together, these four questions will become a powerful tool, namely discourse analysis, to understand who our students are, what they know, and how we can become better teachers. The first question is oriented around code, or what people say. The second question relates to performance or how something is said (Duranti, 1997). The next two questions have been developed in Gee's (2008) research on discourse analysis and language ideologies. Semiotics is the question of what people mean. The fourth question really tries to get at the cultural and historical issues underlying meaning, or ideologies. Of central concern to teachers and researchers is that discourse analysis is one of the most important tools for organizing and assessing learning and development especially from a cultural historical perspective.

In this chapter we will walk you through an example of discourse analysis applied to a short conversation. Then we will discuss discourses, or ways of being in this world. Finally, this chapter will discuss how discourse analysis and discursive identities relates to learning contexts.

1. What Do People Say?

The first question, and perhaps the most obvious, is what do people say? For the moment we will look at the first four levels of the structure of language mentioned above. This is the formal aspect of language, called *code*. The study of phonetics begins this hierarchy. This is the study of speech sounds. Phonology or the study of how sounds are organized in a language is the next step. The third level is morphology, or the study of words and word formation. The fourth step is syntax, which is the study of the rules that govern sentence formation in a language. Together these four steps create what is referred to as the code of a language. When we think about code, really we are thinking about what people say. It is the

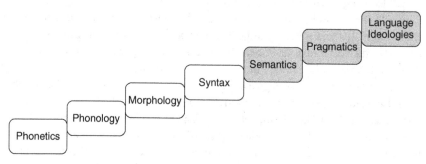

FIGURE 1.1 Seven Levels of Linguistics

structured study of language without respect to context. We will be using this idea of code to analyze some language samples so that we can see some of the benefits and limits of the tools used to analyze these levels of language.

While for linguists these utterances do not typically take place in naturalistic situations, the idea that this is the most descriptive aspect of language form applies, and all discourse analysis necessarily accounts for this dimension. More specifically, this refers to the most apparent features of language such as sounds, pronunciation (phonetic and phonological aspects), words (lexical choice), morphology, and grammar (syntax). If we extend this dimension to typical interactions, this would include the spoken utterances attributed to each speaker and the obvious turns that speakers take within an episode of talk.

STEP 1

1. Listen to the audio sample of a mechanic talking about the hydraulics of a car found on the accompanying DVD. Transcribe what is being said. Pay attention to the pronunciation, words, and grammar used by the mechanic.

2. Write about what is being said in this clip. Here are some questions to consider: What do you notice about the words that are used? What parts of speech are employed? Who is speaking?

   • The following is a transcription of the conversation:

   01 So if you wanted to make a car a lowrider, like make it so that it is lower.
   02 On a regular car you would actually have to do a lot of suspension
   03 work. One of the first things that you want to do- there are different
   04 things that you want to do. You can start with airbags where you
   05 compress the air. You know, and then they're actually bags itself
   06 where you just compress the air, it deflates em and increases the air
   07 and that'll make the car go up and down. The other one is
   08 hydraulics and that's actually based on fluid. Fluid is actually
   09 what's going to go through there. It's going to actually put pressure
   10 on the cylinder. Once the fluid puts pressure on the cylinder, the
   11 cylinder will go up. [inaudible] makes the cylinder go down. So

12 basically you have those two. Do you want to go with airbags or do

13 you want to go with hydraulics.

- Here is our analysis.

  If we were to analyze this brief exchange just based on the code, we can say that there are two speakers: one is asking a question and the other is responding. There appears to be a clarification in the initial question (line 1) where the concept of "lowrider" is extended, "like make it so that it is lower" (line 1). Structurally, the words that are being used are obviously English following basic rules of English morphology and syntax. The transcript clearly allows us to identify the various parts of speech (nouns, verbs, prepositions, etc.), word order, subject/object functions, modals, and even the logical connectors.

2. How Do People Say what they Say?

If the analysis were to stop here, it would clearly be insufficient in terms of the second and third questions that are central to discourse analysis which are: how do people say what they say? And what do they mean? The second question has historically been the domain of applied linguists and sociolinguists and traditionally referred to as *performance*. In general, this is actual language use in real communicative situations and is concerned with how speakers draw on contextual cues to communicate. In addition, performance also consists of prosodic dimensions of language use like tone, intonation, loudness, pitch, and rhythm. This can also include gestures, facial expressions, and other non-verbal acts which make transcription quite challenging and impossible without video. Prosody offers an initial glimpse into the affective stances speakers assume within discourse frames.

STEP 2

1. Watch the video that accompanies the audio sample from above. Now, note on your transcript how things are being said. Note if the words are drawn out or if rising intonation indicates a question. Note if any words take longer to say or if the speaker rushes or slows down. You might also want to take note of any visual cues that are important.
2. Write about and describe how things are being said. Analyze what you wrote down on the transcription and explain how the speaker is talking.

3.

- Here is an example we found:
  Consider the initial "question" from the same transcript except with more of the speakers' performance is transcribed:
  01 M: [So if you wanted to make a ca:::r (.5) a (.5) a low rider (rapid voice, falling intonation), li:ke (.5) ma:ke it so that it is lower.
  Kid: [kid nodding] [yeah]
- Here is our analysis of this example:
  Clearly, what initially looked like a question followed by a clarification for the mechanic appears to be some type of scaffolding directed at the kid. In comparing the first transcript with the second, one immediately notices the invisibility of the kid as we move from code to performance; hence, the importance of video (but still not sufficient as will be discussed later). The brackets represent overlapping talk whereby the graduate student assumes the floor interspersed with acknowledgements from the kid. Furthermore, there is clear hedging (deliberate pause followed by a rapid voice and falling intonation) surrounding the word "lowrider." If the kid has already acknowledged the use of the term lowrider and from previous turns and interactions all participants use the term freely, what is the purpose of the "clarification"?

3. What Do People Mean?

This leads to the central and arguably most contested interpretive question for discourse analysts and that is: What do people mean? If one assumes that meaning is fixed, absolute, and independent from the situation in which it occurs, then there is little argument; however, the central assumption of *semiotics* is that meaning is situated and necessarily dependent on the context in which the participants engage. In many typical teacher–student interactions, the teacher initiates a question, a student responds, and the teacher evaluates the correctness of the response. Cazden called this type of classroom discourse IRE (Initiation, Response, Evaluation) and the role of the participants is clearly defined: the teachers are the "knowers" and the students are "learners." However, in many real communicative situations the participants' roles are not as clearly defined and are fluid; furthermore, since speakers are assumed to be agents of meaning-making, they are expected to take on more active roles whereby they challenge, produce, and author the content of their talk, also referred to as *text*. These texts consist of all types of verbal, non-verbal, visual, auditory, and symbolic forms that are intended to be interpreted by a real or imagined audience. This more comprehensive notion of language and meaning-making has been referred to as *semiotics*.

Halliday (1993) explained that the process of learning is a semiotic process, built on the use of signs of which language is a prime example. It is through language use, meaning-making, and semiotic activity that our experiences become known to others and ourselves. At this point we are moving from what can be observed from listening and watching speakers to trying to understand the interaction and transaction between speaker and listener. When we talk about communication, we often take for granted that what we say and how we say it still must be understood and interpreted by the listener. How many times have you been misunderstood because "what you said" and "what you meant" were completely different? When we talk about this question of discourse analysis we are looking to see how people interpret signs and negotiate the meaning of signs. Signs, in this sense, include words, but certainly are not limited to verbal and written forms of language. In addition, participants invoke intentions and purposes that are hidden from the immediate and apparent discourse. In order to grapple with issues of purpose and intention, it is essential for us to have a historical understanding of how language use has evolved over time with specific discourse communities. Speakers often draw on multiple signs and symbols in multiple modalities available to them in order to achieve higher degrees of shared meaning or what Bakhtin called *intersubjectivity* (Holquist, 1990).

STEP 3

1. Review the video from above once more. Identify terms and speech patterns from the video and your transcription that might have negotiated meaning.
2. Write about how and why those terms and speech patterns might cause misunderstandings. What assumptions and identity associations might the speaker and listener not have in common?
- Here is an example of the terms and speech patterns we identified:
- We suspect the term "lowrider" to have specific historical roots not shared by speaker and listener. We also think that the hesitation recorded in the example above may indicate that the meaning and associations of "lowrider" is contested.
- Here are the questions we thought of about these terms:
  Does the graduate student, using the term "lowrider," share the same footing with the other participants? One might argue that the hesitation surrounding the word "lowrider" is not about referential meaning or shared understanding, but more about speech rights and identities indexed by the use of the term. Does the speaker feel a right to freely use the term "lowrider"? Does the speaker have a discourse affinity with the term?

4. "How Do Values, Beliefs, and Social and Institutional Relations of Power Mediate Meaning?"

The final component of discourse analysis involves the critical dimension of language use. Every act of meaning-making, language use, discourse, and interpretation must be viewed through the prism of values, beliefs, social, and institutional relations of power, or language ideologies. The importance of this question with respect to discourse analysis cannot be underscored enough. It is the central question when it comes to understanding how some practices are more valued, privileged, and attributed greater legitimacy than others. Identities and ideologies become foregrounded in the analysis of talk and text. Street (2003) calls this the *ideological* model of literacy. In contrast to *autonomous* views of language, the ideological model of language and literacy views meaning-making as fundamentally context driven and grounded in the values of the language users. The autonomous model essentially treats language as independent from context and issues of power. When we treat any kind of symbolic system as universally true, then we are, in practice, invoking an autonomous perspective of language. This is very apparent in our assumptions about numbers and mathematical concepts. For example, the decimal system we use to count and perform everyday arithmetic and accounting functions may be viewed as normative and universal; however, this is not the case. We will later explore some of the important work done in the field of ethnomathematics. The ideological principle could very well apply to almost any area of knowledge or meaning that is assumed to be fixed and absolute. Any time talk is analyzed we must consider how power relations impact the role and identity of the speakers making claims. This leads to questions such as: How do speakers position themselves as experts or novices of knowledge within discourse? How are speech rights negotiated (i.e., who has the right to speak and what kinds of claims are allowable to the participants)?

STEP 4

1. Think about the example we have been working through. Think about the identities each of the participants take on through the conversation. Think about issues of power, even at the institutional level.
2. Write about who these people are and why they may talk the way they do. Who is the expert? What does it mean to be an expert? In what contexts is that expertise valued?
3.
- Here are some things we observed:
  We identified the first speaker as a graduate student, the second as a mechanic. Mechanics are the experts when talking about cars. We

want to know the role of the kid, the status assigned, if the mechanic honors the kid's non-verbal cues, and so forth.

- This is a sample of our analysis:

The mechanic is the expert on cars, and noticing the way in which he speaks this is clear, however as indicated before, the hesitation around "lowrider" may indicate that the mechanic does not perceive the kid as equal status. He clearly assumes the powerful role as knowledge broker as he attempts to explain how to make a car a "lowrider." The fact that the mechanic is entertaining the kid's question, however, may seem to contradict conventional social norms that adults don't engage in such interactions with kids. Thus, the response to the kid's question may be seen as empowering since the mechanic views the kid as a conversation partner. This needs to be revisited in light of other social and institutional identities and power issues.

As we journey toward better understanding the meaning-making of ourselves and others, it is important to bear in mind that answering these fundamental questions of discourse analysis is nearly always an approximation. Our goal is to develop the most authentic account that is possible, always checking our analysis with focal participants as well as considering alternative and even counter interpretations. While the search for authenticity seems elusive, it remains the constant objective. Our analysis of discourse is always tentative and revisions are expected. As new questions, interpretations, and perspectives emerge, so will the need to revise. We must assume that no matter how strange or unfamiliar, what is said and/ or not said is purposeful and meaningful for participants even if the purpose is to deceive researchers and onlookers. In the words of the late Clifford Geertz (1973):

Believing, with Max Weber, that man is an animal suspended in webs of significance he himself has spun, I take culture to be those webs, and the analysis of it to be therefore not an experimental science in search of law but an interpretative one in search of meaning. It is explication I am after, construing social expression on their surface enigmatical.

(pp. 4–5)

The process of interpreting the meaning-making of people is continuous, subject to constant revision, and dependent on how much of an ethnographic perspective the analysis is based on. A teacher as an ethnographer (Moll, Amanti, Neff, & González, 1992) is a powerful metaphor that brings together the aims of discourse analysis and the practitioner in the classroom. All types of meaning-making in typical school subjects areas such as mathematics, science, social studies, history, and language arts are viewed in this light. In the remainder of this chapter, and ultimately this book, we will explore how discourse analysis can be a valuable tool for understanding learning practices as situated local cultural contexts and symbol systems.

Primary vs. Secondary Discourses

When one considers the four dimensions/questions of discourse analysis raised above, it becomes evident that the notion of discourse (as opposed to "language") affords a more holistic view of human meaning-making. Discourse analysts have long argued that learning itself is best understood as shifts in discourse over time, especially the appropriation of discursive identities (Gee, 2008; Wortham, 2003). Discursive identities are those identities that are displayed through language use. For example, in the IRE sequence previously mentioned, a teacher displays her identity as "a teacher" through the type of question she asks followed by the student response and teacher evaluation. In fact, if we were to close our eyes and listen to the sequence of talk, we would immediately conclude that "this is a typical classroom" without observing the physical arrangement of a classroom. Of course, becoming a teacher and talking "teacherese" takes time and is evidence of successful socialization in the community of teachers. The shift in discursive identities is one of the most powerful ways teachers can assess learning as a sociocultural phenomenon rather than solely depending on individual and decontextualized measures of learning (Rogoff, 2003). Or, think back to the baseball example. Even though the definitions for all of the terms needed to solve the problem were given first, some of the teachers still did not know how to do the problem. One student said:

> I used to think that just having a dictionary with all the math terms along with the math book would be enough for an English learner to understand what the book says. When we did the activity in class and we went over the terms of baseball before being given the problem, I still was not able to understand exactly what the question was asking even though it was in English.
>
> (LaFrance, 2007)

So what kinds of discourse constitute classroom learning? More generally, where do formalized discourses (i.e., those that are learned in schools) fit in relation to "everyday" discourses? While human beings undergo a life-long process of language socialization, not all discourses are equivalent both in terms of the process and purpose of appropriation. Discourses that seem more natural or are appropriated as a result of spontaneous interaction, like our native "national" languages (i.e., Spanish, English, etc.), are distinct from those that are appropriated through participation in formalized institutional settings (i.e., biological nomenclatures, formulas, etc.). With regards to this distinction there is a clear delineation between *primary* discourses and *secondary* discourses (Gee, 2008). This distinction is important as we consider the features of what constitutes discourses such as mathematics, sciences, histories, languages, and other subjects valued by the educational communities in schools. According to Gee, primary discourses "are those to which people are apprenticed early in life during their primary socialization as members of particular families within their socio-cultural setting" (Gee, 2008, p. 168); and secondary discourses are "those to which people are apprenticed as part of their socialization within various local, state and national groups and institutions outside early and peer group socialisation, for example, churches, schools, etc." (Gee, 2008, p. 168). Secondary discourses have the properties of a more generalizable cultural model, are more explicitly taught, and are less dependent on the immediate situation for access by a larger audience. If we consider algebraic discourse as an example of discourse appropriated through school, then the symbol "x" in $x + 2 = 7$ is understood by algebraic discourse community members as representing the unknown. Members of this community may also assume that in this case x has a single value and they must follow certain rules to find the answer (all school-like practices). For those who have appropriated "Microbiology" discourses a bacterial strand such as E. coli is more than just an arbitrary name. There is a hierarchical system of classification underlying the label where the name of the genus is followed by the species. These literacies serve as mediational tools in novel problem-solving situations and "the more abstract the literate mathematical discourse, the greater its potential as a widely generalizable problem-solving tool." (Sfard, 2002).

These types of "formal" mathematics and scientific discourses would qualify as secondary discourses. This does not, however, mean that primary discourses are separate and unrelated to the development of secondary discourses; in fact, it is quite the opposite: secondary discourses are best developed in relation to primary discourses. This is especially important as we examine connections between learning in formal and informal settings. Both mathematics and science could be considered specialized secondary discourses developed by people for specific purposes, as can normal everyday practices such as running, driving, cooking, shopping, playing video games, and so forth. It is important to explicitly define the discursive markers of each in order to have such a phenomenon as playing a game or doing a math problem or having a conversation about what counts as a scientific activity or who can call themselves a runner, and so forth. For example, one possible definition is that mathematics is a special type of discourse that deals with quantities and shapes (i.e., a secondary discourse); however, there are many ways in which this can be done depending on the context as many studies have shown (e.g., Cole, 1996; Lave, 1988; Scribner & Cole, 1981). While this definition (or any definition) of a domain of knowledge is not without contestation and would undoubtedly be considered a narrow definition of what counts as math, it is an example of one way that mathematics discourse distinguishes itself from other forms of talk. We will come back to the topic of mathematics and science later in the book to apply these concepts more completely. For now, however, we want to establish that domain areas with agreed-upon markers and boundaries are discourses, or "languages" by which we identify who we are individually and communally. Discourses are the very way in which we mediate reality. We are who we are by our affinities with different discourse communities, and those discourse communities have discursive markers which we can identify.

Connecting Discourse to Learning and Development

In connecting sociocultural views of learning with the discourse analysis issues discussed above, there are five issues to consider throughout this book in order to better appreciate discourse analysis as a tool for assessing learning and development over time and across multiple contexts. We will demonstrate these principles of learning throughout the book, but here is a brief introduction. First, all learning and meaning-making occurs in the context of organized activities with a discernible goal (Wertsch, 1998). Second, all learning is mediated through the use of signs and symbols, with language being the most important meditational tool. Third, learning can be best understood as movement through the zone of proximal development (ZPD), where the ZPD represents the gap between what a learner can do individually with what they can do with assistance. Furthermore, as learners move through a ZPD and become increasingly independent or exhibit greater self-regulation, they depend less on actions, objects, and context to make meaning; hence, they are able to participate in more abstract language practices. This move to abstraction of concrete experiences is described as a shift in the action/object to meaning ratio (Vygotsky, 1978, 1987). This leads to the fourth component which is the move from situated discourses to literate discourses. Finally, rather than thinking about how learning "transfers" to novel problem-solving situations, we consider how discourses are reorganized in new contexts. This distinction allows us to think about learning as continuous across time and space.

According to Vygotsky (1987), all learning proceeds from the interpersonal plane toward the intrapersonal plane through mediation, the active use of symbolic and visual artifacts. The material and ideational tools that human beings draw on are historically and socially constituted and become organized as "Discourses" across generations of actors. In his work on children in play situations, Vygotsky argued that one of the primary measures of development are the shifts

FIGURE 1.2 The Shift in Action—Meaning Ratio

in the action—meaning ratio. In the early stages of learning, the object, the action, or the situation dominates the child's ability to make meaning. For example, the presence of a cup filled with some type of liquid would prompt a child to say "water" because the object/action/situation dominates the use of signs and symbols which are highly context dependent in the early stages of development. However, over time the meaning of the sounds "water" become less dependent on the presence of actions, objects, and situations. Through the mediation of more expert others and the use of symbolic tools, learners develop the ability to regulate meaning without relying on the presence of objects and actions as presented in Figure 1.2.

Once learners exhibit command over meaning, it is said they have appropriated the discourse. In other words, they are able to use language in culturally appropriate ways as collectively determined by the community of language users. At this point discourse functions, such as knowing the nuances of greetings or economic exchanges, feel "natural" when used in real communicative situations. The appropriation of primary and secondary discourses happen in much the same way with one difference: secondary discourses represent a greater level of abstraction which means the ratio of action to meaning is slanted toward meaning. This gives secondary discourses the added utility of having cross-situational applicability. However, when we conceptualize subjects in school as "discourse," then it follows that you cannot reach more abstract levels without the mediation of objects, actions, and prior concrete experiences. A clear implication of this point is how sometimes school-based learning is organized as detached activities (imagine arbitrary vocabulary lists with dictionary definitions).

If we begin to think of schooling, and learning more generally, as the movement from our primary discourses to a secondary discourse, one that is more abstract and symbolic, we will see that for learning to happen we need to mediate this transition. This shift can be aided by teachers, people with more expertise, who understand what learners' primary discourses are and how to mediate the socialization into secondary discourses valued in society. Table 1.1 illustrates how primary and secondary discourses compare with respect to development, the types of mediation, durability, and ranges of applicability. Figure 1.3 emphasizes the dialectical relationship between primary and secondary discourses.

TABLE 1.1 Comparison of Primary and Secondary Discourses (Sfard, 2002)

Characteristic	Primary discourse	Secondary discourse
Development	Spontaneous	Through reflection, that is, at meta-level with respect to the primary
Mediation	Predominantly physical	Predominantly symbolic
Durability	Transient	Lasting
Applicability	Highly restricted	Universal

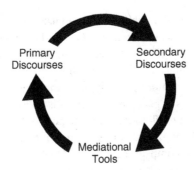

FIGURE 1.3 Interdependence of Primary and Secondary Discourses

Discourse and Learning: The MASS System

Gee offers a framework for discourse analysis for educators in any setting that effectively integrates the key elements of discourse analysis and sociocultural theories of learning and development. The MASS system has four components (Material, Activity, Semiotic, and Sociocultural). Each of these dimensions of meaning-making can occur in one of two scenarios: 1) situated types of meaning and 2) more abstracted cultural models. Social languages are distinct from other types of language (i.e., national languages) in that they immediately draw our attention to the context and purpose of language use.

Activity

Gee compares two language samples that basically convey the same information; yet, have very distinct purposes and thus count as two social languages:

1. Experiments show that Heliconius butterflies are less likely to ovipost on host plants that possess eggs or egg-like structures. These egg mimics are an unambiguous example of a plant trait evolved in response to a host-restricted group of insect herbivores. (professional journal)
2. Heliconius butterflies lay their eggs on Passiflora vines. In defense the vines seem to have evolved fake eggs that make it look to the butterflies as if eggs have already been laid on them. (popular science)

   1. How would you describe sample 1? How would you describe sample 2?
   2. What are the discourse markers that index these two communities and value systems?

Many would describe sample 1 as being more "academic" or more "scientific" when Razfar (2012a) posed these questions to a group of future mathematics researchers and educators. When pushed a little further to identify the discourse markers that index academic or scientific values, some pointed to extra-textual issues such as the genre of the publications (popular science vs. professional journal), thus, the differing discourse communities. Others noted that the language used in sample 1 required greater degree of abstraction from the situation. For example, the choice of subject "experiments show" vs. "butterflies lay" transforms a single observation into a more generalizable proposition. The lexical choice in sample #1 refers to classes of plants and insects. It is no longer about what a single instance of Heliconius butterflies do, but what can be concluded about all Heliconius butterflies. Some pointed that there is an unnecessary formality to sample # 1 especially when one compare "egg mimics" to "fake eggs." This might be indicative of the nominalization tendency of mathematics and scientific discourses to use nouns rather than adjectives and nouns (Morgan, 1998; Pimm, 1987, 1995). Sample #1 is also better suited for predicting future behavior which is a value of scientific discourse. Sample #2 is more descriptive and observable and does not require additional inductive reasoning beyond the situation. By examining the two samples it became evident that the difference between samples #1 and #2 is about not only the linguistic forms but also represent differentiated learning and thinking (i.e., higher order cognition). Both samples can be considered part of the scientific process with the discursive form of sample #1 representing a more durable and universal type of discourse (secondary discourse). The empirical question one might ask, especially if we consider the importance of discursive identities in learning, is which form would a child have more affinity with? This is a critical question for discourse researchers and practitioners because discursive identity, who does a person project themselves to be socially through discourse, is a powerful purveyor of learning and development (from Razfar, 2012a).

Using the MASS system the central unit of analysis for understanding learning and development has four parts:

1. Material: The who and what in an interactional frame (the actors, place, social space, time, and objects present (or referred to) during an interaction).
2. Activity: What's happening and how is it organized?
3. Semiotic: What are they using to make sense and communicate? (This includes gestures, images, or other symbolic systems).
4. Sociocultural: What are participants thinking, feeling, and being?

Summary: Where We've Been and Where We're Going

So far, in this chapter, we have seen how the field of linguistics has developed from the minds of Chomsky to the social contexts of Hymes. We have begun to expand the notion of language from discrete national languages like English, Spanish, and Chinese to the social languages, or discourses of our daily lives. The very tools that linguists have used to study language have been built upon and added to in order create the powerful tool discourse analysis. This method has been applied to talk in a way that we can see the different layers of meaning, identity, and power.

As a tool for teachers in schools, researchers in the field, and inquisitive people watchers on park benches, discourse analysis brings the field of linguistics to a practical and engaging place where we can begin to understand language and its use in context. As we move on in this book we will continue to build more specific understandings and refine our tools to become more reflective and better equipped researchers, teachers, and language users. We will create a way to talk about language and discourse. We will connect the dots of code, performance, meaning, and ideologies.

QUESTIONS/ACTIVITIES

1. What discourses have you partially or fully mastered?
2. Describe features of the discourse that marked membership.
3. Which discourses do you consider "primary" and which ones do you consider "secondary"?

2

NEUROLINGUISTICS

Rethinking Language in the Flesh

LEARNING GOALS

1. Identify the biological components of the brain usually associated with language.
2. Identify major disorders, illnesses, symptoms, and causes affecting language learning and use.
3. Summarize recent research on neurolinguistics.
4. Understand different theories within neurolinguistics and language learning.
5. Identify differences between deafness, aphasias, and cognitive disabilities.
6. Summarize the learning and the critical age hypothesis.

KEY TERMS/IDEAS: neurolinguistics, Broca's aphasia, cognition, embodied cognition, epigenetics, Wernicke's aphasia

Introduction

Neurolinguistics is the study of how language processes are connected to the brain. It combines the fields of neuroscience as well as cognitive linguistics. Neuroscience as a whole is mostly concerned with the physical and biological aspects of language. Its approach to language and learning is for the most positivistic which means it aims to dissect language into experimentally isolatable variables which is a problematic starting point. This lends itself to a "FLESH" based perspective on cognition and language where questions related to interaction, culture, history, and ideology are ignored at best and rejected at worst. The central questions of *what is language?* and *what is the nature, function, and purpose of language?* are answered in terms of code and performance (questions 1 and 2 from Chapter 1). For the most part, there is little attention to questions 3 and 4 outlined in Chapter 1: the *semiotic* and *ideological* dimensions of language, the "HEART" of language.

Given its assumptions of human nature and nurture as external to cognitive activity, language is reduced to an internal, intrapersonal process where meaning making and relational aspects such as affect/affinity in the sociocultural sense are often not taken into account. Furthermore, the notion of context within neurolinguistic approaches is virtually zero. Neurolinguistics draws heavily on biological and cognitive sciences where the brain is treated as a self-contained, independent entity. The dominant metaphor of mind is *embodiment*, whereby all cognition is rooted in physical, sensory experience. The brain is like an advanced machine that executes complex yet ultimately binary logical algorithms that reduce all thought to a series of 1s and 0s, ON or OFF, TRUE or FALSE. It is assumed that language and cognition are inseparable with some suggesting that cognition is bound by language.

In this chapter, we will review some of the typical ways in which neurolinguistics and cognitive neuroscience more generally has approached the study of language and human development. It is important to note that the field is emerging and dynamic, undergoing major transformations with the advancement of new technologies especially related to the study of electromagnetic fields, synaptic networks, and neurological processes. Much of the insights from neuroscience are relatively new. Most linguistic programs do not cover neurolinguistics and neuroscience; however, we think it is important to know about this emerging field of language study, both its possibilities and limitations.

The study of the relationship between language and the brain, language and thought, as well as cognition and mind, are long-standing philosophical questions that have started to receive scientific attention through the development of neuroscience. On the surface, this has been both a welcome and challenging development for sociocultural approaches to language and learning. Since neuroscience privileges a sensory and flesh based approach to language, there has been a tendency to want to explain ALL of language and cognition through the prism of CAT scans, fMRIs (functional magnetic resonance imaging), and other electrode induced methods. After all, it is difficult to employ these devices in naturalistic and longitudinal interactional frames. Authentic human language use is nearly impossible to examine under experimental conditions. The experimental conditions become the context and activity system of the interaction. We should remember one of the early critiques of experimental approaches to human language: children being observed in a lab are displaying the language and actions of "children being observed in a lab."

Despite these challenges, the developments in neuroscience should not entirely be viewed as an affront to the sociocultural and ideological foundations of language. In fact when the lessons of neuroscience are combined with the lessons of *epigenetics*, the sociocultural and ideological view of language becomes more compelling. Epigenetics is an emerging, yet alternative scientific view of genetics that is not deterministic and privileges the centrality of interaction in language and human development. This chapter has immediate and long-term implications for teachers. Given the importance of metacognition and metalinguistic awareness, discussion of neurolinguistic research addresses the following issues: (1) since much of the current language and learning policies are influenced by neuroscience, teachers need to be critical consumers of this research; (2) when we critically think about learning and its relationship to cognition we can be informed advocates for our students; and (3) by understanding the assumptions of this work, we can have another lens by which to assess learning and academic performance; (4) finally, it is important to consider how neuroscience impacts our understanding of ontological questions such as: what does it mean to be a human being. This question puts us in a continuum of human being as advanced animal bound by biology and detached reasoning or human being as an aesthetic and metaphysical being asking questions about its existence and purpose in life. This undoubtedly impacts how we view our students: Do we see them as implied mechanistic brains carrying out arbitrary computations? Or, are they human beings acting, being acted upon, and struggling with their hearts and minds to author meaningful lives?.

The Brain and Language

Many different methods have been proposed to study the complex relationship between language and the brain. The most difficult challenge about scientific studies of the brain is the fact that it is impossible to directly observe "thoughts." Even if we can get in the head to study the biology of the brain, there is no direct access to thoughts. For most of human history, externalized language in the form of speaking, writing, and paralinguistic devices were/are the principal ways of accessing thoughts. Of course, it is not the actual thoughts themselves but a representation of thoughts, a snapshot of the effects of thoughts. With modern technologies such as fMRIs and CAT scans, we can now measure the physical properties of brain activity. These technologies, however, are expensive and difficult to use. They are housed in laboratories and hospitals with little connection to authentic communicative situations. Thus, many old-school methods are actually the preferred method for studying language and cognition as it unfolds in its natural environment.

One prominent way to study cognition is through eye movements. Eye movements have been helpful in many different areas of work including therapy, linguistics, and cognitive studies. In fact, within popular, folk science, people assume that someone will look to the left if they are lying. While this is obviously not a failsafe lie detector, cognitive scientists have found that, generally, people do unintentionally gaze in certain directions when performing different mental tasks. For instance, one of the early empirical neurolinguistic studies argued that right-handed people have predictable eye gazes when accessing their memory (Bandler & Grinder, 1979). Table 2.1 presents some general findings found across a number of studies in this field.

Table 2.1 shows that there are generalities in the way people's eyes move during a given mental activity. These studies did not take into account variation in

TABLE 2.1 Eye Movement Patterns and Cognition

	Looking to the left	*Looking to the right*
Looking up	While imagining an image.	While remembering an image.
Looking parallel	While imagining audio information.	While remembering audio information.
Looking down	While remembering a feeling or action.	While having an internal dialog.

interpretation, the sociocultural context of subjects, and relied on the assumption of homogeneity of people. They concluded that imagination and visualizing of images led to eye movement in an upward and leftward direction. Similarly, they will look directly to the left if imagining or constructing auditory information. Contrarily, when remembering concrete events, the eyes will gaze to the right. Thus, there seems to be some validity to the folk theory that people that lie will look to their left. With a peer, imagine the following six thought experiments and record how your partner's eye movements:

1. Think about a pink elephant.
2. Think about the color of your first house.
3. Think about the sound of a UFO with Martians on board.
4. Think about the sound of your mother's voice.
5. Think about how a piece of sandpaper feels.
6. Think (seriously) about the pros and cons of moving to Australia for a job offer.

Eye movement patterns have not been limited to memory and imagining alone. There have been a number of studies that have examined the connection between eye movement, reading, and information processing. Think about a magazine cover. Where are your eyes drawn to first? Where to second? As you read this paragraph, what is your eye actually looking at? Contrary to some of our common sense understandings and "folk" theories of reading, our eyes do not smoothly scan words on a page in a linear fashion. The evidence suggests that we rarely see individual letters and words when we read. Instead, we tend to subconsciously chunk phrases and anticipate the shapes of the words. There are instances when we focus on letters and words. This tends to happen when we are engaged in metacognitive and metalinguistic activity whose purpose is to focus on structure or some type of error in pronunciation or comprehension.

The movement of the eyes, however, should not be correlated solely with cognition since other physical stimuli-response factors are also at play. It is empirically difficult to isolate cognition from other physical responses. We would need direct access to the brain if we really wanted to understand thoughts in action. How can we hear the "voices" or "images" in one's head? As of today such technology only exists in the movies, which is not to say it is impossible to have such tools in the future. One methodological challenge in neuroscience is that observing the brain at work requires non-invasive procedures. This has become more palatable with PET/CAT scans and fMRI scans as the brain is engaged in simulated cognitive tasks. Prior to these technological advances, brains were studied in surgeries or posthumously after tragedy and trauma, but still they could never show how cognition unfolded in the brain. These new machines have been used to observe the same phenomenon: physical manifestations of thinking and brain activity. This specific type of cognition is induced in laboratory conditions. It could not be observed without prompting, which occurs through language.

One of the methods used to examine cognitive functions was through the use of the *positron emission tomography* or more commonly known as *PET scan*. PET scans are conducted by injecting (or otherwise administering) small amounts of radioactive material. When there is increased chemical activity in the brain, either due to disease or increased stimuli, the radioactive material will gather (Mayo Clinic, 2011). For example, as research subjects are tested with flashing words to read or engaged in prompted speaking activities, the PET scanner registers where the chemicals in the brain accumulate. This would, by experimental design, indicate that the areas activated were more responsible for the cognitive task being administered.

A much newer technology is the *functional magnetic resonance imaging* scanner, or the fMRI. These machines are large tube-like structures that use magnets to scan the body, often used to produce a 3D image of the body or a part of the body for close analysis. Increasingly, it is being used to look at things like brain function by mapping the changes in the blood flow of the brain. Functional MRI (fMRI) scans are presented similarly to PET scans, however, instead of giving the participant small amounts of radiation and then scanning for the radiation, the fMRI shows images of oxygen moved by blood flow. So, increased activity in the brain would require more oxygen from the blood, and hence more blood would be allocated to these areas. The fMRI would show this, but the same basic method would be used (Noll, 2001). The brain would be observed while performing a linguistic related actions (listening, speaking, and reading), and then they would subtract baseline data established while the brain is in a resting state. The remainder in the images reveals the active area that was related to the language actions.

There are still philosophical questions as to whether these scans reveal consciousness. They may show physical reactions to stimuli, which could, in some circles, be defined as cognition. However, consciousness is another issue altogether. In most studies of this type, human cognition is supposed to be observed through the physical, traceable effects on the brain. Thus, in each of these various types of research, parts of the brain can be seen being activated when certain activities are happening or have happened. So, if a person is asked to read words flashing across a screen, certain parts of the brain appear to be active. There generally is a delay in the observed effect and the actual cause, which is presumed to be thoughts delivered through linguistic actions.

The fundamental question remains, how do we separate the thought from its linguistic delivery mechanism? One way this is done is through the different modalities of language like comprehension and production. If subjects are asked to read words out loud, other parts are activated. This presumably filters out the activity related to the physical coordination of language. By subtracting the second image from the first, we are left with only those parts of the brain that are activated by the motor act of speaking out loud. One critique of this method is that it assumes a brain that compartmentalizes cognition. Cognition is in one place and the control of sensory-motor functions is happening in another place. The problem is, even in the most controlled experimental conditions, it is impossible to reduce cognition to a single stimulus. "Think" about it, can we imagine having just one thought in our heads at a time? It is likely that the subjects in the study, while watching the words flash, trigger other thoughts related to their lives. If we were to account for more complex thinking like saying a synonym while we see a word flashed, you can, perhaps, pinpoint where language occurs in the brain.

Neurolinguistics and Bilingualism

From a cognitive approach to language, language, whether one language or more than one, is compartmentalized somewhere in the brain. The traditional cognitive view of monolinguals and bilinguals is essentially the same. In both cases language is stored in a special language area of the brain and the main difference between a monolingual and bilingual is that a bilingual is essentially "two monolinguals in one" (Grosjean, 1989). One of the major consequences of this view is bilinguals become defined by their fluency or balance in both languages. They may be "true" or "balanced" bilinguals if they know both languages equally well. It is impossible to measure languages; furthermore, most bilinguals do not know both languages the same way. As a result, they would be held in a deficit view of not really being bilingual. If languages were indeed separate in a person's mind, then any contact between them, like code switching for example, would be viewed as a problem. If bilinguals are viewed as two monolinguals combined, and their language competence is assessed separately, then all of the interaction between the languages is ignored.

An alternative to the compartmentalized view of bilingualism is an integrative view of multilingualism and the mind. Bilinguals and multilinguals are not the sum of two parts, instead all languages are nested within each other and embedded throughout the brain. Their language competency cannot be assessed as a monolingual, but rather as a specific bilingual. Each of the languages have situated purposes, but the use of one over the other doesn't mean they are separate. We also often use hybrid linguistic forms, where new combinations of two languages are used to perform a wide variety of functions like cooking, relationship building, and even academic literacy. Thus, looking at the bilingual as speaking two different languages monolingually inhibits our understanding of the complex interactions between the languages in the mind.

Often, traditional views of cognitive science do not take into account these different situated practices of bilinguals. For example, if a bilingual person has suffered damage to the brain through a stroke, as in the case of aphasias, their linguistic limitations must be assessed based on competencies in which each language is used. The limitation of many forms of cognitive science is that they do not fully examine the context of language use. However, one area that the cognitive sciences, specifically neurolinguistics, have provided much insight in is language impairment.

Language Impairments

The subject of "language impairment" and its twin cousin "speech pathology" are controversial topics in the study of language and learning. As one can imagine, the controversy is rooted in the fundamental assumptions about language. If language is viewed as being housed in compartments within the brain, then it follows that if those physical parts of the brain are damaged, then language is damaged or impaired. Thus, to repair language pathology means to consider the problem a disease that is sometimes curable and other times not. Either way, a "disease," or "pathology," is a serious condition requiring special care, quarantine, and hospitalization. Given this assumption, and the studies conducted under this premise of language and learning, the research on impairment is inconclusive. They have, however, mapped out different areas of the brain based on purposes and function. This has given us some idea of how our brains coordinate some actions, thoughts, and perform a complex array of functions. We have gained most of these insights, not as the brain performs these actions, but after the fact. It is usually when something goes drastically wrong, in terms of language use, that cognitive scientists inductively reason and hypothesize what areas of the brain might be causing the observed problems.

We will review a couple of language disabilities that have led cognitive scientists to locate language in localized areas of the brain, but first, Figure 2.1 shows where the cognitive scientists have found to be associated with various functions of language.

One of the major language impairments is called *aphasia*. There are actually many types of aphasias and many causes. According to the National Aphasia Association, any damage to the brain that results in language impairment is termed aphasia. However, aphasia impairs speech and communication more generally. It can affect both the production of language (speech, writing, or signs) and/or

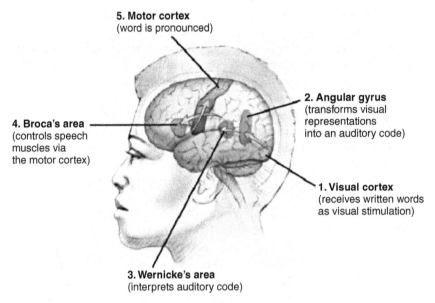

5. Motor cortex
(word is pronounced)

2. Angular gyrus
(transforms visual
representations
into an auditory code)

4. Broca's area
(controls speech
muscles via
the motor cortex)

1. Visual cortex
(receives written words
as visual stimulation)

3. Wernicke's area
(interprets auditory code)

FIGURE 2.1 Language Areas of the Brain

comprehension. Usually aphasias occur due to a stroke, but may be brought on by trauma to the head, infections, or even tumors and growths.

Two major types of aphasias are *Broca's* aphasia and *Wernicke's* aphasia, named after the two parts of the brain shown in Figure 2.1 above. Broca's aphasia seriously impacts speech production. The damage done to Broca's area generally leads to slowed or severely stuttered speech. Often vocabulary is not easily accessed and patients with this aphasia are unable to fluently produce sentences. Usually, if this is the only damage done to the brain, the patient can hear, read, and understand fairly well. It is the production areas of language that are impaired (National Aphasia Association). In the following transcript with a Broca's aphasia patient we can see how the language impairment slows speech:

> Cinderella ... poor ... um 'dopted her ... scrubbed floor, um, tidy ... poor, um ... 'dopted ... Si-sisters and mother ... ball. Ball, prince um, shoe ...
> (Bucknell University Department of Linguistics)

As this example shows, the words are not tied together, the speech is slowed, and there is a lack of coordinating words like articles and prepositions that logically connect phrases together. Many of the more referential terms like nouns, adjectives, and verbs are spoken.

Wernicke's aphasia, on the other hand, largely affects comprehension. Usually speech may sound fluent, not choppy and broken. However, the speech is often rattled off in non-cohesive sentences. The speaking is filled with irrelevant words, an incoherent logic, and to a listener seems unintelligible. Writing and reading is usually impaired as well. This type of aphasia occurs when there is damage to Wernicke's area. In this transcript of speech, the patient speaks fluently, though the patient has much difficulty with nouns, adjectives, and verbs.

> Uh, well this is the ... the /dødøü/ of this. This and this and this and this. These things going in there like that. This is /sen/ things here. This one here, these two things here. And the other one here, back in this one, this one /gÞ?/ look at this one.
>
> (Bucknell University Department of Linguistics)

In this example, the speech is much more rapid; however, it makes little sense, because there are few nouns and verbs. The speaker may perceive that they do indeed make sense. We generally ask students if they were to be stricken with either Broca's or Wernicke's aphasia which one they would prefer. It is a question of whether you would rather talk but not make sense, or talk little but be understood. Perhaps, this is a good question to gauge egocentric and narcissistic tendencies!

Humor withstanding, there are many more types of aphasias, and their effects on language and cognition is far more complicated than simplistically dividing them into production and comprehension issues. Given the complexity of how the brain functions through interconnected synaptic networks, there is quite a bit of variation with patients who have aphasia. Someone may have difficulty naming some objects, reading some texts, or speaking in some situations, yet be able to do the same literacy functions in other situations. While Wernicke's aphasia is supposed to affect all comprehension, it may be more nuanced whereby the patient comprehends some linguistic functions but has difficulty with others. The problem is that the study of these aphasias concentrates on the recorded and produced words, within the frameworks of "normal" people's linguistic conventions. They don't ask, "How are these patients making meaning in their own way?" The real unit of analysis is not speech production, or comprehension (i.e., what happens "in the head") but rather how does communication in the social relational plane unfold.

In many severe cases, however, there is almost no observable ability to communicate. The term "observable" is significant here because we tend to judge communication through available tools and expected norms. However, in many language impairment cases, we simply might not have the proper mediational tools to access the thoughts of the aphasia patient. In the movie *Johnny Got His Gun* (Trumbo, 1939), a nurse discovers an alternative signing system to communicate with a comatose patient who was presumed to be brain dead and lacking thought. In a similar but "real" life story, a man named Rom Houben was trapped in a 23-year coma, but it was revealed that he was conscious the whole time! This became known only through high-tech scans that revealed brain activity that was previously presumed to be non-existent (Hall, 2009).

Other impairments and diseases certainly do affect people as well. Broca's and Wernicke's aphasia are two of the most famous. Aphasias, in mild cases, may go away without treatment, although usually the symptoms are salient enough that treatment is provided. Usually, when an aphasic is diagnosed, speech-language therapists would work with the patient to regain control over the remaining speech functions. Rarely do patients return to pre-injury language capabilities. However, the presence of aphasia doesn't necessarily mean that the lost skills or abilities could not be "re-learned" through a reorganization of the neurological networks. Many studies have demonstrated that significant progress can be made, especially in the first few months. As time goes on, however, complete recovery tends to be less likely. Family members are also trained in how to work with aphasia patients. This often includes speaking in shorter sentences and other types of language modifications designed to ease the burden of communication. The general focus of therapy is to learn to utilize the remaining language functions in the absence of those that are lost, not a full cure (Yavuzer, 2012). This brings up more questions about cognition and the relationship to language. If language is impaired, in some cases severely, does cognition still occur? The case of Rom Houben above suggests that it is better to assume "YES!" than to prematurely declare someone "brain dead" while their mind is conscious even though we might not have the means to know it.

The Case of Embodied Cognition

Associated with neurolinguistics is a movement often called *second wave cognitive science*. This is a major step in a different direction for the field. Whereas the first wave of cognitive scientists assumed that language was a discrete entity in the brain and was acquired in a location named the "Language Acquisition Device" (LAD), the second wave of cognitive scientists viewed language more holistically. Language, they speculated, is not found in the brain as language, but rather builds off of bodily experiences in this world. Hence, they introduced a new metaphor to think about language, *embodied cognition*. All of our thoughts emanate from our sensory experience with the physical world. Abstract thinking, in the Platonic sense, where abstract mathematical or philosophical ideas had a form/real existence in a metaphysical plane was rejected by embodied cognition. There is no abstract meaning with another existence based in a metaphysical reality. All cognition begins and ends in the circle of our material experiences—metaphysics is dead. This has implications for the location, pun intended, of meaning, meaning-making (*semiotics*) and values (*ideologies*) when it comes to the nature, function, and purpose of language. We will revisit this ideological tension in the remainder of this book, but for now we will discuss some of the key findings and implications of the embodiment movement in light of recent neuroscience developments.

Whereas the first wave of cognitive scientists assumed a compartmentalized location (LAD) for looking at speech, reading, comprehension, and so forth, the second wave studied how words related to the bodily experiences we have. Even narratives of "out-of-body," "near-death," or other transcendent experiences that is seemingly beyond the five senses are accounted for through metaphors of concrete physical entities. For example, the symbolism in many "near-death" stories are grounded right here on earth such as a staircase, light, or descriptions of angelic figures with wings. It either exists in its current form, or it is a rearrangement of what we have physically experienced.

While advocates of embodiment reject the philosophical underpinnings of meaning and language as metaphysical entities, it is worthwhile to revisit an ancient counter-argument that still provides a vivid illustration of how we might think about the nature, function, and purpose of language in ALL human experiences, especially those symbolic interactions that seem to transcend three-dimensional time and space. We draw your attention to Plato's Cave allegory. In this allegory three people are trapped in a cave and all they see are the shadows. The shadows themselves are not reality but a reflection of a different reality, in Plato's view, a metaphysical reality where the *Platonic forms* exist. As far as they are concerned the shadows are the reality they experience. One day one of them escapes and sees a world of colors, trees, and the scent of flowers. He realizes another reality that the shadows were simply pointing to. Upon returning, he has to describe what he has experienced in the language of the shadows, otherwise he won't be believed. They will call him "Crazy!" This individual finds it impossible to describe in the language of the shadows, the existence of colors, trees, and flowers.

Language, at least in its form (the shadows), is limited and bound by its physical dimensions (sight and sounds); however, this doesn't preclude it from being able to point to metaphysical realities that are beyond sight and sounds (abstract meaning). Here "abstract" doesn't mean detached, just like the trees, colors, and flowers are not detached from the shadows. Neither side denies the shadows, but the disagreement is whether they point to something else or not. Are the shadows realities unto themselves or do they point to a "higher" reality? This is the central dilemma of language and cognition. The worlds of embodiment (Cognition as Flesh) and what we might call *inspirited* cognition (Cognition as Heart) seem to have antithetical positions on the surface, and are the heart, pun intended, of Western intellectual and ideological debates that pit the secular against the sacred, form against function, rationality against emotion, and literalism against symbolism. These positions are not necessarily mutually exclusive; nevertheless, they are not only long-standing philosophical debates, we see how they manifest themselves in everyday *langua*cultural practices with implications for how we think about language, learning, meaning, and cognition (Razfar, 2013). While some embodiment linguists overstate their claims and declare the argument moot, it is a claim that is not falsifiable in the best tradition of positivistic science. It is impossible to say that the metaphysical understanding of language and meaning is false, even if its truth is subject to debate.

Regardless of where one stands on the philosophical and ideological implications of embodied cognition, there are several points of convergence that need to be highlighted. First, recent evidence from neuroscience increasingly shows the link between linguistic form and function as well as literalism and symbolism. We have long known anecdotally that language evokes different affective experiences both between people and within them. These experiences lead to increased brain activity and leave a physical footprint within areas of the brain associated with that experience. For example, in an fMRI study, it was found that the word "kick," when presented as a word in isolation, actually activated parts of the brain that are responsible for motor control as well as other areas associated with different aspects of language. When the word "kick" was used as part of a literal sentence, it also activated the motor areas of the brain, but somewhat less than the isolated word. In a final trial, the scans showed that there was no activation in the motor area of the brain, but only in the language areas when "kick" was used in an idiom (Raposo, Moss, Stamatakis, & Tyler, 2009). This indicated that language is not a separate function of the brain, but is connected with other bodily experiences. This brings

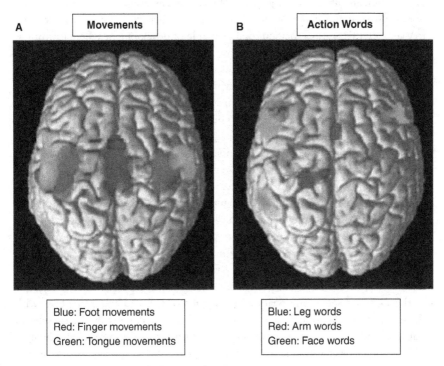

FIGURE 2.2 Movements vs. Action Words

a new hope for the rehabilitation of aphasia patients, children who have passed the "critical age" of language learning, and others who have language impairment.

The second wave recognized that cognition, itself, is embodied. Our thoughts are related so closely with our experiences in this world that we think not through "language," but through a much larger set of meaning-making resources. Our brains are not involved only in the "language" of a word, nor in the movement of the eyes or mouth when reading and speaking; the brain is stimulated by associated physical acts. In a study conducted by Hauk, Johnsrude, and Pulvermüller (2004), fMRI scans showed that the brain was acting differently when a research subject was reading the words *kick*, *lick*, and *pick*. The areas of the brain associated with actions of the legs, face, and arms were activated simply through reading. This would indicate that the brain connects the language more to bodily physical experiences than to the structure of words. After all, linguistically these words share the same category (all are verbs) and have similar phonological characteristics (they all differ by only one sound). In Figure 2.2, Hauk, Johnsrude, and Pulvermüller have indicated where the brain was activated during these tasks. Note the similarities between simply reading the words *kick*, *lick*, and *pick* and actually doing these actions.

It is in this type of embodied thinking that Montessori and other "Hands-On" types of organization of learning seem to have a scientific basis for learning through manipulation of physical objects. In this way, thinking is done on a bodily-physical and concrete level before the abstract-language level. According to Vygotsky, this is also a sociocultural principle of development where learning is movement from the concrete to the abstract.

Another related study to neurolinguistics is the study of neurophysiology more generally. There is much research regarding disorders such as autism. One of the connections, however, between autism and second language use is that of *intentional attunement* or *we-centeredness*. This is tightly connected to the relational function of language in that the primary purpose of language is to form bonds of affiliation and become legitimate members of a community. Many symptoms of autism, and related disorders like Asperger Syndrome, tend to be rooted in a more general problem of not being able to establish bonds of affinity and affective, or heartfelt, connections with others. Patients who are unable to connect and show empathy with others are often said to lack social competence.

While scientists have not been able to pinpoint the cause of this incompetency, one hypothesis is that there may be damage to the mirror neuron system, which would then lead to the malfunctioning of embodied simulation. As an example of this process, we can think of a person who is in pain. When we look at this person in the face and see agony written all over it, we feel bad and empathize with them. However, on a much deeper level, our face may contort by the muscles in our forehead contracting. The convergence of physical pain, emotional solidarity, and sensory motor movement is *embodied simulation*. This process begins in the neuro-network with mirror neurons. So, if there is damage to the mirror neuron network, embodied simulation would not be possible, and empathy, or feeling someone else's pain, joy, anger, and so forth would not be possible. Intersubjectivity or "we" centered action does not occur (Gallese, 2006). So, when considering language use by autistic students, we must be aware that the social competencies of language interaction occur on a much deeper, neurological level. Language, as used in the "we-centered" space, is hindered by the lack of mirrored embodied responses. So, it is not the language or the competency of language alone that makes us feel, think, and communicate. It is, rather, the embodied stimulatory experiences that allow for communication to happen.

Physical reactions to work, whether minor eye movements or startled jumps and jerks, are associated with this concept of embodied simulation. This is made possible by the mirror neurons, which are activated in our brain when we observe something in the outside world. Thus, in any social interaction emotions must be considered. Whether it is reading a novel, looking at a piece of art, or talking with someone, our brain is activated on this emotional-empathetic level. Our bodies are involved in all of these interactions (Freedberg & Gallese, 2007). Thus, for children with disorders inhibiting this emotional connection, language use is also impaired. Language, void of the emotions and "we-centeredness" makes social competency much more difficult to achieve. In fact, many people who are diagnosed with a deficit in social competency have to explicitly learn how to read face gestures and also how to mimic face gestures so that they can enhance communication. We generally share painful stories with someone who can feel, empathize, and demonstrate solidarity by showing they also feel some pain. While most people do this without even thinking about it, some people, with impairments to their mirror neuron system, may need to practice being aware of facial expressions in order to show they share the pain.

Epigenetics

For much of the 20th Century, eugenics and genetic determinism have dominated our understanding of human nature, language, and learning. This perspective has had negative impact on educational policy and practice, especially as it relates to non-dominant populations. Genetic determinism constructs learners as passive and their abilities are rendered unchangeable. Further, it has led to deficit views of entire populations when it comes to academic ability and performance. In recent years a more agentive and cultural model of genetics has emerged with significant implications for learners and teaching.

The field of *epigenetics* examines how our environment and our choices directly impact our genetic code. The human genome project has aimed to map out the genetic code of human beings. For the most part, this approach has fostered a "gene fetish" culture whereby we try to find a gene for every imaginable trait and practice. If genes were found to determine hair color, height, nose shape, skin color, and even personality dispositions, certainly, genes could be responsible for language. Particularly with the mapping of the genome, scientists could more accurately theorize about biological evolution with neuroscience making connections to the evolution of language and cognition. They assume that the human brain developed the innate ability to acquire language precisely due to genetic evolution. No one, not Chomsky, Pinker, or even famed geneticists could, beyond doubt, explain how language was related to biology. That is, until a 2001 study found that mutations in the FOXP2 gene was responsible for several speech and language impairments and related diseases (Lai, Fisher, Hurst, Vargha-Khadem, & Monaco, 2001). The study suggested, then, that the FOXP2 gene was responsible for language and speech. This was widely seen as a "smoking gun" for Chomsky's claims of linguistic nativism. Though Chomsky didn't look much beyond observable language, his followers, like Pinker (1994), had long suspected a gene of this type must exist.

As geneticists continued to study the genome, there was increasing interest in how the genes were expressed. Most are familiar with our genetic code, the genome, and how it expresses itself through observed traits (phenotype). However, our genotype which is the complete code is also impacted by our choices and interactions with the world. The result of our genome's interaction with the world is what we call the *epigenome*. So if identical twins have the same genome, they don't have the same epigenome. Thus, our cultural practices, thoughts, and lifestyle choices affect our epigenome (Sinha, 2006). Epigenetics offers a bidirectional view of how genetics influences our behavior and abilities, but most importantly, how behavior influences genetics. This is a view that places greater responsibility on individuals, learners, and teachers. Our genetic "fate" really is in our minds and hands. Since our language uses are so intimately connected with our thoughts and actions, we can say that language use affects our genetic code.

TEACHER CASE STUDIES

Sandra: Bi-monolinguals

It was Sandra's first year teaching. She was a little nervous about having her own classroom, but was confident she had been prepared well. She went to one of the best schools in her state. In addition to teacher certification, she also pursued a math endorsement. Now she was finally returning back to her hometown in a rural community. She was relieved to be close to family and away from the stress of college life. She settled into her classroom and soon her fifth grade students came in.

Most of the students were from working-class, White households, but she knew that three of her students, Jose, Juanita, and Hector, were immigrants from Mexico. Jose's family had moved recently from a large city. His mother was a nurse in a local clinic serving migrant workers, and his father had been hired as a manager at a nearby factory where there was an influx of Spanish-speaking employees. At home they spoke both English and Spanish, and, quite necessarily, they needed both for their jobs. Hector and Juanita were twins. They had moved to the United States on their father's work visa. They spoke only Spanish and their parents did not know English.

As the year went on, Sandra noticed that when these three would speak to each other, it was in Spanish, which she didn't see too much of a problem with if it didn't cause trouble in the classroom. Jose, however, would switch back and forth between Spanish and English depending on who he was talking with. Sometimes he even switched in the middle of a sentence with Hector and Juanita. When Jose's parents would pick him up from school, they also would speak to him in a mix of Spanish and English "¡Vamos! rápidamente! Get your backpack!" And Jose would respond with both Spanish and English. Sandra thought about this. She did not understand how Jose could switch so much. Hector and Juanita made sense. They speak Spanish at home, but in school mostly it was English. It was as if they were monolingual in one language or the other. They would switch, but not in the middle of a sentence like Jose. Sandra thought this was very interesting, and decided that the following day she would ask Jose about it.

"Jose," Sandra said, "Can I ask you a few questions? How do you switch between Spanish and English so quickly?"

"I don't know. I just do."

"Isn't it more difficult for you? Wouldn't it be easier to just stick to one at a time?"

"I don't know. I just say it like it is comfortable. Sometimes it feels more right in English and sometimes in Spanish. But sometimes it is just better to use both."

"Even when you are talking with your parents? Don't you all speak Spanish?"

"Yes."

"Well, how do you think? Do you think in Spanish or English?"

"I think like I talk."

"Oh, ok. Thank you for answering the questions. Go ahead and catch up with your classmates on the playground."

Slightly unsatisfied with the response, Sandra decided she would ask Jose's mother the same questions. They had built a rapport over the past few months, and occasionally Sandra would see her around town running errands.

"Hi Gloria. Can I ask you a question? I am new to teaching and was very curious about your child. I don't understand why he mixes up Spanish and English. He is a high performing student, but doesn't mixing the languages just cause more difficulties?"

Gloria giggled for a moment and said "Oh, Sandra, it isn't difficult to switch! We just do that because the languages are both in our mind. We don't keep them separate. Some things we do in English, others in Spanish."

"Oh, I see. So, like, you might do math in English, but cook in Spanish?"

"Well, that too, but more than that. Sometimes we don't even notice we are switching."

"You never spoke to me or other teachers in Spanish."

"I know, I know. But that is because you don't understand it, so why would we talk to you in it?"

Sandra thought about that a little later that evening. She thought about how she had assumed that the mind of Jose split the two languages. She never thought that they may have been combined! However, from what Jose and the parents said, it seems like the languages must be working together. The same, she thought, would be true of the other two students. They may also not be two separate language users in one mind. Sandra thought how this may affect her teaching, and for one, she could see now sometimes it might be best for her to let her students speak like they wanted to. Very few times did the three Spanish speakers ever use Spanish in the classroom. They always spoke so everyone could understand them. It just made sense. Perhaps they aren't just two monolingual people all wrapped up in one.

Li: High Functioning Autism and Bilingualism

A young mother walked out of her child's speech therapist's office, confused and discouraged. It had been a long and difficult road to understand her child's diagnosis, but this last meeting just destroyed Li's world. Li and her husband, Ben, had moved to the United States from China for a business venture. Ben was actually his English name, to help him relate to his English-speaking colleagues. Li worked in the computer industry and had accomplished quite a bit in her new job. Their son, Jimmy, had been born in China but they moved when he was very young. They decided to stay near family and had an extended Chinese community because they knew their Chinese heritage was important, and they were proud of it. They decided that they would speak Chinese in the home.

As Jimmy grew, his parents noticed that unlike the children around him, he was not speaking. They thought this was abnormal, and, as first time parents, had him evaluated by experts. Jimmy had been diagnosed with high functioning autism (HFA), and the family knew that meant there would be some delay in his language learning. However, although Jimmy was communicating non-verbally, the speech therapist recommended that the family only speak to him in English. She rationalized that for Jimmy to learn two languages would be difficult in and of itself, but since he seemed high functioning the therapist thought this could be done. The bigger issue, however, was that, at some point, Jimmy would need to understand the different rules of using Chinese and English and when to switch. This is where the therapist said that Jimmy would have difficulty, and it would bring on more stress, and he would likely not learn the social cues needed to be bilingual in dominant English society. Li was frustrated, but left to tell her husband what the therapist had said. The therapist also gave her the contact information of a support group for parents of autistic children.

Li and Ben had never accepted help from anyone, but they knew that it would be best for their child if they at least visited the support group. While they were there, they noticed another family that appeared to be immigrants and began talking. Chan and Esther, a Korean couple, had received the same advice as Li and Ben. For them, this meant that they changed everything in their home to English. They only spoke to their child in English and even stopped going to their Korean church. Well, they did sometimes attend functions there, but their child could not really relate to the Korean speakers. Li asked about how their system worked at home, and Esther said that the family would speak Korean to each other, even often to their other children. The HFA child, however, knew no Korean and seemed to zone out when family members spoke Korean. While the child had no desire to know Korean and considered himself American, Chan and Esther knew he could at least live a "normal" life in the United States.

After the group meeting, Li turned to Ben and told him that that was simply too high a price to pay. It would be very difficult for Jimmy to learn two languages and to know when to use them, however, with the support of the family, she thought it was a better option. She could not imagine her only son growing up without knowing Chinese! How would he take care of his aging grandparents? How would he communicate at their numerous functions with their Chinese co-workers? How would he identify with his parents? To Li, there was simply no choice. Being bilingual was the only option.

As Jimmy grew, he certainly did learn both languages. In fact, he was able to function in both monolingual and bilingual settings. Though stigma of HFA did cause some social repercussions, and he did take longer to learn to use Chinese and English, he grew up to live quite a "normal" life between the borders. His father's company promoted him to oversee operations in China, and this required a lot of traveling. Often they returned to China as a family. Jimmy had a deep amount of respect for his grandparents, and was able to build a sincere relationship with them. He was proud of both his Chinese heritage and his American identity.

Though many speech therapists (and other professionals) recommend that HFA children grow up monolingual, for many these stakes are too high. Kremer (2005), the study from which the idea for this case study is drawn, indicates that for HFA children bilingualism is extremely beneficial. Monolingualism would only suppress HFA children's access to parent–child interactions.

Conclusion

With major advances in the cognitive sciences and medical research, our understanding of how our brains work continues to evolve. Specifically, our understanding of how language relates to our brains has changed significantly. In this chapter we have provided many viewpoints ranging from our brain as a processor of information to some of the most advanced considerations in genetic and epigenetic theory. We have considered how our entire body is involved in the process of language use. Some common language impairments have been presented in this chapter, and in the coming chapters we will show that often the "mistakes" in language are not necessarily due to some hard-to-diagnose "learning disability" or "cognitive" issue. In fact, many of the "errors" or "mistakes" we encounter in our classrooms are predictable when we understand the nature, function, and purpose of language. In addition, many of the learning difficulties we observe may not be "difficulties" at all, but may have emerged from sociocultural contexts and relationships. We will now turn to the formal and structural levels of linguistics so that we can better understand how to think about language use in our classrooms.

QUESTIONS/ACTIVITIES

1. Look at a partner and ask them the following questions. In what direction do their eyes move as they are thinking?

   - What was the name of your first pet?
   - What was your first grade teacher's name?
   - How big was your third grade class?
   - Imagine a unicorn flying through the sky. What color is the horn?
   - What does your grandmother's voice sound like?
   - What did the unicorn sound like?
   - What does your sofa feel like?

2. Look at a partner and ask them to tell you a story of something sad. Note the expressions on their face. What facial expressions are you making? Now try to share a story that is exciting and happy. Try looking at a piece of artwork now. What are the expressions on your face?

3. A popular e-mail circled around the web several years back with the following text. It claims to be from Cambridge University, but there is not substantial evidence for this claim. Read the text anyway!

   Olny srmat poelpe can raed tihs. I cdnuolt blveiee taht I cluod aulaclty uesdnatnrd waht I was rdanieg. The phaonmneal pweor of the hmuan mnid, aoccdrnig to a rscheearch at Cmabrigde Uinervtisy, it deosn't mttaer in what oredr the ltteers in a wrod are, t he olny iprmoatnt tihng is taht the frist and lsat ltteer be in the rgh it pclae. The rset can be a taotl mses and you can sitll raed it wouthit a porbelm. Tihs is bcuseae the huamn mnid deos not raed ervey lteter by istlef, but the wrod as a wlohe. Amzanig huh? yaeh and I awlyas tghuhot slpeling was ipmorantt! if you can raed tihs psas it on !!"

Was it difficult to read? Was it easy? Did it get easier as time went on? Why do you think you could read it even though the letters were misplaced?

While there is not substantial evidence it is from Cambridge (www.snopes.com), there is a paper published which does suggest that we can still read texts when letters are transposed (Shillock & Monaghan, 2003).

Additional Resources (multimedia)

http://www.nimh.nih.gov/index.shtml [National Institute of Mental Health]
http://www.radiolab.org/2010/aug/09/#.T-sqDxSFWgs.gmail [Stroke]

3

PHONOLOGY

Why Languages Sound Different to Second Language Learners

LEARNING GOALS

1. Summarize the basic concepts of phonology.
2. Understand potential challenges in learning English.
3. Perform basic contrastive analysis.
4. Use phonological analysis to inform teaching practices.
5. Understand the different types of alphabets and spelling conventions.
6. Use a phonemic chart to design language learning activities.
7. Create a case study to analyze a particular topic in phonology.

KEY TERMS/IDEAS: allophone, alphabet, contrastive analysis, grapheme, logographic/pictographic orthography, orthography, phoneme, phonemic awareness, phone, phonology, minimal pairs

In the previous chapter, we learned about the inventory of sounds used in human speech. In this chapter, we will turn our attention toward how those sounds are organized in language. Traditionally, phonology is the study of how speech sounds are structured based on rules in a given language. Linguists have long pointed to these phonological rules to explain many of the differences between human languages. They look at the form or structure of a language to further explain how language is ordered in the human mind. From this perspective, phonology affords a useful analysis to break down language into its smallest units, the sounds that a speaker recognizes.

Of course, for our purposes here, we are not so much concerned about the structure and form of a language for a descriptive analysis, but rather to give us insight into how we can understand our language-learning students in a classroom context. Therefore, in this chapter, we will focus on how phonological analysis can inform our understanding of reading, learning a second language, and identity. We will briefly introduce how to study the phonology of a language. Then we will discuss how to use that analysis in understanding alphabetic systems and reading English, specifically. After learning how knowledge of phonology can be used in classroom language learning, we will look at how the phonology of a language is used as an identity marker which is often the basis for stigmatization. Finally, we will provide case studies of teachers who used phonological analysis to address specific issues of language learners they identified.

Introduction

Every language has specific structural rules, which, in a way, govern the way sounds are allowed to come together to make words. To understand how sounds work together in a system can be a valuable resource in a classroom in which students speak multiple languages. When we learn language, we learn these rules, which become tacit or implicit. We don't really think about the sounds we make as we speak, and besides learning to read, we rarely think about the sounds in language at all. Take a moment and try to describe the sounds you use when you say your name. Don't spell it out in letters, but think about the way your tongue, lips, and other parts of your mouth move. Think about the airflow. How are the sounds organized? How can you tell when one sound begins and the other ends? Why is it that you can use letters to represent them? This is very much like the job a linguist would perform when studying the phonology of a language. Perhaps he or she would use a machine to track the vowels and maybe time the length of each sound. However, one doesn't need to go into great depth to glean a massive amount of information that can be useful in identifying language issues in your class. You don't need to be a professional linguist to assess your students, but you do need a way to talk about the sounds in a language.

Phonetics

Back in Chapter 1 we presented a seven-level hierarchy of linguistics. The first and most basic level is phonetics. Phonetics is the study of speech sounds. It is the most basic level of analysis that seeks to describe the physical features of sound. In a formal phonology class, one may experience drills on how to form the sounds of all the languages in the world and how to describe them. All of these sounds have been summarized in the International Phonetic Alphabet (IPA).

In the IPA, each symbol stands for a distinct sound in a language. No language makes every sound on this chart. Refer to the IPA chart in Figure 3.1. Notice that the chart is divided both horizontally and vertically. Along the top are different places of articulation, or where in the mouth the airflow is most

THE INTERNATIONAL PHONETIC ALPHABET (2005)

CONSONANTS (PULMONIC)

	LABIAL		CORONAL				DORSAL			RADICAL		LARYNGEAL
	Bilabial	Labio-dental	Dental	Alveolar	Palato-alveolar	Retroflex	Palatal	Velar	Uvular	Pharyngeal	Epi-glottal	Glottal
Nasal	m	ɱ		n		ɳ	ɲ	ŋ	N			
Plosive	p b	ɸ ɓ		t d		ʈ ɖ	c ɟ	k ɡ	q ɢ		ʡ	ʔ
Fricative	ɸ β	f v	θ ð	s z	ʃ ʒ	ʂ ʐ	ç ʝ	x ɣ	χ ʁ	ħ ʕ	ʜ ʢ	h ɦ
Approximant		ʋ		ɹ		ɻ	j	ɰ				
Trill	ʙ			r					R		ʀ	
Tap, Flap		ⱱ		ɾ		ɽ						
Lateral fricative				ɬ ɮ		ꞎ	ʎ̝̊	ʟ̝				
Lateral approximant				l		ɭ	ʎ	ʟ				
Lateral flap				ɺ		ꞎ						

Where symbols appear in pairs, the one to the right represents a modally voiced consonant, except for murmured ɦ. Shaded areas denote articulations judged to be impossible. Light grey letters are unofficial extensions of the IPA.

CONSONANTS (NON-PULMONIC)

Anterior click releases (require posterior stops)	Voiced implosives	Ejectives
ʘ Bilabial fricated	ɓ Bilabial	' Examples:
ǀ Laminal alveolar fricated ("dental")	ɗ Dental or alveolar	pʼ Bilabial
ǃ Apical (post)alveolar abrupt ("retroflex")	ʄ Palatal	tʼ Dental or alveolar
ǂ Laminal postalveolar abrupt ("palatal")	ɠ Velar	kʼ Velar
ǁ Lateral alveolar fricated ("lateral")	ʛ Uvular	sʼ Alveolar fricative

CONSONANTS (CO-ARTICULATED)

ʍ	Voiceless labialized velar approximant
w	Voiced labialized velar approximant
ɥ	Voiced labialized palatal approximant
ɕ	Voiceless palatalized postalveolar (alveolo-palatal) fricative
ʑ	Voiced palatalized postalveolar (alveolo-palatal) fricative
ɧ	Simultaneous x and ʃ (disputed)
k͡p t͡s	Affricates and double articulations may be joined by a tie bar

VOWELS

SUPRASEGMENTALS

ˈ	Primary stress
ˌ	Secondary stress [ˌfoʊnəˈtɪʃən]
eː	Long
eˑ	Half-long
ĕ	Extra-short
.	Syllable break
‿	Linking (no break)

INTONATION

ǀ	Minor (foot) break
ǁ	Major (intonation) break
↗	Global rise
↘	Global fall

ˈ	Primary stress
ˈˈ	Extra stress

TONE

Level tones		Contour-tone examples	
e̋	Top	ě	Rising
é	High	ê	Falling
ē	Mid	e᷄	High rising
è	Low	e᷅	Low rising
ȅ	Bottom	e᷇	High falling
Tone terracing		ê	Low falling
ꜛ	Upstep	e᷈	Peaking
ꜜ	Downstep	e᷆	Dipping

DIACRITICS

Diacritics may be placed above a symbol with a descender, as ŋ̊. Other IPA symbols may appear as diacritics to represent phonetic detail: ⁱ (fricative release), ᵇ (breathy voice), ˀ (glottal onset), ᵊ (epenthetic schwa), ᵒ (diphthongization).

SYLLABICITY & RELEASES		PHONATION		PRIMARY ARTICULATION		SECONDARY ARTICULATION			
n̩ l̩	Syllabic	n̥ d̥	Voiceless or Slack voice	t̪ b̪	Dental	tʷ dʷ	Labialized	ɔ̹ x̹	More rounded
e̯ ʊ̯	Non-syllabic	s̬ d̬	Modal voice or Stiff voice	t̺ d̺	Apical	tʲ dʲ	Palatalized	ɔ̜ x̜	Less rounded
tʰ ht	(Pre)aspirated	n̤ a̤	Breathy voice	t̻ d̻	Laminal	tˠ dˠ	Velarized	ẽ z̃	Nasalized
dⁿ	Nasal release	n̰ a̰	Creaky voice	u̟ t̟	Advanced	tˤ dˤ	Pharyngealized	ɚ ɝ	Rhoticity
dˡ	Lateral release	n̼ a̼	Strident	i̠ t̠	Retracted	ɫ z̴	Velarized or pharyngealized	e̘ o̘	Advanced tongue root
t̚	No audible release	n̪ d̪	Linguolabial	ä j̈	Centralized	ü	Mid-centralized	e̙ o̙	Retracted tongue root
e̞ β̞	Lowered (β̞ is a bilabial approximant)			e̝ ɹ̝	Raised (ɹ̝ is a voiced alveolar non-sibilant fricative, r̝ a fricative trill)				

FIGURE 3.1 International Phonetic Alphabet (2005)

constricted. The left column explains how airflow in the mouth is constricted. A plosive, or stop, means the airflow stops completely as in a "b" or "k." A nasal occurs when the air comes out of the nose, not the mouth, like "m" or "n." Trills are the continuous stopping and movement of air, like the "r" in Spanish. Taps, or flaps, are a brief stop in the airflow, like the "t" in "little." A fricative is a sound in which the airflow continues, but is constrained, as in the "f" sound. Lateral fricatives don't occur in English, but are similar to the "l" sound if the mouth was flatter and made a hissing noise. Laterals and approximants, or semi-vowels, allow a lot of air through the mouth like "l" or the "w" sound. Some boxes have two symbols. The one on the right is voiced, or the vocal chords are vibrating like "v." Touch your throat when making the "v" sound, now make the "f" sound. Notice how your throat is no longer vibrating, this means that the "f" is voiceless.

The top line specifies the places of articulation. Wherever your tongue, or other articulator, is most constricting the airflow is where we can describe the sound being made. So, if the lips are touching, like the sound [b], it would be called "bi-labial." The "labiodental" position would indicate that the top lip is touching the bottom teeth. The "dental" includes the tongue touching the teeth. As the tongue moves back further, there are other positions, like the "alveolar" ridge, the palate, the velum, and so on. Further back in the mouth are places of articulation that happen in the throat, like "epiglottal" and "glottal."

Every sound has an official name consisting of the voicing, place of articula-tion, and the constriction of airflow. The "b" would be the voiced bilabial stop, or the sound that is made by pressing the lips together, stopping the airflow, and vibrating the vocal chords. The "p" would be the voiceless bilabial stop. We can continue to name these sounds, all of which are consonants. Practice making a few. Practice identifying them in other people's speech.

Vowels allow the most air through the mouth, and that is why they have their own diagram. The vowels occur at different points of the mouth. They are "sonorant" because they allow a lot of noise to come through the mouth. Look at the diagram, and try to mimic some of the sounds by shaping your mouth like the diagram. For example, the long "e" sound in English is a high, closed vowel. The "ah" sound is further back and much more open. Any vowel can be placed on this chart. Indeed, people who study phonetics and the quality of sound have machines that will specify precisely how much air is coming through the mouth and where the vowel was formed. Thus, by looking at how a computer reads vowels, phoneticians can analyze exactly what sounds are made and how they are made.

The point of phonetics in this book is to have a brief introduction into describing sounds. We must learn to think about language, and one part of this is to explicitly be aware of how sounds are made in a language. Languages have different inventories of sounds. Most reading this book have never heard the clicks or ingressives, which are rare, but scattered throughout the world's languages. It is important to have a basic understanding of how to describe and discuss the noises we make.

Phonemes and Phonological Analysis

If we look back at the IPA chart of sounds we can see that there are numerous sounds. Each has a very specific description of how it is formed. In all languages some sounds may be produced in speech, but may not exist from the viewpoint of the speaker. A speaker, unless trained in linguistics, would not be able to speak the "linguistic" language about these, although, implicitly the speaker has a sense of different sounds. This distinction of the physical qualities of the sounds (phonetics) and the sound the language user believes to be there (a phoneme) is an important distinction. The goal of this chapter is that you will be able to talk about these distinctions and use it to inform your teaching, and as you will see in the case studies, teachers that did this were able to develop a deeper understanding of their students.

In linguistic talk, a "phoneme" is a group of sounds that speakers of that language recognize as basically one sound. Prior to literacy, this isn't really a necessary point. It isn't until we have to start thinking about representing these sounds that we must understand what sounds are phonemic. Refer back to the IPA chart and notice that in the alveolar column there are many different sounds that can be created (e.g., [t], [d], [ɾ], [n], [s]). More sounds may be indicated in the IPA that have different features, such as aspiration ([tʰ]). They all share the same place of articulation, and these that have been mentioned are all used in English, but some of them are not recognized once English is written. Look at the following list of words in Figure 3.2 that have been transcribed with the IPA. Try to pronounce them and jot down the word in English.

Notice how your writing of the words compares to the phonetic transcription. The phonetic analysis tells us what physical qualities of the sounds exist, but that probably isn't useful for helping students to learn English. When you wrote down the words, you should have noticed that the letter "t" is in every one of these words, yet the physical [t] sound is not. This is because the phoneme /t/ is actually made up of several different sounds, called *allophones*. Allophones are all the sounds in a language that speakers consider as one phoneme. The crux of phonological analysis is to be able to identify these phonemes and to explain

1. [ˈstap]	3. [ˈlɪɾ l̩]	5. [ˈthul]	7. [ˈbæɾ ɹ̩]
2. [ˈtʰap]	4. [ˈbɹaⁱt]	6. [ˈstraⁱp]	8. [ʌˈthæk]

(1-stop, 2-top, 3-little, 4-bright, 5-tool, 6-stripe, 7-battle, 8-attack)

FIGURE 3.2 Allophones of the English Phoneme /t/

the "rules" they follow. Looking at the example above, when do you see thè [tʰ] sound? How about the [ɾ]? The [t] sound? Chances are when you are speaking or writing you don't even notice that these are different sounds. It would be very difficult for an English speaker to correctly pronounce ['stʰap] because in English the /t/ is not aspirated after an /s/. This rule holds true for the phonemes /p/ and /k/ too.

Through contrastive analysis, linguists attempt to identify which sounds in a language are phonemes. The simplest way to do this is to identify a *minimal pair*. A minimal pair is two different words that have one sound that is different. This sound affects the meaning of the word, and therefore must be a different phoneme. In English, for example, the sounds [tʃ] and [ʃ] are a part of different phonemes. We can tell this by finding a minimal pair. The word "chip" /tʃIp/ and "ship" /ʃIp/ differ in meaning, and contain only one sound difference. Another example would be /p/ and /b/. In many languages, these sounds would not make a difference in the meaning of a word. They may be allophones because the only difference is the voicing, and switching them may sound a little funny, but it won't change the meaning. In English, however, this same switch will affect meaning, as in "slap" and "slab" or "bat" and "pat." Contrastive analysis is one of the easiest ways to identify which sounds may be phonemes in a language.

By now you are probably wondering how any of this is helpful in your classroom with your students, and soon we will discuss how this may be used for reading instruction and working with ELs. First, however, we need to discuss how writing systems, specifically English, are organized and have developed.

The Alphabet

The concept of the alphabet seems so natural and so intuitive because it is all around us. In kindergarten we learn to make letters with clay or in sand, we read alphabet books, we sing the alphabet song. We take for granted that the 26 letters of the English alphabet can be used to store language on a piece of paper, a blog, or a Facebook note. This is actually quite an amazing capability. Think about the last book that you read for fun and how many other people read that book. With the spoken word not nearly as many people could be reached simultaneously and across time. It is nothing short of amazing that we can read the *Diary of Anne Frank* from an attic in one of the darkest moments of human history or that we can enjoy the humor that Shakespeare offered hundreds of years ago.

The technology of writing developed to address different problems facing cultures throughout history. The first writing systems were made of pictures, more or less representing objects in the world. This allowed people to see the picture and associate it with something in the world. Imagine if all writing was like drawing pictures. Some, for sure, may be pretty simple, like a horse, or a feather. What about abstract concepts like love and honor? How would these be represented in pictures? The language would need thousands of pictograms to be useful on a daily basis. They would have to be standardized to some extent if they were to be useful. Yet, some languages have done this. Chinese, for example, has tens, if not hundreds of thousands of characters that more or less represent words or ideas. Interestingly enough, those symbols can be used in multiple languages, as is the case in Chinese where many of the characters are used in Cantonese and Mandarin as well as Kanji, one of Japan's written languages. The efficiency of the logographic system allows readers from multiple languages to understand a text, however, for many cultures, this was not efficient enough for the activities of the people and other forms of writing were developed. Another form of writing is based on syllables. Japanese has a writing system that has one grapheme per syllable.

Alphabets developed later in human history. They seemed to address the need for documentation and widespread communication. Although early on, reading and writing were really only for the social elites and highly special- ized professions. This was an advancement that allowed ideas to spread rapidly. Writing required the ability to describe language through written symbols, whether it was pictures or arbitrary letters. Thus, the alphabet was developed as a way to describe the sounds of a language, so one who knew the symbols could understand the sounds they represented. This required a new kind of lan- guage, a metalanguage. Writing is a way to talk about language. Alphabets were created based on the sounds of a language; however, as seen in the example above, the symbols don't need to represent every sound in a language, in fact, that might even make the alphabet less efficient. It is the concept that these sounds can be collapsed into phonemes that allows alphabets to be created, to varying degrees.

Some alphabets, such as Spanish, have roughly a one letter/grapheme to one phoneme correspondence. Other alphabets such as English have a much more complex orthography. In English, although the writing system is generally pho- nemic, there are many "exceptions" to the "rules." There are many reasons for this. We will look at a few to shed light on the complexities many face learning to read and write English. Alphabets based on phonemes and other features of the language are considered conventional. The spelling is a convention, not necessar- ily a direct representation of sound.

As previously mentioned, English is basically a phonemic writing system, meaning that its system of writing is based on how words sound. This is the fundamental aspect about English that triggers phonics instruction. While the "Reading Wars" between Whole Language and phonics instruction are hotly de- bated, we will look at this a little closer in the next chapter. From a sociocultural perspective, the assumptions about language are so different than either of these approaches that methods and reading strategies from both may be used, but for very different reasons. For example, using phonics instruction should not carry the weight that a set of rules about sounds will eventually add up to proficiency, nor should the assumption be made that inundating a child with autonomous writing will lead to acquiring literacy. Nonetheless, the basic arrangement of English prompts phonics instruction. Anyone having grown up learning from a phonics-based instruction is very well acquainted with the words "Well, this is an exception to the rule." This is primarily because English writing describes much more about the language than just the phonemic inventory.

In English there are some sounds that don't have a single grapheme to represent them, for example /θ/ and /ð/ are represented by "th," two graphemes which individually represent different phonemes that are actually quite different than /θ/ and /ð/. These are often called diagraphs. There are also graphemes which seem to be redundant, such as "k" and "c" which both represent /k/ or "s" and "c" which both represent /s/. And, at the end of many words, "s" actually represents a [z] (for example "buses" is pronounced ['bəsɨz]). If we take a metalinguistic approach to the English alphabet, we can see that these "exceptions" aren't exactly exceptions, but a way of describing different properties of the spoken language.

Take the word "buses" described above. As we will learn in Chapter 6, this is made up of two morphemes, or two different units. The first, "bus" is a noun, the second "-es" is a plural marker. We are very familiar with the concept of making nouns plural by adding "-s" or "-es" to a noun. English writing attempts to describe the spoken language by telling us that there is a plural marker at the end, so it keeps it consistent as "s" because that's how we recognize it in speaking. In speaking, we don't think of the "-s" at the end of "cats" as different from the "s" at the end of "dogs" or the "-es" at the end of buses." The writing doesn't need to differentiate these because the spoken language doesn't. However, because the writing attempts to keep these all looking the same, you can see how it may be difficult for an English language learner to understand that "s" may sometimes sound like [s] and sometimes [z].

Another difficulty is associated with the "ght" that appears in many words like "light," "bright," and so on. This is probably due to a change in English speaking after it had been written down, and sometimes even though spoken language changes, written tradition does not. Even this can provide information about words. Sometimes this information is etymological, and indicates where words came from. Although English is a Germanic language, it is heavily influenced by Latin and the Romance languages, so the writing often resembles those languages, such is the case with the "-cion" and "-tion" endings. These don't "sound" like they are written, but that is because the writing is borrowed from other languages. It isn't that these are "exceptions to the rules" but rather that they are describing a different part of the language. Again, this is quite confusing for students learning to read, and especially students learning to read and write English as a second language.

One other significant aspect of English orthography is that it often preserves word associations. If a word is changed significantly in the way it sounds, the written word may actually remain very similar. For example, the words "medicine," "medical," "medicinal," "medic," and "medicated" all derive from the same root word, but the "c" is a different sound in each usage. If we were to spell the words with an "s" we would lose a lot of information, namely that these words all have related meanings.

From these brief examples, we can see that the English writing system is quite complicated. It is basically phonemic, but also describes many other parts of the English language. This is an important distinction in reading instruction. Since reading and writing is a metalinguistic activity, students need to be able to use the various tools afforded by the writing. Phonics instruction only attends to the phonemic inventory of English. It looks at phonemic awareness, a very important awareness students develop when reading. There is much debate whether phonemic awareness happens before reading or results from reading. Either way, this is the awareness that the language is organized into phonemes, and that this has practical implications for reading. Whether this must be deliberately taught or happens through experience is also left to some debate, but if you take the viewpoint that writing tends to describe English phonology, then explicit instruction can be a useful tool, especially for second language learners. However, students should also attend to the other parts of the written language. Shouldn't they also use the other tools the written language provides? Reading should not be reduced to a rule based phonological exercise, but neither should it ignore that. It should be a combination of using phonemic information as well as graphonic information, or the visual information of the word.

The phonology of spoken English is only rarely violated. This is usually in the instances of borrowed words or proper names. Often, though, even when the words come from another language, we try to make them fit the English phonology. This is pretty common in languages, to make foreign words "fit" our system. Thus, it should be no surprise when our students do this in classes. Students often struggle with English, both spoken and written, because of phonological differences. English just doesn't "fit" their system. Phonological analysis helps us predict many of these areas where it doesn't "fit," especially if we know about both languages. Now we will learn how to do a basic comparison of the phonemes of different languages and see how teachers have implemented it.

Basic Contrastive Analysis: Chart Comparisons

While many issues of phonology seem to be of interest only to linguists, there are some great resources and tools teachers can use in their classrooms to help learn about their English learners. A very useful tool is a comparison between the phonemes of English and those of a student's home language. In the appendix at the end of this chapter (Figures 3.3–3.9) there are several different phonemic charts referred to in this chapter and teacher case studies. Each of these charts shows the phonemes in the respective languages. Remember that the phonemes are not the physical sounds that a speaker would create, but rather the phonological units that make a difference in meaning in a language.

Look at the different charts. Make some comparisons. What do you notice? What differences do you see? Those differences are likely to be areas that must be addressed when working with ELs. Because of these phonological differences, some major issues can be predicted. For example, a Spanish speaker may have difficulty hearing the difference between /b/ and /v/ because in Spanish these are not two different phonemes. The mixing of the /l/ and /ɹ/ in English by many Asian speakers is not just a stereotypical problem, but is rooted in the phonological differences between several Asian languages, Vietnamese being one of them.

These charts can be used to make some major predictions about ELs. Take Arabic, for example. Spend some time contrasting Arabic and English. This can be a significant help, but there are other issues to consider as well. Arabic is a major world language often seen in schools in the United States. It is spoken throughout the Middle East and North Africa and many Muslims whose dominant language is not Arabic are familiar with the language for religious purposes. In many cases, Muslim students learn to read Arabic, usually classical Arabic for religious study. This is a major identity marker, as Arabic literacy remains high. Arabic is also significantly different from English in both its phonology and orthography.

Looking at the Arabic phonemic chart, you will notice that there is not a voiceless bilabial stop [p] but there is a voiced sound [b]. This could lead to both production and comprehension issues if the Arabic speaker doesn't differentiate between "pat" and "bat." The [f] stands as the only phoneme for the Arabic speaker in the area where English has two: /f/ and /v/. This could lead to mispronouncing "veil" as "fail." Another point to notice about phonological differences between Arabic and English is that in English, besides /h/, there are no sounds made behind the velum. In Arabic, however, there is a rich inventory of phonemes made at the uvula and pharynx. These are only a few observations made based on the chart. Take time to consider some other issues that may lead to miscommunication and change in meaning (note specifically where an Arabic speaker may confuse minimal pairs in English).

Also in Arabic, the vowel system is less complex than English. Where English has several vowels all making minimal pairs, such as "bid," "bed," "bad," "bead," "bowed," and "bud," Arabic doesn't necessarily have all of these. For the Arabic speaker learning English, it is not uncommon to find /I/, /i/, or /e/ substituted for /ɛ/, as in "peat" for "pit" or "hair" for "her."

Another consideration, not seen from the charts, would be the orthographic differences. Arabic, as with other Semitic languages like Hebrew and other languages using the Arabic script (e.g., Farsi, Urdu), do not represent vowels in the writing. Because the vowel system is less complex than English, it is easy from context for the reader to decide which vowel would be inserted when reading. This may play somewhat of a role in learning to read for the Arabic speaker because English writing uses many cues for vowels, including the silent "e," multiple vowels clustered together, and semivowels like "w" and "y." Literate Arabic students most likely will tend to focus on the graphemes representing consonants because it is similar to their own language. In Arabic, words are changed in many ways, but usually contain three consonants. The word for "writing" and "book" both contain the Arabic letters "ktb." Various forms of these letters with vowels change the meaning. So, for the Arabic reader, identifying the consonants is much more significant than vowels when reading. This shouldn't be too difficult to imagine, however. An English reader would probably not have too difficult of a time reading the following sentence, even though it has no vowels: "Stdyng phnlgy hlps m ndrstnd my stdnts bttr."

In this chapter we reviewed some major points of phonology that may be useful in understanding the language learning of ELs in your classrooms. These are not just theoretical assumptions derived by linguists, but can provide a powerful lens for studying your own students and seeing where new forms of mediation are needed. Next we will present some case studies based on teacher experiences in real classrooms.

In a linguistics class, students were asked to identify an EL they work with and to study the phonological differences between their language and English. The teacher was also asked to converse with the student and develop a case study about the student's language learning. By using the phonemic chart for that language, the teacher was to predict where some language issues may arise in learning English and to write about how this analysis helped them understand the student. Other things to consider are orthography differences and whether the language allows consonant clusters, or multiple consonants, to be strung together. Many languages do not allow this, making words like "blanket" and "straight" difficult to produce. Take time to read through the below case studies noticing some of the observations these teachers made.

TEACHER CASE STUDIES

Janet: Spanish

Spanish is the most common language spoken at home in the United States besides English. In many communities, it is the dominant language. Despite the predominance of Spanish in homes and around certain communities, the language of instruction in schools frequently remains English. In communities where both languages are used, different forms of subtractive bilingualism are generally instituted in the schools.

Janet is a teacher in a predominantly Hispanic school. She teachers sixth grade in which most of the students speak Spanish as their home language. Janet has a basic understanding of Spanish, but is not fluent. Many of her students come from transitional programs or a year or two of intensive ESL for those who have immigrated to the United States after third grade. Janet was seeking an ESL endorsement as well as her Masters degree in bilingual education, but had been a teacher for several years. She maximized the usefulness of this classroom assignment as she wrote:

> I wanted to select a student from my school that I felt I needed to learn the most about. The student I selected is named Maria. I believe she has been misdiagnosed with a learning disability because of language barriers. Maria is in sixth grade. She was diagnosed with a learning disability in fourth grade. Over the past two years she has received services in my classroom for Language Arts. When she came in she was reading at least two grade levels below her own, and lacked basic comprehension skills.

She took an explicit look at the phonological differences between English and Spanish. While there are many resources for teachers regarding Spanish-speaking ELs, approaching the phonological differences was a new experience for the teacher. She had never really been able to talk about language sounds. Janet, however, suspected that this was not the case, that, in fact, the trouble was due to language learning, specifically reading, not what the school had previously identified.

After studying the IPA phonological charts for English and Spanish, Janet counted 11 consonant phonemes in English that are not in Spanish, as well as four that occur in Spanish but not in English. Some of these may be in points of articulation that are similar, therefore creating an "accent," but others may lead to production and comprehension issues that could cause misunderstanding. The vowel system in Spanish is much less complex than in English as well. The five vowels in Spanish may correspond slightly with the representation in English orthography, namely that English has five vowels: "a," "e," "i," "o," "u"; however, the graphemes don't take into account that there are both long and short English vowels. Thus, the Spanish speaker learning English must learn to distinguish between several more vowels.

The vowel system becomes a major issue in reading, as Janet pointed out. Because Spanish orthography is more phonemic than English, the Spanish speaker must learn the complex representation of silent vowels and long and short sounds. Janet explained that many of the Spanish speakers she worked with had difficulty on precisely this point. However, she also noticed that often she could encourage Spanish speakers, who couldn't read Spanish but could read English, to try reading Spanish, and they picked up how to read the Spanish orthography with ease. She was able to reflect on this by describing the phonemic differences between the languages, carefully noting that the English vowel system is more complex.

Another area she described were the interdental sounds /θ/ and / ð/. Since these do not occur in Spanish, the nearest sound would be the alveolar stops /t/ and /d/, which are contrastive phonemes in English. Thus, a substitution could lead to one not understanding or changing the word completely. For example, when the sounds [θ] or [ð] appear in the intial position of a word, Spanish ELs often pronounce it with a [t] or [d]. This changes the word "this" to "dis," or, more significantly, "thumb" to "tum." Another teacher pointed out that her students frequently wrote "v" instead of "b." She recounted one such mistake as the student wrote "graves" instead of "grabs." The teacher didn't really have a way to discuss this other than it was a "mistake" until she learned that Spanish doesn't have a [v] sound, it only has an [f] and a [b]. The [v], therefore, since it has a similar point of articulation and is voiced, may sound very much like a [b] in certain contexts. The English speaker would immediately distinguish these sounds, whereas the Spanish speaker may very well hear them as the same sound.

There are many other phonological differences between Spanish and English, including word initial blends, the glide [ɹ], among others seen on the chart. These were just a few of the problem areas this teacher had noticed when studying phonology. She noticed many of the production and comprehension issues before, but didn't know specifically why those issues appeared the way they did. It wasn't until she learned how to talk specifically about phonology that she was able to realize that many of them were predictable. The ELs in her class were using the language they knew to make sense of this new sound system, and they were doing it in systematic ways.

This analysis further supported Janet's claims that Maria did not have a learning disability. The previous language programs she had been through did not place consideration on the phonological differences between the languages, but rather just assumed that over time Maria would spontaneously learn English, and if it didn't happen on the time schedule, it must be a learning disability. In fact, Janet explained that the school system had systematically put her at a disadvantage:

> Maria does not feel like she is completely fluent in reading, writing, or speaking in either language. This is obviously a huge problem, since she has been living in the United States since she was born, and been in our school since kindergarten (seven years) and does not speak, read, or write well in any language. I feel this is a systemic issue that needs further review by the urban public school administration.

Mariane: Portuguese

Unlike Spanish, which is often the dominant language in urban communities with schools that have many Spanish speakers, Portuguese is rarely the dominant language. There are relatively few speakers of Portuguese in US schools compared to Spanish, and therefore it does not share the same level of acknowledgment. There are fewer resources to help Portuguese speakers, and since it isn't a "major" language, it often gets brushed to the side. Furthermore, since many assume that it is basically similar to Spanish, there is little tendency to focus on it in its own right, especially if the Portuguese speakers are mixed in with the Spanish speakers. Yet, there is still a great need for teachers to understand phonological issues of such minority languages as Portuguese.

Alice has been a teacher for several years. She has traveled extensively, including to Brazil where she learned Portuguese. In addition to Portuguese, she speaks Spanish and French as well. Previously, she had been exposed to the academic linguistic discourse, but in this case, she had to specifically consider her students in the analysis, not the language itself. She had a student who had immigrated to the United States from Brazil several years ago. The student, Mariane, still spoke Portuguese at home, and the teacher wanted to investigate in more depth some of the experiences she had as an EL. Alice, herself, speaks several languages, including Portuguese. She was able to reflect on the student's language learning having gone through it herself, but Mariane is an interesting case because Spanish, not Portuguese, was the dominant language in her community. Since in Brazil, many of the Portuguese speakers have some familiarity with Spanish, Mariane frequently relied on the Spanish speakers in the United States to provide the assistance she needed prior to learning English and even watched television with Spanish subtitles. However, as she waited for ESL classes to help her English learning, she spent most of her time in a very isolated context, because even though she understood Spanish, very few Spanish speakers could understand her. It wasn't until being in a class with mostly Spanish speakers that she began to communicate more effectively in Spanish, and eventually English as well. Learning to read was the most difficult part of language learning, although she was highly literate in Portuguese before she came to the United States.

Alice identified that some of these language-learning issues may have been due to phonological differences between the languages. Portuguese, for example, does not use the sound [ɹ], but does have a phoneme for a flap, [ɾ], which has a similar place of articulation, and in some dialects, the orthographic representation "r" is pronounced as an English /h/. Portuguese has /ɲ/ whereas English has /ŋ/. Portuguese also includes a uvular sound absent in English as well as a lateral /ʎ/. There are no affricates in Portuguese. While English uses the semivowels /j/ and /w/, Portuguese seems to prefer diphthongs. The Portuguese vowel system is more complex than English, and notably, the schwa [ə], is absent.

Alice wrote: "One issue includes the distinction of minimal pairs, especially for English phonemes that are Portuguese allophones and vice versa. In certain positions within a word, the sound [ɹ] may be equivalent to [h] or [χ], depending on the speaker's dialect." She identified a particular minimal pair, "raw" and "haw," that may provide some production issues. The substitution of [h] or [x] for [ɹ] sounds normal in Portuguese under specific phonological contexts especially because [ɹ] doesn't exist in Portuguese as a phoneme. Therefore, they are allophones of the same phoneme. In English, however, [ɹ] and [h] are contrastive sounds, being a part of separate phonemes. In Portuguese, substituting one sound for another may sound a little funny, but it will not change the meaning. In English, however, the same switch could sound so different that it may be misunderstood.

One of the biggest challenges for a Portuguese speaker learning English is the schwa [ə]. Since it does not occur in Portuguese, when speaking English, Mariane tended to substitute a similar vowel to replace it, usually corresponding to the place of articulation of surrounding consonants. This provided major issues in production and comprehension because the change in vowel alters the meaning of words in English. What is even more difficult is that the schwa, being such a neutral vowel, is highly variable among English dialects. Thus, this particular sound is very difficult for Portuguese speakers and they tend to hear and produce other vowels. For example, the following English words share the same consonant sounds, but the vowel is different: [bit], [bɪt], [but], [bet], [bət], [bot], [bæt], and [bɔt]. A mispronunciation of "but" [bət] could result in a misunderstanding.

Alice's interview with Mariane provided some very interesting insight into the complex issues of ELs. Through talking with Mariane and studying the phonology of Portuguese, Alice saw many of the problems Mariane had in learning English were explained by the differences in the sound systems of the two languages. She explained that there are identity issues to consider as well. For example, Alice wrote:

> Most people have been patient and nice to Mariane during her English language journey. However, there exists those who identify and punish her as an outsider. Some people upon hearing Mariane's accent and rhythm of speech, become hostile.

Alice pointed out this identity issue, something that is normally not included in a phonics lesson.

This explicit awareness provided Alice with a way to understand problem areas and address them. It is a tool that she can now use to talk about language and specifically English language learning.

Linda: Mandarin

Increasingly Mandarin is being taught as a second language in schools, however, there is also a significant number of Mandarin-speaking students who don't receive much needed support in their dominant language. Many of the

historic Chinatowns in cities across the United States are still Cantonese dominant, but Mandarin is on the rise both in status and in number of students in
schools. Also, there are increasing numbers of Mandarin-speaking students in
schools located outside of the historic Chinese and Chinese-American communities. Meanwhile, Mandarin is a major world language and is becoming quite
popular amongst elementary, secondary, and post-secondary students as an
additional second language.

Linda is a teacher in a school with a predominant Chinese student population. Most of the students speak Cantonese at home; however, over the years
she has noticed more Mandarin speakers coming to the school. In the classroom,
Cantonese can often be heard among students, but for Mandarin speakers there
are few opportunities to receive peer assistance in their dominant language. Linda, a Chinese-American herself, grew up hearing her parents speak Cantonese,
though she does not, nor does she understand Mandarin. She took this opportunity to compare English and Mandarin to gain a better understanding of her
Mandarin-speaking students.

Before analyzing some of the phonological differences between Mandarin
and English, Linda asked for a writing sample from a former Mandarin-speaking
student. Song was in seventh grade, but had previously been in Linda's classroom. Song told Linda that she "had no problems learning math in English, but
English conversation was difficult." Song also struggled with learning science
vocabulary. The journal entry Linda analyzed was interesting because of the
mistakes that were made. Song wrote about a day she and two friends helped
her mom by working in a Chinese restaurant. Every word written was a correctly spelled English word, although most of the verbs were not inflected for
tense (this is an issue we will take up in the next chapter) and Song made many
mistakes with word order (this will also be studied in the syntax chapter). Linda
explained that the phonological insight gained from this sample was that her
spelling in English was impeccable, if Song recognized the word. There were at
least seven examples of Chinese characters being used in place of English words
or concepts. For example, Song wrote "When we finished asking what they
want to eat, we were get the paper go in the 厨 房 to cook out." The Chinese
characters used were all words that Song did not attempt to write in English.
Linda wondered about why she did not attempt to spell the word in English,
certainly she knew what a kitchen was. Thus, seeing that Song made no spelling mistakes but also often did not inflect the words, she wondered if Song saw
the words more as entire symbols like Chinese rather than a string of symbols
representing the phonology of English.

There are many differences between the Mandarin and English phonemic
inventories. Some of the differences Linda identified after she had observed her
Mandarin-speaking students. Many of the phonemes in English do not exist in
Mandarin. Among them is the / θ / and / ð /. These two often are problematic
for Mandarin speakers, and are usually pronounced with a [t] or [d] sound

respectively, at least at the beginning of a syllable. This is most likely because /t/ is the nearest Mandarin phoneme. It is likely that a /f/ or possibly a /z/ would be produced at the end of a word though, depending on the surrounding sounds. This is most likely due to the onset of a syllable being easier to start with a stop, hence substituting /t/ or /d/ for the interdental fricatives is common for many speakers learning English, and indeed English speakers as well. At the end of a word, the fricative continues to let air through the oral cavity, which would allow for a /f/ sound to be used. It is also important to note, however, that Mandarin does not utilize voicing in contrasting phonemes as English does. In fact, instead of the English contrast /t/ and /d/, Mandarin has a /th/ and /t/. Neither of these is voiced, but the first is aspirated. English does not differentiate between aspirated and unaspirated stops; rather there is a rule that tells us when to use one and when to use the other. In Mandarin, these could cause differences in meaning.

A major area of contrast in the two phonologies is the nine sounds between the alveolar and palatal points of articulation in Mandarin and the six in English. For English fricatives, there are sounds made at the alveolar ridge (/s/ and /z/) and at the palate (/ʃ/ and / ʒ/) and also affricates made postalveolar (/t ʃ / and /d ʒ/). In Mandarin, there are none made postalveolar or at the palate, but there are retroflexed sounds and alveolpalatal sounds. The retroflexed sounds are quite difficult for the English speaker because it requires the tongue to curve back in the mouth, somewhat like making a [r] sound while still attending to the restrictive airflow and articulation. The alveopalatal is also quite different from English because it requires the tongue to remain high in the mouth articulating at both the alveolar ridge and the palate. The sounds are difficult for the English speaker, but are normal for the Mandarin speaker. This may cause problems, however, when the Mandarin speaker has to make and hear the postalveolar English sounds / ʃ / and / ʒ /. This sound falls right between the two Mandarin phonemes. The fricatives may have similar issues as the Mandarin speaker will have to move the tongue further back to spread out the three sounds into two points of articulation. Learning how to reorganize the sounds in this part of the mouth from nine phonemes to six, with different voicing and different articulations, is quite a challenge.

English uses glides much more frequently, such as /w/ and /j/. This is a challenge as well since glides can be quite similar to vowels. As mentioned above, however, perhaps the most problematic phonological issue that may affect meaning is the voicing strategies of the two phonological systems. Because Mandarin doesn't contrast between voiced and voiceless, it is possible to find a Mandarin speaker using /f/ for /v/. This is because /v/ doesn't exist in Mandarin. So "life" and "live" may very well be confused. The same problem may occur for /p/, /t/, /k/, and /s/.

Mandarin has a very complex set of phonemes made in the center of the mouth that do not exist in English, and there are several sounds that Linda's students struggled with. However, she developed an awareness that helped her to understand why she was hearing mistakes in speech and seeing the writing errors. Song's current teacher had attributed all errors to "word error confusion" and claimed, "it indicates she is not at a beginner's level" although had "noted that her writing was 'good.'" Linda was able to realize that there was some impressive evidence that the writing was a lot better than Song was being given credit for by attending to the phonological considerations.

Sarah: Polish

In many large cities, there are long established Polish communities where the primary language spoken in homes is Polish. In some cases, schools provide bilingual programs for Polish-speaking students, as is the case with Diana, whom a teacher wrote about. Polish remains a widely spoken European language with vibrant communities of immigrants, second, and third generation students. This is somewhat unique among the European immigrant groups. The Polish language continues to be quite resilient and has strong religious and cultural institutions associated with it in some urban centers. Therefore, Polish communities still receive consideration for bilingual programs due to the high ratio of Polish speakers.

Diana's family, for example, lived in a community that communicated primarily in Polish, but her schooling was done mostly in English. She had been in a bilingual program and benefited greatly from having a teacher who spoke her language, but she also was looked down upon by other students for being in the bilingual program. Eventually she transitioned out into a mainstream English classroom. A Polish speaker in a teacher education program, Sarah, decided to delve deeper into some of the language issues that Diana faced in her daily education. Diana, having been in a mainstream English classroom for quite some time, now struggles occasionally with and can neither read nor write Polish.

Sarah, an undergraduate teacher candidate in an urban university, did an investigation using the IPA chart for Polish phonemes and comparing it to the one for English. She was finishing up her program and receiving a bilingual endorsement in addition to the teaching certificate. Since she was bilingual herself, having grown up speaking Polish in her home, Sarah already knew many of the production problems for speaking English; however, through this experience, she was able to develop a metalanguage to talk about these issues and to move her embodied experiential knowledge into a theory that she could use to talk about with others in the class. She identified several aspects of pronunciation that seemed to give Diana trouble, but she predicted them from using the IPA chart in the appendix (Figure 3.8). She also, based on her own language learning experiences, critiqued the chart. Sarah claimed:

[ʒ] is post alveolar in English, while in Polish it is alveolar. Although this difference might appear to be minor, it limits the native Polish speaker's ability to achieve English fluency. This sound, along with the other post alveolar sounds, are the most difficult sounds for a Polish speaker to learn in English.

Notice that in the appendix, the Polish phonemic chart has these sounds at the same place of articulation as in English. This is somewhat a disputed point as many charts and phonological analyses of Polish do indicate these sounds are made much further toward the front of the mouth than in English. This may be due to dialect differences or misclassifications of these sounds. Sarah, having gone through the struggle herself, noted that these sounds were very difficult to learn, even though Polish has similar sounds, and explained Diana struggled with them very much.

She identified several other issues that may cause difficulty in English pronunciation for a Polish speaker. In her analysis of the phonology of Polish, she paid particular attention to the points of articulation for sounds; however, this rarely led to issues where meaning was at stake. For example, while she did mention that there was no /h/ in Polish, although it is in English, she only explained that it led to the word sounding different. She did not consider how a speaker of Polish, not recognizing the phoneme /h/, may substitute a sound in English such as the next nearest fricative [x] or delete the sound altogether. A speaker may say [xow] or [ow] instead of [how]. For an English listener, the first would sound more like "cow" and the second like the exclamation "ow." Such contrastive differences may be found in other points of articulation, causing more confusion than just a pronunciation issue.

Sarah noted that one major problem Diana faced was in recognizing these different phonemes. This was most noticeable in reading where Diana struggled with the complex English orthography. In Polish, as Diana was used to reading, the letters had a much closer correspondence to the Polish phonemes than English letters do for English. In English, the letters may "make different sounds" depending on their place in relation to other letters. In fact, English letters may represent different phonemes (the "f" in "of" for example represents the phoneme /v/ not /f/). Coming from a system where the letters represent phonemes much more consistently, Diana struggled. She may have had phonemic awareness in Polish, and while there is evidence that phonemic awareness transfers to a second language when people are literate in their first, Diana still struggled with understanding the English orthography. Once she started to recognize the phonemes in English, her reading improved greatly. Sarah wrote:

When writing the word "stand," a Polish speaker would probably write "stend" because that is how he or she hears it pronounced. When a Polish native speaker learns to read, it is very hard to develop the phonetic and phonemic awareness of the differences between the two languages.

Diana struggled with English phonology; however, through certain teachers in school who spoke Polish, she was able to recognize many of the differences in the phonological systems. Through explicit study of phonology, Sarah was able to recognize many of Diana's problem areas and was better equipped to engage in metalinguistic discussion about some of the differences that hindered Diana's reading.

Conclusion

The study of speech sounds is called *phonetics* and the study of how they work together in a language is called *phonology*. Phonetics is a direct, measurable science that is based on the description of sounds based on articulation, voicing, and acoustic quality. Phonology, on the other hand, is the study of how speakers perceive meaningful sounds within a language. Phonology is predicated on the assumption that languages are rule governed and systematic. The phonology of a language is a system that is predictable and consistent across speakers. When working with ELs, many of the "mistakes" they make in pronunciation are due to systematic differences between two or more languages they speak. These "mistakes" can be predictable. We have demonstrated a form of phonological analysis, called *contrastive analysis*, that can be used to understand the differences between languages and understand our students' actual and potential problem areas. In the next chapter, we will look at how phonetics and phonology have played a major role in some of the most controversial debates in language education over the past several decades: the *Reading Wars*.

QUESTIONS/ACTIVITIES

1. Describe the difference between a phonetic and a phonemic or conventional alphabet. What are some of the benefits and disadvantages of each?
2. Pick two of the languages in the appendix (Figures 3.3–3.9), or visit the Speech Accent Archive at http://accent.gmu.edu/ and compare the phonemes. What predictions can you make, based on the charts, about difficulties speakers of one language may have learning the other language?

3. Working with ELs.

   a) As with the teachers in the case studies, identify an EL. Look at the phonology of the student's dominant language and compare it with the English phonemic chart. What are some differences? Where might be some problem areas?

   b) Have a conversation with the student and/or observe the student reading. Were you able to observe mispronunciations and misreading in English at the areas you identified in part a?

   c) Talk with the student about what he or she finds difficult in speaking English. Does the student identify the same issues you identified in part a or b? Why or why not? Can he or she explain how and why those areas of language learning are difficult? Does the student refer to his or her dominant language?

   d) Do these difficulties affect meaning? Does the student have trouble understanding spoken English or do English speakers have difficulty understanding the student?

   e) Develop a plan to target these areas. Provide a rationale about how you will work with this student to address these issues. What steps will you take? Why? How has learning about phonology helped you make these decisions?

Additional Resources

American Speech-Language-Hearing Association http://www.asha.org/practice/multicultural/Phono.htm

"The speech accent archive" http://accent.gmu.edu/

"Phonetics and Phonology" http://www.dmoz.org/Science/Social_Sciences/Linguistics/Phonetics_and_Phonology/

http://www.phonetics.ucla.edu/course/chapter1/chapter1.html

Appendix: Phonemic Inventories

CONSONANTS (PULMONIC)

	Bilabial	Labio-dental	Dental	Alveolar	Palato-alveolar	Retroflex	Palatal	Velar	Uvular	Pharyngeal	Glottal
Plosive	p b			t d				k g			
Nasal	m			n				ŋ			
Trill											
Tap or Flap											
Fricative		f ʋ	θ ð	s z	ʃ ʒ						h
Affricate					tʃ dʒ						
Lateral fricative											
Approximant				ɹ			j				
Lateral approximant				l							

Where symbols appear in pairs, the one to the right represents a voiced consonant, shaded areas denote articulations judged impossible.

VOWELS

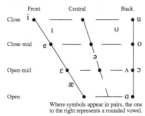

Where symbols appear in pairs, the one to the right represents a rounded vowel.

FIGURE 3.3 English Phonemic Inventory

CONSONANTS (PULMONIC)

	Bilabial	Labio-dental	Dental	Alveolar	Palato-alveolar	Retroflex	Palatal	Velar	Uvular	Pharyngeal	Glottal
Plosive	b			t d				k g			ʔ
Nasal	m			n							
Trill				r							
Tap or Flap				ɾ							
Fricative		f	θ ð	s z	ʃ				χ ʁ	ħ ʕ	h
Affricate					dʒ						
Lateral fricative											
Approximant							j				
Lateral approximant				l							

Where symbols appear in pairs, the one to the right represents a voiced consonant, shaded areas denote articulations judged impossible.

VOWELS

Front — Central — Back

Close   i ——— • ——— u
Close-mid e ——— • ——— o
Open-mid   — • —
            æ
Open   a • ———— •

Where symbols appear in pairs, the one to the right represents a rounded vowel.

FIGURE 3.4 Arabic Phonemic Inventory

CONSONANTS (PULMONIC)

	Bilabial	Labio-dental	Dental	Alveolar	Palato-alveolar	Retroflex	Palatal	Velar	Uvular	Pharyngeal	Glottal
Plosive	b			t				k g			
Nasal	m			n			ɲ				
Trill				r							
Tap or Flap				ɾ							
Fricative	β	f	θ ð	s				χ ɣ			
Affricate					tʃ						
Lateral fricative											
Approximant							j				
Lateral approximant				l			ʎ				

Where symbols appear in pairs, the one to the right represents a voiced consonant, shaded areas denote articulations judged impossible.

VOWELS

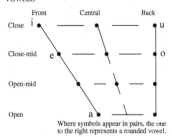

Where symbols appear in pairs, the one to the right represents a rounded vowel.

FIGURE 3.5 Spanish Phonemic Inventory

CONSONANTS (PULMONIC)

	Bilabial	Labio-dental	Dental	Alveolar	Palato-alveolar	Retroflex	Palatal	Velar	Uvular	Pharyngeal	Glottal
Plosive	p b		t d					k g			
Nasal	m			n			ɲ				
Trill									R		
Tap or Flap											
Fricative		f v		s z	ʃ ʒ						
Affricate											
Lateral fricative											
Approximant				ɹ			j				
Lateral approximant				l			ʎ				

Where symbols appear in pairs, the one to the right represents a voiced consonant, shaded areas denote articulations judged impossible.

VOWELS

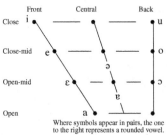

Where symbols appear in pairs, the one to the right represents a rounded vowel.

FIGURE 3.6 Portuguese Phonemic Inventory

CONSONANTS (PULMONIC)

	Bilabial	Labio-dental	Dental	Alveolar	Palato-alveolar	Retroflex	Palatal	Velar	Uvular	Pharyn-geal	Glottal
Plosive	p			t				k			
Nasal	m			n				ŋ			
Trill											
Tap or Flap											
Fricative		f		s		ʂ ʐ	ç	χ			
Affricate				ts		tʂ	cç				
Lateral fricative											
Approximant							j				
Lateral approximant				l							

Where symbols appear in pairs, the one to the right represents a voiced consonant, shaded areas denote articulations judged impossible.

VOWELS

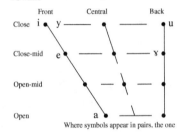

Where symbols appear in pairs, the one

FIGURE 3.7 Mandarin Phonemic Inventory

CONSONANTS (PULMONIC)

	Bilabial	Labio-dental	Dental	Alveolar	Palato-alveolar	Retroflex	Palatal	Velar	Uvular	Pharyn-geal	Glottal
Plosive	p b		t d					k g			
Nasal	m		n					ŋ			
Trill				r							
Tap or Flap											
Fricative		f v	s z		ʃ ʒ						
Affricate			ts dz		tʃ dʒ						
Lateral fricative											
Approximant							j				
Lateral approximant				l							

Where symbols appear in pairs, the one to the right represents a voiced consonant, shaded areas denote articulations judged impossible.

VOWELS

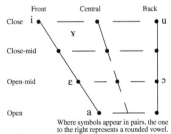

Where symbols appear in pairs, the one to the right represents a rounded vowel.

FIGURE 3.8 Polish Phonemic Inventory

CONSONANTS (PULMONIC)

	Bilabial	Labio-dental	Dental	Alveolar	Palato alveolar	Retroflex	Palatal	Velar	Uvular	Pharyn-geal	Glottal
Plosive				t			c	k			ʔ
Nasal	m			n			ɲ	ŋ			
Trill											
Tap or Flap											
Fricative		f v		s z				χ ɣ			h
Affricate											
Lateral fricative											
Approximant							j				
Lateral approximant				l							

Where symbols appear in pairs, the one to the right represents a voiced consonant, shaded areas denote articulations judged impossible.

VOWELS

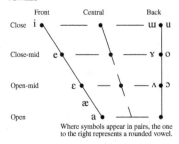

Where symbols appear in pairs, the one to the right represents a rounded vowel.

FIGURE 3.9 Vietnamese Phonemic Inventory

4

PHONICS AND WHOLE LANGUAGE

Linguistic Foundations

LEARNING GOALS

1. Understand major implications for phonology in language learning.
2. Use concepts in phonetics and phonology to critically analyze teaching practices.
3. Understand major debates in phonics and Whole Language education.
4. Summarize the benefits and limits of "sounding out" words versus reading sight words.
5. Critically analyze major debates in reading and language teaching.
6. Create a lesson for student inquiry using concepts from relevant theories.

KEY TERMS/IDEAS: accent, BICS, CALP, language acquisition, language socialization, phonics instruction, Whole Language

Introduction

As teachers, our instructional practices and pedagogical approaches are necessarily informed by how we perceive the nature, function, and purpose of language use. Sometimes we are conscious of our perspectives, especially when we draw on formalized and explicit metaphors of language and learning, generally acquired in teacher education programs. For example, many teachers may invoke terms such as *learning styles*, *basic interpersonal language*, *academic language proficiency*, or *Whole Language* to talk about language learning and instruction (Cummins, 2008; Gardner, 2011). Clearly, these terms our framed by academic discourses and debates; however, most of the time, our explicit knowledge of language functions and learning are mixed with implicit, everyday *folk theories* of language. Sometimes we consciously or subconsciously adopt a pot-pourri of language "buzzwords" and the "latest flavor of the month" to justify idiosyncratic practices even if the perspectives are fundamentally incommensurate or even contradictory.

Regardless of whether our notions of language are explicit or implicit, the fact remains that some perspective of language mediates every teaching strategy, curriculum planning, and educational policy. Our ideas about the nature, function, and purpose of language impact our uses of language not only in the classroom but society at large. We collectively refer to these explicit and implicit ideas about language, whether in-school or in society, as *language ideologies*. Language ideologies (our ideas about language) always directly or indirectly impact our analysis, teaching, and learning of language. Our goal in this chapter and throughout the book is to make the more tacit and implicit language ideologies that impact our lives more visible and explicit which allows for greater reflection. This type of *metalinguistic awareness* allows us to become more purposeful and strategic in how we approach the complexities of language and learning.

In Chapter 3 we presented the foundations of phonetics and phonology as structural approaches to the study of language in the classroom. We also modeled practical methods of conducting phonological analysis through a variety of ways actual teachers used those phonological principles in their classrooms. In this chapter, we will continue our journey up the linguistic ladder and take a broader look at some instructional strategies and classroom activities. The intent of this chapter is to provide a critical framework to unpack, analyze, and differentiate the underlying assumptions of various approaches to language and instruction that are often mandated in schools. This critical framework of language and learning will empower you (the teacher) to exert greater agency in curriculum planning and broader educational decision making that impacts language learners. While as teachers of language learners we are often expected to implement "one size fits all" curricula, we know that this approach severely overlooks the variation and diversity of learners. As professional educators, we have an ethical responsibility to not only implement curricula programs, but to critically analyze and adapt the strengths and limitations of each activity as it relates to our students. This process engenders greater *metalinguistic awareness* that we think is so important to effective teaching of not only second language learners, but ALL learners across multiple contexts of development.

Building off of the last two chapters on neurolinguistics and phonology, we now turn to one of the classical debates in the history of second language learning: *phonics vs. Whole Language*. On the one hand, the "phonics" approach focuses on the development of phonemic awareness through explicit instruction of discrete sounds. Programs like *Hooked on Phonics* target schools, teachers, and parents alike, to provide what they claim to be the best way for students to learn language and literacy skills. In contrast, "Whole Language" advocates are theoretically opposed to discrete language and literacy activities and subscribe to more holistic approaches that emphasize communication. Each of these approaches is premised on fundamentally different views of language, learning, and development.

Implications of Phonology in the Classroom: Accent

While phonics based approaches to phonology emphasize the structural/acoustic aspects of sounds in literacy instruction, there are significant sociocultural dimensions to consider. We often hear second language learners express a desire to "fix" their accents or better yet "remove their accent." Of course, as linguists we know that there is no such thing as an "accent-less" language, so what do people mean? An accent marks one as different from the norm, foreign, or other. Often pronunciation can impact comprehension and meaning. For example, if a student wants a "snack" /snæk/ but instead what comes out of his/her mouth sounds like "snake" /snek/ there will be a problem! Here we would like to focus on those instances where comprehension and meaning are not the issue, but rather how accents and sounds serve as identity markers. How does one's pronunciation mark them geographically, economically, politically, socially, ideologically, and educationally? Listen to how the following three people pronounce the word "snack" (http://www.forvo.com/word/snack/).

Given the inextricable link between accents and identity, how do speakers, consciously or subconsciously, use accents to achieve various identity goal(s)? The social identities invoked by accents often speak to our stereotypical and essentialized views of entire communities of speakers. Politicians often change the way they talk based on the audience they talk with, as noted in several campaign speeches. A "southern drawl" is often used to signal authenticity, hospitality, and warmth; however, the same sounds could be interpreted as homey and uneducated to people from the northern states. The "Queen's English" accent seems to give authority and legitimacy in documentaries and sometimes God speaks that way too! The "lisp" clearly distinguishes the Spanish speaker from Spain and the speaker from Central America. African-American English (AAE) also has a different phonological system from Standard English, which often gets dismissed as "bad" or "improper" English. In the classic *My Fair Lady* (1964), Henry Higgins transforms the local flower girl into a Hungarian princess simply by changing the way she sounds. Notice that the focus of that movie was on phonetics and phonology, not the topics of conversation or the way she acted. These differences are not arbitrary, but are cultural and historical manifestations of speech sounds, the manipulation of phonological features to perform identities.

The manipulation of accent is frequently used in pop culture, mass media, and comedy/satire. These uses signal our collective awareness of speech norms and the exaggeration or violation of those norms to earn the audience's laughter. Russell Peters is one comedian who is famous for engaging in ethnic and racial humor through the use of accents that mark multiple regional and international identities. Michael Scott in *The Office* (2005–2012) often assumes the role of someone else by using an accent to identify them. We have assumptions based on these small speech sounds, and sometimes those assumptions inform decisions about jobs and housing. There is substantial research to show the real life consequences of accent discrimination in housing and employment decisions. One famous example is the *2000 Housing Discrimination Study* where the researchers found that speakers who have foreign or ethnic accents were less likely to be called back by landlords (Zhao, Ondrich, & Yinger, 2006). In another study, attitudes of employers were measured regarding the accents of Mexican-American workers. The expectations (stereotypes), exposure, and language attitudes of interviewers reviewing Mexican-Americans for jobs as supervisors, skilled technicians, and semi-skilled workers, were found to correlate with the actual hiring of Mexican-Americans for jobs (de la Zerda & Hopper, 1979). While we may not have been aware of such studies and the day-to-day effects of accents, most of us have either heard or made comments such as "he sounds so uneducated" or "she sounds like she's from New York." Without hearing the content of speech, or even word choice, our accents serve as identity badges for better or worse. The point here is not to say that these judgments are right or wrong, but rather to become aware of how language, and in particular accents, function in everyday life. Thus, linguistic analysis can provide deeper insight into how identities are being negotiated, manipulated, and contested in classrooms and society at large.

The Reading Wars: Whole Language and Phonics Instruction Debated

Some of the issues in this chapter may seem largely abstract and too big for it to make a difference in classrooms. Speech accent may not be something dealt with in every classroom, but the same phonological tools needed to understand students' language in the last chapter and the complexities of language in this chapter, are also needed to inform the use and development of curricula. Teachers of writing and reading, especially, will benefit from understanding how phonology works and how it can help them organize learning and instruction.

This is particularly salient in the discussions of "Whole Language" versus "phonics instruction." Later, in Chapters 9 and 10, we will discuss more in depth theories of learning that ground these two approaches, but by now you should have learned the tools of phonological analysis to critically unpack the two approaches and extend that into your own classroom.

In the 1990s the lines were drawn in popular discourse between what was called Whole Language instruction and phonics instruction. An article published in 1997 in *Time Magazine* publicized the debate that was ringing in elementary education throughout the nation. The article, *How Johnny should read*, laid out the opposing sides in the conflict dubbed the "Reading Wars."

On one side of the war was explicit phonics instruction. This came under the national spotlight in the 1950s when the nation, as a whole, was reporting low literacy rates. A book published in 1955, *Why Johnny can't read*, placed the blame on look-say teaching methods, claiming that phonics would help reading achievement. Jeanne Chall, an expert in reading instruction, did a review of the research in the 1960s and found that phonics instruction actually was reported to have increased reading. However, she warned that if taken too far, phonics would provide no benefit to reading. Without heeding her warning, students were forced into tedious phonics drills. The letters and sound correspondence was elevated to utmost importance, and reading had everything to do with fluency, but not comprehension. For Chall, and supporters of phonics, however, they noted that a focus on "meaning" of words actually hurt reading scores.

On the other side was Whole Language, the idea that students should read words as a whole, in context. Students, according to cognitive psychologists in the 1960s, read whole chunks of text at a time. They didn't need to rely on specific letters and corresponding sounds because they could predict, based on context, what the meaning was. Over time, of course, students would learn individual words. The battles raged. Whole Language gained ground and support of national associations. Phonics gained support of parents looking for results and major corporate products. Whole Language lost some, phonics lost some, and students' reading didn't drastically improve.

Eventually the concept of "phonemic awareness" was brought to the forefront, and in many ways served as a potential peace treaty. Remember from the previous chapter phonemes were the group of physical sound units that speakers believed were a single sound, or the minimal meaningful unit of sound in a language (*minimal pairs*). If students were aware of the different phonemes in English, then they would be able to understand the relationship between letters and sounds. They would pick up new patterns of letters and sounds as they read through texts. Thus the peace treaty sort of allowed for some phonics instruction to build phonemic awareness, but not too much. This was generally confirmed by the *National Reading Panel* (Shanahan, 2005), which found that phonics instruction was helpful in that it helped with fluency, but it did not help with comprehension.

Teachers need to understand how their reading curricula are situated in these prevailing philosophies. There are benefits and limitations to each. It is our hope that the concepts of phonology can be used to improve your reading curricula or to supplement a school curriculum with what it may be lacking.

Assumptions in Phonics Instruction

There are many different types of phonics products. Often they are presented as games or drills that teach "b" as in "bat" and "c" as in "cat" type of letter recognition. These may come in the form of wooden blocks, electronic games, or worksheets. Often the assumed intent is letter recognition. We assume that if kids recognize a letter, or a set of letters, and the sounds that they stand for, then the student will be able to "sound out" a word. This, then, would constitute reading. Of course, some words, like those that end in "-ght," just can't be "sounded out," so phonics instruction often would teach these three letters together. But eventually the students would catch on and be able to read.

In this view of language, the assumption made is that language, specifically writing, is merely a representational system. The letter represents a sound. If you put the sounds together, you can make a word, which represents something else. The relationship between a sign, like a letter or word, to the world, is that the sign "stands for" something else. The sign "b" stands for the /b/ sound, or the linguistic description of a bilabial stop. The sign "horse" stands for an animal in the world that has four legs and people ride. The point being that the assumption often in reading instruction is that there is a one-to-one correspondence between an arbitrary sign, and an object in the world. As this is applied to phonics instruction, then, our students need to memorize this correspondence between the letters and the sound. Once this is achieved, they can be young readers. Eventually, though, they won't need to read every letter, but at least when starting, this is helpful. Usually explicit phonics instruction ends during the elementary years. Once the students know the sounds, they can begin reading, and hopefully comprehending.

Phonics instruction is not really about comprehension. Usually it is focused on saying words "correctly." Again, what is underscored is the way the word sounds. Teachers who have been trained with a phonics perspective often correct students in read-out-louds. If a student mispronounces a word, they would be corrected, or the word would be modeled for them. This type of reinforcement occurs at the smallest meaningful units of language, or the phonemes. While teachers and students may not call them phonemes, phonics attempts to help students understand what sounds are appropriate where in a language. For this reason, as we saw in Chapter 3, many English learners (ELs) may have difficulties because of the different phonemes. However, even monolingual students may find it difficult to know what sounds are grouped together into a phoneme, and how those are related to written symbols like letters.

Another common difficulty with phonics instruction is the heavy focus on a standard pronunciation that rarely occurs in spoken speech. We typically teach early readers the difference between consonants and vowels denotatively, rather than phonetically. For the most part, children memorize the discrete list of vowels: *a, e, i, o, u* and sometimes *y* or *w* and consonants are simply "not vowels." While this might be a more convenient strategy for defining the difference, it doesn't provide a useful metacognitive strategy for novice readers attempting to pronounce unfamiliar words. This is a place where awareness of the difference between phonetic and orthographic representations could help, especially for second language learners who may be coming from a more phonetically friendly orthographic system (e.g., Spanish). Remember from Chapter 3, consonants are universal sounds that are articulated in specific ways and the *International Phonetic Alphabet* (IPA) uniquely captures each sound with a unique symbol, irrespective of local orthographic conventions. Turning back to the IPA chart, consider how each consonant is articulated (i.e., the placement of the tongue, voicing, and airflow) and how each humanly possible consonant has a unique symbol.

In contrast, vowel production and its representation are relatively more approximate as to its acoustic properties. Any sound that is made with the airflow relatively unobstructed is a vowel. While vowels tend to cluster at certain points, technically they can be made anytime you open your mouth and push air through the vocal cords. For this reason, if you were to set out to study vowels, you would need to do an acoustic analysis of the way the air and sound waves come through the mouth and nose. The "a" /æ/ sound in "cat" /cæt/ for example, actually will be produced by a variety of different vowels. We can call that the English sound for "short 'a'" if it is close enough. Eventually, though, if you move your tongue up, you will begin to recognize the "short 'u'" sound instead. Likewise, all vowels, orthographically speaking are approximations of what actually happens phonetically. The actual sound varies depending on the phonological and sociocultural rules governing the uses of each word. Thus, phonics instruction imposes a sign, or a letter, upon a group of sounds, many of which younger students may not recognize yet. This is the underlying idea behind phonemic awareness, that students need to be aware of what "counts" as an "a" and what counts as a "b." Phonics instruction traditionally attempts to teach this explicitly, decontextualized, and through memorization and repetition.

In languages with different writing systems, phonics may be a moot point. Students don't need to focus on the representation of each sound. Some languages require the reading of each word as a single symbol. Chinese (Mandarin or Cantonese), for example, requires the memorization of many different symbols, perhaps somewhere around 2,000–3,000 to read a standard newspaper. Other languages may benefit from phonics instruction very well. Spanish orthographically is more phonetically aligned with its symbols, and there are not nearly as many "exceptions" as in English. Thus, phonics instruction can be a helpful tool in reading classrooms. It can also be a benefit for working with ELs, as seen in the previous chapter. However, phonics instruction, at least in as far as the major "Reading Wars"/ debates are concerned, should be seen as more of a way to view language than as a specific reading strategy. It is the focus on the linguistic code, rather than meaning.

Assumptions in Whole Language

An alternative approach, as outlined above, is the Whole Language approach. This is actually a wide array of approaches that have some fundamental points in common. Unlike phonics instruction which focuses on the minute sounds of words as they correspond to letters in reading, Whole Language acknowledges that when we read we rarely look at every letter in a word, in fact, we rarely look at every word. Our minds actually begin to fill in the information by taking in context. The more one reads, of course, the better one gets at this. Thus, in Whole Language, the underlying issues are exposure to text. Students are asked to read, and to read often. They will, it is assumed, pick up on the meaning of words as they read for understanding in context. As opposed to phonics instruction, which defines reading in terms of fluency (more or less), Whole Language is much more focused on comprehension.

Whole Language should be seen as a philosophy of sorts, since it could include any number of reading or comprehension strategies. Indeed, proponents of Whole Language underscore that the approach treats language as a "whole," attending to all parts of language. A major benefit of Whole Language approaches is that language is viewed as contextualized, so you don't need a wordlist, per se, nor a worksheet, to practice "bl" blends. The language learning, specifically learning to read, comes as words are encountered in context.

Meaning is centralized, so the specific sounds, letter patterns, and words are observed as text is encountered. Often students may not actually make specific letter sound connections. Perhaps in early versions and strategies students may not even recognize phonemes. The explicit reaction to strict phonics or other explicit teaching tends to be reactionary, a sort of "throw the baby out with the bathwater" situation. All explicit language teaching is avoided so students can construct language as they encounter it. Newer movements, still holding solidarity with Whole Language, do allow for explicit phonics instruction, if, of course, it is contextualized.

One of the major drawbacks of Whole Language is that it seems to be a catchall phrase. Any reading instruction could, after all, be a part of Whole Language. Although the focus may be on comprehension strategies, one may consider any instruction a part of the "whole" of language. Fundamentally, however, Whole Language does not seem to address bigger picture issues, or other layers of meaning. Accents, alternative spellings, and so forth may have some profound meanings that require a scope beyond the initial context or text. For example, the difference between "catalog" and "catalogue" may not be recognized in Whole Language approaches, because readers would know what the word "means," but in phonics, this would definitely be a point of conversation. It could even lead into an explicit discussion about the etymology of words, simplification of American English (from British English), and when and where the appropriate use of the "ue" in words like "catalogue" and "dialogue," or the sometimes very confusing spellings of "theatre" and "centre." These discussions may prove to be very well set in an elementary classroom, and should be covered in high school (at least when reading classics). These alternative spellings may, perhaps, be lost on students in Whole Language where the word–concept relationship is privileged above the phonics letter–sound relationship.

Can we do both?

Phonics and Whole Language instruction are only two of many different teaching styles. It may be best to think more along the lines of a continuum (Figure 4.1) instead of an "either-or" polarized dichotomy. At any given point on that continuum, teachers should be able to understand how phonology can be applied, and how the instructional practice might benefit from phonological insights. For example, we could, perhaps, put phonics instruction near one end (left side of Figure 4.1) where the focus is on language form and explicating phonological rules for students to memorize in order to enhance reading fluency. On the other end, there is a focus on meaning rather than form and categorically rejects any

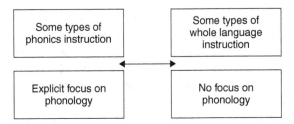

FIGURE 4.1 Phonics–Whole Language Continuum

explicit phonetic/phonemic instruction, preferring sight words until students can construct word meanings based on contextual cues.

On the extreme left we have complete reliance on explicit instruction and knowledge of sounds for reading development, while on the extreme right it is assumed that language will naturally and spontaneously develop implicitly.

Practically speaking, no approach to reading instruction and language learning could ever sit at one end of this continuum or the other since language learners rely on both explicit and implicit knowledge of language while the relationship between the two types of knowledge remains murky (Ellis, Loewen, Erlam, Philp, Elder, & Reinders, 2009). Explicit phonics instruction could be used strategically at any point to foster metalinguistic and metacognitive awareness about sound–symbol relationships. It is more a matter of how much context and what context is considered. A teacher who understands phonology could insert phonics instruction while engaging in joint reading and other context embedded, meaning-making activities like *author's chair*. However, to exist only on the far left side of the spectrum by strictly adhering to form and phonics worksheets is equally worrisome. If one stays in this zone exclusively, then language is reduced to meaningless code and parrot-like recitation where its communicative purpose is lost.

There are potential benefits from explicit phonemic instruction for second language learners (Stuart, 1999). One way this could be done is by having students talk about the phonemes in their languages. They would have to explicitly talk about the differences in the sound structures of languages. Teachers may facilitate this learning by developing activities in which knowledge of phonology is needed to solve problems. By doing so, phonology may be seen as both contextually bound, in that it means something within a context, as well as a part of the context itself, in that phonology is a system which binds sounds together as meaningful. Thus, phonology can be used in the moment-to-moment interactions to help understand EL students' language learning (Chapter 3) as well as a useful analytic tool for social critique and curriculum development on a much broader scale (this chapter).

Phonetics and Phonology in Student Inquiry

Another benefit of understanding phonetics and phonology is that it can be used in student inquiry. Especially in schools with high populations of ELs, having students conduct a phonological analysis may be extremely helpful. In this book we draw attention to student inquiry in instruction. When students are given the tools to study language, they can begin to speak about language, or develop a metalanguage. In Chapter 3 we talked about using phonological analysis in classrooms to understand how the micro level features of phonology may bring difficulties in the classroom. Here, however, we want to look at the bigger picture. Students can engage in this process too. Students hear the differences between different accents and different ways of speaking. Many students probably already know that there are social implications of these different ways of speaking. Teach them, on the level of phonology, to try to describe different ways of speaking. How do people sound in their community? How about in a science documentary you watch during your science class? How about a politician shown in a clip for civics class? Have the students study the way these people sound. Then ask them what that means about them. What do these differences say about their identities? How about their status? Their relationships?

This process can begin informally by asking questions and talking about the sounds of language. Eventually you build a language to talk about language with your students. This awareness is important, but not as important as self-awareness. Can they describe their own speech style? What does that mean? Student inquiry is a great way to get students engaged in asking deep questions about society through the prism of their own language practices. It is also a way to teach them the importance of understanding the language taught in school. There is a place for pronunciation and grammar, but students need to be able to understand what that space is. Facilitate students' understanding of how pronunciation matters personally, socially, economically, politically, and ethically in their daily lives. Phonological analysis can be a window into complex social issues surrounding the lives of all students.

Conclusion

In this chapter we considered further implications of phonology in the classroom. One way phonology helps us is to understand the different ways *accents* are interpreted in society. When we understand the differences in accents we can begin to break down the roots of stereotypical thinking. We also looked at how different teaching strategies like *phonics* and *Whole Language* are based on diverse views about the way language functions. Learning and language are inextricably linked. We can't talk about learning without talking about theories of how language functions. In classrooms around the world, teachers are making decisions to implement curricula and conduct lessons based on the way they think about how language functions and how it is learned. Therefore, explicit discussion about language empowers us to make more informed decisions about learning and instruction. In the next chapter we continue our journey across the linguistic landscape when we closely examine how sentences are formed.

TEACHER CASE STUDIES

Sandra: Rhyming

While learning about phonology in her linguistics class, Sandra created a lesson plan for her first grade students. Most of her students spoke Spanish in their home, but were in an English-only instruction classroom. Sandra, herself, did not speak Spanish. Sandra was trying to teach her students how to read. However, as she was planning her lessons, she realized that the students were struggling with more than "sounding out" the words. The typical letter–sound recognition was just not working with her students, so she decided to investigate further.

Using the principals from Chapter 4, Sandra identified phonological differences between Spanish and English:

> I understand that some sounds that are in English are not in Spanish such as; ŋ, v, θ, ð, z, ʃ, ʒ, h, dʒ, and r. There are also sounds that are in Spanish that are not in English such as; ɲ, x, ɾ, and ſ. Because of these differences I want to know that students are practicing listening to and using these sounds in context.

After analyzing the phonemes, Sandra developed a plan to help her students become aware of phonemes. Many of the resources available to her were either explicit phonics worksheets or leveled reading books. She knew that the phonics wouldn't really help the students understand meaning, but the alternative didn't seem to help students learn many of the differences between English and Spanish, and were somewhat confusing for the students. Thus, she set out to develop her own unit to teach students about the differences in phonology, and how these concepts were applied to reading.

Sandra first recognized that any discussion of phonemic awareness was best done in the context of meaning-making:

> I will read the book [about baseball] to the students with excitement while stressing rhyming words. Students will repeat the line of text after I read it orally. Students will stand and pretend that they are holding a baseball bat and ready to play. Next, I will say two words from the story and if the words rhyme they need to swing their bats.

She was able to make the activity into a game, using a theme, baseball, many of the students already knew about (and had been playing in gym class). However, she knew that understanding rhyming wasn't enough. This wouldn't really help kids understand the importance of the relationship between the words and meaning, nor would it really be beneficial in making explicit differences between Spanish and English, thus making students aware of phonemes.

She then created an activity that would be very explicit about why sounds in language matter. She mentioned in her lesson:

> Students will also practice with words that might be challenging to native Spanish speakers because they might be unfamiliar with certain English phonemes that are not in the Spanish phonetic alphabet. Students will practice using these sounds within the context of the story so they can focus on meaning making. For example, the words "three" and "tree" would allow students to hear the difference between the two sounds and tell the meaning of each word based on contextual clues. Next we would discuss how mistaking these two words could confuse a listener and change the meaning of a statement.

The goal of the activity was not just to recognize that /t/ and /θ/ were different phonemes in English, but to understand how these phonemes could affect meaning. Of course, "three" and "tree" may rarely be confused in context, the mere fact that the students could conceptualize how the phoneme changed the meaning was a profound revelation for the students. They had to put to words why these sounds matter!

Finally, Sandra ended the baseball unit by playing a matching game. Students were given short sentences or clauses about baseball, some from the baseball book they had read. They were to go around the room saying their lines until they found the rhyming lines. This helped contextualize the activity. Because the students knew about and enjoyed baseball, they were able to connect the lines of text to a larger activity. Therefore, the reading they were doing was embedded in an activity which, as Sandra explained, "allows students to engage in the text in many different ways so by the end of the lesson I hope they are very comfortable with it. After students can share baseball stories and connect with the text."

Sandra's understanding of phonology gave her the tools to critique the school's reading materials, understand what was lacking, and ultimately create an entire unit of lessons to help students understand the connection between phonemes and meaning.

Lauren: Vietnamese

Languages like Vietnamese are not as significantly represented in the American school system; however, many students speak languages and find affinity in ethnolinguistic groups which don't have representation in the United States as "major world languages." Vietnamese is a significant language in various parts of the United States. It does not necessarily share the same status as Mandarin or Spanish on the world stage, but is, nonetheless, a very significant language spoken in U.S. schools.

Lauren is a student in a Master's of Education program. She was young, but had recently decided to change careers. She was fulfilling classroom observation requirements in a school where the students spoke many different languages at home. She, herself, had grown up speaking Polish and had experienced being an EL in an English dominant context. She noticed that one of her eighth grade students, an American born Vietnamese boy, was having difficulty interacting with his peers and with accomplishing homework. At this point, since he had gone to English-speaking schools since preschool, the teachers and the principal were beginning to think he had a learning disability. Lauren, trying to figure out how to help this student, set out to study the phonological differences between Vietnamese and English to get a better understanding of where there may be potential production and comprehension difficulties for this student.

She began by interviewing the student about language; however, she was met with an unexpected nervousness:

> He seemed distant and uninterested, very nervous to speak about language at all. When asked to reflect upon the language spoken in his home, now or growing up, he seems lost as to what this "other" language is called. He poses the inability or unwillingness to speak of Vietnamese foods or his own sister's name.

After becoming familiar with the IPA chart for Vietnamese and identifying its differences from the English chart, she began to realize that many of the production and comprehension issues the student had in class were predictable. She could use the IPA chart as a way to talk about language, developing a metalinguistic awareness of phonological differences. She constantly connected these phonological differences to whether or not they could affect meaning. For example, the teacher correctly identified that there was a difference between the English and Vietnamese IPA charts at the voiceless alveolar stop, [t]. In the English chart, there is only /t/. In the Vietnamese chart, however, there is both /t/ and /tʰ/. She interpreted this to be "phonetic" and not "phonemic," thus not being a problem in meaning. Her rationale was that either Vietnamese phoneme would sound the same in English, or at least would not affect meaning. In Vietnamese, however, she found out, these are very different sounds, and by confusing them one word would change into another.

Vietnamese has several phonological differences with English. As seen in the IPA consonant chart, Vietnamese does not utilize affricates as phonemes. Vietnamese does not have a phoneme for a voiced velar stop, [g], but does have voiced and voiceless velar fricatives, unlike English. English does not have stops or nasals articulated at the palate, yet Vietnamese does have the phonemes /c/ and /ɲ/. English contains the fricatives [θ], [ð], [ʃ], and [ʒ], however, Vietnamese does not. The English sound /ɹ/ is also not found in Vietnamese. Thus there are significant phonemic differences between Vietnamese and English. There are also various vocalic differences, though perhaps the most notable are the phonemic differences between rounded and unrounded upper high and upper mid vowels. One other major difference in the phonology of Vietnamese is the presence of six different tones. These tones, absent completely in English, are mutually contrastive in Vietnamese.

As she began to look at the phonological differences of her Vietnamese student, Lauren unpacked many of the language production issues the school had identified. For example, the lack of the phonemic fricative [ʃ] poses issues for this student when he pronounces words beginning with this sound. The production, itself, really does not pose a significant problem except when it impacts meaning, so the aim of a phonological analysis should be to find instances where the differences impact meaning. The substitution of a similar sound, such as [s] for [ʃ], would cause problems in English, as seen in the pronunciation of "shoe" and "sue" or "ship" and "sip." Context, of course, may help the listener understand which was meant; however, the Vietnamese student may easily make these pronunciation shifts because the sounds are not different phonemes in Vietnamese. Lauren reflected on her reading program and noted that the Whole Language approach to instruction, like word walls, wasn't necessarily helping this Vietnamese-speaking boy learn to read English. She knew she needed to do some explicit phonics instruction.

Lauren wrote:

> We begin to see a change, however, in the addition of the dental/interdental sounds of /θ/ and /ð/ in the English alphabet, which Vietnamese does not experience. This could pose an issue with everyday blends found in "these," "this," and "those."

Her association with the English phonemes /tʃ/, /θ/, /ð/, and /ʃ/ as "blends" draws on her knowledge of English orthography which may be challenging for a Vietnamese speaker. In English orthography, some sounds are represented with two characters, although they represent one phoneme. The teacher used the traditional phonics word, "blend," to describe the orthographic representation, although this is misleading. They are really one sound represented by a digraph. However, the teacher correctly identifies this as a potential problem area for the Vietnamese reader, since "c" itself is a phoneme in Vietnamese, but "ch" is not. It may be difficult to associate the digraph "ch" with the sound [tʃ], since the sound doesn't even exist as a phoneme in Vietnamese. Another digraph the teacher mentioned was "th" which her student had difficulty reading. The orthography itself was confusing, but so was the fact that this phoneme did not exist in the student's home language. Thus, in reading, the student recognized "th" as two separate sounds, [t] and [h].

Vietnamese also does not frequently have consonant clusters; most syllables consisting only of a consonant, vowel, consonant (CVC). English, however, in some cases, allows three consonants to cluster at the beginning of a word, like "spray." Students trying to string these sounds together may face difficulty since it is not consistent with the way their language organizes the sounds into words.

Many of the issues the teacher was able to point out after looking at the phonology of Vietnamese were helpful in considering the difficulties of English production and comprehension. There were clearly some instances when this would impact meaning. With this knowledge, she understood how some of those issues this particular student had with speaking and reading were not necessarily due to a learning disability, but rather were probably related to the phonological differences between English and Vietnamese. Despite the length of time he had been in English classrooms, he still made the same mistakes repeatedly, further convincing Lauren that this was a predictable and systematic phonological issue, not a learning disability.

QUESTIONS/ACTIVITIES

1. For younger students, ask them to pick a sound in language (in any language they want). Ask them to describe the sound to others. What does it sound like? How do they make it? One of the major purposes of phonetics is to describe the sounds of language. This will help you and students open up an explicit discussion about language. It is a practice in thinking about language.

2. For older students, challenge them to critically engage in analysis of their networks. What do they notice about accent and the sound of language? What does that mean? This activity should require students to describe language, making them explicitly aware of linguistic differences. Furthermore, students should begin to talk about what the different sounds of language mean. How do they describe the differences? Do they mention class, race, gender, and so forth?

3. What methods of language instruction do you use in your classroom? In your school? Would you describe them as a *whole language* approach, a *phonics* approach, or something else. Think of a critique and a way to improve your classrooms language learning environment.

Additional Resources

http://www.kidzone.ws/kindergarten/consonants.htm [Phonics]

http://www.scholastic.com/teachers/article/lesson-plans-and-activities-teaching-phonics [Phonics]

5

SYNTAX

English Learners Building Sentences

LEARNING GOALS

1. Summarize basic concepts in syntax.
2. Understand different grammatical structures used in languages in the world.
3. Understand the relationship between syntax and meaning.
4. Analyze ambiguity in sentences.
5. Use syntactical analysis to inform teaching grammar.
6. Use syntactical analysis to understand student discourse.
7. Teach students to engage in inquiry using syntactic analysis.

KEY TERMS/IDEAS: syntax, grammar, recursion, phrase structure rules, prescriptive grammar, descriptive grammar, Universal Grammar (UG)

Introduction

"It's you and I, not you and me!" . . . "Don't end a sentence with a preposition!" For many of us, we can still hear the voices of our English teachers correcting our pronunciation, grammar, or writing. We may still be haunted by the red ink splashed over the pages of our writing reminding us to capitalize, insert commas, fix dangling modifiers, and correct run-ons. While we appreciated the feedback and good intentions of our teachers, these errors probably affected our attitude toward speaking, reading, and writing. It may have even caused us to be overly conscious when taking communicative risks—a serious impediment to learning and development. It was these experiences that taught us the absolute, natural, and immutable "correct" form(s) of speaking and writing.

As teachers, we may find ourselves reverting back to the default script of grammar correction we acquired during our "grammar school" days. Many students, especially second language learners, may wonder about the inherent logic of some of these rules. It is natural for them to compare the rules of the language they are learning (L2) with their primary language (L1). For example, a native Spanish speaker may wonder why double negatives are considered incorrect in English, or a native Arabic speaker may wonder why we don't just drop the "is" altogether in contractions. If we are pushed by our students to provide a rationale for some of these grammatical rules, how do we respond? Do we appeal to the authority of convention ("that's the way it is!") or do we engage in an explicit discussion about the situated nature of what is considered correct language use? The purpose of this chapter is to provide you with more tools to take up the latter strategy with regards to the complex functions of grammar or syntax. In this chapter we will examine the differences between stylistic conventions and linguistic notions of what constitutes grammatical correctness.

Reading this book, and in particular this chapter, can be a little challenging and perhaps uncomfortable. It won't be because the material is too academic, abstract, or "jargony"; it will be because we will need to temporarily suspend our "common sense" notions of correctness. Sometimes these ideas about language function can be so engrained that it may be difficult to imagine an alternative possibility to the comma, tense, subject-verb agreement, voicing rules that have regulated our language use since the formative years of our lives. If you are one of those English teachers who really relishes using the red pen to insert commas, cross out double negatives, and make passive voice into active voice (or vice versa), then we invite you to put the pen back in the holster (at least temporarily) as we examine the alternative universe of linguistic syntax and grammar of the mind.

Morphosyntax

For the sake of following a traditional linguistic approach, we have separated this chapter and the following into two separate chapters, one on syntax, and the other on morphology. Together, these two could be grouped into morphosyntax, and, realistically, should be studied together. Morphosyntax is the study of how speech sounds are used to make words and sentences. In languages around the world there is much variety about how words and sentences are formed. In fact, much of our own awareness of words comes from our use of writing. We see individual words, in English, separated from others by blank spaces. In oral speech, however, the separation between words is not as clear-cut. Think about the times you have paused to think if two words should be hyphenated or if they should be written as one word or two words. This is just one example of how we come to understand what constitutes a word.

In many languages, words can contain an entire expression of a sentence, as we will see in the next chapter. In others, words are very short and must be placed in the correct grammatical order in a sentence. There is so much variation in the way that languages allow for communication that linguists have set out to understand how languages develop their grammar. Several major theories have emerged, some of which you have been exposed to in this book already. Here we will discuss two approaches as they relate to morphosyntax. The first is Chomsky's Universal Grammar (UG), also called the "language instinct" by Pinker (1994). This is based on the assumption that there are universals in the grammar of all languages.

Theoretically, even if a linguistic form violates the grammatical rules of a particular language, it is assumed that it doesn't violate the rules of UG. While linguists are far from describing all that is structurally possible in human languages (less than 20% by some estimates), UG serves as a metaphor for the human linguistic potential, at least structurally speaking. If something assumed to be universal in language is missing, then linguists search for it or explain it away as a pragmatic or cultural irregularity, not a structural one. This, it could be said, is a deductive approach to linguistics. Linguists start with assumptions and work from those assumptions.

A second vein of linguistics, which is becoming increasingly popular, is that the grammar of language emerges from cultural systems and is a social construction (Sampson, 2005). We have seen this theme emerge in the first four chapters of this book as well. Language is a tool used to accomplish goals of people, who are cultural beings. Therefore, morphosyntax must be studied in the context of cultural activity systems. One cannot assume that studying language can be done in the absence of socially organized activities that are mediated by history, rules, and goals. The ways languages organize sentences, and the way languages build words, are embedded within cultural practices. Thus, it is not sufficient to ask, "How do my students use language?" Instead, it is more complete to pursue answers to two questions: "Why do my students use language this way?" and, reflecting on one's own assumptions, "Why do I think this is incorrect?" The first question is the realm of traditional, structural linguistics, and the second set of questions move us into the domains of meaning and understanding language as a situated, cultural phenomenon, which has been the domain of applied linguists, linguistic anthropologists, and other applied communicative fields.

We will begin to look at morphosyntax from a traditional, structural linguistics point of view. Just like the phoneme charts in Chapter 3, the intent is to think about language itself, namely how to describe sentences and words. Once we have a way to talk about the language structures, however, we will move to the sociocultural approach to morphosyntax. The sociocultural approach foregrounds the central role of cultural activities in the organization of morphosyntactic rules and how people actually use language in everyday contexts. It is important to note, though, that the relationship between language form and culture is not so easily explained. Many have proposed that language, in fact, creates culture, not the reverse. This is best explained in a "both/and" paradox, a dialectic understanding where "language" and "culture" mutually inform one another. That discussion, however, will come later. For now we turn to the workings of morphosyntax by talking about syntax, specifically. We begin by looking at it in the theory of UG.

Linguistic Approach to Universal Grammar: Prescriptive Versus Descriptive Syntax

The grammar we learn in schools is called prescriptive grammar because it usually consists of a set of rules that tells us how to form, or prescribes, phrases and sentences. Some of these rules can also be a matter of convention or style (e.g., the use of double negatives, dangling modifiers, etc.). This stands in stark contrast to the immutable, innate principles of how human beings universally give order to words to form meaningful sentences irrespective of the language they speak (something linguists are more concerned with). It is important to understand this basic difference. In this chapter we are concerned with describing the way language (linguistic form) works; therefore, we will be talking about the way languages make sentences as syntax. We will be building a set of tools to use for descriptive analysis of language.

What Is Universal Grammar (UG)?

During the middle of the last century, Noam Chomsky revolutionized the fields of linguistics and cognitive science with his pioneering work on Syntactic Structures (Chomsky, 1957). Chomsky is arguably one of the most influential scholars in modern times (Foreign Policy, 2005; MIT News, 1992). His approach to syntax and ALL linguistic and cognitive functions were predicated on the idea that the human brain was inherently inductive and rule governed. Human beings are genetically predisposed to form rules of language through inductive experience. He hypothesized that all linguistic structures were innate to the human species and these structures were acquired through the Language Acquisition Device (LAD). The LAD was not intended to be an actual location in the brain, but rather a metaphor for how the mind innately functions. One of the implications of the LAD is that some aspects of language should be universal, especially syntax. For example, it is assumed that all languages have different parts of speech, like nouns and verbs, or more accurately noun phrases (NP) and verb phrases (VP). Thus, reasoned Chomsky, by studying the very structure of language (phonology, morphology, and syntax), one could map the function of the human mind. He championed the theory of *generative grammar*, that language structure is generated in the mind through a systematic application of rules. While many today question the assumptions and implications of generative grammar, no one can deny the importance this theory had on other theories of linguistics and cognitive science more broadly. Many of the assumptions Chomsky originally made are still a standard part of linguistic study.

UG assumes that humans are hardwired with the basic information for language development. The grammar of the mind functions at two levels: deep structure and surface structure. There is an assumed deep structure of language in the mind that, once processed with the proper rules, becomes what we think of as a conventional sentence (surface structure). These two levels of grammar are what distinguish linguistic approaches to grammar and the notion of grammar that has been popularized through school based language activities. The theory of deep structure attempts to account for the similarities between sentences such as:

1. The man hit the baseball.
2. The baseball was hit by the man.

Chomsky's theory posits that sentences 1 and 2 are equivalent in meaning and perhaps identical at the deep structure level before being transformed through syntactic rules. The result of this mental transformation is the observed difference on the surface level. One of the problems with thinking of these two sentences as basically the same is that they actually can be interpreted quite differently. We will return to this point when we discuss meaning and discourse analysis, in which active and passive voice has considerable impact on interpretation. In sentences, the subjects and objects play different roles, and therefore, the meaning of the sentence could be significantly different depending on what role is being performed. Here we will discuss the surface structure, or the phrase structure, on the level of syntax. Later we will attempt to understand how the syntactic analysis may actually help us understand identity, social relationships, and social structures. Therefore, while UG is a highly vetted theory in the field of linguistics, it is considerably limited when dealing with one of the major semiotic and pragmatic questions addressed later in this book: "What is meaning?"

Syntax and the World's Languages

Word Order

On the basic level, syntax is concerned with how languages build sentences. The first most noticeable feature of a language is the order of the words. Languages are often categorized based on the order in which they organize the different words. There are six ways languages may order subjects (S), objects (O), and verbs (V). Some languages require certain orders. Others simply prefer certain orders but may vary in use. According to the World Atlas of Language Structures Online (WALS.info), the breakdown would look like what is displayed in Table 5.1.

The WALS provides a vast amount of information on many of these languages, including examples. There is also a map that shows where the various word order types are dominant. There are two types that are most prevalent among the world's languages. It is quite possible that they are more prevalent because many cultures have found it useful to state the subject of the sentence first, and then either the verb or object. This is clearly not a universal among the languages, but may have been a developed technology.

TABLE 5.1 World Atlas of Language Structures (WALS)

Word Order	Number of languages (out of a total of 1377 analyzed)	Percent (out of a total of 1377 analyzed)	Example languages
SOV	565	41.0	Gujarati, Hindi, Japanese, Tibetan
SVO	488	35.4	Arabic, English, Hebrew, Mandarin, Polish Russian, Spanish, Vietnamese
VSO	95	6.9	Hawaiian, Irish, Tagalog, Zapotec
VOS	25	1.8	Kiribati, Wari'
OVS	11	0.8	Tiriyo, Urarina
OSV	4	0.3	Kxoe, Nadëb, Tobati, Wik Ngathana
No dominant order (though there is preferential order for simple sentences)	189	13.7	Dutch, German, Hungarian, Yupik

As can be seen from the chart, the English word order is not the most common. This may be a consideration when teaching English learners (ELs). Many of the languages they speak may typically order words differently. English always begins with a subject and then contains a verb. This is why most English grammars split the English sentence into the "subject" and "predicate." If the verb is transitive, then the object follows after the verb and is in the predicate. This is a fairly basic rule of grammar that most of us are taught early on in school. However, one distinction between the grammar taught in schools, as prescriptive, and the grammar here, which is descriptive, is that the description is generally more concerned with function in a sentence. Thus, linguists explain how words or phrases are operating in the sentence.

Lexical Categories

Languages are made up of different types of words, also referred to as lexical categories. In Chapter 6 we will talk about how these words are formed and how we can analyze which category they belong to. Here, we need to know the basic categories. In traditional, structural linguistics, there is an assumption that language is made up of a lexicon and syntax. The lexicon is divided into different categories, and the syntax tells us where words from a particular lexical category may go. We may know them as "parts of speech" instead. The typical categories are nouns (N), verbs (V), adjectives (A), prepositions (P), adverbs (Adv), and determiners (Det).

These are relatively standard across languages, though by no means universal. These may serve as a guide, however, as we begin to think about languages. In Table 5.2 we have defined some basic parts of speech. These definitions are by no means standard, but are a way of helping us think about syntax (Bickford, 1998). The function can only be known once a specific interaction is analyzed, but here, at least, some basic functions are given.

For a sentence to be grammatical, it is assumed that for every position in a sentence, any word in the same lexical category may be supplied. A lexicon is actually more complex than the above categories. Not all nouns, for example, are interchangeable. Some are mass nouns (e.g., water, milk, grass, etc.), which are not counted. You couldn't really say "a water," "two waters" or "a lot of waters." You can, but it would be assumed that there is a unit of measure attached as in "a *glass* of water," "two *gallons* of water," or "a lot of *bottles* of water." Context would supply that information. However, these nouns would be in a different lexical category than, say, puppies or icecubes. These can be counted. So, when linguists talk about lexicons, they are more defined than the parts of speech we are used to.

Another example would be adjectives that are found in different places of the sentence. "Large, purple apple" would not be spoken "purple large apple".

TABLE 5.2 Parts of Speech (English)

Part of Speech	Definition	Function	Examples
Verb	The core of the clause, usually an action.	Links other words together usually by indicating a relationship, action, or state of being.	Run, swim, think, throw
Noun	A person, place, thing, idea, or abstract concept.	Can be the subject of the verb, an object of the verb, or an object of the preposition.	Dog, bicycle, Chevrolet, Jimmy, ice cream
Adjective	A description word that can be applied to a noun.	Can be used to modify a noun or to describe the properties or characteristics of a noun.	Beautiful, ugly, tall, green, cold, angry
Adverb	A description word.	Can be used in multiple ways including to modify verbs, adjectives, adverbs, clauses, or a sentence.	Quickly, too (as in "too fast"), possibly, well, very
Preposition	A grammatical relationship word.	Can be used to indicate the relationship between the noun phrase associated with the preposition and the rest of the sentence.	With, to, by, from, in

Nor would one say "brown big camel." The color words are always closer to the noun than the size words. These would be in different lexical categories. So, all size words could be exchanged with each other, but they may not always be exchanged with the color words.

In this theoretical framework of sentence building, you may notice that the concern is not that the camel is brown or the apple is purple. For a "big teal camel" sounds much more correct than "brown big camel". Obviously this doesn't make much sense though, for camels are quite rarely teal, but often are brown. The reason the former sounds better is because the words are arranged in a grammatical word order in English.

If, then, descriptive syntax is not concerned about meaning but rather about how languages construct sentences, then we can create grammatical sentences like Chomsky's famous "Colorless green ideas sleep furiously" (Searchinger et al., 1995). The sentence is completely grammatical, but also completely senseless. Ideas cannot be green, and they certainly cannot be green and colorless at the same time. Nor do ideas sleep, and certainly they do not sleep furiously. Therefore, the ingenuity of human language is that a sentence may sound grammatically correct, but not mean anything.

Furthermore, you don't even need real words to make a sentence! The following sentence is made up of mostly senseless words: *The brank fimled in the hinkled bram.* We know that there is something called a "brank" that did something in the past, namely "fimled" while in a "bram" that at some point had been "hinkled." We don't know what this means, but we know a lot about the sentence from its syntactic structure.

If two words can be exchanged, then they are most likely in the same lexical category. For example, of the following sentences, only two are grammatical:

1. I want to read a book.
2. You want to read a book.
3. ★But want to read a book.

"I" and "you," then, are in the same lexical category. They can be interchanged and the sentence remains grammatical. "But," on the other hand, would make the sentence ungrammatical.

Agreement

Languages often show agreement in case, number, person, gender, tense, and so forth. Different languages do this differently. For example, in English the verb needs to agree with the subject in number:

1. Elizabeth eats granola every morning.
2. Elizabeth and her sister eat granola every morning.

In the first sentence, there is a singular subject, therefore the verb must agree in form. In the second there are two people, so the verb must also reflect plurality. In Spanish, adjectives must agree in both gender and number with the noun.

1. Las blancas camisas   "The white shirts"
2. *El blanco camisas   "The white shirts"

In the first phrase, all three words have the morphemes "-a" and "-s." The first morpheme, in Spanish, indicates feminine gender, whereas the second indicates plural number. Components of a noun phrase, in Spanish, will agree in gender and number, so all components will be inflected with these morphemes consistently. The second phrase is incorrect. It is the literal translation of the English to the right. The English noun, "shirts," does indicate number (it is plural), but it is unnecessary in English to change the other words of the phrase. English also does not show gender. Therefore, the unmarked words "*el*" and "*blanco*" are used, albeit incorrectly.

In the technical sense, agreement is actually an issue dealt with in morphology since the words are changing (see Chapter 6). However, because many languages don't rely on word order for meaning the agreement between cases may be important. For example, in English, we know that the subject is the subject because it comes first in the sentence. Direct objects would come later in the sentence. However, in some languages, like Russian, Greek, Hebrew, and Arabic, for example, word order is not essential toward determining whether or not the word is functioning as an actor/subject or direct/indirect object. We can identify the subject or object because the word changes depending on the case. We can know whether or not a word is functioning as a direct or indirect object, regardless of where it is ordered in the sentence. This is called case agreement. Even Old English had some form of case agreement, which has found its way into modern English in instances like the use of "whom" instead of "who." When you are referring to the object of the sentence, you would use "whom," but when referring to the subject, you would use "who." While case agreement is also probably best framed in morphology, it is critical to syntax. Again, morphology and syntax must be studied together, under the realm of morphosyntax.

Greek case agreement, for example, shows us how words are related in a sentence, much the same as English word order does. In English, the order of the words would tell us what is the subject, direct object, addressee, or object of preposition. The noun would look the same in all of these instances. We may call these different cases. Greek, however, changes the word to show *nominative* or *accusative* case and it varies depending on the gender of the word (neutral, masculine, and feminine nouns). Consider how the Greek words "fish," "bear," and "shark" change depending on whether or not it is the subject (actor, nominative case) or the object (acted upon, accusative case). Because the word "fish" in Greek is neutral, when it changes from nominative to accusative it stays the same. However, in

TABLE 5.3 Nominative and Accusative Case in Greek

Greek word	Example sentence			Nominative	Accusative
ψάρι (fish, singular)	Το ψαρι	εφαγε	το ψαρι	Το ψαρι	το ψαρι
	The fish	ate	the fish.		
ψάρια (fish, plural)	Τα ψάρια	έφαγε	το ψάρι.	Τα ψάρια	το ψάρι
	The fish	ate	the fish (sing.).		
αρκουδα (bear, fem.)	Η αρκουδα	εφαγε	την αρκουδα	Η αρκουδα	την αρκουδα
	The bear	ate	the bear.		
καρχαριας (shark, masc.)	Ο καρχαριας	εφαγε	τον καρχαρια	Ο καρχαριας	τον καρχαρια
	The shark	ate	the shark.		

masculine and feminine words, like bear and shark respectively, there are changes depending on whether it is nominative or accusative as presented in Table 5.3.

Agreement is considered to be a universal syntactic principle of language; however, not all languages have the same agreement system. English syntax calls for agreement in number between the subject and verb; however, in Mandarin, for example, subjects and verbs need not agree in terms of number. So, as one might suspect, the following sentence, though ungrammatical in English, may sound correct to a Chinese EL:

*Elizabeth eat granola every morning.

In fact, many Chinese ELs do find number agreement in English confusing. So, while we may recognize this as ungrammatical, it is actually impressive that the word order is correct and the meaning can be understood. For the EL first learning the language, agreement may take some time to learn. This does not mean that they do not understand the language, but rather may be unfamiliar with the structural variation needed by agreement.

Phrase Structure and Hierarchy

The conventional and stylistic grammar that we learned in school is fundamentally different from the descriptive grammar of linguistics in two fundamental ways. First, conventional grammar is nondescript and the fundamental unit is individual words. It avoids trying to describe words in terms of clusters and relationships to other words. In other words (pun intended), this grammar is not interested in accounting for what linguists call *constituency* and *dependency*. Chomsky believed that the fundamental unit of grammar is *phrases* because each word intrinsically carries with it morphological and syntactic information that dictates how it relates to other words (i.e., *constitution*). Secondly, conventional grammar and diagramming, which is primarily focused on the surface structure, is arranged in a linear fashion; in contrast, phrase structures are arranged in a hierarchy, in order to describe the deep structure and show the rule-governed, logical arrangement of words. While the tree diagrams of conventional grammar can only describe a particular language, linguistic tree diagrams are theoretically capable of describing any language. Thus, the tree diagrams of English, Spanish, Mandarin, and Arabic would be similar when it comes to the basic relationship of noun phrases and verb phrases. Of course, their surface structures are obviously distinct. In the remainder of this chapter, we will demonstrate how this type of hierarchical diagramming works and by applying it to various languages, you will have a strategy for understanding the grammar of any language. More importantly, you will see how the study of syntax can provide insights into how the mind works and shed light on the inductive nature of learning.

So, what do we mean when we say phrases are built through hierarchical rules? Consider the simple noun phrase (NP): *green apple*. We know that *apple*, the noun, is the most important part, or the *head*, and that *green* is an adjective which modifies the noun. In English, like many languages, the adjective comes before the noun. In Spanish and many other languages, however, the adjective comes after as in "manzana verde." While the sequence on the surface is different, the functions are exactly the same. In both English and Spanish the *head* is apple/manzana and the modifier (adjective) is green/verde. We notate this as a NP (noun phrase), and in both cases the NP is constituted of a N and an A, where the modifier "A" is below the N. We can further notate this by NP→A N (in English) and NP→N A (in Spanish). Regardless, A is always attached to N, or *dependent* on N. Why is it important for our minds to parse phrases hierarchically as opposed to linearly? Consider the sentence: *I eat green apples*. The word "green" is in between the words "eat" and "apples." However, when we think of this sentence in hierarchical terms, the word "green" in terms of its modifying function is actually **below** apple. It is this hierarchical arrangement that allows for systematic linguistic functions to occur. In Figure 5.1, you will notice that the hierarchical structure is the same, although in the final noun phrase the adjective (A) and the noun (N) are in a different linear order.

As phrases become more complex, we can continue to build on these phrase structure rules. The rules for a verb phrase may look something like VP→ V NP

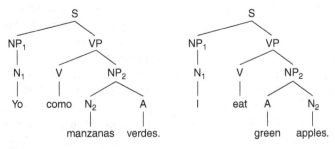

FIGURE 5.1 Spanish and English Tree Diagram Comparison

PP, meaning that the verb phrase is made up of a verb, a noun phrase, and a prepositional phrase. An example of a sentence like this would be:

hit   the baseball   into the pond
V   NP   PP

The NP and PP can additionally be broken down because they include their own constituents. Thus, we can begin to see a hierarchical ordering to the phrases.

A useful tool to show the hierarchy and phrase structure rules is the tree diagram. Tree diagrams may be intimidating; however, they can also be useful in studying language. In fact, they can also be useful in teaching grammar in classes, as in the case study of Jamie at the end of this chapter. Simple sentences may be easily diagrammed with a two- or three-tiered tree, in which the sentence is made up of a NP and VP and each of those are made up of smaller constituents, as in "The man ate" (see Figure 5.2).

More complex sentences can be diagrammed as well; the following contains a direct object (NP$_{DO}$). When a triangle is used, rather than individual branches, it simply means that individual constituents of a phrase are not analyzed. This is intended to simplify the tree diagram, though each of the noun phrases are, indeed, made up of their own constituents (see Figure 5.3).

As the sentences become more and more complex, the tree diagram begins to reflect the relationship and hierarchy (see Figure 5.4).

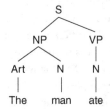

FIGURE 5.2 Simple Sentence Tree Diagram
[[the   man]   [ate]]

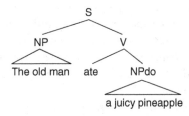

FIGURE 5.3 Triangle Tree Diagram
[The old man] [ate [a juicy pineapple]].

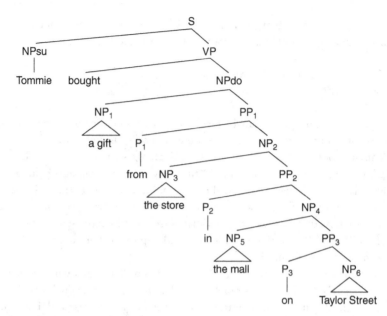

FIGURE 5.4 More Complex Tree Diagrams

[[Tommie] [bought [a gift] [[from] [the store] [in [the mall]] [on [Taylor Street]]]]].

Sentences, at least in English, can theoretically go on forever. This may happen by recursion, which we will discuss in a moment, but first we should note how other languages can also be analyzed by tree diagrams. Notice in the following diagrams how you can analyze the different relationships between words in other languages. What are some differences in these languages?

English, as discussed above, is an SVO language. This allows English tree diagrams to be very tall, like the example above. This is because the NP (subject) and the VP make up the two constituents of the sentence. The NP (direct object) is a constituent of the VP. In many languages the trees may be more flat, especially if the word order if different. For example, in Palantla Chinantee, a language from Mexico, the word order is VSO. Therefore, in the tree diagram in Figure 5.5, the sentence has three constituents.

In this example, we can see how other languages order words differently. While they are still hierarchical, some languages are organized differently. Palantla Chinantee, for example, organizes the direct object on the same hierarchical level as the subject and verb. English, as seen in the examples, does not. One of the assumptions of Universal Grammar is that lines in these trees do not cross, therefore, the trees from SVO and OVS languages tend to be taller and not as wide as SOV, OSV, VSO, and VOS languages.

Tree diagramming may seem like a fairly mechanical process, and it is in the sense that diagramming sentences focuses on structure alone, and not necessarily meaning.

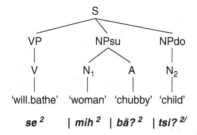

FIGURE 5.5 Palantla Chinantee Tree Diagram
"The chubby woman will bathe the child."

Language trees and phrase structure rules are the basis of computational linguistics. As a logical algorithm, language can be built into computer programs both for production of language and also analysis. The Institute of Language and Communication at the University of Southern Denmark has a website with software that will actually analyze the syntactic structure (http://beta.visl.sdu.dk/). The tree diagrams in this chapter have been created by *phpSyntaxTree* (Eisenbach & Eisenbach, 2003) by typing in the bracketed version into a text box. The trees can be built like any logic tree or computational program. Computational linguistics is a quickly expanding field using set types of algorithms that mimic natural language. Many automated voice programs organize and substitute words into the correct slots based on the phrase structure rules of a particular language. The universe of computational linguistics is expanding very quickly, just think that at the time this book was written digital book platforms, like the Kindle, can read text out loud (with various limitations), and Siri, on the iPhone 5, can assist oral questions and can even hold rudimentary conversations (in a variety of languages and dialects). She (Siri, that is) is even able to express tones of language to mimic emotion. This entire field really was based on the assumption that language follows these hierarchical models, and that will continue to propel the computational linguistic field into the future.

Tree diagrams can be useful beyond simple structural analysis though. Often in language there is ambiguity in meaning. Sometime this may be because of the words themselves. This is often the case with puns, which draw on lexical ambiguity:

1) To write with a broken pencil is pointless.
2) A rule of grammar: Double negatives are a no-no.
3) He said I was average—but he was just being mean.

(Pun of the Day, 2011)

In these examples, as with all puns, there is an ambiguous word that gives the potential for a double meaning, one that is literal, and the other that is figurative. Usually one of the meanings has a sense of humor to it. In the first pun, the pencil is indeed pointless because it was broken. However, "pointless" may also mean useless. It is humorous because there is a double meaning. The other two are similar, with "double negatives" and "no-no" (sentence #2) and "average" and "mean" (sentence #3).

Another type of ambiguity comes from the structure of the sentence, or the way the words are organized. In this type of ambiguity, understanding how the words relate to one another is very important. The following examples are well-noted newspaper headlines that are structurally ambiguous:

1) Teacher Strikes Idle Kids
2) Child Teaching Expert To Speak
3) Chou Remains Cremated
4) Complaints About NBA Referees Growing Ugly

(www.ling.upenn.edu, 2012)

For each of the sentences above, they are humorous because initially we do not know how the words relate to each other. Using tree diagrams we can map out the meaning. The following example is diagrammed in two different ways, showing the two ambiguous meanings (see Figure 5.6).

Notice that the two examples are quite different. In the first, the free legal advice is poor. In the second, the poor are given free legal advice.

Using the tree diagram can be very helpful in understanding ambiguity and clarifying the different meanings of a sentence. It also can be very useful in understanding differences in languages and how they organize meaning through syntax.

Recursion

An amazing feature of most languages is their potential most languages is the potential for *recursion*, or the embedding of phrases within phrases. One of the most dogmatic assumptions by cognitive linguists like Chomsky and Pinker is that what makes human language different from other forms of communication,

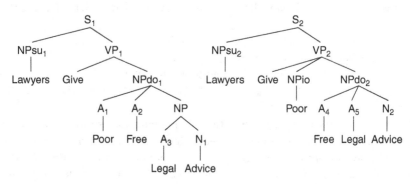

FIGURE 5.6 Tree Diagram "Lawyers Give Poor Free Legal Advice"

and thus makes humans different from animals, is the ability to embed phrases within phrases, as we have seen in the tree diagrams already. The mind is assumed to be able to process and contain the information in long and complex sentences because it is all organized in a grammatical system in which phrases are a part of other phrases, or sentences may be found within larger sentences. This allows, theoretically, at least, for a sentence to continue on forever. This was long assumed to be one of those universals of generative grammar. The idea is that, for example, a noun phrase (NP) may include a prepositional phrase (PP), which, in turn, may include another noun phrase. The rule would look like this:

NP→N (PP)
PP→P NP

This recursive structure allows us to create the following (see Figure 5.7).

Not only may phrases be embedded, but entire sentences may be embedded (see Figure 5.8).

While embedding occurs worldwide and allows us to speak of people, events, and objects that are not in our immediate context, the assumption that embedding is universal was challenged recently by Daniel Everett. In his study of the *Pirahã* language, he found no evidence that the speakers used recursive embedding. In fact, to the contrary, he found that no embedding occurred in this language, and many other assumed universals (e.g., color words and numbers) were not used in this language either (Everett, 2009). This limit in language restricted the people to only talk about the immediate context. This challenge is perhaps one of the most surprising claims in linguistics to have been made in recent history.

Despite the questions about the universality of recursion, it is a very useful tool to understand. In fact, through recursion we can often note how people position

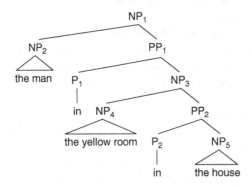

FIGURE 5.7 Recursive Structure

[the man	[in	[the yellow room	[in	[the house]]]]]
NP	PP	NP	PP	NP

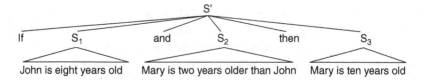

FIGURE 5.8 Tree Diagram of Embedded Sentences
[If [John is eight years old] and [Mary is two years older than John] then [Mary is ten years old]]
S' S   S   S

themselves or others. For example, in the sentence "The boy who is from Kansas came over our house for dinner" tells us not only that the boy was from Kansas, but that the speaker consciously decided to describe him as being from Kansas. This may bring to light issues that relate the speaker to this boy. Most likely the speaker is not from Kansas because the speaker is positioning the boy from there (and note that our use of "from there" most likely indicates that we are not writing while in Kansas). Recursion, then, can help us to understand how people, including our students, are framing their world through the grammatical relationships in which they speak. This also will become more important as we continue analyzing language in our classrooms.

Syntax and the Classroom

Punctuation and Written Language

Often grammar is reduced to proper punctuation. When we think of grammar, usually we think about the written form, though we do realize that in speaking there is a grammar as well (remember being corrected "It's Jane and I not Me and Jane!"). In Chapter 9 we will focus more on written language, but here it is important to see how prescriptive grammar, like the rules we teach in schools, relates to descriptive grammar.

Indeed, eventually in human history, it became important to standardize writing so that there could be wide readership. Grammars were formed to describe languages so that the spoken language could be written. Thus, it became important to know how to write the difference between the following two sentences:

1. The men who were riding the bus got to the hotel quickly.
2. The men, who were riding the bus, got to the hotel quickly.

In the first sentence, the men riding the bus were only a part of the entire group of men heading toward the hotel. In the second, all the men were riding the bus. The commas tell us where we would pause in spoken language and what we would mean. The commas are actually descriptions of spoken language.

Perhaps a more controversial example is needed for the true grammarians reading this book. The Oxford comma, or the comma used in lists, is generally a standard practice. However, in conventional grammars, whether a comma is needed after the word "and" is debated. For example, if one were to write "the sunset was orange, yellow and red" there is no ambiguity. There is no real need for a comma after "yellow." Note the change in meaning in the following two sentences though:

1. I want to thank my parents, Jill and Steve.
2. I want to thank my parents, Jill, and Steve.

In these two sentences, both conventional and grammatically correct, there is a major difference. In the first sentence Jill and Steve are the parents. In the second, they are two other people. The extra comma is needed. Again, the commas, in a conventional way, describe spoken language. They signify that there needs to be a longer pause after Jill. Of course, punctuation alone does not produce meaning. As noted above, it is not difficult to find examples of phrases and sentences that are ambiguous even without commas. Nonetheless, punctuation is a system developed to describe language, and is used in schools to prescribe it.

English Grammar Rules

To show an example of a grammatical analysis of a language, we will go over the syntax of English. Theoretically, it is possible to generate an infinite number of sentences through using these rules. If you follow the steps and plug in the words from the correct lexical categories, all English sentences can be created, or analyzed. Again, this is a theoretical point within generative grammar; however, it may be useful to understand how English is structured. Other languages are different, so their rules would vary significantly. In the Appendix, the first line is a formal notation, the second is the formal reading of the notation, and the third is our explanation.

Based on Appendix A, attempt to plug in words to make a sentence. In many ways this operates like a computer, as we discussed above. From this template, any English sentence may be generated. You can pick, almost at random, any of the rules, and generate a sentence. For example, start with the first line:

S→NP[SU] VP

Now, pick what you want to fill in the VP with, perhaps:

VP→V NP[DO] PP

Now pick your PP rules:

PP→P NP

Finally pick your NP:

NP[SU]→ D N
NP[SU]→AdjP N
NP→ D N

Since we included an adjective phrase, we now have to select one:

AdjP→Adj

Now, let's plug in the words.
   Pick a transitive verb: kick
   Pick a preposition: in
   Pick a determiner: a
   Pick a noun: ball
   Pick an adjective: small
   Pick a noun: kid
   Pick a determiner: the
   Pick a noun: park

The sentence would be: The small kid kicked the ball in the park.

   The point of this exercise is to demonstrate the complexity of language, at its structural level. When we speak and write, we are following these rules often. In fact the rules are merely descriptions of what people actually say in a language. Now that you are aware of the rules, perhaps you can identify where your students may be having difficulties. Try to describe their grammar. Are they consistently leaving out determiners like "a" and "the"? For English learners, this may indicate that in their first language determiners aren't used, or at least not the same ones. What about your students that have difficulties with word order? It may be that in their first language, the order is different.

Rethinking Syntax in Classrooms

Meaning and Context

One thing you are probably used to hearing in this book is that context matters. While syntax, as a traditional area of study, generally ignores the context of language, it is important to remember that meaning is always contextually bound. Disaggregating syntax from the social and cultural relationships that govern its communicative uses severs the connection between linguistic form, function, and meaning. Apart from the social and cultural relationships that are mediated by syntax, language is reduced to a set of discrete formulaic rules and/or meaningless code. Without meaning and connection to real social structures, the grammar in schools, the syntax of an Indonesian sentence, the grammatical relationships in Constitutional Law, are essentially pointless.

Remember earlier in this chapter when we discussed "colorless green ideas sleep furiously?" The sentence sounds right, but it's considered nonsense. For us to really understand how to use syntactic analysis, we need to understand how those "colorless green" ideas are related to the rest of the ideas, or how the "furiously" sleeping differs from normal sleeping. Therefore, we are going to briefly look at the different functions that words play, not just their grammatical category.

Functions of Words

Earlier, we mentioned the different parts of speech, or the different lexical categories. That will tell us the type of word, and the phrase structure rules will tell us where they go in a sentence, but neither of these tells us how words function in a sentence. The way a word functions in a sentence tells us much more about the way we conceptualize the word. For example, the following are both grammatical sentences, and John is the subject in both of them:

1. John hit the ball.
2. John was hit by the ball.

Even though John is the grammatical subject in both of these, he is having two distinct experiences. In the first he is doing an action; he is an agent. In the second, something is being done to him; we can call him the patient. Likewise, the ball functions differently too. In the first it is the patient, but in the second it is what we may call an instrument, or the object involved in the action, but not the agent. These different roles show us how words are being used. Notice, however, this is different from sentence structure. For example, two nouns can play the same role in vastly different sentences. In the following sentence, John is the agent and the ball is the patient:

1. John hit the ball.
2. The ball was hit by John.

Regardless of whether the sentence was passive or active, John was the one doing the action to the ball.

There is not a single, hard-set list of roles; in fact, many people disagree on what roles are possible in English. Other languages also have the same phenomenon, namely that different roles are expressed in the sentence. However, different languages may do this differently. The roles in English may not be exactly the

TABLE 5.4 English Roles (adapted from Tserdanielis and Wong, 2004, p. 193)

Role	Definition	Example
Agent	The person doing the action.	*Tina* tackled the wide receiver.
Patient	The thing the action happened to.	Kyle ate the *donut*.
Instrument	A thing involved in the action, but not the agent.	Sam hit the golf ball with the *club*.
Theme	A thing that is in a state or undergoes a change.	*Tom* slipped. Jerry heard *the noise*.
Experiencer	An animate being that has a perceptual or mental experience.	*Kendra* learned the science concept.
Source	The person, object, or place change starts from.	My cat is scared of *your dog*.
Recipient	The person that gains possession of something.	Tammy gave the book to *Billy*.

same as roles in another language. Table 5.4 displays some of the major roles we observe in English.

Syntax Used to Study Identity and Power

An example of this being used in a real situation comes from critical language studies. Consider the following news headlines:

1. Argentinian police forces kill 20 protesters.
2. 20 killed in Argentina.
3. 20 die in Argentina.

What differences do you see? Who is doing what? The grammatical subject of the sentence can actually tell us a lot! First, all three headlines are referring to the same set of events. Although these headlines are *referentially* equivalent, the differences in syntax and lexical choice lead to three very different interpretations. In headline #1, the Argentinian police forces are doing the killing, and it is clear who the responsible actors/perpetrators are and who are the "innocent" victims, namely "the protesters." Because the verb "to kill" is active and transitive, then someone must be responsible for doing something to an object, in this case the protesters. The police forces, we can say, have agency in the sentence. The second headline, on the other hand, is passive and the responsible party and victims are invisible. However, the verb "kill" is transitive in contrast to "die" which is intransitive, so we can still presume that a person did the killing (X kills Y). If we compare this headline with #3, where the past tense of the verb "to die" is used, we can see that the verb choice alone would affect the interpretation because "dying" just happens (X dies, no object Y).

The differences in agency may reveal blame, indicate causation, or show some other social relationship between who is doing what to whom. Generally, in public relations, for example, passive voice is used so as not to indicate fault. If a major supermarket chain was to say "We sold bacteria-infested spinach," we may not choose to shop there anymore. However, to say "The spinach was contaminated" admits no fault. We may be more likely to forgive the store even though what actually happened remains the same. Likewise, if you are trying to diffuse an argument, it rarely helps to yell "You hurt my feelings because you called me stupid!" while better results would probably be achieved if you were to say "My feelings were hurt when I was called stupid." The passive voice avoids placing direct blame on the name caller.

Understanding these relationships can be a useful tool in the classroom. For example, you can use something like agency analysis with your students by having them evaluate the headlines of different news sources. Ask what viewpoints or *ideological stances* are being constructed. You can also elicit alternative possibilities by manipulating the lexical choice and/or transitivity. Perhaps assign intentionally conflicting reports from politicians and ask the students to judge who is to blame. You can also apply this type of analysis to other genres of text like literature and visual images (see Fairclough, 2003). This type of syntactic analysis is purposeful, meaningful, and situated in real life experiences. Grammar is no longer presented as an arbitrary practice with little consequence; instead, it is understood as a phenomenon embedded in social, cultural, and ideological relationships.

Student Inquiry and Learning

While traditionally few students get excited about learning grammatical rules, we believe this is because grammar has been stripped of its social functions. It is important to engage students in the study of syntax through providing them with meaningful activities. In our experience working with teachers, many students are not only intellectually stimulated by syntactic puzzles, but they also get excited discovering that politicians, sports broadcasters, or TV shows are making judgment calls on the grammatical level. The small, micro-level grammatical choices people make may have very large social implications. When students become aware of this reality, they become linguistically empowered. It is significantly more relevant for students when they realize the social implications of syntax. Whether it be the use of active voice, or punctuation rules, the social and ideological dimensions of syntax make for a more empowered consciousness of writing.

This is not a simple task for teachers. To provide opportunities for students to learn through their own inquiry requires that teachers know the rules well enough to know when meaning is affected. However, there is no better way for a student to learn about grammar than for a student to be put into an activity in which grammar is necessary to accomplish the goal, assuming of course the goal is not just a grade on a test. When teachers recognize the importance of grammar beyond its form, they can engage students in discussions about the grammar of social relationships. This requires a *metalanguage* which this chapter has attempted to provide, a way to talk about language. If we cannot look at language and study it, then we cannot critique its use.

Language is best viewed as a tool, a tool for mediating activities, relationships, assignments, discussions, and identity(s). Therefore, it is when we examine that tool, look at its affordances (and limits) that we can truly understand how it works. A grammar book can only explain to us how we are expected to use language, but the tools to analyze language can provide us opportunities to see powerful relationships between speaker and hearer, author and audience, friends, family members, students and teachers, and so forth. These tools should be passed on to students in our classrooms. Therefore, it is an essential point of this chapter that we don't look at language as a set of grammatical rules, but rather that language is seen as a tool to build different types of social relationships. Language, in context, has meaning. Commas, periods, verbal agreement, in context have meaning. The rules themselves don't have meaning without social context and relationships. It is only within particular social contexts that it is wrong to begin a sentence with a conjunction, or that run-on sentences are marked wrong. In Chapter 14, we will consider questions regarding corrective feedback, repair, and its implications for ELs. We will particularly examine the structural and sociocultural dimensions of this pervasive practice.

Conclusion

The study of words and sentences is in a combined field of morphosyntax. In this chapter we studied syntax, specifically, and in the next we will review morphology. The field of syntax is traditionally limited to studying how words in a sentence are related to each other, as based on the organizational structure of the human mind. However, syntax, from a sociocultural viewpoint, is not only the relationships between words and phrases in a sentence. It is also a useful area of study when investigating learning and teaching of ELs. Furthermore, by studying the syntax of language use, we can make some observations about its function in society, specifically how it positions people, as we looked at with agency analysis. Syntax is more than simply a technical area of linguistics. It is also a useful, practical area in which we can understand how speakers and communities see the world.

TEACHER CASE STUDIES

Tanya: Syntactic Questions

Tanya is a special education teacher. Last year she had a student, Danielo, who was in her special education class and scored very high on the language assessment test. During a staffing meeting the decision was made to move him out of the bilingual program into English-only instruction, both for his general education classes and the special education support. Tanya studied his language background and noted some potential syntactic difficulties Danielo may face. He spoke Spanish at home and for his first year of school he spoke mostly Spanish as well. He was in a transitional program, so he began to learn more English in school in first and second grade. She wrote about him:

> I have known Danielo since the 2009–2010 school year, as I was his special education teacher last year when he was in third grade, and this year as well. Danielo is a really sweet and considerate boy. He works really hard in both the general education classroom and special education classroom. Danielo's mother really cares about his education, last year she had Danielo and his brothers in many after school activities, both academic and athletic.

Danielo had a difficult time learning to read. In second grade his classmates made fun of him because he took so long to sound out words and sometimes mixed up Spanish and English while reading. Over time, he practiced English in school and began to use English most frequently for reading and writing, although at home he spoke mostly Spanish. Tanya wanted to investigate some of the differences in Spanish and English syntax so that she could understand more of Danielo's language learning story.

Spanish, like English, is an SVO language. The normal pattern of sentences required the subject, then the verb, and finally an object if the verb is transitive. However, Tanya noted some major differences in word order, one being that in Spanish the adjective follows the noun. More notably, however, Tanya wrote:

> In Spanish one would say "caballo blanco." There are also differences in question structure. An English speaker would say "Do you want to go to the movies tonight?" while a Spanish speaker would say "¿Quieres ir al cine esta noche?" The Spanish speakers would likely leave out the "do" from their questions. These differences in English and Spanish are important to keep in mind, so we can understand where our students "errors" are coming from, and provide explanation for the pattern in English. If we help them understand, then they can apply the rules to their own experiences.

Thus, in Spanish, the auxiliary verb "do" is not necessary. The question "¿Quieres ir al cine esta noche?" directly translated into English would be "You want to go to the movies tonight." In fact, the Spanish statement would be identical to the question except the intonation would be different. Tanya pointed out that this helped to explain why some of her students (including Danielo) often leave out "do" while forming questions.

Another note Tanya made was that questions in Spanish can be formed by adding "no" to the end of the statement with rising intonation. For example, "Tienes muchos amigos, ¿no?" is translated "You have a lot of friends, no?" This is not a typical way of forming a question or asking for confirmation of a statement in English, although one might find a similar idea using "You have a lot of friends, right?" Tanya observed Danielo and many of the Spanish speakers at her school asking questions in English by creating a statement and adding "no?" In this way the Spanish syntax was visible in the English learner's speech in her classroom.

Tanya recognized that many of the "errors" in grammar in her classroom were directly related to the differences between Spanish and English. This allowed her to better understand her students and provide helpful mediation in their language learning.

Jamie: Ambiguous Trees

After a midterm in her linguistics class, Jamie decided to try out one of the activities with her fifth grade students. She had attempted to diagram an ambiguous sentence using the tree diagram seen in this chapter. Knowing that there were at least two plausible meanings, she had correctly diagrammed the sentence. However, she did not think that this activity would work with her students. Nonetheless, she took on the challenge to teach her fifth graders about hierarchies in sentences.

Jamie began her lesson by writing the words "the electric light orchestra" on the white board in the classroom. She asked the students what were possible interpretations of the phrase. She recounted their responses:

> Right away, I had one of my students raise his hand and say, "The orchestra lights are electric," and I wrote it down under the original phrase on the chart paper. Then, I had another student say, "The light orchestra is electric" and I wrote that one down below, too. And finally, I had another student say, "The orchestra is filled with electric lights."

She then showed the class how to diagram these, explaining the hierarchical relationship between the different words (see Figure 5.9).

After modeling an example, Jamie split her class up into groups of four or five students. Each group received a notecard with an ambiguous phrase on it. At first, some of the groups struggled. Jamie was quite fascinated by the questions that were asked. For example, group 2 had the phrase "stolen painting found by a tree." The group asked if the sentence had to make sense, recognizing that, while a tree finding a painting was grammatically possible, it wasn't realistic. So, Jamie noted that her students were aware that though a sentence may be grammatical, it may not be meaningful. She encouraged them to continue to diagram it, and draw a picture of what it would look like. Thus, group 2 drew two pictures, one with a painting by a tree, and the other with a tree (with eyes and a mouth) holding a painting.

Group 5, Jamie said, had the most difficulty. Ironically, however, the trouble did not stem from the grammatical connection of the two phrases, but from not

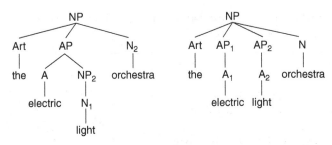

FIGURE 5.9 Teacher Making Tree Diagrams in the Classroom
The orchestra lights are electric.   The light orchestra is electric.

understanding what a particular word was. The phrase was "eye drops off shelf"; however, the students, all of whom spoke Spanish at home, didn't know what a shelf was. Jamie had to explain what a shelf was and then they were able to see that an eyeball fell off of the shelf. However, the noun phrase "eye drop" was not one they easily saw. Jamie had to mediate once more and explain to them what eye-drops were. Once she had done this, they were able to see the grammatical relationships of the two possible interpretations.

Reflecting on the lesson, Jamie wrote:

> Surprisingly, all groups were able to understand the ambiguity of the sentences and diagram them correctly through the use of tree diagrams. The hierarchical relationships seemed to come very easy for at least one or two students in each group, where the other ones seemed to take a little more time to process what the others were doing. But once a team member explained what they were doing, they had no problem understanding what they did.

Some of the students did have difficulty understanding the hierarchical relationships of the phrases. So, Jamie decided she might have to re-mediate the activity. She attempted to show the students another way to see what was going on. This time, instead of using the tree diagrams, she showed them how to bracket the phrases, which, according to Jamie, "really helped students to understand the different combinations of words they could use to come up with different sentences."

The students seemed to enjoy the activity and asked Jamie if they could do some more. She told them that many more activities would come up in the following weeks as they explicitly looked at language. Reporting back to her college class, Jamie shocked the other teachers when she told them the students not only understood the grammatical relationships, but also enjoyed the activity! She told the teachers that letting them solve the problems themselves through discovery and inquiry achieved a deeper understanding than the grammar worksheets they had been working with.

QUESTIONS/ACTIVITIES

1.   Diagram the following sentences:

(1) The waitress gave the check to Kevin.
(2) The waitress gave Kevin the check.
(3) Sandy went to a beach in Florida to relax.
(4) Sandy went to a beach to relax in Florida.
(5) Sandy went to Florida to relax on the beach.

Now, describe how the trees are different. What do you notice about the phrase hierarchy?

2.   Each of the following phrases is ambiguous. Identify whether they are ambiguous because of the meaning of a word (lexical ambiguity) or the structure of the sentence (structural ambiguity). Diagram the sentences with structural ambiguity to indicate the differences in the hierarchical relationships.

(1) the plastic egg basket
(2) The girl hit the boy with a ball.
(3) Frank had the will to be the executor of the estate.
(4) I ate pumpkin butter and toast for breakfast.

3.   With the following 12 words, create a sentence. If you can come up with an alternative sentence do so as well. How did you come up with this sentence? Which words did you start with? Compare the sentence with the class. How many sentences can be made with these L2 words? Across, And, Boy, Down, Hall, Large, The, The, Threw, Skunk, Walked, A.

4.   Mad Libs can be a fun way to teach about parts of speech. You can use them to prompt discussion about what words mean. The reason Mad Libs and other games are so funny is because they sound like real stories (the story is grammatical) but the actual words are chosen at random.

5.   Observe the phrase structure rules of English and Arabic in the Appendix. What are some differences between the languages? Where might learners find the phrase structure rules confusing?

6.   Compare the two sets of phrase structure rules in the Appendix. What differences are there? What challenges may a speaker of English have with Arabic syntax? How about an Arabic speaker with English syntax?

Additional Resources (multimedia)

http://beta.visl.sdu.dk/ (This site will analyze phrases and sentences into trees for you, in several different languages)

http://fora.tv/2009/03/20/Daniel_Everett_Endangered_Languages_and_Lost_Knowledge#fullprogram (Recursion)

http://www.ling.upenn.edu/~beatrice/humor/headlines.html#structural-ambiguity (Humor)

Searchinger, G., Chomsky, N., Newmeyer, F.J., Gleitman, L.R., Miller, G.A., Thomas, L., South Carolina Educational Television Network., ... Ways of Knowing, Inc. (1995). *Discovering the human language: Colorless green ideas.* New York, NY: Ways of Knowing, Inc.

http://www.npr.org/templates/story/story.php?storyId=9458681 (NPR argues against embedding)

http://www.wordlibs.com/

http://ironcreek.net/phpsyntaxtree/?

FP Foreign Policy (2005, Oct. 14). The Prospect/FP Top 100 Intellectuals. Retrieved from http://www.foreignpolicy.com/articles/2005/10/13/the_prospectfp_top_100_public_intellectuals

MIT News (1992). *Chomsky is citation champ.* April 15, 1992. Retrieved from http://web.mit.edu/newsoffice/1992/citation-0415.html

Appendix: Arabic Syntax Rules

Grammar Rules for English (Adapted from Bickford, 1998)

Included is the phrase structure rule, how the rule would be read, and an explanation of the rule.

$S' \rightarrow (C)\ S$

An English sentence prime may contain a clause and must contain a sentence.

$S \rightarrow NP_{[SU]}\ VP$

An English sentence consists of a noun phrase[subject] and a verb phrase.

English sentences must contain both a noun phrase and a verb phrase.

$VP \rightarrow V\ (NP_{[DO]})\ (VP)\ (PP_{[IO]})\ (\{NP\}\{PP\}\{AdvP\})^*\ (S')$

An English verb phrase consists of a verb and may contain a noun phrase [direct object], a verb phrase, a prepositional phrase [indirect object], and may also contain one or more of the following: noun phrase, prepositional phrase, adverb phrase. The VP may also contain a sentence prime.

English verb phrases must have a verb and may contain a direct or indirect object, another verb phrase, or adjectives, adverbs, or other noun phrases after the verb. Another sentence may be recursively embedded in the phrase.

$PP \rightarrow P\ NP$

An English prepositional phrase consists of a preposition and a noun phrase.
Prepositional phrases must have both a preposition and a noun phrase.

NP→ ({D}{NP$_{[Poss]}$}) (QP) (AP)★ N (PP) (S')

An English noun phrase may consist of a determiner or a noun phrase [possessive], a quantifier phrase, and one or more adjective phrases; it must contain a noun and may contain a prepositional phrase. The NP may also contain a sentence prime.

Noun phrases must contain a noun that may be modified by adjectives, numbers or quantifiers, and determiners or possessives which appear before the noun. Additionally, noun phrases may contain a prepositional phrase which appears after the noun. Another sentence may be recursively embedded in the phrase.

AP→ (DegP) A

An English adjective phrase consists of an adjective and may contain a degree phrase.

Adjective phrases in English must have an adjective and may contain a degree phrase like "very" before the adjective (traditionally in English grammar we call this an adverb, as in "it was *very* hot", where the adverb modifies the adjective).

AdvP→ (DegP) Adv

An English adverb phrase consists of an adverb and may contain a degree phrase.

Adverb phrases in English must have an adverb and may contain a degree phrase before the adverb.

QP→ (DegP) Q

An English quantifier phrase consists of a quantifier and may contain a degree phrase.

Quantifier phrases in English must have a quantifier like "many" and may contain a degree phrase before the quantifier.

DegP→ . . . Deg

An English degree phrase consists of a degree.

A degree phrase must contain a degree like "very" or "super."

Arabic Phrase Structure Rules

Based on a Jordanian Arabic speaking Language Associate
(Rumenapp, 2007, unpublished fieldwork)

S'→ (C) S

An Arabic sentence prime may contain a clause and must contain a sentence.

S → NP$_{[SU]}$ VP

An Arabic sentence consists of a noun phrase [subject] and a verb phrase.

VP→ (Neg) V (AdvP) (NP$_{[DO]}$) ({NP}{PP}$_{[IO]}$) ({NP}{PP}{AP})$_{[NAC]}$(S')

An Arabic verb phrase may contain a negation, will contain a verb, and may contain an adverb phrase, noun phrase [direct object], noun phrase [indirect object], or prepositional phrase [indirect object], and a noun phrase, prepositional phrase, or adjective phrase that operate as non-active clauses. The VP may also contain a sentence prime.

NP→ ({D}{QP}) N ({NP$_{[POSS]}$}{AP}{PP}) (S')

An Arabic noun phrase may contain a determiner or quantifier phrase; it will contain a noun; and it may contain a noun phrase [possessive], adjective phrase, or a preposition phrase. The NP may also contain a sentence prime.

AdvP→ . . . Adv . . .

An Arabic adverb phrase consists of an adverb.

PP→P NP

An Arabic prepositional phrase consists of a preposition and a noun phrase.

AP→ ({Neg}{D}) A (DegP)

An Arabic adjective phrase may contain a negation or a determiner, it will contain an adjective, and may contain d degree phrase.

DegP→ . . . Deg . . .

An Arabic degree phrase consists of a degree.

QP→ . . . Q . . .

An Arabic quantifier phrase consists of a quantifier.

6

MORPHOLOGY

Building Words with English Learners

LEARNING GOALS

1. Summarize the basic concepts of morphology.
2. Identify morphological processes.
3. Understand different types of morphological systems in the world's languages.
4. Understand the difficulties ELs may have in learning English morphology.
5. Use derivational and inflectional rules in the classroom.
6. Create a case study to analyze a particular topic in morphology.
7. Use morphological concepts in discourse analysis.

KEY TERMS/IDEAS: Morpheme, lexeme, lexicon, derivation, inflection, agglutinating, fusional, isolating, nominalization

In Chapter 5 we discussed the syntax, or grammar of language. Morphology is a related field in linguistics. Sometimes it is very difficult to distinguish what belongs to syntax and what belongs to morphology because there is much overlap. What one language does in syntax, like through changes in word order as seen in the last chapter, another may do through morphology, by changing the word itself. Therefore, it is often better to think about both fields together, as *morphosyntax*. In Chapter 5, we focused more on how words (in the discrete analytic sense) relate to each other. In this chapter, we will examine how words are built internally to create distinct meaningful units. Morphology is the study of a language's morphemes and the rules governing its transformations for communicative purposes. Morphemes consist of words, affixes, intonation, stress, and their implied or explicit contexts of use. In this chapter we will see how the traditional concept of "word," especially in the isolated sense, constrains our view of how we learn, develop, and actually use language to make meaning.

As we learn about the ELs in our classrooms, we need to be aware of the complexities of languages in the world. If we look at language only through our "English eyes" we will certainly misunderstand the way language is used by ELs. In this chapter we will attempt to build a way of thinking about words, how they are formed, and how they are used in a language system. We will also look at some common difficulties for ELs in English morphology and attempt to understand the underlying issues as well as how to mediate classroom instruction for ELs.

Introduction

Many forms of linguistics operate on the assumption that language is made up of two major pieces of information, a grammatical code and a lexicon. Last chapter we talked about the grammatical code, and in this chapter we talk about the lexicon. In certain linguistic circles, the lexicon consists of all of the words in a speaker's mind, so that when applied in a grammatical code, sentences can be formed. This is assumed to work very much like a computer program. You plug in words here and there and voilà! You have a sentence. This may seem very familiar to those of us who have sat in classrooms with workbooks containing a "word box" and sentences with blank spaces we are to fill in or "word walls" with seemingly random words hanging all around the room. What we hope to explain in this chapter is what words are, and how this computer-like view of words is actually misleading. We hope to provide ways for you to understand and develop ways to learn about words, and to teach your students about them.

When we talk about words we often suppose we are talking about nouns, verbs, adjectives, and so forth specifically. However, to understand what a word is, we need to look much deeper at how they are formed. In classrooms, we often find word lists, vocabulary tests, and other examples of words plastering the walls of our education system. As educators it is necessary to understand how these words work. We often give specific rules about making words, like adding -ed or -ing, however, when those rules don't work we tell the students "That's just English" or give a list of sight words for memorization.

Languages have a fairly predictable set of rules that can help us make words; however, we need to understand what these rules are, how they work, and how to teach them. Many of these rules seem so natural to us because we grew up learning them from grammar books and in songs. For this chapter, it might be helpful to, just for a moment, suspend our ideas of these rules so that we can learn to describe them. Then, after describing these rules we can see how they differ from different languages. Once we see that the rules aren't so "natural" but that we learned the complicated set of English word rules through a long process, we can begin to learn how to work with students, specifically ELs, to help them understand how language, in this case, English, works. We must become students of morphology before we expect our students to grasp the multitude of words and rules in the classroom.

The concept of a "word" is fundamentally abstract. They are easy to see in writing because of the spaces we put in between them, but in rapid speech, they are not always so easy to identify. Sometimes we slur words together; sometimes we drop off parts of words. When we are teaching students about words and our focus is the 'words' themselves, then we might be losing sight of the more critical element: meaning. This is a tough balance to hold, for we want our students to attend to the typical speech style of, say, mainstream American English, but we also want them to develop competence in meaning, developing ideas, and effectively communicating them. Therefore, this chapter is really organized to help us understand how many of the overlooked processes in language-use demonstrate a linguistic competence on the part of our students that is not seen if they are only evaluated from the point of view of Standard American English. In fact, many of the "mistakes" our students make actually may provide us with deep insight into language learning.

Morphemes and Morphological Analysis

In linguistic talk, a "morpheme" is the smallest unit of language that is meaningful. In written language we can see words, either like the ones you are reading now or characters as in Chinese or hieroglyphics. There are conventional spellings or pictograms for those words, and we can recognize them when we see them. However, in spoken language, words work a little differently. In fact, there are multiple language systems that use morphemes in a variety of ways. In English, for example, each word consists of at least one morpheme, but many words contain several morphemes. Think of the word "cat." When we teach our students to make this word plural we tell them the English rule is to add an "-s" to make "cats." This basic rule is an example of how English combines two morphemes into one word. The first morpheme is "cat" which we, in English, identify as a noun. The second is the plural marker, which we can add to most nouns to make plural. This constitutes a morphological rule. As we have said previously, linguistic rules are different from prescriptive rules found in school-based grammar books. For linguists, it is a rule because we can use it to describe how a language works, even though the rule is not always true. We could call English, then, a *fusional* language in that many words can be made up of multiple morphemes, or they are "fused" together.

Not all languages have a morphological structure like English. In some languages, like Mandarin, almost every word is only a single morpheme. We might call a language like this isolating. In English we would change the word to show past tense, but in Mandarin the word doesn't change at all. Another word is simply added to the sentence. The morphological rules in isolating languages are quite simple compared to English because tense, case, aspect, number, and other grammatical concepts are understood in the context of the sentence or conversation, and not in the word itself.

Another category of languages may be called *agglutinating* or *polysynthetic*. Similarly to fusional languages, agglutinating languages combine different morphemes to form what we would call a word. However, these words sometimes may contain so much information that it would be similar to an entire sentence in English. Many Native American languages are polysynthetic, including Inuit languages. For example, in one Inuit language, "*katimaqatigijunnaqinnga?*" roughly translates to "Can I meet with you?" (Pirurvik Centre, 2012). This entire sentence is made by morphemes attaching to each other to form a single word.

In English and other fusional languages a morpheme might include person and tense (like "-ed" which is used for first, second, and third person). In agglutinating languages, however, these would likely be two separate morphemes. When studying these languages we may need to observe many morphological rules, but we might not be as concerned with concepts like word order that we learned in the last chapter.

As we continue to learn about morphology, it is important to keep in mind that understanding how languages differ in the way they make words is significant because our EL students may speak languages that have different systems. So, when we tell them the "rules" of English grammar, we need to remember that making nouns plural or verbs past tense are not universal rules. They are English rules. We can consider that many of the problems ELs have in not using past tense properly, misusing plural markers, and so forth are related to their linguistic background. Therefore, conducting morphological analysis and understanding these differences can help our students understand how English works.

Building Words

Formal linguists identify two types of morphemes, "bound" morphemes and "free" morphemes. It should be pretty straightforward to guess what the difference is. The "bound" morphemes need to be combined; they cannot be used on their own. The "free" morphemes, however, may be used alone. They can form an entire word alone, like "cat," which we discussed above. In the lexicon, or for analysis, people speak of "lexemes." A lexeme would include all forms of a word. So the lexeme "jump" would include "jumping," "jumps," "jumped," and so forth. In the lexicon, similar to some dictionaries, the word exists in only one form, but then, once it is used, adding bound morphemes according to the grammatical rules of the language can change it. For the purpose of this chapter, however, we will try to steer away from the more technical jargon of "morphemes" and "lexemes" and discuss three parts of words. The first is the root, or a "free morpheme," the second is a prefix, and the third is a suffix.[1] The second and third are "bound morphemes," meaning that they cannot exist unless they are attached to a root word. As teachers and language users these terms seem pretty common sense, and we are likely used to them already, as they are pretty standard in English and grammar classes. Roots, or base words, are the word if it would stand by itself. Prefixes are added to the beginning of a word, suffixes to the end.

---

1. Note: In some languages there are also *infixes* which are inserted in the middle of a word.

In many schools, at least when most of us were growing up, we were given worksheets or workbooks with boxes of words and asked to match the root word with a prefix or suffix. Sometimes we may even have been asked to match two words together to form a compound word. In some more entertaining lessons we may have had to match two pictures together to form words, like butterfly. What is often left out of these lessons is "how" these words are formed. Here we will discuss two of the processes, namely inflection and derivation, of how the prefixes, suffixes, and roots are used to form words.

Inflection

The first process words undergo is *inflection*. Words are inflected to add, or mark, grammatical information. This does not result in changing the part of speech of a word, and does not result in changing the word's meaning. An example, as we showed above, is that words in English are inflected to show plurality, or are inflected for number. The word "cat" is inflected by adding a suffix "-s" to make "cats." We noted in Chapter 3 that because of phonological processes that also occur in language, sometimes the addition of a morpheme, or a suffix, will change the sound of the suffix. For example, the same morpheme that marks plurality for "cats" cannot simply be added to "bus." "Buss" is not the form of the word acceptable in English. So, what happens, then, is that there is the suffixing of "-es" instead of just "-s." This isn't a change in the morphology, but rather the phonology. In reality all of these systems are related, but for analysis it is helpful to separate them. One of the assumptions in linguistics is that the word undergoes changes in morphology first, and then phonology, at least in theory. So, one could say lexical item "bus" is inflected for "number," or bus + -s, and then changes to match the phonology of the language, thus resulting in the word "buses." So, we can say that -s and -es are the same morpheme, or the plural marker.

Inflection usually is seen, consistently, throughout a particular language. If the language inflects for person (i.e., first, second, third), then, usually, all of the verbs will be inflected. Even in instances where there is irregularity in the language, the verb would contain the grammatical information of person. In English, for example, though not every verb is made past tense by adding "-ed," almost every verb does show that past tense information in some way.

This is a significant point to note when working with students who are learning language, and especially English learners. For the student who consistently makes "mistakes" in adding suffixes, say, perhaps, adding an "-s" to sheep and therefore saying "sheeps" is actually doing a quite impressive task, applying the morphological rules consistently. Likewise, the student who says "looked-ed," "take-d," or "build-ed" for "looked," "took," or "built" are also impressively using inflections, though in English we would say they are wrong. There are many reasons why English may have these exceptions. Some are phonological, some historical, and some may not be easily explained. Nonetheless, it is important that, as teachers, we understand these are not "wrong" in the sense that our students don't know how to use English, but rather the students understand the rules of morphology in an impressive way, but perhaps haven't mastered what is socially and culturally acceptable. Indeed, to the average person, a mistake like this would sound wrong, but they would probably understand what the student was saying. We will discuss implications for ELs later in this chapter.

Languages inflect for different reasons, and to different degrees. In languages like Mandarin, for example, there is very little inflection. Thus, it would seem quite new for a student from a Mandarin-speaking background to have to change the word when it is past tense. Other languages, like Spanish, inflect words for gender. Many languages in the world even inflect words for case, which would allow words in a sentence to change places. In Chapter 5 we showed an example of Greek case inflection. Latin and German, among other languages, also inflect, to some degree, for case morphologically. All of these different systems of changing words are quite different from English. All of these changes, however, theoretically do not change the word into a different lexical category. If the word does not change, most likely the meaning would still be communicated. Notice the "mistake" that many ELs, or young children for that matter, make:

Sam kick the bucket. Sam kicked the bucket.

Notice that the basic meaning is preserved. We know there is someone named Sam, and that person kicks the bucket at some point in time. Of course, depending on what is said this could affect the meaning, but the context should help us to know when this event would have occurred. It is also important to point out that almost everything about the first sentence is "correct." The syntax and morphology are correct. It is meaningful. So the one error is an error in morphology. Therefore, a closer inspection of the morphological process is needed when working with ELs to understand why this error, specifically, is made.

In some cases, then, inflection could cause confusion. If a student doesn't change "dog" to "dogs," then the following sentence would surely change: "My dog ran away." We wouldn't know how many dogs to look for. This, however, still, is not a change in the topic, or what is being talked about. We merely lose "number" or "tense." As teachers, we need to know when meaning is affected through these mistakes and when it is not. When does the student really understand there are four lost dogs, and when does he or she not? Does the student understand past tense and just didn't inflect "kick," or does the student need to work on conceptual ordering? Understanding how words are inflected may help us identify deep issues in student learning.

Derivation

A second process of word building is *derivation*. Similarly to inflection this usually happens through adding prefixes and suffixes. However, unlike inflection, in which the word remains in a single lexical category, deriving a word changes the meaning of the word. This may result in becoming a different part of speech. In English this is most commonly seen in changing nouns into verbs or adjectives into adverbs, and so on. We know by adding "-ly" we can change an adjective into an adverb, from describing a noun (the quick boy ran to the store) to describing an action (the boy quickly ran to the store). Notice that these two sentences are quite different. The meaning may change significantly. The boy is quick in the first sentence, but not necessarily in the second.

In derivation, unlike inflection, words sometimes change meaning over time. It is as if the derived word takes on a life of its own. This frequently happens when a verb or adjective is changed into a noun. We will study the implications of "nominalization" in a later chapter, because it can have severe social repercussions, but for example here, take the word "populate." As a verb it is rarely used. Perhaps in video games like *SimCity*, ecology, urban planning, and so forth one may talk about populating the environment. However, in common usage, populate isn't really frequent. "Population," however, is a very frequently occurring word. We talk about the population of a country, a city, or a classroom, but we changed it into a noun by adding "-tion." Furthermore, there is "populace," a different noun. They have different meanings, but they been derived from the same root word. In contrast to a root, the "stem" is a word that has derivational affixes, but has not yet been inflected. So a word like "reactionary" is made up of a root word and derivational affixes, but is still considered a stem. Derivation is an effective process, changing words into different words.

In traditional English schooling, prefixes and suffixes are more or less taught in the same way. However, as we have seen, inflection and derivation are two distinct processes, and their implications can be significant for both language learning and for language analysis. It is also important that we are careful not to limit our concept of "word" to those which are written on paper. Even in sign languages the signs have inflections and derivations. Changing a sign may add important information, grammatical or lexical, to the sign.

Analyzing Morphological Structure

There are many ways to study morphology. We will provide one way that may be useful, namely by creating a morphological chart (Table 6.1). Charts like this can be used to explain how morphemes are combined in words. We can start by identifying the parts of the word "elevators."

The following word must follow a certain path because "reinstitute" is different than "re-institutionalize," which are different from "reinstitution." So, we know that we are talking about something that has happened to someone in which they were put back into an organizational structure like a mental health facility. Something isn't being re-instituted, so we know that "re-" must occur after the other derivations. Inflectional suffixes will almost always be last (Table 6.2).

TABLE 6.1 Morphological Chart

elevate	-or	-s	
Root	Derivational Suffix	Inflectional Suffix	Notice that when the derivation is happening the word changes parts of speech and meaning. Indeed, "elevate" is general, but "elevator" is a specific noun.
verb-to go up	makes a verb a noun	indicates number	
stem word		inflectional suffix	
Elevator		-s	
Noun-something that goes up		indicates number	
Elevators			Notice that inflection does not change the part of speech and adds grammatical information.
noun-more than one of something that goes up			

TABLE 6.2 Inflectional Suffixes

re-	Institute	-tion	-alize	-ed
Derivational Prefix	Root	Derivational Suffix	Derivational Suffix	Inflectional Suffix
to do something again	verb-to organize or implement something	nominalizes a verb	makes a noun into a verb	-past tense marker
	institution (stem)			
	noun-a place with an organizational structure			
	institutionalize (stem)			
	to make something or put something or someone into an institution			
re-institutionalize (stem)				
to make something or put something or someone into an institution again				
re-institutionalized				
to have already made something or put something or someone into an institution again				

These processes seem quite normal to the native speaker. In fact, we often wouldn't think much about the word "institutionalized" because it has conventionally been used to refer to someone who has been put into a mental health facility. The stem word, "institutionalize," is not merely a sum of all the previous parts, it is a word in its own right. It has been derived and takes on its own meaning and uses. So, it is easy to understand what "re-institutionalize" and "institutionalized" mean. For many ELs, however, this process is not as straightforward, especially when prefixes and suffixes are taught as parts, added together to make a whole.

It is important that we can break words apart into the different morphemes and identify meanings, but it is also important that we do not fall into the trap of relying solely on assuming that these parts of words have meanings that can be added together like a math equation. This is often the assumption school curricula implement in workbooks, worksheets, and even some standardized tests. In fact, even tests like the SAT and GRE base their verbal tests, in many instances, on the notion that words have specific definitions and that prefixes and suffixes will help you to know that meaning. This may be true, but only in part. Indeed, words take up a life of their own and are used for various reasons. They are not limited to only the dictionary definitions.

Morphological Processes: Reduplication, Alteration, Suppletion

There are several other morphological processes that are important to be aware of, namely *reduplication*, *alternation*, and *suppletion*. These processes help us understand both regular and what some people think of as "irregular" forms of a language, based on the grammatical rules. Not all languages share the same morphological processes, and understanding the differences helps us pinpoint potential challenges for second language learners. For example, there is a major process that English doesn't use but many other languages do. *Reduplication* is a process where a whole or part of the word is doubled. In Indonesian, for example, to make something plural, you double it. "House" becomes "houses" by doubling *rumah* into *rumah-rumah*. Tagalog also uses reduplication, but by duplicating only part of the word. To morphologically change the word "buy" to "will buy," Tagolog changes *bili* to *bibili* by duplicating the first part of the word (Tserdanelis & Wong, 2004).

Another morphological process called *alteration* is found widely in English "irregular" verbs. Many of the verbs that "break the rules" of past tense, for example, actually go through a morphological process in which the word changes, usually through a vowel change. Note the following examples:

"man" [mæn] → "men" [mɛn]
"woman" [wʊmn̩] → "women" [wɪmn̩]
"foot" [fʊt] → "feet" [fit]
"sing" [sɪŋ] → "sang" [sæŋ] → "sung" [sʌŋ]

In these examples there is usually a change in the vowel and they are relatively consistent for the process throughout English. For example, the words *sing, ring, swing, spring*, and so forth all would follow a very similar alteration process.

Another process creates "was" from "am." This is called *suppletion*, these tend to be irregular and there are very few of them in English. Suppletion is the use of one word as the inflected form of another word when the two words are not cognate. They do not, like the other processes, seem to be as widely used. There are more examples like "good," "better," and "worst" that do not resemble each other, though they are clearly related.

These types of suppletions are not predictable and seem like "irregular" forms, especially for ELs. They are usually taught as "exceptions" to the rule. While it may appear this way from a structural point of view, there is generally an etymological, sociocultural, or historical reason. For example, in English the past tense of "go," which is the seemingly irregular "went," is actually derived from the old term "wend." One of the most challenging and "irregular" features of English, especially for non-Indo European language speakers, is the verb "to be," also known as *copula*. Many non-Indo European languages do not even have such function. The different forms of "be" such as "is" (present tense) and "were" (past tense) originally come from several different roots and are not structurally connected. In other words, we shouldn't expect the same generative rules of grammatical structure to apply here. They are, however, etymologically tied together—coming from what linguists call the *Proto-Indo European* (IE) language. A *proto-language* is a hypothetical language linguists construct to discuss languages that have a common ancestor, or what we prefer to call a historical relationship. For example, in the cases of IE languages and the verb "to be," *be* comes from the prototypical form *bhu-*, *am/is/are* from *es-*, and *was/were* from *wes-*. While a proto-language didn't historically exist, it is a useful tool for understanding the non-structural rationale for what appears to be irregular. We believe, as we have stated throughout this book, that it is important to engage in an explicit discussion about etymological underpinnings of "irregularity" as opposed to providing the more simplistic, less accurate, and less satisfying generative explanations that native speakers tend to provide ELs.

Etymology

The Aztecs had a fruit called *ahucatl* after their word for *testicle* (see Figure 6.1 and perhaps you can imagine why!), and when the Spaniards tried to pronounce the Aztec word it sounded like their word for "advocate" which was *avocado*.

The dictionary defines "hazard" as "danger," but did you know it evolved from the Arabic term *al zahr*, meaning "dice." Since games using dice signified risk, deception, and corruption, the word came to be associated with danger during the Middle Ages (Figure 6.2).

Similar stories can be told about the days of the week (e.g., Wednesday), the archaic spelling of "February," and *quarantine* (referring to the 40 days a crew had to forego all contact with the shore if they were suspected of having a contagious disease, see Figure 6.3). Words are one of the most dynamic purveyors of historical information and serve as living artifacts of human history.

Etymology is the study of word origins, and in contrast to definitions, it provides cultural, historical, ideological, and political information about language and

FIGURE 6.1

FIGURE 6.2

FIGURE 6.3

the human communities that used it. One example would be borrowing words from other languages, and then, of course, making them sound like English. As the sounds of a language change, as well as the needs for language use change, as languages come into contact with each other, and so forth, the words of a language change. Words have a history. They are part of a cultural system and historical development. Much can be found out about a word if one were to look into the history of the word. The Oxford Dictionary actually gives basic etymological information for words. At http://oxforddictionaries.com or in a print edition, you can look up a word and find out the word's origin. It will tell you if the word came from Old English, Latin, German, and so forth. Another resource, which compiles other sources, is http://www.etymonline.com. Note the different ways word origins are traced historically. Different dictionaries often trace words differently. Nonetheless, this information can be important to understand word meanings and word development. In spelling bees it is often customary to ask for the word's origin because those that study for the spelling bees often know how the development of words into English change the spelling and meaning over time.

Etymology is an important concept because it can help us to see that words do not simply "mean" something, the same thing, every time we see it. Meaning changes because of context. Over time the meaning develops and changes. Words are at the same time historically linked to previous usages, but also vitally dependent on their current context. For example, take the word "dragon." Imagine a dragon. What does it look like? Is it scary? Is it nice? Does it breathe fire? Is it long and slender? Does it bring good luck? All of these different images of dragons we have are held together, somehow, by the term "dragon." Yet, dragon, both the idea and the word, have histories. Dragons in the Middle Ages were fearsome creatures that flew and breathed fire. The word, however, comes from "Middle English (also denoting a large serpent): from Old French, via Latin from Greek drakōn 'serpent'" (www.oxforddictionaries.com). The flying creature was named dragon, changing "drakon" from serpent to the flying dragon that in English has little connection to a serpent. We will turn more to how words mean next chapter, but the etymology may help explain how words are formed, why they don't fit typical English morphological rules, and how students may be clued into meaning based on the form of the word.

Cognates

Because words are historically developed, there are often similarities between languages. Words that look or sound like words in other languages are called *cognates*. Many times these words are used similarly (though pronounced differently), like "miserable" in English, which is very similar to misérable in French. However, we shouldn't always rely on the appearance of words only, for many are false cognates. The word embarazada has pained many English speakers learning Spanish because it appears to be the same word as the English "embarrass," so a girl who falls off her bike and scrapes her knee and says "estoy embarazada," may not get the response she wants, which, to the speaker's demise, is actually a declaration of pregnancy.

While we cannot rely on cognates all of the time, they are often useful to ELs. The word looks and often sounds much like the same word in Spanish or French. ELs may find cognates helpful in language learning. Usually the English word will follow English morphology, the Spanish word the Spanish morphology, and so forth. The root, however, may provide clues to students on meaning. It may even be helpful to point out some cognates and show how they are inflected differently in the different languages. This way, students can see some of the differences, though there is a common root word.

Structure, Myth, and Ideology—Moving Forward

As we have seen throughout this chapter, words are complex linguistic units, they change, they are made up of morphemes, and they inflect and derive differently from language to language. Indeed, people often look at words and assume they have meaning. This has been the cornerstone idea of debates in law, religion, and education, that words hold power because they mean something. One of the big questions of the 20th Century, how language and culture are related, revolved heavily around words. The American linguist Benjamin Whorf addressed the question in the early and mid 20th Century. He, following his mentor Edward

Sapir, understood that the structure of language (as surveyed in the first half of this book), deeply affected thinking. For example, in the Hopi language, which Whorf studied, there were no words for time, and verbs were not inflected for tense, as they are in English. Hopi verbs are inflected for aspect instead of tense, or the length of duration of an event. They wrestled with the question, then, if the Hopi experienced time the same way modern societies experienced it and how language impacted thought (Whorf, 1956).

Other studies arose during this time whether cultures experience colors differently, as some languages have many color words (think of the box of 108 crayons, or trying to decide on paint in a hardware store), while others had only three or four (e.g., Berlin & Kay, 1969; Kay & McDaniel, 1978; Levinson, 2000). These studies suggested that there seemed to be predictable patterns across language as to what colors would be named. Those following Whorf's hypothesis assumed that language structure essentially creates culture and restricts thinking to that which we were able to speak about. That language structure dictated thinking became both a milestone in anthropology and caused major reaction in other social disciplines.

Recently, linguist Daniel Everett (2009) has studied languages like Pirahã in which every verb must be inflected to show how one knows the action has happened. Everett calls them hyper-empiricists because they have to inflect verbs according to how evidence of an action came to be known. So, the speaker would have to identify how they know what they know through instantaneous morphological transformations. In Pirahã abstract concepts, including abstract numbers, were not attested in the language structure, prompting the question of whether the people could count, think of ideas outside of the immediate realm of existence, and so forth. This realization further raised questions about how language and culture work together. The Pirahã language is also noted as having a possible 16 different morphological process occurring for each verb. This would yield the possibility of 65,536 forms of the verb since each suffix may or may not be present. English usually has only five different forms (e.g., swim, swam, swum, swims, swimming) while Spanish and Portuguese may have some 40 or 50. The Pirahã language, then, has a highly complex morphological structure; although its syntactic structure is observed to be one of the simplest in the world, apparently not even structurally allowing for recursion in the sentence (Everett, 2009).

An example from closer to home may be the inflection of gender in Spanish and the derivation of diminutives. In Spanish adjectives are inflected for gender, usually ending in "-o" to describe a masculine noun, and ending in "-a" to describe a feminine noun. We may talk about these as marked and unmarked. The unmarked word, or the assumed form, is masculine, and it becomes "marked" or different if it is changed to feminine. By marking it, a difference is noted between masculine and feminine. So, we can note a difference between señor (Mr.) and señora (Mrs.) in Spanish. The word is marked for gender. Further, we can note the difference between señora and señorita (miss). The second is marked for diminutive, meaning an unmarried woman. When addressing a woman in Spanish, one has to make the decision to call her señora or señorita. If the woman's marital status is unknown, it is likely she will be addressed based on age. She will be called señora if of married age and señorita if younger. Now, for an older, single, Spanish-speaking American woman the options are somewhat limited. Either she is called a married woman, or she is called a young unmarried woman. In English we differentiate on marital status, regardless of age, but we also include "Ms." if the marital status is unknown or left ambiguous. These names not only reference marital status and age, but also social standing. People most likely assume an older woman is married, noting a cultural norm. By marking señora with -ita, there may be social implications.

From this point on in this book we will be looking at these social meanings. What is the relationship between language structure, as we have studied, and the social relationships we build around us? How do words relate to social status? We have attempted to develop tools for linguistic analysis, not to learn about language per se. Rather we have attempted to develop tools to understand how language relates to student learning and the construction of social relationships in classrooms and society at large. Therefore, we will now turn to studying how language is used to make meaning. The next chapter, if you recall from the levels of linguistics in Chapter 1, is about semantics. This is the first level that actually studies meaning. In many ways what follows in this book may be more difficult to see concretely, however, in many ways it will be more useful in understanding the implications of language in our classrooms.

Conclusion

Over the past several chapters we have examined layers of structural linguistic approaches to the study of language. In this chapter we took a closer look at the study of how words are formed, or the field of *morphology*. As teachers we often observe "errors" in the way ELs form words. In this chapter we have provided tools to break down some of these "errors" and understand how these errors make sense from the point of view of the learner. It helps us understand how second language learners struggle to make meaning in a new language. We also expanded the use of morphology through a sociocultural framework in order to better understand how word formations function in society. Specifically, when English morphology is privileged and normalized, other ways of forming words are ignored. In classrooms with diverse learners, it is helpful to understand the different ways languages create words.

TEACHER CASE STUDIES

Stephanie: Science Words

Stephanie, a kindergarten teacher, was teaching a science lesson. She had been learning about language socialization in her Master's level course and recognized that there was something more going on in her classroom than what originally had met the eye. She began to recognize that as she taught science, she expected the students to talk and act like scientists. However, many of the words the kindergarteners were using were not "scientific" words, so Stephanie attempted to introduce different words into the classroom activity.

She created a lesson about observations. Students were asked to describe properties of different materials like cork, wood, and cloth. Stephanie explained:

> As students started to describe their objects I offered words from science to be used as observational terms. For example one student said "the tube is bendy," so I introduced the term flexible. To do this I asked the students other words that mean the same thing as bendy and listed them on the board. I even had a student draw a picture of bendy. Then I said "is that kind of like flexible?" I asked "Where have you heard flexible before?" hoping they might relate that word to gym class. We had similar discussions with many different properties they brought up.

Stephanie had planned the lesson around students learning a secondary discourse, however, to begin using the secondary discourse (science) they first made sense of the classroom science activity through primary discourses (both Spanish and everyday language like "bendy").

The students correctly observed that a certain material could bend, and therefore, they described it as "bendy," correctly making "bend" into a description. Stephanie's lesson, however, was not oriented around whether or not students could inflect words, which apparently they were doing, rather she was attempting to socialize them into the scientific discourse, something usually left out of morphological analysis. Stephanie didn't call their word "bendy" wrong, though it might not pass in certain contexts, rather she recognized that students were applying morphological rules to the words they knew to describe materials. Therefore, she began introducing other words from science into the activity, which the students began to use.

> Students started by describing things using words such as bendy, round or 2 sided, see through and not see through. And by the end they started to use terms such as flexible, cylinder, opaque, transparent, etc. When they discussed how they sorted their objects they use their new secondary discourse to describe their sorting. When a student would use a term like bumpy other students would say "Oh, you mean rough."

Through understanding the context of words and allowing students to make sense of the activity in their primary discourses, Stephanie allowed them to build words like we saw in this chapter. Students applied the morphological rules to descriptions and then Stephanie, or peers, could offer in the contextually appropriate words. This gave students the opportunity to talk and use words to mediate understanding.

Stanley: False Friends

After a discussion that arose in a college linguistics course about cognates, Stanley took it upon himself to develop and teach a lesson to his class oriented around learning about the students' home language, in this case Spanish. So many of the students had been recognizing that the words in English sounded like words in Spanish. However, Stanley correctly identified that some of these words were false cognates, or falsos amigos. They may have sounded and looked similar, but their meanings were not a 1:1 correspondence. In fact, some of them could cause major confusion in the wrong context.

Stanley identified his objective as "The goal is to improve students' communication abilities by making sure that they are able to use English in the clearest manner. Students will be able to recognize various false cognates and use contextual clues during communication to clarify meaning if they are unsure." In his classroom the workbooks were mostly created for English speakers so issues like cognates never were addressed. For the ELs, however, cognates were a very important part in their language learning experience. Thus, Stanley had to undertake a close study of words in English and Spanish to understand how they are used. To do this he tapped into his sociocultural understanding of the students in the classroom, realizing that the grammar in the school curriculum would not provide the critical information of social contexts of speaking.

Some of the false cognates Stanley identified and used in his classroom lesson were as follows:

False Cognates—Falsos Amigos

1. You don't have a fever, why don't you want to go to school today? The *actual* reason is that I don't want to take a math test today.
2. I didn't *realize* that you were having a hard time with math.
3. Where do you usually find *hay*?
4. Would you be *embarrassed* if you spilled horchata on your pants?
5. We are going to the new basketball *arena* to watch the Chicago Bulls beat the Lakers.

Explain the following: actual, realize, hay, embarrassed, and arena.

1. Actual in Spanish means present day. The equivalent English word in Spanish is efectivo.
2. Realize is similar to realizar, which in Spanish means "to achieve a goal." The equivalent phrase in Spanish is darse cuenta de.

3. Hay in Spanish means "there is/are." The equivalent English word in Spanish is paje.

4. Embarrassed is similar to embarazada, which in Spanish means "pregnant." The equivalent phrase in Spanish is avergonzado.

5. Arena in Spanish means "sand." The equivalent English word in Spanish is estadio.

Some of these words simply look the same, while others have a similar etymological history. Yet, they all could be confusing to the EL. Stanley intentionally sought out to study these words and learn from his students as well. He identified this as an activity to learn about how his EL students talked about language. Students had to talk about cognates from the teacher as well as come up with their own that they have observed. Stanley provided a space that students could talk about words that may have been confusing without the risk of being told if they were "right" or "wrong." They could have an open discussion about language.

QUESTIONS/ACTIVITIES

1. Attempt to create the longest possible word you can by combining as many suffixes and prefixes you can to a base word. What part of speech is it? How would you define it? Use it in a sentence. For example: anti-anticonservationistic (Table 6.3), adjective, being against those who are against conservation. My brother Tom is an anti-anti-conservationistic politician. Now, use a word another student created. Make a chart like we saw in this chapter and see if you can identify a potential definition.

2. Observe one or two EL students. Use their written and spoken language as data. How do they change their words? Are they inflecting and deriving words the typical English way, or are there inconsistencies? Note all of the differences. What do you notice? Can you predict "mistakes"? Talk to your students about what you have observed. Can they explain the process (i.e., "add -ed to make something past tense")?

3. Pick a language, other than English, which has relevance in your classroom. Study the morphology of that language by looking at online recourses, talking to students, or from your own personal experience with the language. Attempt to make a chart of the different inflectional prefixes and suffixes. Make a short list of some derivations. What are some similarities and differences between this language and English? What might be some issues ELs may face? Were any of these observed in activity 2?

TABLE 6.3 Morphological Chart

anti-	anti-	conserve	-ation	-ist	-ic
Derivational prefix against/ opposite	Derivational prefix against/ opposite	Root verb—to save or protect	Derivational suffix makes a verb a noun	Derivational suffix makes an adjective into a noun, a person who does	Derivational suffix makes a noun into an adjective

noun—the act of saving or protecting the environment

noun—one who protects or saves the environment

noun—one who is against those who protect or save the environment

noun—one who fights against those who oppose conservationists

adj.—describes one who fights against those who oppose conservationists

Additional Resources

http://www.etymonline.com/

http://fora.tv/2009/03/20/Daniel_Everett_Endangered_Languages_and_Lost_Knowledge

www.oxforddictionaries.com

http://www.sil.org/linguistics/GlossaryOfLinguisticTerms/ComparisonOfInflectionAndDeriv.htms

7

SEMANTICS

The Beginning of Meaning

LEARNING GOALS

1. Understand how words mean.
2. Explain different theories of how meaning relates to signs and words.
3. Use dictionaries to critique word/meaning relationships.
4. Understand difference between semantic meaning and pragmatic meaning.
5. Understand role of context in word/meaning relationships.
6. Analyze classroom practices and how to teach about meaning.

KEY TERMS/IDEAS: semantics, semiotics, cohesion, metaphor, idiom, index, icon, symbol, framing

Introduction

For the past several chapters (3–6), we have been studying the structure of language. In Chapter 4 we studied how language is composed of physical sounds (in oral communication) that are created by the physiological workings of our bodies (phonetics). Then we studied how speakers of a particular language organize those sounds into meaningful units (phonology). In the next chapter, we studied how sentences are made up of hierarchical ordering of words (syntax). Finally, in the last chapter, we studied how words are formed (morphology). This structural understanding of language helps us as practitioners to understand and describe how students use language in the classroom. We can observe the structure of language, compare the structures between languages, and can use linguistic analyses to help mediate student learning. However, up until now, the linguistics analysis we have done has been more focused on structure and form, not on *meaning*. In contrast to the explicit, objective, and quantifiable dimensions of language, the study of meaning is more implicit, subjective, and qualitative. However, the study of meaning, *semantics*, is what gives impetus to a more relevant and comprehensive study of human language use.

Semantics is the study of the relationship between language and the objects, events, and relationships referenced by words, phrases, and sentences. However, this is all too restrictive in the grand scheme of human communication. In fact, there are many ways we know and there are many ways we mean. When we consider all of these linguistic and non-linguistic ways of meaning, we are talking about *semiotics*. Semiotics is a diverse field of study that reaches into gesture study, music, art, linguistics, and many other fields. The big question in all of these areas is "what is meaning." That, in a nutshell, is what we will be studying in this chapter.

Framing and Intersubjectivity: Meaning-Making as Ongoing Approximation

As we move from the study of linguistic form to the study of function and meaning, there are three principles to keep in mind and we will develop these points throughout the chapter and remainder of the book:

1. the stability of linguistic form in relation to function and meaning;
2. stability and variation in meaning-making;
3. meaning-making as the achievement of *intersubjectivity* through ongoing approximation by interlocutors (speakers).

First, linguistic form is relatively stable and objective compared to meaning. There is considerably more agreement about the phonetic, phonological, and morphosyntactic aspects of language amongst speakers than semantics and semiotics. As we have shown in previous chapters, we can more objectively and scientifically describe the physical properties of sounds, quantify word order, but it is more challenging to do the same thing with semantic and semiotic processes. When we consider the images and emotions evoked by words, no two people have exactly the same experience. Furthermore, those mental images and emotions are virtually inaccessible to instruments of science. However, communication is still accomplished, and it is done in fairly efficient manner both synchronically (in the moment) and diachronically (across time and space—e.g., transmission of oral history). This highlights the relative stability of meaning making. Of course, miscommunication or misinterpretation also occurs with regularity, and this reminds us of the variability and variation in language use.

Meaning-making is difficult to pin down in fixed terms because it's so dynamic and constantly moving at a rate that is beyond our collective consciousness. While difficult, the question of meaning is the most worthwhile to pursue because it makes us who we are as human beings. In order to even discuss "what people mean?" or "what was intended?" or even more philosophical levels like "meaning of life" type questions, we have to come back over and over again to other words and images in order to gain more satisfying answers to these questions. Consider the following scenario: Three people are witnessing the burning of a forest and exclaim, "The forest is on fire!" The first person sees smoke from a distance and says, "The forest is on fire!" The second person is much closer and sees the raging yellow flames. The third person is actually in the forest! Clearly, the same set of words, while referring to the same event (referential meaning), are being experienced differently (i.e., varying levels of affective intensity). Figures 7.1–7.3 illustrate the point.

The second principle in the study of meaning requires us to simultaneously pay attention to both the stability and variability of language. Communication is only possible when the interlocutors share at least a partial, common understanding of the words being uttered. This serves as the common ground and could be considered the more *denotative* aspect, or literal definition of the words. This would be what speakers implicitly agree to. For example, when it comes to the naming of objects in the world like colors and material objects we have near unanimous agreement about the definitions of the words. The variation arises in the more subjective or *connotative* aspects of meaning. For example, how do colors make you feel, what is your favorite color, or what does it remind you of?

FIGURE 7.1 The Forest is on Fire!

FIGURE 7.2

FIGURE 7.3

This brings us to the third principle. Since meaning-making amongst people is fundamentally interpersonal, the process of achieving interpersonal understanding or *intersubjectivity* is always an approximation and an ongoing process. Intersubjectivity drives the engine of semantics and semiotics. It represents the broader objective of communication and language use. It points to both the private machinations of meaning (i.e., inner voice, reflection, presentation of self) and the public display of thought (re-presentation). Intersubjectivity is not synonymous with "common understanding" because it presumes a more critical view of "understanding." It is always approximate, partial, and stable yet varied. It is simultaneously agreement and disagreement, coherence and contestation.

One way to think about these three principles of meaning-making is in terms of *framing*. Framing and *frame analysis* was introduced by the late sociologist Erving Goffman (1974). Goffman was one of the pioneering figures in presenting macro sociological forces through the prism of micro interactions like face-to-face talk. He is credited with inspiring an intellectual current that aimed to describe the "grammar of society" and social relationships. In his seminal work, Goffman drew on the metaphor of a picture frame to illustrate how language works. The frame represents linguistic structure and the boundaries of meaning. It is the stable aspect of language, which provides a common anchor for communication to begin. The picture itself is the context and lived experience. It is experienced subjectively and is necessarily varied. The frame sets the stage for the picture (i.e., language) to be interpreted, and allows the audience to collectively focus on a common subject. Framing is apparent in all language use, but it is even more vivid in institutional talk. Consider how framing works in the production of news events: the editorial decision making on newsworthiness, the headline, the location of the headline, the positioning of the principal actors, the ideological slant of the news agency. If the President of the United States delivers the State of the Union address, and the news agencies frame it as an economic speech, the audience will tend to focus on the economic parts.

Framing also occurs in everyday language use. Semantic framing is necessary to understand the meaning of words and is used by speakers to organize meaning for their intended audience. For example, if someone were to utter the word "table" without any framing, it could conjure multiple types of tables. However, if we framed it with the concept of "picnic," then we would almost surely understand the conceptual framing of this word as a particular table. Likewise, if we indicated we were talking about a picnic, and we mention the word *basket*, then we would likely think about certain types of items. The conceptual frame helps us to relate these words together and develop a coherent picture. Without framing, words become jumbled pieces of a puzzle with a scattered range of possible meanings. Without framing, the likelihood of miscommunication and misunderstanding is also increased. Of course, technically, there is no such thing as "without framing," what we "mean" is if the speaker doesn't do the framing, then the listener will do it.

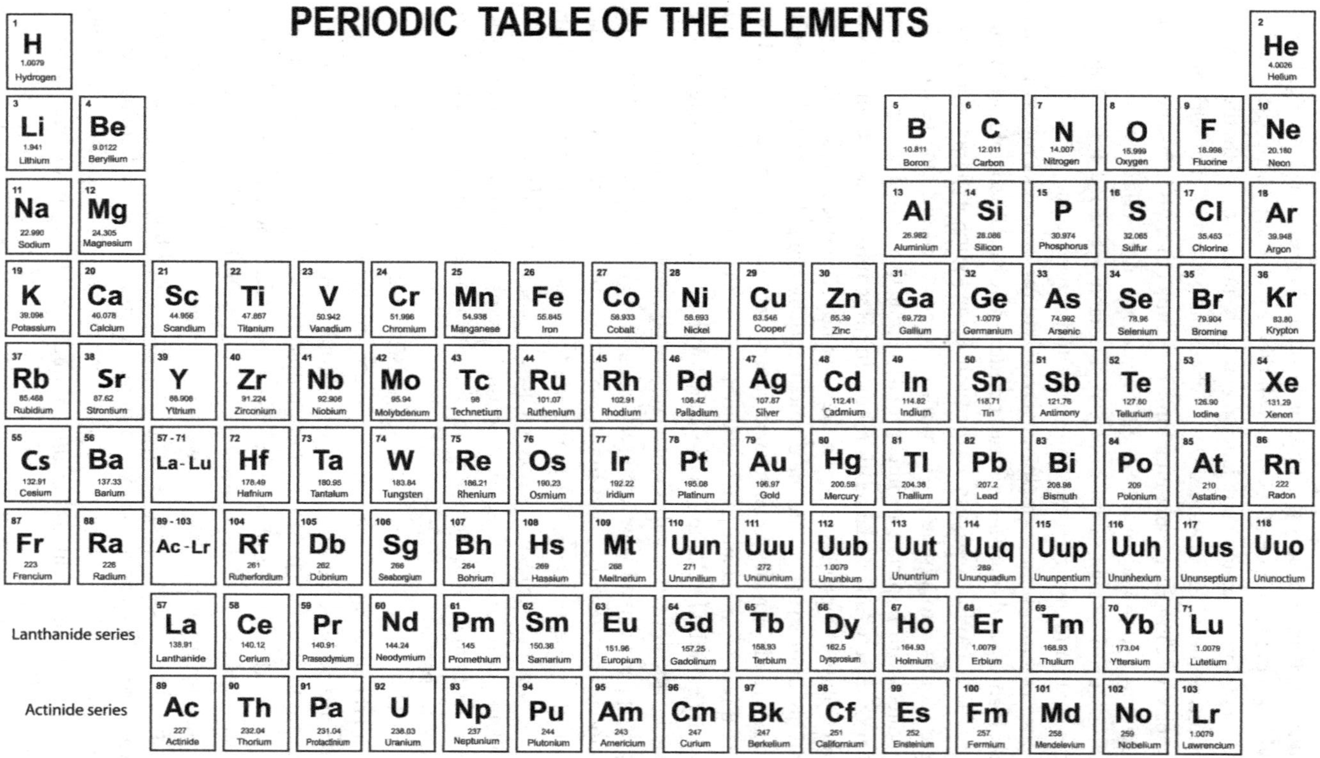

PERIODIC TABLE OF THE ELEMENTS

FIGURE 7.4 Periodic Table of Elements

FIGURE 7.5 Table Mountain, New Zealand

We could say that words have a semantic range, and framing reduces the range of possibilities during communication. There are a lot of possible meanings evoked by a word, but these possibilities are not infinitely relative. Think back to the *table*. When you think of the word table, what comes to mind? Think of all the examples of tables you know and perhaps don't know of. There are card tables, coffee tables, dining tables, picnic tables, religious altars, conference tables, ping-pong tables, database tables, tablespoons, Table Mountain, and of course the periodic table of elements just to name a few. Each of these images could be invoked by the word "table."

Framing provides the context for greater precision and specificity of meaning. For example, in the sentence "John set his cereal, bowl, and spoon on the table before he poured some coffee," a certain table is mentioned than in "John sat across the table from the head of sales in the morning meeting." These different ways to frame the situation bring up different conceptual contexts.

Consider the following sentences (see Gee, 2008):

1. I spilled my coffee and mopped it up.
2. I spilled my coffee and swept it up.

What is the difference between these two sentences? All the words are identical with the exception of the second verb (mopped vs. swept). How does the different lexical choice change the frame of interpretation? In the first one, the coffee is certainly a liquid. In the second, it is probably still in ground form. Consider the following two as well:

3.   I spilled my coffee and wiped it up.
4.   I spilled my coffee and brushed it up.

Again, in these two sentences, as with the first two, the difference is in the form of the coffee, whether it is liquid or not. But, there is also a difference between 1 and 3 and 2 and 4. This difference is in the quantity and location of the coffee spilt. In the first two, it is likely the whole cup spilled, and obviously on the floor (since we generally don't mop the countertop—it has probably been done though!). In the second two, the quantity may be less, but it likely happened on a table or counter.

These examples show how subtle shifts in frame alter the meaning and interpretation in significant ways. If such complexities and subtleties arise for primary speakers of a language, consider the implications for second language learners. Understanding the semantic shifts through the shifts in framing is grounded in the language socialization experiences of speakers. These shifts have to be explicitly discussed and contexts for experiencing the differences need to be designed for second language learners. For example, perhaps an EL child has never been on a picnic nor has seen one take place. How might they understand "table" in a given context? Likewise, with the coffee examples, if the student doesn't understand the framing around the coffee, he or she may not understand whether the coffee was liquid or not or if it was a big spill or not.

Semiotics

In this section, we would like to provide a more in-depth account of various approaches to the study of *semiotics*, or the formal study of meaning-making processes. It is impossible to present the vast range of semiotic studies from around the world,[1] nevertheless, we think educators and practitioners should at least have some familiarity with some of the core issues, concerns, and questions of semiotics in order to better understand and perhaps counter some of the common fallacies of meaning-making that permeate the world of second language instruction.

As you read the various approaches to semiotics, consider some of the pervading assumptions surrounding translation. Sometimes we assume that there is a one-to-one correspondence between the words of one language and the words of another. Moreover, those equivalent terms are understood cross-culturally in almost identical ways. We call this the *fallacy of equivalence*. For example, the word "education" in English is translated into Spanish as "educación." However, the framing of each is slightly different. For English speakers, the word "education" generally refers to formal schooling and/or certification. So if someone is "well

---

1. See Rauch and Carr (1994) for a deeper coverage of semiotic approaches from around the world.

educated" it means they have matriculated and graduated from some type of schooling. In addition, the level of what is considered "well educated" has shifted over time, so that someone with a high school diploma would not be considered "well educated" today. For Spanish speakers, generally, the concept of "educación" provides a frame beyond schooling. The Spanish equivalent of "well educated" or *buen educado* refers to one's refinement, manners, and social sensibilities. Thus, equating education to educación is misleading and ignores the underlying cultural ethos of each. Understanding the nuances of these differences is important pedagogically, and semiotics helps develop our metalinguistic awareness of such salient issues in meanings that are *lost in translation*. It further allows us to engage students in these types of discussion about how meaning functions both within language and across languages.

European Approaches to Semiotics

Linguistics in the Western world is generally traced back to the Swiss linguist, Ferdinand de Saussure, also known as "Father of Modern Linguistics." He is considered to be one of the most influential intellectuals of modern Europe and laid the foundation for the study of meaning. Saussure considered the basic unit of meaning across all human languages to be the *sign*. Each sign consists of two parts:

1. the *signifier* (the spoken word, or symbol); and
2. the *signified* (the word's referent).

In the example below (Figure 7.6), the sign is made up of the signified (the tree) and the signifier (the spoken word "tree").

A sign represents an external object in the world. An artist draws a landscape, which represents a real landscape in the world (or an imagined landscape). A photograph represents the person that was in front of the camera lens. A word refers to an object (*referent*) that has an objective existence beyond language. While this is a very intuitive understanding of the relationship between signifiers and that

"Tree"

FIGURE 7.6 Signifier and Signified

which is signified, this oversimplifies how language and meaning function. One of the major critiques of this view of semiotics is that the sign is not grounded, or stabilized. For example, think of the English word/signifier "tree." What comes to mind? Try to describe or draw it. Depending on the geographic climate you grew up in, you probably have different images. If you grew up in a desert climate, the signifier "T-R-E-E" may evoke images of palm trees, while more jungle environments might evoke images of kapok trees with vines.

While all the different images that come to mind are considered "trees," only one signifier ("T-R-E-E") represents them in English. If we look cross-linguistically, the signified image of a tree could be evoked by other signifiers such as "arbol" (Spanish), "木"(Chinese), and "شجرة" (Arabic). Thus, a simple one-to-one correspondence between a sign and something in the world does not explain how we can all use the same signifier (in this case "T-R-E-E"), and yet have different ideas and images of the signified tree in the world.

Systemic Functional Linguistics

In the early chapters of this book, you were exposed to language as a system of grammatical rules and regularities. However, as noted by one of the most influential linguists, Michael Halliday (1978), language is not only systemic, it is functional. Language is the interrelationship between form and function to constitute culture, "Indeed, we can define a culture as a set of semiotic systems, a set of systems of meaning, all of which interrelate" (Halliday & Hasan, 1985, p. 4). Thus, Halliday and other functional linguists see grammar not only as a system of tools and signs, but as a resource of potential meaning. This brand of linguistics that focuses on how language systematically produces meaning is better known as *systemic functional linguistics*. Systemic functional linguistics has impacted how we view second language learning. In particular, it has led to a more situated perspective of English pedagogy like English for Special Purposes (ESP) and provides a detailed framework for describing the variation within languages.

From a systematic approach to language, Halliday drew on Saussure and suggested that any unit of language only can "mean" when systematically connected to other units. So, a word, in and of itself, means nothing, unless it is situated in relation to other words. Words may be part of an arbitrary syntactic category, but we don't know what they mean until they are in a system of other words. Halliday also suggested that the nature of a system means that each word was based on a choice. So, the very decision of what we say and how we say it implies that we had a choice out of a number of options. Therefore, choice implies intentionality and meaning. Halliday's approach to language allows us to look for cohesion among larger stretches of language use. We can look for consistency among language use and expect that there is some sort of cohesion holding text, spoken or written, together. This is how language maintains stability and systematic variation across speakers, time, and space.

Pragmatism

Charles Sanders Pierce (pronounced like "purse"), a contemporary of Saussure, was a logician and mathematician who turned his interests to philosophy later in life. He is known as the "Father of American Pragmatism" and developed a theory of semiotics that differed greatly from Saussure. Unlike Saussure, who saw a sign representing something else, Pierce thought that a sign was actually a process called *semiosis*. One of the major differences between the two theories was that Saussure believed that the signifier and the signified remained the same, corresponding to each other. Pierce, on the other hand, believed that in order for a sign to be meaningful, it had to be grounded and stabilized; otherwise, we would never know what it represented.

Pierce developed a system in which the sign was made up of three parts (as opposed to Saussure's two). There was the *representamen*, which was similar to Saussure's concept of the sign, which does the representing. There was also an *object*, which was similar to Saussure's concept of the signified, that which is represented. In Figure 7.7 this works much the same way as Saussure's system.

As noted above, however, there is nothing to ground the representamen and the object. The ground represents our conceptual understanding of the relationship between the representamen (sign) and the object (signified). The relationship between the sign and signified is something separate and abstracted from the initial experience. This conceptual image is something novel in the mind of each interpreter. They do not look alike, sound alike, and there is nothing about the intrinsic properties of the word "T-R-E-E" and an actual tree that make them related. However, the word "tree" is meaningful. Thus, Pierce saw that we needed to ground the relationship between the two. The third part of the sign, then, is the *interpretant*, or the concept we have when we see or hear the representamen (Figure 7.8).

So, now we can see that the word "T-R-E-E" does not necessarily mean a tree out in the world somewhere, but it does bring a concept to our mind of a tree we, at some point, experienced. This process happens again. The next time we hear the word "tree," we now are interpreting the relationship between the word "tree" and the concept "tree" (see Figure 7.9).

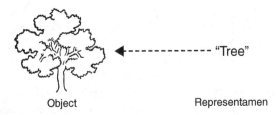

Object   Representamen

FIGURE 7.7 Reprentamen and Object

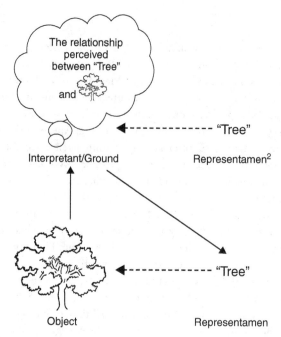

FIGURE 7.8 The Interpretant

As can be seen from Figure 7.9, the only reason we can agree that the word "tree" actually means something is because we have all had an experience with the object, tree (Parmentier, 1994). This experience could have been conceptual rather than material. Many people have never experienced the Great Wall of China, yet we have in some way experienced the concept of the Great Wall. Likewise, no one truly experiences an object, in and of itself, when we talk. However, we all do draw relationships between the words we use and the concepts we have.

Thus, unlike what Saussure thought, a sign does not mean something on its own. A sign only means in relationship to our concepts. Perhaps the most famous illustration of the relationship is the painting *The Treachery of Images* (Figure 7.10) by surrealist painter René Magritte.

Indeed, this is only an image of a pipe. It is not the pipe itself. Thus, meaning must be conceptually grounded in the minds of speakers. It is grounded not only in convention or some otherworldly arbitrariness, but also in our experiences and interactions with the material world. This includes the material world and world of ideas. Semiotics is concerned with meaning, and we have to understand how meaning is constructed between and within speakers. As Pierce pointed out, something means because we have grounded a relationship between the sign and that which it represents. This connection between the sign and that which it represents is not random but systematically organized as conceptual schemes.

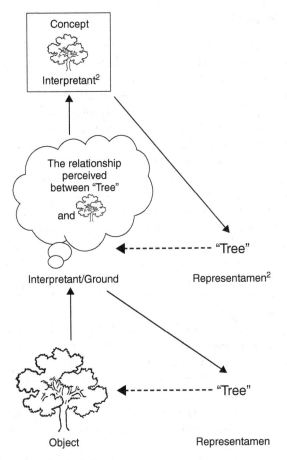

FIGURE 7.9 Complete Semiosis Process

FIGURE 7.10 "This is not a pipe" Magritte, R. (1929)

Index Icon Symbol

From Pierce's semiotics, there can be three types of signs based on the relationship between the three levels (Parmentier, 1994). For example, look above to Figure 7.4. In the most basic of relationships between a sign and the world, the object is merely represented. In this figure the word "tree" and the actual tree are not grounded. So, if someone from a different language was looking at this, they would see no relationship. However, if, perhaps, you were to show a picture or even a drawing, they may see the connection. We would call this an *icon* because it looks like the object it is representing. Icons are all around us. Indeed, even Magritte's pipe was an icon of a real pipe. Icons are symbols that stand for objects, events, and relationships in the world.

The second type of sign is an *index*. An index, like the index finger, points to other objects, sets of actions, events, ideas, and/or relationships. Consider how we learn the meaning of "the wind is blowing." If we look out the window and see the leaves of a tree moving, we interpret our observation as "the wind is blowing." How come we don't say "the leaves are moving?" We don't know this from direct experience of seeing the wind, but we are inductively interpreting that the movement of the leaves must be attributable to the wind. The wind is the cause of the movement because leaves don't have volition of their own. The arrows on a compass or weather vane are examples of indices. They have meaning because they point to inferred causal relationships.

Finally, the third type of sign is a symbol. This is something that is entirely conventional. Look at Figure 7.9. The word "tree" has become symbolic because people can agree that the word means something. Most of language is considered to be symbolic and conventional. An exception would be onomatopoeic words which generally sound like what they mean.

Later in this book, these relationships will be very meaningful, especially when working with diverse classrooms. It is important here to understand that language does not work in a one-to-one correspondence with the apparent, temporal, and physical world. Rather, language is a system of symbolic representation and *re-presentation*. The hyphenation of **re-**presentation refers to how language users display agency by taking existing symbols and using them for novel purposes and functions. Language is meaningful because relationships are drawn between words and our interpretations of the relationship between words and objects.

Metaphors

A *metaphor* is a non-literal, rhetorical device used to convey abstract and symbolic meaning. Traditional linguists thought that metaphors worked because they were accepted conventionally, on a symbolic level. In fact, metaphors were assumed to be "on the margins" of language because they were not "clear" and transparent. The sign did not seem to have any resemblance to that which it signified. In fact, according to traditional linguistics, plain speech is crystal clear. Since each word represents something in the world, then communication worked very smoothly, as it does for the most part in our lives. However, because metaphors essentially say that one thing is something else, they are confusing. Language is a means for communication. Metaphors don't work like normal language. They must, therefore, exist only on the fringe of language.

Traditional linguistics sees metaphors as relatively insignificant, the most imperfect part of language. Newer fields of linguistics and other social sciences have come to understand that metaphors are at the very core of our existence. They are how we understand, and how we live. It is important that a distinction is made between linguistic metaphors and conceptual metaphors, though linguistic metaphors being a typical metaphor when we say A is B (meaning A is like B or has some quality of B-ness) (Lantolf & Thorne, 2006). Linguistic metaphors, then, are a misalignment between the signifier and the signified. It is what we think a sign means, or doesn't mean.

Conceptual metaphors, however, are not the same as linguistic metaphors. In fact, conceptual metaphors build a theory. They create and hold up our cultural models, or the ideas and understanding we live by. Conceptual metaphors are so engrained in the way that we live our lives, we hardly notice them! For example, in the United States there is a conceptual metaphor that the *mind is a computer*. This metaphor is much more than the simple linguistic equation. At the very essence of our culture, the mind is considered a computational device that algorithmically processes information. Thus, the metaphor is extended to various aspects of cognition and development. *Mental processing, input/output*, are all a part of this larger conceptual metaphor. The mind as a "computational device" provides a dominant frame for how we discuss and think about human learning. The metaphor shapes the way we understand instructional practices, policies, and so on. Other metaphors we invoke to frame learning and/or language include: "children are like sponges," "planting flowers or seeds," "switching on a *light bulb*," "peeling an onion," "savings account," or "clean language" (see Lawley & Tompkins, 2001). Until these conceptual metaphors are challenged, we continue to live by them. Therefore, contrary to traditional linguistics, metaphors are not on the fringe of language at all. They are very much at the center of our cultural models.

We have cultural models that white is good and innocent, hence why we wear it at weddings. Black is the color used for grieving and mourning, which is why we wear it to funerals. These color metaphors are not universal in the world. In fact, in many Asian cultures, white is the color worn to funerals, and traditionally, Indian brides would not wear white to a wedding. Blue is for boys and pink is for girls—another color metaphor. Theories are structures that lay the foundations of how we live and make sense of our lived experiences. This is yet another cultural metaphor that we use frequently (Lantolf & Thorne, 2006). Thus, cultural metaphors are so common in our daily lives that we rarely notice them outright.

Metaphors are also cultural because they are developed historically. Many of the metaphors we use in colloquial speech are rooted in literal historical meanings. Likewise, idioms can often be traced to historical practices. *Idioms* are figurative units of language that cannot be translated word for word into another language. Idioms can be divided into two types:

1. *transparent*
2. *opaque.*

Transparent idioms are relatively more literal and connected to concrete entities, events, or actions. For example, "hand" metaphors such as "lending a hand" are considered transparent because "the hand" is literally connected to providing assistance. Transparent metaphors can be easily demonstrated through gestures and explicit definitions. In contrast, *opaque* idioms are less clear and their meaning is probably better understood through etymology. For example, the idiom "kick the bucket" means to die; however, the meaning is not apparent from the literal definition of the words. Like metaphors, idioms have meanings beyond the direct sum of the meaning of the parts. Idioms actually work like a single lexical unit. They work together as one. So, "kicked the bucket" isn't the sum of "kick" plus "the bucket." It has a meaning beyond the denotation. Opaque idioms can often be traced back historically to concrete events. The idiom "kick the bucket" actually comes from a time when executions were performed by hanging. The bucket, on which criminals would stand, would be kicked out from underneath them, thereby killing the criminal. The opaque idioms require an explicit discussion about the cultural and historical context of use. For example, the *Bucket List* is a film about two terminally ill patients who have six months to live and they put together a list of things they want to do before "kicking the bucket." Showing and discussing films such as this are valuable cultural resources for mediating ELs' understanding of English idioms.

Embodied Metaphors

Many metaphors are learned through physical experience. They are embodied, or rooted, in our physical experience with the world. At the most basic level we can call these primary metaphors. They are so basic to the way we understand the world because we have experienced them in a real, physical way. Often, these metaphors are relatively universal around the world because they are experienced physically. For example, metaphors like "reach for the stars" to talk about achievement and "lend a hand" are both rooted in the physical experience of extending your physical arm to obtain an object. One feeling metaphor, "anger is bottling up inside," for example, is extremely common around the world. The physical experience of anger feels like there is pressure inside of a container, therefore the metaphor arises that pressure is building. In the United States, this includes an

FIGURE 7.11 Idioms of Anger in English

expression of heat. "He is hot headed," "My blood is boiling!" are just a few examples of anger being compared to building pressure. Chinese metaphors about anger do include a sense of building pressure, but the idea of heat is not attached. Thus, these bodily metaphors seem to be more universally applied around the world because we, as humans, experience them physically in a similar way. Though not each of these metaphors is an exact replica of another (Lantolf & Thorne, 2006).

George Lakoff and Mark Johnson (1999) explain that so much of our cultural selves are rooted in our physical experience with the world. These *primary metaphors* are ubiquitous cross-culturally because our material experience is universal:

> Primary metaphors are part of the cognitive unconscious. We acquire them automatically and unconsciously via the normal process of neural learning and may be unaware that we have them. We have no choice in this process. When the embodied experiences in the world are universal, then the corresponding primary metaphors are universally required. This explains the wide spread occurrence around the world of primary metaphors.
>
> (Lakoff & Johnson, 1999, p. 56)

It is important to note that while primary metaphors are universal, they are not innate. They are the result of human beings having similar needs, purposes, problems, and interactions with the world around them. As a result, human be-ings engage in similar *embodied meaning*-making practices because they are trying to figure out the same type of problems. Lakoff and Johnson state, "Universal conceptual metaphors are learned, they are universals that are not innate" (p. 57). These primary metaphors are not the result of complex logical reasoning or en-lightened literary license. Rather, they are a basic part of our biology that may be expressed in our language and our cultural models. In Table 7.1, there is a chart of several primary metaphors. These tend to be fairly universal in languages and cultures around the world, with some variation.

There may be hundreds of other metaphors that we can map on to our physi-cal understanding of the world. The metaphors are not arbitrary relationships between words and concepts, rather, there is already a physical understanding of the concept, which is taken up and applied linguistically.

Therefore, when we think about the way we think, we realize that so much of our understanding of the world is based on metaphors. Surely, we do have literal

TABLE 7.1 Universal Primary Metaphors

Primary metaphor	Example	Physical experience
Affection is Warmth	"A warm hug"	Think of the feeling of being held affectionately.
Important is Big	"It's your big day!"	Think of being a child and all of the important things are big.
Intimacy is Closeness	"This is my closest friend"	Think of being physically close to those who are important to you.
Bad is Stinky	"This movie stinks!"	Think of being repulsed by a foul smell.
Difficulties are Burdens	"This assignment is weighing me down"	Think about trying to lift or carry something heavy.
More is Up	"The stocks soared"	Think about observing piles rise and fall as things are added or taken away.
Categories are Containers	"Bats are in the mammal class"	Think about things that are similar being in near proximity.
Time is Motion	"Time flies when you are having fun"	Think about time passing as you move.
Help is Support	"I support the Breast Cancer Foundation"	Think about some things (and some people) that need physical support to help them function.
Understanding is Grasping	"The students finally grasped the concept"	Think about getting information about something and physically manipulating it.
Seeing is Touching	"She picked out the dress she liked"	Think about the connection between seeing and touching.
Knowing is Seeing	"I see your point"	Think about getting information through sight.

talk, however, when we talk from our subjective experience, we almost always draw on metaphors. Therefore, understanding how these metaphors are formed is important to teaching second language learners.

When working with second language learners, we can assume that many of the experiences we go through in life, regardless of where we grew up, are similar. This provides the starting point for making connections. At the same time, however, we also need to assume that there is cross-linguistic (i.e., between languages) and intralinguistic (i.e., dialects within a language) variation. The experience of growth extending upward, reaching out to grab something, time moving, pain of loss of someone close, and many other experiences are common across human cultures. These are experiences that can be shared between teachers and students from various cultural contexts in order to achieve intersubjectivity. For example, the metaphor "reaching for the stars" can be explained through the bodily act of reaching. "Aiming high" is another example that can be explained in terms of physical success being associated with growth and height. "Striving for excellence" can be explained as movement forward. Students can connect with these metaphors because it is grounded in common experiences. "Reaching out to help" is associated with a bodily experience. These concepts can easily transfer across languages and cultures. So, while, traditionally, metaphors cannot be translated word for word, in primary metaphors, the concepts can be translated via the actual physical acts (e.g., reaching, looking up, etc.).

Metaphors and Second Language Learning

Metaphors have typically been difficult to teach to second language learners. This is, at least in part, due to the fact that all metaphors are generally assumed to be the same. As we have indicated, there is also variation in metaphors across cultures. Some metaphors are linguistic metaphors, and can be arbitrarily invented. For example, a child may use a simile and say "he balled up in the blanket like he was a rollie pollie in the dirt." This concept would be very difficult to understand unless you had knowledge of being physically rolled up under a blanket and what a "rollie pollie" does. So, a word-for-word translation would only be beneficial if the student has knowledge of these two domains.

A cultural metaphor, as described above, could be a conceptual model that is local to the United States. For example, metaphors about hats are rooted in cultural practices. So, taking your hat off for respect is a cultural practice that helps us understand "Hats off to you." These metaphors are difficult to understand for second language learners who do not have the same cultural context and understanding. For example, French second language learners had difficulty with guessing the meaning of English "hat metaphors" in the absence of cultural cues (Boers & Demecheleer, 2001).

Primary, or *embodied metaphors*, on the other hand, seem to be rooted not only in cultural practices, but also in our physical, bodily interactions with the material world. Thus, second language learners probably have these embodied experiences with the world. Teaching metaphors becomes a matter of connecting the linguistic expressions to physical experiences.

Working with second language learners requires knowledge of our own cultural practices and those of our students. We need to understand what those cultural metaphors are, how we use them, and how they differ from those of our students. If we continue to speak and talk as if metaphors are neutral parts of language, then we won't be able to understand why second language learners often have difficulty with some and less with others. The difficulty is not because metaphors are not transparent or are too complex. In fact, much of the difficulty is in the intuition with which we use them. Cultural metaphors are learned, as are embodied metaphors.

Conclusion

In this chapter, we have taken a critical step in our linguistic journey by moving from the study of linguistic form to the study of linguistic function. We have discussed the basis of human language use: semantics (meaning) and *meaning-making processes* (semiotics). We have learned that in order to understand the how and why of human semiotic practices, we have to attend to three principles:

1. the stability of linguistic form in relation to function and meaning;
2. stability and variation in meaning-making;
3. meaning-making as the achievement of intersubjectivity through ongoing approximation by interlocutors (speakers).

These three principles are best understood through the concepts of framing and embodiment. For second language learners, communication in a new code is an ongoing struggle that requires metalinguistic mediation. This chapter provides you with tools to think about and "frame" critical discussions with students about the nature, functions, and purposes of the embodied metaphors we live by.

TEACHER CASE STUDIES

Juana: Idioms

Juana is a middle school teacher in a classroom where the majority of students spoke Spanish at home. As a bilingual herself, she knew that she sometimes found idioms difficult to grasp. However, though she found them difficult, she knew she could never escape them in her relationships with English speakers. So, she thought it would be a good idea to make it a point to teach idioms in her class. Of course, this would mean she would have to step out of her own comfort zone.

Juana started to collect idioms from her English-speaking friends, the news, books she was reading, the Internet, and so forth. Many of these she recalled having heard in conversation, but didn't know what they meant. She knew they were supposed to be literal, but didn't understand them. She then created a game for the students that was designed to:

> draw my students' attention to the elasticity of language by showing them how silly or absurd many of our familiar sayings are if taken literally. By examining idioms and describing them in both literal and metaphorical terms, students see that what gives words their useful meaning depends on our ways of thinking about idioms.

The game was intended to get the students to think about meaning.

Juana introduced the lesson by explaining what idioms are. She then gave some examples, like "Blind as a bat" and "clear as a bell." She explained that neither of these was meant to be taken literally. However, she explained both the literal meaning and the metaphorical meaning. Gradually, she released responsibility, and asked them about what "hit the hay" meant. After asking them about both the literal and figurative meaning, she then asked them to get into groups.

The students were to think about the idioms they heard. Each player needed to have four idioms. They wrote the idiom down on a piece of paper and then drew a picture of the literal meaning on one index card. If they didn't feel comfortable drawing, they could find a picture online or in a magazine. On a second index card they were to try to draw the metaphorical meaning. Since the students in a group were coming up with different idioms, many of the students did not know all of the idioms.

In the next step of the activity, students placed all the cards upside-down. They then played a game of "memory." As they turned over the cards, they had to think about how the literal meaning related to the figurative meaning. This gave students an opportunity to think about how the idioms mean.

Finally, Juana brought all the students together to share about some of the idioms they used in their groups. She asked what was difficult and what was easy about the game. Many of the students had difficulty drawing the figurative use of the idiom. Also, she asked how they felt when they heard idioms in everyday language. Some of the students said they often felt like they knew what was being said, but didn't understand the meaning. Juana felt like she grew closer to her students. They felt the same way.

Tamara: Similes

Tamara is a third grade teacher in a predominantly Chinese-American school. One day she was reading a book to her students called *Poppa's new pants* by Angela Shelf Medearis.

While reading this book, they were discussing similes and other metaphors. The students asked if they could make their own similes. This really surprised Tamara! The students wanted to make their own similes?

So, Tamara went home that evening and designed a week-long language arts unit in which the students would create metaphors. Using the book as an example, the students worked in groups to rewrite the similes that were in the book. They drew pictures, typed their story, and put them into bound volumes. Each group had a read-out-loud and the students discussed their metaphors. Some of them had quite imaginative similes! Tamara was impressed and looked at the example a little more closely. She noticed that the groups had very different similes! Very few of them were duplicated. She was amazed that the students were getting across the same idea with such different words. This led to another discussion about how the similes mean things. The students talked about how they envisioned the pictures and could "feel" and "see" the metaphors. The words themselves seemed to come to life, to have texture. Figure 7.12 shows a couple of the similes the students created.

Tamara noted that in this first simile, based on *Poppa's new pants*, the simile was clearly something they had never experienced first-hand before. She knew the students learned about the Nile. They knew it was the longest river in the world. However, the Nile was something far from their experience, though a knowledge shared relatively universally through formal education.

She compared this to a second simile (see Figure 7.13).

This simile, "It was a relief to him like a kid that gets money on Chinese New Year," is one that was very common to the students' experience. Tamara had certainly never experienced this herself, and was very surprised that this simile was so different from the first. The first one, she could find herself relating to and understanding the simile. Here, however, she knew what it meant, but couldn't "feel" like the kids felt.

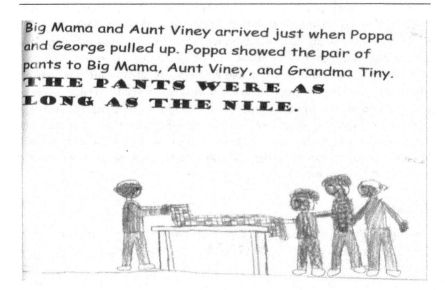

FIGURE 7.12 As Long as the Nile

George woke up and heard someone say his name. It was Grandma Tiny. Grandma Tiny told George to wash up before he could say anything. It was morning, George checked if his limbs were all in place. His limbs were all in place. *It was a relief to him like a kid that gets money on Chinese New Year.* Grandma Tiny told Poppa to come in the kitchen. There was a surprise in Grandma Tiny's arm.

FIGURE 7.13 Like a Kid that Gets Money on Chinese New Year

QUESTIONS/ACTIVITIES

1. Ask your students to use several different dictionaries, in print or on-line, to look at the meaning of certain words. What are the differences between the dictionaries? Do the words always "mean" the same thing? Have students evaluate the dictionary definitions and give critique to their misuse.
2. Ask students to create and analyze metaphors using the website below.
3. Ask students to draw images (or point to images) as they hear the following words or see the following symbols: heart, liver, stomach. The goal is to generate multiple frames for each. You can even discuss these in multiple languages by having student provide "an equivalent" in their primary language.

Additional Resources (multimedia)

http://www.dailymail.co.uk/news/article-2165620/Colorado-32-000-evacuated-dozens-houses-destroyed-blaze-DOUBLES-size.html [Experiencing Fire, Colorado Springs Fires, June 2012]

http://blogs.transparent.com/english/make-a-metaphor/ [Transparent Language, Making a Metaphor]

www.engrish.com [Documenting Misuses of English/Comedy]

http://www.phrases.org.uk/ [Idioms and Metaphors]

8

WRITTEN LANGUAGE

Historical Developments in Literacy

LEARNING GOALS

1. Understand different types of written languages.
2. Understand the connection between written and spoken language.
3. Understand the historical development of written language.
4. Use written language as a tool for analyzing learning.
5. Use written language as a tool for analyzing social relationships.
6. Summarize basic concepts in literacy studies.

KEY TERMS/IDEAS: orthography, grapheme, metalanguage, literacy, orality, literacy practices, multiliteracies, typography

Introduction

"In the beginning was the word . . ." Was it spoken or written? While the answer to this question is a contentious theological debate, and in linguistic circles it takes the form of the primacy of orality vs. literacy debate, we know for sure that throughout human history, the written word has mediated complex social, historical, and genealogical relationships transcending time and space. From hieroglyphics, the ancient Elamite tablets, the Dead Sea scrolls to the printing press, typewriters, spray paint graffiti, carved initials in the bark of a tree, faxes, dot matrix printers, SMS, e-mail, and now Tweets, the written word has proven to be a social practice grounded in goals and governed by cultural rules. Writing has always been more than simply recorded code—it serves as an index for identity, ideological cohesion, status, and solidarity. From national spelling bees, to "misspelled" text messages, there is a tremendous need to understand the written word as a sociocultural practice and move toward what Sebba calls the "sociolinguistics of orthography" (Sebba, 2012).

Perhaps one of the most dramatic technological shifts in human history is the development of writing. Three major technological shifts have profoundly contributed to the purpose and function of writing in human society:

1. *the phonetic alphabet*;
2. *the printing press*;
3. *digital text*.

Writing essentially allowed information to be more widespread and standardized than oral communication, reaching wider audiences and even crossing the span of time. Prior to writing, many societies kept historical records in the form of oral history; however, with writing, societies could develop standard historical accounts and regulate large areas with written decrees from a central location. The earliest recorded writing systems were *logographic* ("images of words") and were found in ancient Mesopotamia around 3200 B.C. The proto-Elamite is the oldest known writing system from Iran. Its script was logographic, consisted of more than 1000 signs, and was principally used for accounting purposes and management of large masses of territory (Figure 8.1).

The earliest hieroglyphic systems also emerged in ancient Egypt, Greece, and China—but were highly cryptic and difficult to teach. The most significant literacy

FIGURE 8.1 The Proto-Elamite Script

development was the advent of the phonetic alphabet—each symbol stood for a consonant. Its ancient ancestors were the Canaanites of Egypt, which was the forerunner of Semitic languages (i.e., Arabic, Aramaic, Hebrew). It is interesting to note that in contrast to the elitist roots of logographic systems, the alphabet was the invention of nomads, shepherds, and laborers of the ancient world (around 1850 B.C.). Their principal purpose was the transmission of sacred texts and the survival of their cultural practices in the face of dominant empires. The phonetic alphabet fundamentally altered the accessibility of literacy to a wider population. Below are samples of the earliest alphabet (Figures 8.2, 8.3, and 8.4).

Writing not only served accounting functions of large empires, it was also used to promote ideas, worldviews, and even serve aesthetic functions. With the spread of Islam, the aesthetics of writing in the form of calligraphy permeated the arts, architecture, and culture of the Middle Ages (A.D. 600 to A.D. 1250) (Figure 8.5).

The second major technological advance in the history of writing was the printing press. The moveable type printing press dynamically changed the organization of the world. While the earliest presses were perhaps made in China, Gutenberg's invention in 1440 proved to be revolutionary and spawned a major sociological shift in the Western world. Prior to the presses, each copy of a paper or book was handwritten, which made it an expensive and exclusive commodity. While literacy had become ascendant in the East, in medieval Europe, many people could not read or write, and since there were no mass produced materials, there was little need for mass literacy. With the ability to produce books and other written works more efficiently, writing became more accessible to the layperson. This fueled religious movements like the Protestant Reformation. Ideas, letters, and even the Bible could be spread so much more quickly and widely than ever before, stripping the power, in many ways, of the elite. The layperson could now access the writing that had so long been available only to the rich and powerful.

A third major technological shift, we could perceive, is the advancement of the computer and Internet (Razfar & Yang, 2010). Presently, information, ideas, communication, and so forth can be spread more quickly and efficiently than ever before. The accumulated writing of an entire library prior to the printing press can be contained on a single flash drive. An entire library from after the printing press can be displayed in one database. Writing can be modified in real time. Instantaneous written communication can be sent (and stored) from almost anywhere to almost anyone. Relationships can be built globally. An e-mail originating in Chicago can almost instantly be sent to Beijing. Encyclopedias that used to house the standards of information on a given topic are giving way to *wikis* and other interactive knowledge bases (www.wikipedia.com). A single Tweet on a cell phone could reach people around the world and bring outcry, rage, and possibly even revolution (www.twitter.com).

In this context of writing and literacy development we need to expand our understanding of what counts as literacy as well as its social functions.

FIGURE 8.2 Ancient Phoenician

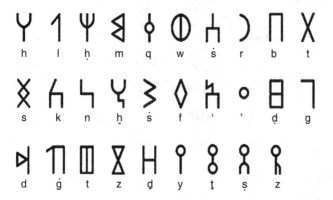

FIGURE 8.3 Yemeni Phonetic Alphabet

Letter Name	Proto-Sinaitic	Early Phoenician	Greek	Phonetic Value	Letter Meaning
'aleph			A	[']	ox
beth			B	[b]	house
gimmel			Γ	[g]	throwstick
deleth			Δ	[d]	door
he			E	[h]	
waw			Y	[w]	hook/peg
zayin			Z	[z]	
heth			H	[ḥ]	fence
teth			Θ	[ṭ]	
yodh			I	[y]	arm/hand
kaph			K	[k]	palm of hand
lamedh			Λ	[l]	goad/crook
mem			M	[m]	water
nun			N	[n]	snake
samekh			Ξ	[s]	
'ayin			O	[']	eye
pe			Π	[p]	
tsade			M²	[ṣ]	
qoph			Φ³	[q]	
reš			P	[r]	head
šin			Σ	[š]	
taw			T	[t]	mark (?)

FIGURE 8.4 Stages of Phonetic Alphabet

FIGURE 8.5 Writing as Art: Qur'an from Al-Andalus

Literacy is more than school based reading and writing serving discrete academic purposes. In this chapter we will discuss the wide variety of modalities, technologies, orthographic systems, rhetorical styles, and ideologies of literacy that have contributed to our collective experience with writing.

Orthography

In Chapter 4 we discussed the development of the alphabet in relation to phonology. Here we will consider the relationship between writing and language more generally. The study of signs and symbols is called *semiotics*. When people study the relationship between writing and meaning, they try to understand how a person makes sense of the sign. There are several approaches to understanding how one makes sense of a sign (written or spoken). Once spoken language is written down, it changes the sign significantly. One approach, then, is that writing is a sign representing another sign. In this way, reading is a metalinguistic activity. It is a way of thinking about language.

Different writing systems are used for different purposes. The writing systems that are more logographic, like Chinese, have roughly a sign–word correspondence. So, mostly each sign stands for a word though sometimes there is a combination of signs for a word. Generally, historical linguists think these logographic systems developed first. Logographs have an iconic quality; they usually look like, or resemble, the thing they are standing for. As they develop, they become more conventional and symbolic. For efficient communication it is impractical to draw every word into a picture. Many concepts can't be expressed well in a picture. For example, only the effects of actions and feelings can be depicted visually; therefore, a writing system becomes established through conventions and rules determined by a community of users. When literacy practices need to reach a more global audience, the symbols can't just resemble local images and material objects. This would seriously limit access to meaning-making.

There are very few truly logographic writing systems today. The writing of Chinese is really the only widespread language that has retained such a degree of logographic writing. It is used in various parts of Asia, though has some notable differences. For example, one of Japan's writing systems utilizes the symbols in Chinese, though not exactly. Hieroglyphics, the Ancient Egyptian language, isn't truly a logographic system either. While it does have some logographic qualities, it also contains phonetic features as well. Although ancient Mayan script also appears to be logographic, it also contains a complementary syllabic script. Thus, Mayan symbols could be used to represent morphemes or syllables. As we can see, no writing system is completely logographic. The conventions of a pure logographic system would not allow for the standardization needed over long distances, nor would it be able to easily adapt to new words.

Another type of writing system is syllabic where each symbol roughly represents a syllable. Hiragana and Katakana (Figure 8.6), two of Japan's writing systems, are syllabic systems. These types of writing systems can be very efficient for languages that have a small phonemic inventory and restricted syllable length. Japanese, for example, has only five vowels, so the number of syllables that can be generated would be about 50. The 46-character Hiragana system is larger than the English alphabet, but much smaller than the Chinese logographic system. Japanese also uses two other writing systems including Kanji, an adapted Chinese logographic system. Together Hiragana and Kanji are used frequently in everyday writing with Katakana used for foreign words. Another writing system, based on the phonemic inventory, uses Roman script. It is used mostly when Westerners learn Japanese. This is called Romanji. Other languages that have used syllabic systems are ancient Persian, Sanskrit, and Cherokee (Tserdanelis & Wong, 2004).

hiragana	katakana	reading
あ い う え お	ア イ ウ エ オ	a, i, u, e, o
か き く け こ	カ キ ク ケ コ	ka, ki, ku, ke, ko
さ し す せ そ	サ シ ス セ ソ	sa, shi, su, se, so
た ち つ て と	タ チ ツ テ ト	ta, chi, tsu, te, to
な に ぬ ね の	ナ ニ ヌ ネ ノ	na, ni, nu, ne, no
は ひ ふ へ ほ	ハ ヒ フ ヘ ホ	ha, hi, hu, he, ho
ま み む め も	マ ミ ム メ モ	ma, mi, mu, me, mo
や ゆ よ	ヤ ユ ヨ	ya, yu, yo
ら り る れ ろ	ラ リ ル レ ロ	ra, ri, ru, re, ro
わ を ん	ワ ヲ ン	wa, wo, n
や ゆ よ っ ゛゜	ヤ ユ ヨ ツ ゛゜	

FIGURE 8.6 Hiragana and Katakana

Logographic systems have roughly a symbol–morpheme correspondence, and syllabic systems a symbol–syllable correspondence, but alphabetic systems have roughly symbol–phoneme correspondence. We can look at alphabets as another development in writing systems. They served as a tool to accomplish goals and meet needs that logographic systems could not. They also changed the way language is thought of. Some alphabets, true alphabets, have a symbol for the different phonemes in a language. Others, like Arabic and Hebrew, do not have independent symbols for vowels, though there have been some developments in these writing systems to use vowels when necessary in the form of diacritics. After the alphabet, we could think about words as compilations of different sounds. Spelling grew to become important because people used the symbol to make sense of sounds, together, which formed words. Of course there are still "sight words" and evidence that people don't read every single letter, but rather chunks of letters, or even whole words themselves. Consider the following example, a popular quote from Steve Jobs, without the vowels:

Crtvty s jst cnnctng thngs. Whn y sk crtve ppl hw thy dd smthng, thy fl a lttl glty bcs thy ddn't rlly d t, thy jst sw smthng. t smd bvs t thm ftr a whl. Tht's bcs thy wr bl t cnnct xprncs thy'v hd nd synthsz nw thngs.

Even without the vowels, we can still read the words, albeit with some difficulty. The phonemic alphabet facilitated the creation of new words because there was not an iconic relationship. There was no need for the symbol to look like an object, or indicate an action. The symbol stood not just for a sound and could be put with other symbols in ways to represent sounds together, forming words.

Indeed, symbols do represent sounds and things in this world, but they do much more than that. They are cultural tools that not only neutrally represent words, but play more complex roles in meaning-making. They are conventionalized and governed by rules. While in the 1700s there were not such strict conventional spellings for words, soon rules for spelling were developed. In English, for example, there are also significant differences between British spelling and American spellings, designating both a simplification of English spelling, but also a cultural shift away from British standardization.

However, though there are no purely logographic systems of writing, there are some logograms used in many languages, thus no language is completely alphabetical or syllabic either. The Arabic numeral "1" is pretty standard regardless if it is read as *one*, *un*, *uno*, *eins*, or *wahid*, though in contemporary Arabic the numbers are often written differently now. In this way, numerals, mathematic symbols, and other conventional symbols have logographic qualities. We shouldn't look at writing and reading as one or the other. Rather, we should look at reading and writing as social practices utilizing symbol systems for specific purposes. We may use multiple means as a social group to write or communicate through writing.

Typography and Penmanship

Another area of study, not a part of linguistics, but more a part of wider semiotics studies, is *typography*—the art of letter formation, like fonts, colors, and other arrangements. It is a popular field in marketing, news editing, and other relevant fields in which the aesthetics and visual appeal of written language are as important, if not more important, as the written language itself. Different fonts, sizes, and so forth can be used to signal different meanings, especially emotions. Some indicate something comical is being communicated, others something scary or sad. Notably, all capital letters can indicate anger, a mistake often made via chat or text.

Visual appeal is important in communication, and typefaces can convey attitude, mood, and identity of the writer and their intended audiences (Brumberger, 2003). What can often be done via speech cannot be done as easily in written language. There are different affordances. However, written communication can allow for different messages to be communicated. College professors may find it odd to read an academic paper written in Comic Sans font! Every professional community has its own literacy norms when it comes to typeface. For example, lawyers are required to use particular fonts, and they vary from state to state and court to court (see www.typographyforlawyers.com or www.ca7.uscourts.gov). One way written communication is regulated is through professional standards.

A related topic is *penmanship*, or handwriting. The mechanics of writing is often assessed in young grades, and again as students learn cursive, usually around third grade in the United States. These mechanics, again, are important because there are cultural models of what "good" and "bad" penmanship is. Students may be judged on how their handwriting looks. They may even have emotional connections with the handwriting. There is probably even a reason seventh grade girls draw a circle above their "i" instead of a dot. We study these practices of handwriting and typology as literacy practices that are grounded in issues of identity and culture.

Literacy

Literacy is a major field of research. However, literacy has been defined in various ways. These different views have profound influence on the ways we teach and the ways we understand how reading and interpreting signs and symbols works.

Literacy as Reading and Writing

Walter Ong, with his classic *Orality and literacy: The technologizing of the world* (1982), built on the long tradition of literacy-as-technology. In this tradition, *orality* was seen as human thought through sound and *literacy* was seen as human thought through sight. Ong argued that literacy, in contrast to orality, had the unique potential to bring about individual cognitive change as well as broader cultural change. When an oral people learn to write, as a widespread practice, they begin to change the way they think. There is no longer as much of a need for long-term memorization and transmission of stories and information. They can write down stories and songs to be passed on or distributed. However, this may dynamically change the way the stories and information are organized in the mind of literate peoples (as opposed to oral peoples).

Goody and Watt (1963) in "Consequences of literacy" also distinguished orality and literacy; however, they point out we should view literacy as additive to oral tradition rather than subtractive. The change was a cultural change in that literacy enables a built history and allows events to live in the memories of the culturally literate.

David Olson (1991) reviewed several different definitions of literacy and orality, but eventually he posed the hypothesis that literacy is a *metalinguistic activity*. Writing makes us think about the nature, functions, and purposes of language use. Another way written language may affect the mind is by transforming oral speech into discrete words and letters. In spoken language, there is not a real separation between words and it is continuous. There isn't a blank space separating one word from another, instead they flow together in a continuous string. Likewise, there are not individual words or sounds, a concept that is not intuitive for oral peoples. Literacy may deeply transform the psychological state because after one learns to write, whether in pictograms or in an alphabet, the language then is thought of in light of sounds and individual words. This is a fundamental psychological shift in the mind of the literate, signaling a new linguistic and cognitive consciousness. Oral cultures have no need to think of words as abstract, arbitrary, and/or autonomous signs in the world. As a result, they don't develop "higher" metacognitive functions.

All three of these views toward literacy are heavily text based (i.e., the written word). They are heavily set on the distinction between literacy and orality in which the difference lies in the subject's mind. Culture and the reorganization of culture are extensions of literacy's effects on an individual's mind. Thus, these three views are generally grouped together because of the dichotomist view of literacy and orality, their relation to cognition, and the potential misrepresentation of oral cultures as more primitive than literate societies. Literacy, due to its highly privileged status in this tradition, is viewed as a technology or tool of modernization, advancement, and progress.

Related to the question of whether literacy is limited to reading and writing, is the traditional view of literacy as the ability to read and write a language. In society, we generally categorize people as either literate or illiterate based on whether they can or cannot decode, recite, and record words. We assume that reading and writing will lead to major societal changes due to the "education" of the illiterate mind. Street (1985) critiqued the *autonomous* view of literacy represented above, because it presumed literacy to be detached from the social, cultural, and historical context in which it is practiced.

Arguably autonomous views of literacy, if not explicitly, implicitly privileged literate practices over indigenous oral literacies. This tradition of literacy has sustained deficit views of non-dominant populations by constructing literate peoples as cognitively more advanced, and essentializing "non-literate" peoples as naïve, simplistic, and perhaps less intelligent. As far as their potential to participate in modern society, their cultural norms were framed as an impediment to success. An alternative to this deficit model of literacy was pioneered by more ethnographic, situated, and socioculturally based views of literacy, culture, and human development. Drawing on a *cultural historical activity (CHAT)* approach to literacy, Scribner and Cole (1981) were among the first to challenge the deficit and primitive view of oral cultures by showing the sophisticated uses of multiple literacy practices. Nevertheless, the institutional inertia of autonomous views of literacy remains firmly entrenched in classrooms, curricula mandates, and policy debates wherever nation-states attempt to standardize schooling for a diverse population. In much of our discussions of standards and high-stakes testing, we separate language into four skills: speaking, listening, reading, and writing; furthermore, reading and writing are given more status in relation to oral language functions (e.g., story-telling, rapping, singing).

Literacy as a Social Practice

While these hard and fast approaches to literacy, taking "literacy" to be a single, or dyadic, construct (i.e., reading and writing), grew into one literacy research tradition, there was also a movement toward defining literacy as social practice. Rather than literacy changing culture, literacy is seen as a social practice that arises out of cultural needs and goals (e.g., Heath, 1983; Scribner & Cole, 1981). Scribner and Cole (1981) found that the Vai people systematically used a variety of scripts (Arabic, English, and Vai) for different purposes in society. Furthermore, they found that the Vai were learning and using these different writing systems in non-school settings. This study helped broaden the notion of what counts as literacy and bring awareness to the complex literacy functions which so-called "primitive" peoples engaged in. These literacy functions served purposeful goals and were embedded within culturally organized activities such as religion, business, and politics. Thus, literacy was developed within a social context. For example, the Vai people needed to read the Quran for religious purposes; as a result, they developed literacy of Arabic script. They needed to use English for commercial purposes, so they used English in order to engage in certain business markets. They used their indigenous Vai script for more personal and local political functions. Contrary to how literacy was usually conceived, a formalized system taught in schools, Scribner and Cole found that schooling was not only unnecessary for literacy, but perhaps was peripheral for the particular literacy practices of the Vai.

Shirley Brice Heath (1983), likewise, recognized through her ethnography of Trackton, Roadville, and Maintown that different groups of people use literacy for diverse ends. Heath's study was one of the first *language socialization* studies of literacy practices in diverse U.S. communities. *Language socialization* is defined as the "interactional display (covert or overt) to a novice of expected ways of thinking, feeling, and acting ... through their participation in social interactions, children come to internalize and gain performance competence in these sociocultural defined contexts" (Ochs, 1986, p. 2). Language socialization is the process by which children become competent members of language and literacy communities through the use of language by interacting with adults. It is a process that is life-long and life-wide because human beings are continuously using language across their lifespan and in multiple contexts, transitioning between novice and expert roles. In Heath's comparative study of literacy in three communities, she showed how sometimes these literacy practices were in alignment with school literacy practices, and sometimes they weren't. In roughly ten years of fieldwork, Heath learned about the different literacy practices in two rural communities and a town. The communities varied in terms of class and race. One rural community was predominantly working class, African-American (Trackton), the other working class White-American (Roadville), and the third middle class White-American (Maintown).

The ethnography was conducted just following racial integration of schools, so it provided an opportune time to observe how different literacy practices in these communities resembled or did not resemble school literacy practices. Heath found that the children from the town were involved in literacy practices, like reading bedtime stories at home with their parents. These stories resembled the practices of storybooks in schools. Thus, in bedtime stories, she noted the differences, namely that the townspeople used school-like literacy practices in the home while Trackton and Roadville used different literacy practices. Most notably different were the African-American children who were engaged in complex performative storytelling that was very unlike school, but were complex literacy practices nonetheless. Literacy, again, was conceptualized not as a skill or task learned in formal education, nor as a metalinguistic activity alone, but rather as practices of social interaction which may or may not be school-based. One of the key ideological consequences of Heath's work was the fact that literacy practices in school were shown to be not objective or neutral. The children of Maintown performed better in school, not because they were more intelligent or more "literate," but because the literacy practices of school mirrored those of home. In other words, Maintown children were at home, while in school, whereas Trackton and Roadville children found themselves strangers in their own schools. This obviously gives Maintown children an advantage in achievement, success, and school-based learning opportunities.

From the ethnographic language socialization studies of the late 1970s and early 1980s, emerged a more critical view known as the *New Literacy Studies (NLS)*. This ideological view of literacy allowed literacy to not only be studied as social practices, but also attend to issues of power and social stratification. For Street as well as Gee (2008) the everyday ideas of what literacy is and how it constitutes social relations are not neutral. NLS represented a paradigm shift in the study of literacy. The shift from autonomous to ideological models of literacy included a shift in the unit of analysis from the individual to the social, ideological, and critical (Hatano & Wertsch, 2001). The ideological character of literacy is predicated on the idea that what counts as literacy is inextricably connected to how some symbolic resources become dominant and others subordinate. It focuses on literacy as cultural capital and a purveyor of asymmetrical relationships between "haves" and "have nots" of dominant literacy practices (Gee, 2008; Luke, 1996; Street, 1993).

From the beginning of this book we have asked four questions regarding the nature, function, and purpose of language. With regards to the third of "what is meaning?" an autonomous view of literacy is predicated on a literal and denotative notion of meaning. Autonomous views of literacy have led to the view of literal meaning in texts (Lähteenmäki, 2004; Street, 2003). As we have shown throughout the book, texts are inherently contextualized. Even when texts appear to be autonomous, the reader imposes a context in order to make meaning. For example, if we see the word "red" on a page, we probably would interpret it in light of our notions of color. This would be the most literal and denotative approach. However, we could easily interpret it affectively and symbolically, as in red representing passion, anger, or love. In both cases, one contextual frame may be considered more dominant and the other less; however, without context interpretation is impossible. Neither the more literal or symbolic interpretations are absolutely "correct." It depends on the context and the reader.

Within NLS, *multiliteracies* emerged as a term to encapsulate the multiple texts used for meaning-making. *Text* here is more than the written word, and more encompassing of multimodal semiotic resources (e.g., Kress, 2000, 2004). This necessitates an approach to literacy that teaches adaptability and higher-order thinking skills, or *embodied meaning-making*, rather than a traditional reactive response to the needs of the day. Historically, educational policies and debates have reacted to literacy and achievement crisis by going back to "basics" and discrete forms of literacy. Teachers teach students what is needed to navigate printed text and, more recently, basic media and games (Chandler-Olcott & Mahar, 2003). However, these strategies are ineffective and literacy education must shift focus from simply understanding text (in the autonomous sense), to *texts* in the ideological sense.

As technology changes the nature of literacy practices available to students, teachers will need to be equipped to better engage the *digital native* generation (sometimes called the *millennial generation or Generation Y*). From the vast array of social media sites to hip-hop, Generation Y students have already surpassed their teachers in many of the new literacies of this millennium (e.g., Alim, Ibrahim, & Pennycook, 2009). Thus, a comprehensive approach to developing students is needed in which they can learn to use familiar literacy practices strategically. Literacies are found all around us, we just aren't always as perceptive of them because many are tacit and our definition of what counts as literacy may be too dependent on what we see in school settings. For example, Gee discusses the higher-order literacies found in video games (e.g., 2003), many of which have superbly developed story lines, require high levels of reading and synthesizing information, and require split-second judgments based on evidence gathered in the virtual world— all advanced academic practices.

Literacy understood as encompassing more than just traditional reading and writing sees understanding and synthesizing images as a literacy practice. Some have even considered the image to surpass the written word in importance (e.g., Stephens, 1998). Much of the reading and research done on the computer violates the laws of traditional reading, in which text is bound and linear, and requires the ability to understand texts embedded within texts and texts hyperlinked to other texts. These are literacies, which are generally left out of the official curriculum, though they may involve higher-order academic type problem-solving. There is still a need for understanding how students are using multiliteracies in their daily lives both in and out of school (e.g., Moje, 2000).

Since literacy is a social practice, it is essential to understand what types of literacies are available and needed in a community. Some communities have high need for digital literacies. Students need to know how to access online content in schools, stores may be highly dependent on credit and debit card services, jobs may require digital knowledge(s) even for basic entry-level positions. On the other hand, other communities may have little access to digital products. As teachers, it could be valuable to take an inventory of the available literacies and epistemological expertise, or *funds of knowledge*, within our students' communities.

What do the students do? What do they have access to do? What do they need to read? How do they read? What types of literacies are necessary for basic survival?

Some literacies in the community or used in families are not valued in schools. Some of these may be in different languages, as in the case of many EL homes. Maybe community literacies involve graffiti or gang symbols. These are still literacies, even though they are not the type valued in schools. How do we deal with these types of literacies in schools? Literacies used in society don't always "fit" into our school curricula and often make us uncomfortable; however, that does not mean that it isn't a conventional and cultural system of literacies. As teachers, how will we analyze these? How will we understand them? How can we leverage those literacy practices to develop our school-based literacy objectives? While these are tough questions, we believe the linguistic perspectives, activities, and tools provided in this book facilitate answers that are specific to each classroom context.

Metalanguage Development as Practice

While these two types of traditions approach literacy very differently, there is a dynamic relationship between culture and literacy. In fact, the very fact that one tradition looks at literacy as *metalanguage* is indeed a significant point. However, metalanguage is only significant as it related to larger social and cultural structures. Metalanguage, the way we think about language, is transformed by the way we write, and writing is enveloped by communicative purposes and social needs. There is a dialectic relationship between culture and literacy, specifically between the way we think about language and literacy.

Writing systems are conventional systems of signs that serve purposes in social practice, but once they are used as a cultural tool, they do change the way we think about language. For example, the orthography used by a language plays a large role in how we think about how language works. In the conventional alphabet, like English, we may often tell students to "sound it out," working with the assumption that each letter represents a single sound, as discussed in Chapter 4. Because we look at words as a compilation of sounds, we can "sound out" words until we say the correct one and understand it. Other writing systems are not like this. In logographic type systems the sign corresponds not to a set of sounds, but rather an image or action. People who read and write that language think about language in a different way. Instead of "sounding out" words, we may think of this as "showing out" words. This has implications for how we organize literacy learning for different populations.

There are several possible areas where this may arise in literacy education for ELs. One is with English speakers who struggle with reading and come from families whose literacy practices are different from schools (i.e., dialect speakers from non-dominant populations). While this is not the traditional definition of

"EL," it is a student who struggles with learning an aspect of English, namely the written parts. This can be exemplified by this reflection by an after-school tutor:

> I was working with an 8th grader who read at roughly a second grade reading level. I was talking with his aunt in his home about his school grades. The student and aunt were sitting on the couch and the aunt, getting frustrated about the grades, turned visibly angry about the reading grade. She called the student "stupid" and threw a book to him. Covering half of a word on the cover, she told him to read it. He began to tear up and didn't answer. His aunt yelled "Come on! This is easy, just sound out the first two letters." She continued to yell until he made it through the word, as she slowly unveiled individual letters.

In this reflection, the student was being forced to read a certain way, in what the aunt assumed was a typical literacy practice of schools, namely "sounding out" words. However, she was covering half of the word and the student never saw the rest of the word. In the case of this student, the school literacy level in his home was limited. Several members in the student's home read only functionally and others had not graduated high school. Their implicit assumption about reading was that the letters merely represented sounds, which is not completely true. Writing does more than represent oral language. It is in itself an entirely different, but related, social practice.

In languages that have alphabetic writing systems similar to English, its speakers tend to construe language as a chain of sounds. As a result, the literacy practices of reading and writing are often focused on sound level reading techniques. While some advocate for a whole word reading strategy, the letter symbols can be recognized even in other languages as representations of sounds or phonemes. In many alphabetic systems there is the understanding that the letters represent sounds. Likely there are similar literacy practices associated with reading and writing language. This may include alphabet books, developing acronyms or acrostics, and so forth. These types of practices arise from the convention of a written alphabet. These literacy practices are prevalent in English, but are not universal to all alphabetic languages. For example, Farsi uses an alphabetic system; however, the use of acronyms, abbreviations, and acrostics is not a pervasive social practice. Thus, we cannot assume that these literacy practices are universal.

Another example would be of students who are learning English but are literate in a language that uses a logographic writing system like Chinese, in which each sign roughly represents a word. The basic foundation of how language is represented through writing is fundamentally different. In one language (i.e., Chinese), the word is a whole unit, and in the other (i.e., English), it is made up of multiple units. So, beyond explaining the different phonemes in a language, understanding how phonemes are represented in written form may be a challenge.

This point would not be as intuitive, and it may require developing phonemic awareness from the ground up.

An interesting example of how logographic writing systems work is Chinese. For the most part, Mandarin and Cantonese Chinese (two different languages) use the same writing system. If you can read one language, you would understand most of the writing in the other, though it may seem ungrammatical or rough. You would be reading words in your own language, although they were written in another. Of course, there are limitations, again, mostly with the syntax. So, if one is used to reading a sign as pointing to a word, then the sounds don't really matter. You could read the word and understand what it means, regardless of how it sounds in your language. An example of this would be "Happy New Year!" They are written exactly the same in Mandarin and Cantonese, but there are different readings (Table 8.1).

In many ways, pictures, or emoticons, function like logographic writing systems. The happy face emoticon on Internet chat or email (☺) is roughly understood in different languages (with some cultural differences). This is an amazing cultural tool not afforded by an alphabetic system. For the most part, if you can read Spanish or English or another system that uses a Roman script, you may be able to "sound out" words in another language, or at least you would understand the concept with some variation. However, those words would not make sense because you are reading the phonological representation of the oral language not the written. These differences highlight how writing systems are sociocultural tools that mediate meaning.

Finally, an EL who comes from a language with no writing system may have difficulties developing phonemic awareness, which is shown to help improve reading and writing. The very concept of reading and writing might be so foreign that the literacy practices required for formal education may need to be taught all together. Imagine a refugee adult from Burundi who speaks a language with no writing. The concept of writing may be so foreign there may be larger issues that need to be learned beyond the alphabet. They would need to be socialized into a literate culture. This is a real issue that arises in the United States. Many refugees fall through the gaps of ESL programs because the foundations of writing, the cultural and social needs, are never realized. Perhaps, in the end, they would develop the literacy practices they would need to get along in a literate culture, but perhaps this would not be reading and writing as we traditionally think about it. There are other ways these communities accomplish the same literate functions as the dominant society. For example, some may pay rent or buy groceries not

TABLE 8.1 Mandarin and Cantonese Writing/Reading, "Happy New Year!"

Characters	恭	禧	發	財
Mandarin	gong	xi	fa	Cai
Cantonese	gong	hey	fat	Choy

through reading individual letters and words, but relying on trusted friends to help. They would recognize the symbols on money and rather than calculate exact amounts understand it in terms of buying power (e.g., five dollar bill = bread and eggs, not $5.00). These literacy practices are developed as tools to make sense of situations and accomplish goals. They are not inferior to conventional forms of reading an alphabet per se, but usually it is necessary to be socialized into the literacy practices of the dominant social group. This means learning to read and write the dominant script, either alphabetic or logographic system.

Errors in Reading and Writing

If we look at reading and writing as social practice, then we can look at formalized schooling subjects, like spelling, composition, and reading, as social practices as well. We can begin to see "errors" not as isolated, structural mistakes that need correcting, but as sociocultural practices that can be *re-mediated* through new literacy activities. These activities would be consciously designed to leverage the full spectrum of a student's linguistic, cultural, and epistemological repertoire in order to socialize them to the dominant types of literacy. It becomes equally important for teachers to critically analyze and discuss the reading and writing errors using sociocultural principles in order to gain insight into how the students understand the nature, function, and purpose of their own language practices. This metalanguage then becomes an important tool for further learning and cognitive development.

Certain mistakes made in spelling, for example, may help us understand how a student is using language. If they are consistently missing vowels in a word, as is very common with young readers and writers, they may not have developed the phonemic awareness of vowels yet. Quite often students will write only the consonants and not the vowels, which isn't surprising since vowels are *sonorants*. They are much more versatile than consonants because their boundaries are quite blurry. In English, many words could be understood if the vowels were centralized to the schwa /ə/, even though it is a phoneme itself. There is not a clear boundary when the /i/ becomes /e/, even though they are clearly phonemes with contrastive distribution. So, if a student is writing only the consonants, we should be sure to affirm the correct consonant use. The vocalic awareness will likely come later in development.

Mistakes in consonants, like "d" for "th," likely means that the student does not understand the phonemic contrast between "d" and "th," in which case the teacher should put the student into situations where this contrast makes a difference. It is possible that the student has not been made aware of the phonemic difference, especially if, as with many children, "th" is substituted with "d." "Th" usually develops later in language learning, and is, indeed, a rather rare sound in the world's languages, so it may be difficult for many ELs. The writing could very well indicate that the student does not have the phonemic awareness of "th" rather than simply is making a spelling mistake. These are two different errors: The first error is a metacognitive and developmental issue, while the second is more of a motor sensory or mechanical issue.

Another prevalent type of spelling mistake is following the phonetic form rather than conventional spelling. Students may, for example, spell "bought" like "bot." The difference in the words is in one sound, though the spelling is different. The first is /bɔt/ while the second is /bot/. However, the vowel /ɔ/ in the first word is not written with a single English letter. It actually could be written as "aw" or "awe," neither of which would make sense in the spelling formation beginning with "b" and ending with "t." Therefore, the student may be selecting the closest vowel letter to put in the word. Given that "bought" is spelled using a conventional spelling that has little direct correspondence to the phonemes, due to historical language change, the spelling put forth by the student, "bot," is actually the most reasonable spelling pattern. Unfortunately, it is not the correct one based on the conventional English spelling. Thus, we do need to provide the correction for students because they do need to understand how to conform to the conventional spelling system for social and communicative reasons. However, we should be very careful to understand that the error is actually an error only because the conventional system has defined it that way, not because the student doesn't understand basic spelling rules. Usually we would refer to these words as "sight words" or words which have spellings that need to be memorized.

Table 8.2 summarizes the three types of spelling errors mentioned here. There are many others that could be explained, but many of the errors you may find in early grades, or with ELs, may be explained here.

Punctuation

Another feature of written language is punctuation. Punctuation is a convention that helps us read written language. Often what is salient in spoken language are *supralinguistic* features, like intonation and pauses. We notice these features in speech, but simply cannot in written language. Therefore, there are conventions that are used to indicate the way words would be spoken. Actually, punctuation can operate in two different ways:

1. it tells how to speak what is written;
2. it shows us the grammatical relationships.

Punctuation in written language tells us when sentences stop, when we should pause, and when we should change intonation. The difference between a sentence and a question in speech, in English, is the intonation. In a question, the pitch of the voice goes up, whereas in a statement it does not. In the following sentences, the words are the same, they are in the same order, but when we see the question

TABLE 8.2 Typology of Spelling Errors

Spelling error type	Explanation	Example
Absence of vowels	Words are spelled with correct consonants, but there are few, or no, vowels. Students likely have not learned vocalic phonemic awareness. This is most common in very early readers and writers.	cts—"cats" str—"store"
Consonants or vowels switched	A consonant is switched for another consonant, or a vowel is switched for another vowel. It is likely that the student had not developed phonemic awareness of the switched letter, or that the student cannot (or did not) differentiate between the sounds.	da—"the" ant—"aunt" (in some dialects where they sound different) teef—teeth (common if students pronounce it this way)
Phonetic, not conventional, spelling	Likely the student understands the relationship between letters and phonemes, but does not know some of the spelling conventions that are not directly phonemic.	jem—"gem" lite—"light" kichun—"kitchen" ant—"aunt" (in some dialects where they sound the same)

mark at the end, we can imagine the intonation going up. In the third sentence there is an exclamation mark. In that sentence, how do you imagine hearing the intonation?

1. The monkey climbed that tree.
2. The monkey climbed that tree?
3. The monkey climbed that tree!

Sentence (1) is a statement that provides us information that the monkey climbed a certain tree. Sentence (2) is a question. Read it out loud, how does it sound? The question could be interpreted in two different ways, depending on emphasis. Reading the sentence emphasizing the "monkey" brings the verification of the monkey into question. If "that" is emphasized, then the verification of that particular tree is in question. Notice that in both, however, the intonation rises. In sentence (3) the intonation again changes to express surprise or some other affective feature of the sentence. Without the punctuation, the only way to know how to read these sentences would be the context.

A second use of punctuation is to help us see the syntactic relationships between words. For example, in the following sentences, the commas tell us how the words are grouped together.

4.   My parents, Jill and Steve.
5.   My parents, Jill, and Steve.

Of course, if we were to read these sentences out loud, we would say them differently. But the commas can tell us how the words relate to each other. In (4) Jill and Steve function as an appositive identifying the parents. Syntactically speaking, the phrase "Jill and Steve" is subordinate to the phrase "My parents" (i.e., it is lower on the tree diagram). In (5) the comma after Jill signals that Jill and Steve are different people from the parents, so there are four people in total. This time, syntactically speaking, "my parents," "Jill," and "Steve" are on the same level. In Chapter 5 we discussed how words in sentences are hierarchically related, and commas help to indicate that relationship. Punctuation can help us understand these hierarchical relationships.

When we teach punctuation in schools, we should be sure to explain how it relates to both written and spoken language. Rather than explaining a set of punctuation rules, of which there are hundreds, punctuation should be taught as a system working with the written form of language. There is a standard conventional use, which needs to be taught; however, more important than the actual correctness of the use of punctuation is the awareness of the relationship between the words. That awareness allows for the manipulation of the rules for creative purposes as well as the conformity to the rules to show adherence to a larger system.

When teaching punctuation, then, we might want to think about why certain "errors" are made. It may be possible that students are unaware of certain rules because they have rarely found a need for them. We should be asking ourselves if "meaning" is affected. Does the meaning change because of the error? This would probably be a significant opportunity to teach the rule and why it is there, namely as a tool to avoid confusion. If an error is made but meaning is not affected, then teaching a punctuation rule would require a different kind of explanation, one that appeals to convention and authority. We can give examples of instances where commas, colons, semicolons, and so forth do not affect meaning; nevertheless there could be sociocultural consequences (i.e., deficit judgments about ability, performance, etc.). These are good opportunities to open a discussion about language and engage in student inquiry. Students can discuss examples of common, or even obscure, punctuation errors and how meaning could be affected. They can even be tasked with developing their own punctuation system (e.g., digital literacies), to be compared to the conventional punctuation.

Conclusion

Written language is extremely complex, and a single chapter doesn't do justice to the topic. However, to study the use of written language in our classrooms, we should keep in mind several key principles. First, literacy is a social practice that mediates our relationship with the world. Second, these literacies are varied and situated depending on the goals and meaning-making needs of the participants. Written symbols are cultural tools that can be phonetic, logographic, or visual images with each serving different purposes. Orthographies are cultural systems rooted in historical and cultural meaning-making practices. Third, power, privilege, and ideology shape the functions and uses of literacy across contexts. Dominant scripts are highly conventional, standardized, and regulated by nation-state institutions. Non-dominant and indigenous forms of literacy are often marginalized and dismissed in schools and other spaces of "official" life. As teachers, we need to understand the complex variation inherent in literacy practices, whether they are the ones we assign to our students or the ones they use at home, the skatepark, or the Internet. Formalized, school-based literacies serve specific academic functions and are an essential tool for cultural cohesion in large-scale societies. In order to foster optimum learning environments for ELs and non-dominant populations, teachers must critically examine non-school literacies and design activities that leverage them as mediational tools to develop formal, school-based literacies.

TEACHER CASE STUDIES

Sally: Google Translator

Sally, an elementary teacher in a school with any ELs, decided that the students should make Earth Day fliers to send to parents and other community members. This activity would give the students a chance to practice their writing and would be fun. Sally even thought this would be an ideal opportunity to draw on the students' other languages to give them an opportunity to use multiple languages. They would think about topics like audience, presentation, and cultural awareness.

Sally's school was on the north side of Chicago where, due to immigration, resettlement of refugee families, and strong ethnic enclaves, many communities are extremely diverse, socioeconomically, ethnically, and linguistically. Some of these communities include speakers of hundreds of languages. In Sally's classroom, alone, there were well over a half dozen languages, besides English, that were spoken in students' homes. So, for this activity, Sally would draw upon many of the students' languages to create these posters.

In Sally's classroom students were asked to work in groups and develop their Earth Day awareness posters. They were encouraged to use the languages that their parents and other community members would use. Sally asked her students which languages they could read and write:

SALLY: First of all, we know that Earth Day is March 28. Today, we are going to make a poster that will hang in the hallway. Now, our task is that we want to spread the word because, here, in our school, we have a lot of languages. How many of you can write in your native language, not just English?

(Some students raised hands; one was hesitant)
SALLY: If you can do in Spanish, talk to each other, help each other . . .

Students took the fliers home that day, and when they came back some had different languages written on them. Sally asked the students to share what was written on the fliers.

SALLY: Very good. Now, can you say that in another language?
STUDENT 1: I can't read it. (Looking at T) Sorry.
SALLY: Huh? (Tone of surprise)
STUDENT: It's hard. I can't read it.
SALLY: You can't read in your own language↑? (Surprised voice)

It dawned on Sally that many of these students didn't know how to read in their own language. They used it all of the time, but never learned to read or write it. She reflected:

> I had trouble getting them to put it in different languages. Some of them didn't know it in other languages. They understood it, their parents spoke it but they couldn't *write* it. So, to help with the *writing*, they got their parents' help and they kind of helped them write out some of the flyers, or the bilingual teachers.

So, Sally thought about this for a while, and realized that there were other resources for writing in different languages. For example, the bilingual teachers, parents, and so forth could help. However, even in her own classroom there were some students who did know how to read and write in their own language and could help peers. She even recognized that the Internet provided a great resource! The students could use web-based translation services to help them translate the writing. The students were directed to Google Translator on the classroom computers and were able to use the computers to type in their own written language (which they could not read) and would then get the English translation. For many of them, as soon as they saw the English translation they knew exactly what the writing said in their own language! Additionally, the students could type in English sentences and get their own language in writing!

This opportunity allowed them to have the experience of working with literacy in their own language. Many of them could draw on their parents' literacies while others had to find new ways to mediate written language. For Sally, she realized how complicated it is in learning to be biliterate. Many of the students would not have this opportunity in school to learn to read and write in their parents' language, but they at least had the experience of interacting with their own language on a new and deeper level.

Linda: Chinese in the Writing

Linda had assigned a journal assignment to her seventh grade class. She asked them to write about the best day of summer because in narratives the students write about meaningful experiences. In fact, Linda even noted that these narratives were actually a construction of reality, as Bruner (1991) stated. One of her students, Song, was a second language learner. She had only been in the United States for two years, though it seemed like she was making huge progress in written English. It seemed, from previous assignments, that Song was still writing in English with noticeable Chinese morphosyntax features. For example, few of her words had inflection, although she did use helping verbs like "was" to indicate something was past tense.

This particular writing assignment was very meaningful to Song. She had had a great summer and was even able to work at her uncle's restaurant by passing out menus to earn money! In the figure below, Linda noticed that Song wrote a Chinese word above the word "afreid," which was misspelled and should have been "afraid." Linda was not pointing out spelling or grammar errors. She saw these journal assignments more as a social practice and warm-up exercise for class. However, she was taken aback by the Chinese symbol.

Linda asked Song about this, "When I asked her why, she said she wanted to make sure it was clear that she meant afraid in Chinese and English!" So, the added Chinese symbol was intended to clear up confusion. This was very interesting to Linda, because, given the space of the journal, Song was able to treat the writing as a social practice, with an assumed audience. Thus, writing itself, as Linda noted, was something meaningful and contextual. Writing, especially for those who are biliterate, can take on different meanings in different languages. Linda was even more impressed by the fact that the two languages used such different orthographies. Chinese words were logographic, and could not be inflected, something that Linda took note of. English, on the other hand, was almost phonemic, and the spelling and inflection was very important. However, by using Chinese in the place of unknown English words, or to further explain, seems to show that Song's writing practices drew on whichever language was more efficient for the social context. Certainly she needed to use English because Linda didn't read Chinese; however, she also could draw on Chinese when she was unsure of herself or knew something was incorrect. Linda was able to provide opportunities for writing practices that were meaningful to her students.

QUESTIONS/ACTIVITIES

1. Conduct a literacy survey of your community. What types of writing are around the community? What newspapers? What libraries, what access to computers and books? Do households own books? How

many? Magazine subscriptions? Which ones? What types of graffiti are there? How about stickers on poles? Do you see different types of trash with writing? In this community, what types of reading skills are necessary? What is needed to interpret all of these different signs and symbols?

2. Make a log of every time you read or write anything for three days. Remember looking at a clock and reading the time, signing a check, and typing in a pin number all are literacy practices just like reading a novel or writing a journal. What literacy practices are valued in schools?

3. Have students in one of your classes bring in pictures of signs or different types of writing in magazine and newspaper ads. What are the different fonts used? Why? What does the design of writing mean? Have students make their own ads using different styles. Interchange the styles, what is the effect?

4. Analyze a student's writing. What are some common errors? Are they consistent? Why do you think the student may make those errors? What is the underlying assumption about language the student is making?

Additional Resources (multimedia)

http://www.ancientscripts.com/elamite.html

http://www.childrenofthecode.org/interviews/shanahan.htm

http://goodcharacters.com/newsletters/gong-xi-fa-cai.html [Mandarin and Cantonese Writing]

http://islamic-arts.org/2011/islamic-calligraphy-600-to-1250-a-d/

http://www.japanese-symbols.org/japanese-alphabet [Japanese Syllabic Alphabet]

http://www.typeculture.com/academic_resource/movies/

http://www.typographyforlawyers.com/?page_id=2254 [Lawyer Typography Standards]

www.ca7.uscourts.gov/rules/type.pdf [Professional Standards of Typography]

9

LANGUAGE LEARNING

Basic Principles and Debates

LEARNING GOALS

1. Summarize major differences between language acquisition and language socialization.
2. Summarize different approaches to bilingual education.
3. Summarize recent trends in literacy learning research and pedagogy.
4. Analyze dominant models of second language learning in the field.
5. Analyze different pedagogical concepts as they relate to second language learning.

KEY TERMS/IDEAS: language acquisition (SLA), language socialization (SCT), BICS, CALP, structured immersion, dual immersion, transitional bilingual programs, heritage language

Introduction

Up until now we have been presenting different domains of language, specifically we have looked at the linguistic hierarchy beginning with phonetics and phonology, and ending with semantics and pragmatics, leaving a fuller conceptualization of the ideological level for later in this book. We have interspersed the chapters with different learning theories, and will develop a fuller theory of learning in Chapter 10. Here, however, we would like to outline some typical approaches to language learning, specifically to second language learning or acquisition depending on the perspective. These approaches and methods are very commonplace, but often take on different names, features, and material components. It is important that we, as teachers and researchers, are able to identify the underlying theories of the different approaches. The theoretical underpinnings of these programs and approaches are often not analyzed and a selective mix of metaphors of second language learning emerges. While teachers often feel pressured to advocate for one program or another, as they are accepted at a school, district, and even state-wide level, a strong theoretical understanding of second language learning would empower you to strategically reorganize any mandated curricula to best serve students.

Traditionally, the terms "L1" and "L2" have been used to refer to native and target language, respectively. It is important to understand what these notions imply about how we conceptualize the nature, function, and purpose of language as well as learning. The L1–L2 dichotomy assumes that languages are self-contained, compartmentalized, and isolated entities housed in the brain. In addition, the idea of an L1 or L2 overgeneralizes the functions of a language and assumes the languages are independently functioning based on a separate underlying proficiency (SUP) (Cummins, 2000). The concept of *interlanguage* was one of the first attempts to present the mind/brain with respect to language as more integrated (Selinker, 1972). As we discussed in Chapter 3, research from cognitive science as well as neurolinguistics suggests that the brain is a complex set of neural networks that crosses organic boundaries. Language and its various dimensions permeate throughout the brain and are difficult to isolate to a particular part. Instead of the L1/L2 label to refer to languages, we prefer to describe languages with respect to the particular context of use (i.e., discourses).

Bilingualism in the United States

Bilingualism and multilingualism in the United States has had a long, contested history (Crawford, 1995). Over the last 15 years, we have seen a public revival of debates and "controversies" about dialect use and the status of bilingual education (Razfar, 2012b). From bilingualism being encouraged for nearly 300 years to the rise of linguistic restrictivism at the turn of the 19th Century, there has always been an inextricable link between English-Only movements and national identity. Whether it was slavery or wars of conquest in the Southwest, English-Only legislation and English proficiency served as a litmus test for political loyalty and being a "good" American. These policies have undoubtedly impacted the educational trajectories of non-English-speaking populations (e.g., Gandara & Contreras, 2009; Padilla & Gonzalez, 2001).

The Civil Rights era of the 1960s provided a glimmer of hope in the history of language and bilingualism in the United States. Not coincidentally, this was also the time when language scholars began to view the nature, function, and purpose of language in social and sociocultural terms. This significant revolution in the study of language is known as the *Hymes* turn, named after the late sociolinguist Dell Hymes (Hymes, 1964). While the term sociolinguistics was originally coined by Thomas Hodson in the late 1930s, it was Dell Hymes, John Gumperz, William Labov, and

Basal Bernstein who pioneered a profound movement against the structural and nativist assumptions of Chomskyan linguistics. Their work collectively focused on the context of language use and the languages of non-dominant populations.

The *Civil Rights Act* of 1964 legislated that all citizens should receive equal treatment in regards to government funded services, including education. This has, therefore, been foundational in the arguments presented in favor of bilingual education. If the students do not speak English, then are they receiving an equal education if they are in a classroom in which content is only taught in English? This was the major question to be addressed in courts regarding bilingual education (Valdés, 2001).

In fact, in 1974 the Supreme Court decided on the case *Lau v. Nichols* in which some 1800 Chinese-American students sued for not having equal access to education. Since all education was in English, Chinese-speaking students were effectively erased in the eyes of the San Francisco school district. The lawsuit made it to the Supreme Court docket, filed because the school district was violating the 1964 *Civil Rights Act*, denying the students equal access to education. In the opinion of Justice Douglas, the petitioners asked only that they were provided with equal access to education. Douglas wrote:

> Teaching English to the students of Chinese ancestry who do not speak the language is one choice. Giving instructions to this group in Chinese is another. There may be others. Petitioners ask only that the Board of Education be directed to apply its expertise to the problem and rectify the situation.
>
> (*Lau v. Nichols*, 1974)

Thus, the Supreme Court demanded that language minority students had language support in schools, but what type of support was left up to the interpretation of schools, districts, and states. The *Bilingual Education Act of 1968* did not specify which type of approach should be implemented either.

Transitional Bilingual Programs: The Dominant Paradigm

The bilingual education programs ushered in by the Bilingual Education Amendment of 1974 were largely "weak" forms of bilingualism. In other words, they were not designed to raise a bilingual population where all members of society were fully proficient in two languages. The Amendment allowed for use of a student's primary language to transition into English proficiency as well as study content matter like mathematics and science in their first language. English remained the target of instruction and the student's primary language (L1) was used to scaffold English development. When the time came to implement bilingual education in schools, most programs turned to linguistics for answers. Actually, it was some linguists who seized the opportunity to provide lightning in a bottle, a panacea for language learning. While most linguists were not traditionally interested in questions of learning, acquisition, and bilingual education, many of the lessons from structural linguistics led to the conclusion that language is naturally acquired and not learned—after all, the morphosyntactic transformations that were assumed to be happening spontaneously in the mind were far too complex to be learned.

Krashen and Terrell took this line of reasoning to a whole other level (pun intended!). They stipulated that given there is something like a *Language Acquisition Device (LAD)*, and children appear to spontaneously acquire their first language with little effort, then second language acquisition (SLA) must be an identical process (Krashen & Terrell, 1983). The explicit instruction of grammar or any part of linguistic structure was not only viewed as ineffective, but also potentially harmful to second language development. The best way to acquire a second language was not to analyze language into discrete parts, but rather engage the language naturally, holistically, and using it for communicative purposes. This idea of a *Natural Approach* to second language acquisition that aimed to recreate the conditions of first language acquisition in formal learning environments formed the backbone of the *Whole Language movement*. This movement was also supported by Jim Cummins' notions of *common underlying proficiency (CUP)*, *basic interpersonal conversational skills (BICS)*, and *cognitive advanced language proficiency (CALP)* (Cummins, 2000).

These metaphors of second language acquisition have dominated bilingual education and teacher preparation for three decades. The Whole Language movement combined with weak forms of bilingual education provided a context for teachers throughout the country to throw the baby out with the bath water. Many schools abandoned direct instruction of grammar and placed teachers of second language learners in a vulnerable position. They were less trained to engage in metalinguistic activities and explicitly discuss linguistic form, morphosyntactic rules, semantics, and other complex sociocultural aspects of meaning. There was an expectation that if teachers simply created a print-rich environment, a culture of pleasure reading, and comprehensible input—then English would spontaneously be acquired. After nearly two decades of implementation, the results were inconclusive at best. English learners continued to lag behind and bilingual education and its theoretical foundation, *Whole Language/natural approach*, came under attack from both language and literacy scholars and the public. Of course, some of this attack was political opportunism veiled as concern for bilingual children (see the Unz "English for the Children" initiative)[1]; nevertheless, Whole Language and the natural approach proved to be inadequate and an oversimplification of language development.

In the late 1970s, sociocultural theory (SCT) provided an alternative perspective to the role of language in human development. Vygotsky, whom we have encountered elsewhere in this book, and will continue to trace his legacy (in the next chapter especially), helped to form the notion that all language, and indeed, all cognition, was first social, embedded in cultural contexts, hence "sociocultural

---

1. http://www.languagepolicy.net/archives/unz.htm.

theory." Contrary to the acquisition assumptions of Chomsky, and by extension the SLA models presented by Krashen and Cummins, SCT looked at language as a form of mediation, or a tool used for learning. SLA and SCT offer contrasting views of how we conceptualize the learner and the role of language in learning; however, in recent years, many teachers and the texts they study during teacher education present SLA and SCT as compatible perspectives, freely mixing and matching metaphors of language learning.

SCT scholars have long argued that the differences between SCT and SLA are so fundamental that these perspectives are essentially incommensurate with each other (Razfar, Khisty, & Chval, 2011). The differences are not trivial and we would like the readers of this text to consider the profound implications for how we organize learning and instruction. Our beliefs about how language functions, how it is learned, and how we talk about it clearly mediates how we teach. Consider two fundamental ideas that are often treated as equivalent:

1. *the zone of proximal development (ZPD)* from SCT; and
2. *comprehensible input (i+1)* from Krashen's SLA.

The following table taken from Razfar et al. (2011) shows the definitions side by side (Table 9.1).

The two definitions differ fundamentally in how each conceptualizes the goal of learning and the process through which it occurs. In SCT, language is never the target of learning. Instead, it is the means, or the *mediational tool*, through which learning unfolds. In contrast, the definition provided by SLA assumes that linguistic structures are the target of learning. In other words, the mind explicitly parses word segments at an interval of i+1, where "i" represents the current level of understanding and "+1" represents the subsequent level. In SCT, learning occurs through interaction with more expert peers, whereas in SLA language acquisition is primarily an individual process. Of course, this is not to say that the SLA position is absent of social interaction, after all the comprehensible input has to be received from the environment; however, the process is for the most part spontaneous and passive. SLA also assumes that everybody learns or acquires language in roughly the same way, whereas SCT assumes that learning is fundamentally

TABLE 9.1 ZPD vs. Comprehensible Input

Zone of proximal development	*Comprehensible input*
"The distance between the actual development level as determined by independent problem solving and level of potential development as determined through problem solving under adult guidance or in collaboration with more capable peers" (Vygotsky, 1978, p. 86)	"We move from i, our current level to i+1, the next level along the natural order, by understanding input containing i+1" (Krashen, 1985, p. 2).

varied. Thus, in SCT, learning is defined by variation whereas SLA assumes the process to be relatively more universal.

This has implications for how learning and instruction is organized. In SCT heterogeneity is a critical organizing principle while in SLA there is a tendency toward homogeneity since everybody acquires language in a similar fashion. For example, if we were organizing learning activities using SCT, we would want to create a context where the mediational tools available to the participants were specific to their current and potential development. This would be much more differentiated in accordance with the individual we were teaching. With SLA, we could design the same activity for everybody. For example, SLA assumes that everybody learns the present tense before the future tense; therefore, present tense lessons would precede the future tense.

Another important distinction between the two perspectives is that SCT posits that learning through the ZPD is often contentious, frustrating, and sometimes stressful. Vygotsky believed that children learn more complex, abstract, and scientific ideas through the tension that emerges between their everyday ideas and the scientific ones. Imagine struggling to solve a difficult puzzle and how frustrating it can be. For example, to understand how dice work a child would have to develop a sense of probability. Razfar (2012d) shows how children in an after-school club develop an explicit probability strategy through mediation with parents, graduate students, and peers using multiple languages and discourses as mediational tools. These tools were situated and organized through the *Counters* game. In contrast, one of the major tenets of SLA is the idea of the *affective filter*, which stipulates that language acquisition only occurs in low-stress environments. This is a major difference in the types of learning activities we would design. With SCT, we would design challenging activities that might cause anxiety, stress, and frustration, but we also provide the mediational means to solve the problem. While activities may be "high anxiety," they would consciously designed with high support as well. In SLA, we would not want to inhibit the acquisition of language in this way. In SCT, our measure of learning is directly correlated with the shift in the mediation. As the learner moves from being a novice to an expert, the types of assistance and tools also change. Thus, our assessment of learning is not the outcome but the process itself. In SLA, language is learned when language is produced. SCT emphasizes a focus on the learning process, while SLA focuses on the outcomes of learning (i.e., language production). When teachers focus on the individual learner rather than the activity and the quality of the mediation, they may develop a deficit view of the learner if she/he is unable to successfully negotiate the problem. As a result, instead of changing the mediation, they may change the problem, preferring an 'easier' one.

SCT vs. SLA: Language Learning and Vocabulary

For many teachers the discussion and debates between SCT-ers and SLA-ers may seem like an ivory tower polemic that has little relevance to the trenches of classroom teaching. On some level we agree with this; however, we have attempted to highlight those aspects that directly impact instruction with real consequences for student achievement. We hope that we have convinced you that being atheoretical and apathetic about language and learning issues is not a viable or even ethical option.

Vocabulary development is an integral part of every language teacher's activities. If you think about it, every teacher is developing vocabulary specific to a domain of knowledge, what we've been calling "discourses." One of the most critical points of divergence between SCT and SLA are the notions of "target language" and what counts as "vocabulary." In SLA, lessons and activities are designed to target linguistic form since that is the type of input necessary for the presumed "Language Acquisition Device." The LAD automatically extracts the phonological and morphosyntactic rules of the target language through induction. One familiar expression of this approach is the direct instruction of "target words" that are posted in a discrete and decontextualized manner on word walls (Figure 9.1).

Artifacts such as word walls and worksheets suggest language, and in particular words, are treated as isolated entities. In this framework language is the target of instruction instead of the means to solving problems and making meaning. In SCT, language form is not really the target of instruction; it serves as the primary mediational means to accomplishing concrete goals within culturally organized activities. If language is the object or learning goal of an activity, it is purposefully designed to develop greater metalinguistic awareness, enhance metacognition, and greater independent problem solving or *self-regulation*. The SLA approach leads to an overt focus on fixed definitions rather than situated meaning.

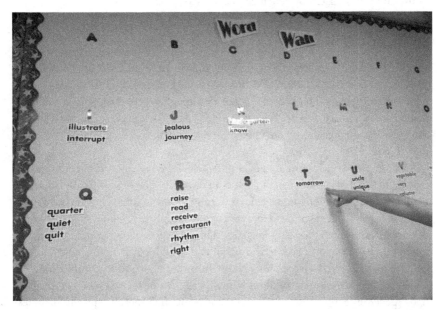

FIGURE 9.1 Discrete Vocabulary "Word Wall"

In both SLA and SCT, meaning and understanding is central to language learning; however, one fundamental difference exists. In SLA meaning is made by the individual while in SCT meaning occurs socially. The instructional implication is clear: in SLA, the teacher is expected to provide repeated "comprehensible input" at a rate of "i+1" and the learner will eventually acquire proficiency with the words. There is only one major problem with this approach, the teacher doesn't really know that comprehension has happened and, furthermore, it is virtually impossible to determine "i+1." The problem is that "i+1" is theoretically supposed to be the same for everyone, but there is no empirical evidence to support this assumption. The only way to even come close to assessing learning is when the student actually used the vocabulary that was targeted. Even then, does the use of the word actually suggest learning? A parrot can also produce words it hears repeatedly, but we would never consider that authentic communication.

SLA research is now starting to recognize this limitation and has moved more toward a social and interactive understanding of language and learning (e.g., Mc-Cafferty, Jacobs, & Iddings, 2006). The concepts of *cooperative learning* and *interlanguage* are examples of this theoretical shift. The concept of interlanguage allows for "incorrect" forms of the target language (L2) to be housed in the brain, an idea that undermines the L1/L2 dichotomy and challenges static notions of linguistic correctness. The process of language learning becomes more about trial and error, which is very much a sociocultural and constructivist position. This concept also brings into question the myth surrounding the idealized, native speaker who speaks correctly and who language learners are expected to emulate in classrooms. From an SCT perspective, the "correctness" of language depends on the context of use and is negotiated by actual language users.

SCT vs. SLA: From "Basic" to "Advanced" Vocabulary

One of the most pervasive metaphors in SLA is the distinction between BICS and CALP. The BICS/CALP continuum consists of two axes to rank the difficulty of vocabulary. The horizontal axis distinguishes between context, reduced academic vocabulary and context embedded "basic" vocabulary, and the vertical axis provides a range from "cognitively undemanding" to "cognitively demanding" (Figure 9.2).

In this framework, as one moves counter-clockwise from quadrant A to quadrant D, the level of the language increases in difficulty. The most difficult language would be in quadrant D. Language learning also follows a similar linear pathway—first we learn context-embedded and cognitively undemanding language then develop cognitively demanding language. This perspective suggests that words are inherently basic or advanced. It also suggests that all learners follow an undifferentiated and natural developmental path—from simple words to complex ones.

Given the staircase view of development, there is a heavy emphasis on "simplified" speech in early stages of development. Simplified speech typically includes

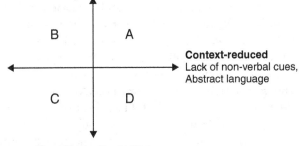

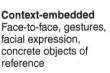

FIGURE 9.2 BICS vs. CALP

elongated pauses and the use of non-verbal cues to scaffold meaning-making. It is assumed that the readiness to engage in linguistically and cognitively complex tasks emerges from biology and time rather than the quality of the mediation. This can lead to an underestimation of what learners can accomplish with or without assistance. For example, beginning ESL students may not be expected to engage in writing or sophisticated grammatical analysis since the learner is assumed to be not ready. Similar to how mothers speak to their infants through oversimplification and clarification, older second language learners are assumed to follow a similar path. Thus, instructors adopt similar practices in the classroom.

The progression from BICS to CALP may seem intuitively correct because of our reliance on oral production to assess learning. After all, children first produce single utterances, then phrases, then sentences, etc. Older second language learners do the same thing, right? However, what is actually happening neurologically and developmentally is quite complex and multidirectional. This intuitive, common-sense model presents a convenient and static perspective of learning. In reality, learners move in and out of novice/expert roles depending on their role within an activity.

Rather than labeling words as basic or advanced, we should think about the process and purpose by which we learn to use words. Many students learning a second language through grammatical methods do well on traditionally "decontextualized" testing tasks and struggle with basic interpersonal conversation skills. The reverse is also true where students master conversational language and struggle with the academic. Instead of rating the difficulty of language, let us consider how words are learned from an SCT perspective. The word "dude" may seem like a simple, BICS type of word. In one of his skits (see link in multimedia section), the comedian Rob Schneider parodies all the different functions the word "dude" can accomplish simply by altering the way one says it. It could be a greeting, approval, disapproval, or a question to name a few. While this may be funny to someone familiar with the uses, understanding the nuances of such a word is difficult for second language learners lacking sociocultural experience. Of course, no one would consider "dude" to be an academic term, but in isolation, all words become "academic" in the sense of being decontextualized because the context has to be provided by the listener. Without contextualized experience, words are never learned.

We first experience words (signs and symbols) in concrete conditions where actions and relationships are experienced. As we become expert users of these sign and symbols, we become adept at referring to them in the absence of those conditions. For example, we first learn the words for counting numbers or describing colors in the presence of the concrete conditions that make the use of counting or color terms meaningful. Consider when a child first counts numbers using his/her fingers, he/she has a difficult time counting beyond 10 because there is no difference between the object, in this case fingers, and the symbol representing the meaning of numbers. In fact, without the fingers, there are no numbers as far as the child is concerned and the object dominates the meaning carried by the symbol. As the purposes and contexts for numbers change, the child begins to transform the symbols for numbers to be applied in novel situations (e.g., counting marbles, cards, or candy). At this point we can say the learner is now focused on meaning and has learned the functions of the words.

This developmental process is described in SCT as a shift in the *object/action to meaning ratio*. This transformation is the result of situated, meaning-making activity and is necessary for **ALL** the words we learn. So, it is not the words themselves that are basic or advanced, but the type of thinking that is occurring. Vygotsky gives the example of a child who transforms a stick and the act of riding it to mean riding a horse and thus the stick comes to represent a real horse. This shift from object to symbolic use is precisely the point where the "ratio is inverted and meaning predominates, giving meaning/object" (Vygotsky, 1978, p. 98). As far as the mental perceptions of words are concerned, the actions and objects are never truly separated from the meaning. Children arrive at meanings and "definitions" through the transformation of situated actions/objects. In the early stages of learning, the object(s)/action(s) dominate the child's ability to make meaning. This is the stage where learners rely on contextual cues surrounding the signified. The signifier (word) has little meaning beyond the sounds for novice learners. The following example adapted from Razfar (2012a, p. 51) illustrates the point. The presence of a cup filled with some type of liquid would prompt a child to say the signifier "W-A-T-E-R" because the set of object(s)/action(s) dominate the use of signs and symbols which are highly context dependent in the early stages of development. However, over time the meaning of the phonetic sounds for the word "W-A-T-E-R" (/wɔtər/) become less dependent on the presence of object(s)/action(s). Through the mediation of more expert others and the use of symbolic tools, learners develop the ability to regulate meaning without relying on context (see Figure 9.3).

FIGURE 9.3 Form to Function Ratio Shift (adapted from Razfar, 2012a)

Consider this process in light of how human beings learn the specialized discourses of baseball, medicine, and law. While we may think that these specialized discourses remain in their local domains, often specialized discourses find their way into other fields of life. In his book *Baseball as a second language*, Harry Lewis provides numerous examples of how American culture draws on baseball metaphors to talk about love, politics, economics, and social life (Lewis, 2011). "It's the bottom of the ninth and it's time to step up to the plate!" "It ain't over till it's over!" "I hit a home run last night!" As discussed earlier in this book, understanding these words requires more than definitions, it requires sociocultural context. Many fields have recognized the sociocultural aspect of word meaning and have begun to provide discourse specific dictionaries (e.g., UMLS, the Unified Medical Language System). Online resources such as the legal dictionary (http://dictionary. law.com) provide useful tools to engage students in a discussion about the social context of words.

It is interesting to note that in recent years, Cummins (2000) has sought to clarify and respond to some of the misconceptions and critiques surrounding his model of BICS/CALP. Perhaps, the movement from decontextualized, cognitively undemanding to context embedded, cognitively demanding can be viewed in a similar fashion to the shift in action/object to meaning ratio. Cummins argues that this model should not be used to oversimplify instruction but to make tasks that are cognitively challenging, holistic, and develop a critical awareness about language functions (p. 98). While many still dispute this, he states that BICS/CALP "essentially is a Vygotskian perspective on language and academic development" (p. 92). The SCT perspective has had substantial influence on how we think about words and language learning.

Types of Bilingual Education Programs: Implications for Classroom Pedagogy

The two theoretical approaches mentioned here, SLA and *language socialization* (or more broadly sociocultural theories (SCT) of language learning (Schieffelin & Ochs, 1986), play out very differently in the classroom. However, there is also a host of political and ideological factors that drive policies of second language learning. As previously mentioned, in SLA the second language is usually called a "target" language, and the first language is often the "primary" or "first" language. Additive bilingual programs are those that view the second language as "adding to" or further enriching the language of a child. In these programs the second language is not considered to be the ideal, but rather is taught because of either a desire to learn or impending social issues for which it is required. The underlying assumptions are important to understand because the structure and curriculum tend to support either SLA theories or SCT theories. In Chapter 10 we will dive more deeply into SCT and its implications for reorganizing learning; however, here it is important to note the dominant organizations of language learning.

There are several types of bilingual education, but broadly speaking, we can place them along a continuum of "strong" and "weak" forms of bilingual education (Baker, 2006). The goal of weak forms of bilingual education is assimilation and monolingualism (or a very limited bilingualism). We will call these *subtractive* because they essentially privilege the L2 over the L1, which ultimately leads to a loss of L1. In contrast, the goal of *strong* programs is *additive* because they seek to develop the L1, including literacy, as well as develop the use of L2. In additive programs the L1 and L2 are treated with equal status and all segments of a population can be expected to be fully bilingual. The following table (Table 9.2) summarizes several of these approaches, but we also want to make the connection they have to the wider theoretical base of SLA and/or SCT. Ultimately, even though teachers are in programs that may be structured along these lines, teachers can, when necessary, and do, resist the dominant theories of the system to reorganize learning in their classrooms. Examples of this will be shown in Chapter 10, but first it is important to understand the types of programs language teachers often work in Table 9.2.

Structured Immersion (Submersion)

Structured immersion is sort of a sink-or-swim system based on the extreme assumptions of SLA. Students will learn English quickly when immersed in a predominant English-speaking environment. This may or may not be accompanied by explicit English instruction, often depending on whether schools are proponents of phonics or Whole Language instruction we learned about in Chapter 4. However, this type of learning is subtractive in the gravest sense. In fact, often-official policy bans the use of the L1 for any type of assistance in the classroom. There is little scaffolding using the students' L1, and there is no teaching of content in the L1 so that skills could be transferred into L2 once the vocabulary had been acquired. This program is often practiced in schools and classrooms where the official policies call for transitional bilingual education. Often, the prevailing folk beliefs of teachers, that more exposure to English will result in faster acquisition of the language, prevents the maximized use of transitional programs, which could at least provide mediation in the L1 to learn content and language. The folk assumption that more exposure to language results in faster acquisition is actually counter to SLA research, which suggests that it takes between five and seven years to develop academic proficiency (Cummins, 2000).

This opens up the larger SLA debate regarding the ease and quickness of language learning. As shown above, the differences in SLA and SCT rest primarily on

TABLE 9.2 Types of Bilingual Education (adapted from Baker, 2006)

Type of program	Typical children in a classroom	Languages used in the classrooms	Additive or subtractive	Outcome
Structured immersion	Mostly language minority students	Society dominant language	Subtractive	Monolingualism
Sheltered English	Mostly language minority students	Society dominant language	Subtractive	Monolingualism
Transitional	Mostly language minority students	Begins with L1 and moves to society dominant language	Subtractive	Monolingualism (some may preserve L1 and develop bilinguals)
Immersion	Mostly language majority students	Bilingual with emphasis on L2	Additive	Bilingualism and biliteracy
Heritage language	Mostly language minority students	Bilingual with emphasis on L1	Additive	Bilingualism and biliteracy
Dual language	Language majority and language minority students and bilingual students	Languages of both language majority and language minority students	Additive	Bilingualism and bilitreracy
Mainstream bilingual	Mostly language majority students	Two languages in a diglossic society	Additive	Bilingualism and biliteracy

the object of the activity. Structured immersion programs emphasize the object of English language proficiency, through the acquisition of language structure. With the pressure of standardized tests in the content area, the urgency with which these immersion approaches target English instruction often results in very explicit language teaching techniques, or ESL classes, for a short period before they are mainstreamed into an English-only classroom.

Sheltered English

Like structured immersion, sheltered English instruction is done almost completely in the society's dominant language. Students who struggle with that language are pulled out for specific instruction in the language they are learning. This often results in students missing valuable class time learning content areas such as mathematics and science. Driving sheltered English is the idea that second language acquisition in the classroom may need to be supplemented with explicit language support. This also may lead to stigmatization of the kids that are pulled out. The object of instruction, here, is clearly English, especially as students are pulled out specifically for direct instruction in the target language.

Transitional Bilingual Education

As noted above, one of the major approaches to bilingual education in the United States, perhaps the most dominant, is the *transitional* approach. The primary focus in transitional programs is for the student to become competent in the L2 while mastering content (in the L1 if needed). This approach can take place in several different formats, but most often leads to the mastery of English but not the L1. In fact, in many schools, L1 literacy isn't even valued. This can be considered a subtractive approach to bilingual education because the L2 is privileged at the expense of the L1. There is generally the opportunity to learn content in one's L1 while acquiring English. This relieves the stress of the student trying to learn language and content at the same time. It is a slow immersion process with added support using the L1 for 1–3 years. While competence in the L1 is possible, it is not the objective. Usually by the end of the transition process, students are not able to use the L1 in later academic work, and often do not use the L1 in school at all. An example of a model would be that instruction may take place in L1 for the first two years of school, with the third and fourth years moving to English instruction with L1 support, and finally, English-only instruction. There are differing amounts of time the languages should be taught, and the percentages in which they should be used while transitioning, but the driving theory remains the same.

The assumption in these programs is that students take a long time to learn a second language. They come to school speaking BICS, often, but need to learn the academic language CALP. Since most of their daily language practices at home are assumed to be in L1, the focus of school is English needed for CALP. Often students only receive direct English instruction (or indirect instruction, for that matter) toward the end of learning CALP. This transitional type program is the dominant SLA program.

Immersion

Immersion programs are an additive type of bilingual education. They are usually created for students who speak a society's dominant language but are learning a second language. In these programs the second language is viewed as enrichment. In Quebec, Canada, in the 1960s, for example, English speakers were put into French immersion programs. Instruction would be in French as well as English, often giving preference to the French instruction in the early years. The aim was for the English speakers, the dominant language in Canada, to be able to speak the language that marked the cultural identity of Quebec. There are various models, with different ratios of English and French instruction, but the immersion programs aim at majority language speakers learning a second language (Lambert & Tucker, 1972).

While the immersion metaphor follows the SLA tradition, the methods of SLA are not necessarily strictly based on acquisition models. The language, in the Quebec case, was usually not the immediate goal of instruction. French was the medium of instruction used to teach content. So, one of the outcomes was proficiency in French, but that was not the sole focus of instruction.

Heritage Language

Another type of bilingual program is called heritage language. In these programs, in addition to learning English and content, there is a focus on learning the language of the students' parents. Occasionally this happens with students who may not really speak the heritage language, though often the students come into these programs using the heritage language frequently. Behind these programs is the assumption that language connects to identity, and that students should not forget their heritage language at the expense of the dominant language in society. Often these programs are found in areas where a language group may be in the middle of revitalization, though it could very well be in any situation where the school is set up to have an explicit focus on the language of students' families. The focus in these programs is on the language itself, so often this presents itself in explicit teaching of language form, not social practice. Again, there are tendencies toward SLA in these programs over SCT. However, once again, we cannot generalize that every heritage program or every heritage classroom takes an SLA approach. In fact, the focus on identity in heritage language programs may make them more compatible with SCT principles. If the teacher or administrators are amenable to sociocultural theories of learning, it is possible to organize learning to develop heritage language and English through the content areas.

While the heritage language program is considered an additive approach, the dominant language of society can still be privileged. Nevertheless, in heritage language programs, unlike the transitional program, the heritage language is viewed as an asset and a goal, not just as a means toward English proficiency. Whereas in transitional programs, the use of the L1 beyond the transitional years is not encouraged and the continued use of the L1 is not desired (subtractive bilingualism), the use of the heritage language is a desired outcome (additive bilingualism).

Mainstream Bilingual

Mainstream bilingual education usually takes place when there are two high status languages in use, or a language that is locally dominant and regionally dominant. The students are usually a part of the majority language group; however, because these societies are often *diglossic*, many of the students use both languages in so-ciety to some extent. The schools, therefore, provide ways for bilingualism and biliteracy to be a part of the curriculum. These types of schools actually tend to model society in that both languages are used or desired. In instances where an indigenous language is used along with an international language, the intent is to create a bilingual society. In contrast to immersion programs where monolingual-ism is dominant, bilingualism is the dominant norm.

Dual Language Immersion

The most effective type of bilingual education programs are dual immersion pro-grams (Howard, Christian, & Genesee, 2003; Lindholm-Leary, 2001). Dual im-mersion programs are generally implemented in contexts where there are two languages with relative equal status, and more importantly community support. In the United States these are often Spanish and English programs, even though the status is unequal in the broader society. The goal is that all students should be bilingual and biliterate. Since English and Spanish have an asymmetric relation-ship in society, these programs go to great lengths to create an environment where the languages are equally used in schools. The student population is often a mix of dominant language speakers (English), and speakers of the non-dominant lan-guage (i.e., Spanish). This equal time can be achieved through either successive or simultaneous arrangements. The school may alternate days or times to use one language or the other. Perhaps half the day would be in English and the other in Spanish, or maybe mathematics would be in English in one unit and Spanish in the next unit.

Programs like these are often based on SCT theories of learning, that language is the mediation for learning, but the direct goal is the curricular content, not the language form itself. Again, the aim for all students, both language minority students and the students who already speak the society's dominant language, is bilingualism and biliteracy, as well as the curricular content.

Implications for Practice: Constraints and Opportunities

Given the different approaches to bilingual education and the political/ideologi-cal constraints within schools, teachers have to be adept at negotiating multiple tensions. Since the advent of No Child Left Behind (NCLB), mandated curri-cula with narrow views of language and learning have been imposed on teachers throughout the United States (Razfar, 2012a). These "one-size-fits-all" approaches have seriously limited teachers of ELs (Pease-Alvarez, Samway, & Cifka-Herrera, 2010). One particular program, *Open Court Reading* (OCR), was used by many of the teachers Pease-Alvarez et al. interviewed and is a common scripted literacy curriculum used throughout the United States. The findings suggested that most teachers believed that OCR was ineffective and did not meet the needs of their

ELs. Nevertheless, they felt pressured to implement it even though it conflicted with their ideas of best practice. Even though the mandate was often at the district level, principals differed in how strictly they wanted OCR implemented. In fact, when some teachers tried to modify the curriculum, some literacy coaches and principals actually supported them.

Despite the constraints, teachers are in a position to exercise a tremendous amount of agency in their classrooms, especially when they have an articulated theory of language and learning. More experienced teachers can be expected to display greater agency than more novice teachers. Because of the high stakes (for both teachers and students), it is important to discuss pragmatic strategies for negotiating the complexities of restrictive teaching environments. In this book, we assume that teachers are curriculum designers, not simply consumers, and must develop pragmatic strategies for implementing best practices. In any of the bilingual programs identified in this chapter, teachers still have the capacity to simultaneously work within and *without* the system that restricts sociocultural tenets of language and learning.

In one case study, Shannon (1995) offers an example of a bilingual classroom in a transitional program where learning was reorganized to reflect SCT practices. Normally, in these classrooms, English maintains a higher status; after all, within a few years all students would be mainstreamed into English-only classrooms. Shannon described a classroom in which the teacher (and students as well) went to great lengths so as to make Spanish valued as much as English. They adopted a successive approach, where sometimes English would be used first and then translated into Spanish, and sometimes vice versa. The teacher identified seven points that were helpful in resisting English dominance:

1. Thinking *language* when preparing *every* activity of the day.
2. Thinking *language* when giving directions, asking questions, answering kids' questions—in *every* interaction with any student, coworker, parent, or visitor. Even when thinking out loud in front of the kids.
3. Not allowing in the classroom any materials in Spanish that do not have the *same* quality as the English counterparts.
4. Working hard to convince all kids, some parents, and school staff that Spanish is fun and beautiful.
5. No allowing racist comments from *anybody*.
6. Consciously talking to kids in their second language.
7. Taking a lot of *risks*.

(Shannon, 1995, p. 196)

These seven points were used by a teacher to resist the dominant teaching models of transitional programs. This demonstrates that teachers do have agency in their classrooms, and may, in some instances, resist the dominant models. So, teachers who value the use of language as a mediation tool, adhering to a SCT approach to understanding learning, can challenge and even resist SLA models. Whereas the transitional bilingual model seeks only English proficiency and monolingualism, the teacher sought to promote bilingualism and biliteracy. This took much planning because the system was already set up to devalue Spanish, therefore, she needed to make sure Spanish was included and seen as beautiful as well. The dominant program would implicitly teach that Spanish is less valuable than English because all of the English resources were better and instruction was only in English. When the language and cultural resources of ELs are viewed as vital mediational tools then it is incumbent upon teachers to design activities that leverage a student's entire linguistic repertoire.

Conclusion

Competing language ideologies underlie different types of bilingual education. In this chapter we have focused on two major theories of second language learning, namely *language socialization* and *second language acquisition*. These theories inform many of the bilingual education programs implemented today. How we think about language has major implications for how we plan programs, design curricula, and organize learning in the classroom. Across the globe, people are trying to understand how to best organize learning for diverse learners. This has led to newer movements that engender stronger versions of multilingual education. While bilingualism gains greater status in many parts of the world, more restrictive versions of bilingual education have taken root in English dominant societies like the United States. In the next chapter we will make connections to learning theories in order to provide insight into the social organization of our classrooms and development of curricula.

TEACHER CASE STUDIES

Tom: Teaching Adult Refugees

Tom was a teacher in an ESL classroom for adults. There had recently been a significant increase in refugees coming from several countries that were going through civil wars or other hardships. He had outlined his objectives for the day and was prepared to teach students how to count in English, how to greet others, and finally, the colors. Since it was the first day of class, he knew he should begin with greetings. Then, because many of the students were beginning jobs, paying rent in a new country, and otherwise needed to know numbers, he thought counting would be important. Since it was a three-hour class, he wanted to break it up with something fun, namely colors.

As students filed into the classroom from all different backgrounds of life, Tom greeted each one with a generic "hello." This was his first teaching strategy. He then stood in front of the class and said "hello" and waved to the students, hoping they would get the idea that he was greeting them. Many of the students caught on and replied. Tom said "My name is Tom" and pointed to himself. "What is your name?" he said in long and drawn out speech, pointing to a student Mu Ler, from Burma. He repeated with gestures "What is your name? My name is Tom." Finally, Mu Ler spoke up and said "Mu Ler!" Tom repeated back to him "My name is Mu Ler." He repeated this activity with the rest of the class. And then drilled them a little longer on greetings. Finally, he left the room for a moment to grab the secretary from the office of the small site and demonstrated with her:

TOM: Hello
SUZIE: Hello
TOM: My name is Tom.
SUZIE: Nice to meet you, Tom, My name is Suzie.
TOM: Nice to meet you, Suzie.

Then Tom asked Suzie to greet each of the students. She then went back to the office.

After a short break from the activity, which he knew he would have to repeat the following day, Tom began to teach them counting. He held up numbers, which he hoped they would be familiar with, and called out the names. After going through 1–10, he started again, this time gesturing the class to repeat. Tom would call out "One" and the class would do their best to mimic. "Two" and the class would repeat. After going through all the numbers, he showed small quantities that corresponded to the numbers. These were pictures on large flash cards like five ducks and seven kittens. He repeated the activity. Then he motioned for the class to stand in line. He taught them a game that would be very common in his classrooms. The students would have to point to a number when he called it out, very much like a game of memorization. Sammy, a refugee from Sudan, came up to the board and Tom called out "three." Sammy correctly responded by pointing to the number three. The class clapped. They repeated the activity with the quantities.

Finally, after a long two hours of greetings and numbers, Tom decided to lighten the mood by teaching colors. Tom had placed color words around the room on different items. So, the wall had the word "white" on it whereas the window shade had the word "blue" on it. Again, Tom held up flash cards with the words of the color written in the corresponding color. As he showed a word and said its name, he walked around the room pointing to items that were that color. The class practiced saying the words and then he indicated to Ahmed to stand up and point to the color green. "Green" Tom said. "Point to something green." And Tom pointed to the green chalkboard. "Green" Tom said again. "Point to something green." After a moment of blankly staring at Tom, Ahmed hesitantly pointed to the chalkboard. "Yes," said Tom, "Can you point to something else that is GREEN?" Ahmed lifted his finger to his table and pointed to a green notebook. "YES!" shouted Tom as he began clapping. The rest of the class joined in. The game continued as a sort of "eye spy" game until the time was up. He dismissed the class and said "goodbye, see you tomorrow" to each of the students leaving the room.

Sandra: Teaching Lemonade

Sandra was a teacher in a second grade classroom. Most of her students were English learners. The students spoke several different languages at home. In fact, many of the children were refugees, new to the country. A new refugee resettlement center opened in the community, so the elementary school was trying to grapple with this new influx of students and meet their needs. She knew that the beginning of the school year was always difficult, so she decided to begin by planning a community activity. She knew that the only way for the students to learn how to interact with people was for them to actually do it. So she designed an activity that would require the students to interact with other school and community members.

Sandra got permission from the principal to create a lemonade stand of sorts one day after school. She had fliers explaining it to parents and invited them to come. So, after school there would be sort of a little fundraiser. The money, she indicated, would be used to help pay for a field trip later in the year.

While it was difficult explaining the concept to the students, they did practice recognizing coins and dollar bills. They practiced making change for one-dollar bills. Since each glass of lemonade would cost only 10 cents, they focused on dimes. Watching the students practice managing a lemonade stand in the classroom was an interesting sight. It was like a game to them. While they often made change incorrectly, at least they were having fun.

As the day of the lemonade sale approached, Sandra had an idea. The students would not only learn how to greet people, they also would have to make change. However, if she introduced a slight variation, they would have to think critically about how money works. She could provide three different sized cups and price them at 10, 20, and 30 cents. With the help of the adult "pourers" the students could negotiate the price. After this, Sandra, the all too ambitious teacher, thought that she could also use this as an opportunity to teach colors, which was in her next ESL unit. She knew many of the students knew their colors, but the recent newcomers didn't yet. So, in addition to the lemonade, she explained to the class that the customers would be able to choose between blue lemonade (which was actually a blue raspberry lemonade), yellow lemonade, pink lemonade, and green lemonade (which was actually lemon-lime flavored). Now the students would have to really take orders and provide the customer with the correct product. They would have to charge them and even make change!

The day came and the students all stood behind the lemonade stand at the school with adult helpers for pouring. The adult helpers were only there for pouring from the gallon jugs. So, the students were the ones doing the interacting, sales, and math. Sure enough, the 2:30 bell rang and parents were already waiting around. Students from other classrooms were filing down the halls. People were lining up for small Dixie cups full of lemonade. Sandra could overhear the "customers" asking for "big" sized cups, "large" sized cups, "small," "tiny," and "regular" sized cups of different colors, and she started to panic! She didn't teach all these terms to the students! She just showed them how to recognize the money and make change! She thought they knew the colors, but never even thought that some people might actually call them differently! Also, many of the parents were speaking to their kids in their own language, and the kids were responding both in their own language and in English! All she could do now was watch closely and help if necessary. As she watched, she focused in on one boy, Alvin, who greeted each customer how she taught him, "Hello, what can I get for you?" But the responses were all so different! One customer said "I'll have one of each."

"One of each!" Sandra thought, "Poor Alvin!" But as she watched closely she saw Alvin struggle with which cup to give the customer. After handing one pink-lemonade in a small cup, he stood there. "One of each please," the customer repeated. Alvin stood there for a moment. Finally the customer said "a green one, a yellow one, and a blue one." It was as if a light came on in Alvin's eyes, and he handed the customer three more cups. The customer handed him a dollar. "Oh no!" Sandra thought, "I only taught them how to do 10, 20, and 30 cents." Alvin counted the cups, and "seemed to know that he needed four dimes, but how was he going to make change? Does he know 100 minus 40?"

Alvin stared at his small cash register, a model to hold the dimes. After a few moments of pulling dimes out and counting he put the dollar bill on the counter, pulled out ten dimes and placed them next to the bill. He then took four of them and put them in the cash register with the dollar bill and gave the six dimes back to the customer. Sandra was amazed! She didn't know how the class would handle it, especially when faced with these unpredictable situations! Yet, even though it was a struggle, and some kids sure did struggle, peer assistance, help from the customers, and their own creativity helped them to solve the problem. The class made nearly 50 dollars in profits that day! She congratulated them and marveled at how they learned to solve problems about counting and simple arithmetic, colors and sizes, and interacting with people.

QUESTIONS/ACTIVITIES

1. Have students watch a video about the *Natural Approach* (e.g., https://www.youtube.com/watch?v=4K11o19YNvk) and ask them to reflect on key components such as *comprehensible input*, the *natural order*, and the *affective filter hypothesis*. What are the strengths and

weaknesses of this approach? How might it benefit academic literacy development in a second language?

2. In small groups have students select one of the bilingual education programs in Table 2. Discuss the pros and cons of each. Design a mini-lesson based on the program orientation and present it to the class.

3. Using the BICS/CALP quadrants (Figure 9.2), brainstorm examples for each quadrant. How might those same language practices be re-arranged? Have students reflect on the process of how we learned each with a special emphasis on quadrant D. Trace one example from quadrant A to B.

4. Shift in Action/Object to Meaning Ratio—watch a video of children engaged in pretend play and discuss the movement from actions and objects to meaning. How do the children use the objects in symbolic ways? (for examples of scenarios www.ChildCareExchange.com).

Additional Resources (multimedia)

http://www.angelfire.com/az/english4thechildren/krashen.html [Critique of Krashen]

www.ChildCareExchange.com [Children Engaged in Pretend Play]

http://dictionary.law.com/ [Legal Dictionary]

http://www.eslprintables.com/vocabulary_worksheets/general_vocabulary/Thematic_Vocabulary_125420/ [Thematic Vocabulary for ESL]

http://www.youtube.com/watch?v=77v_Q0mhbZU [Rob Schneider-Multiple Meanings of "Dude"]

10

LEARNING AND CONTEXT

Language and Activity

LEARNING GOALS

1. Analyze and critique various definitions of culture.
2. Identify differences between primary and secondary discourses.
3. Gain insight into learning about students' funds of knowledge.
4. Use funds of knowledge for curriculum development.
5. Examine the relationship between content (mathematics) and literacy.
6. Explain what activity systems are, both as a framework and analytic tool.

KEY TERMS/IDEAS: funds of knowledge, ethnomathematics, culture, discourse communities, Cultural Historical Activity Theory (CHAT)

Introduction

In Chapter 9, we introduced some of the fundamental differences between sociocultural theories of language and learning (SCT) and second language acquisition (SLA). One of the most distinguishing terms that captures the essence and practicality of this difference is *context*. SCT scholars always foreground the social context of learning and development. While all SCT approaches emphasize the social, the cultural, and the context of development, there is some variation regarding what constitutes context. In this chapter, we will provide some of the details of varied understandings of context and how it has evolved historically. A second objective of this chapter is to also present *Cultural Historical Activity Theory (CHAT)* as a model for thinking about second language learners and designing optimal learning environments.

Culture and Language

While some speak about language and culture separately, since the social turn in language, there is a general consensus that language and culture are inextricably linked and impossible to separate in real life. Michael Agar has coined the term *languaculture* as a way of merging the two ideas into a single signifier (Agar, 1994). The attraction of sociocultural theory (SCT) is that it is predicated on the convergence of three fundamental constructs in the social sciences: language, culture, and cognition. Prior to SCT, the dominant theories of learning minimized the role of language and culture. The focal point of learning was the individual's developmental pathway in terms of time and linear biological stages (e.g., Bandura, 1986; Erikson, 1950; Piaget, 1952; Skinner, 1957). In the United States, John Dewey was a pioneer in looking at learning as a social and experiential phenomenon (Dewey, 1916). In the early part of the 20th Century, the Russian/Soviet psychologist Lev Vygotsky developed a more empirically based theory of social psychology and human development grounded in Marxist ideas of dialectic materialism. In contrast to his Western peers, human development was primordially driven by social interactions with the material world and entailed multiple directions. The human being acts on the environment as the environment acts on it. Thus, the human being can never be separated from the context of development.

Learning could be considered a movement from the outside (interpersonal) toward the inside (intrapersonal). The emphasis on context in human development begs the question, how do we define *context*? Since the days of Dewey and Vygotsky, we can see how our understanding of context has expanded. In the early phases, social psychologists would focus on the interaction between two people, or a dyad. Over time, it was noted that dyads are nested within larger socially organized activities. These cultural activities include literacy events in the homes and classrooms like bedtime stories and author's chair. It can also focus on the broader ideological, historical, and political aspects as well.

The role of language in these socially organized activities becomes fundamental to how learning unfolds through interactions. If we think about it closely, all interactions are taking place through language, in the broadest sense of the word (all signs and symbols). The speech that occurs between people and the speech that happens within a person (inner speech) are the systems. Learning can be thought of as outside-in rather than inside-out, moving from the interpersonal to the intrapersonal. This process happens through the exchange of signs and symbols (language) in purposeful activities. As signs are used in consistent and coherent ways across situations, meaning and intersubjectivity is achieved amongst people. Language functions as the primary mediational tool through which human beings solve problems and develop (Wertsch, 2008).

Cultural Historical Activity Theory

Learning is perhaps the most innate human characteristic and it is life-long and life-wide. It spans multiples social spaces and timescales—learning never stops.

Is there a distinction between "language learning" and "learning"? We can say that when a child first enters the world, he/she begins to interact with the world through sounds. They communicate their physical and emotional needs through crying sounds and gestures that are interpreted by primary caregivers. These initial sounds may not be a formally recognized language; however, it is language nonetheless. Thus, the onset of learning and the use of language, broadly defined, are mutually dependent. While the child is learning *through* language (cognition), the child is also learning *about* language (metacognition and metalinguistics). If learning happens through language (signs and symbols), then language learning is simultaneously a goal and a tool of learning. We can think of learning as movement toward a goal mediated by signs and symbols. As the child develops, he/she learns to manipulate signs and symbols that are grounded in culturally and historically organized activities.

Cultural Historical Activity Theory (CHAT) is based on the idea that learning is semiotically mediated where language is used to make meaning. Rather than thinking of language in terms of its structural properties (i.e., phonological, morphosyntactic), the fundamental unit of analysis of language and meaning is the activity system in which these structures are embedded. One can never abstract language from the activity systems that govern its use. Activity systems are bound by cultural rules that have been shaped by communities. Learning is movement and change through stable yet fluid activity systems. It is a movement of learner identity: from *novice* to *expert* of meaning-making. As we discussed earlier in Chapter 7, meaning-making relies on both stability and variation. According to Wertsch (1981), human activities can be understood at multiple levels and have the following properties:

1. All activity is *goal* directed.
2. All activity is *mediated* by culturally constructed tools and artifacts.
3. All activity is *historical*, which includes genetic and epigenetic factors.

Thus, we can think of learning and language through the prism of the following activity triangle (Figure 10.1).

Most theories of learning place the individual learner at the center; however, in this activity triangle the center is the nature of the problem or task that is being solved by multiple actors (subjects). The subjects, who are the participants within an activity, are jointly moving toward a goal or *object*. This process unfolds in multiple directions through *mediation*. If we consider this to be a typical classroom, then the students would be jointly solving a problem and, through mediation, moving toward a solution. Mediation can be materials (e.g., paper, pencil, abacus, electronic technology), ideas (e.g., English grammar rules, geometric theorems), and assistance from more expert others. Mediation and the quality of the mediation is the most important indicator of development. Mediation is dynamic and fluid. If subjects are not moving toward the object, then the mediation has to change. This becomes the core aspect of assessment for learning, in which, in

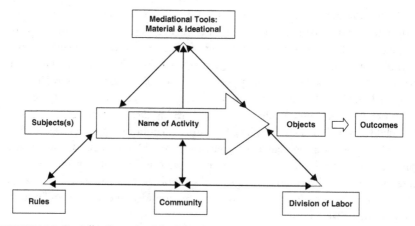

FIGURE 10.1 Socially Organized Activity System

contrast to most traditional assessments of learning, the focus is on the process not the outcome of learning. While the other dimensions of an activity can also change, they are relatively stable. Rules may be explicit and/or implicit. For example, rules can determine how participants take turns, are they selected by someone with more authority or expertise or do they self-select? There could be rules governing the language choices participants make. Beyond the immediate subjects of an interaction, how do members of the broader community impact movement within an activity? Finally, the division of labor is the roles taken up by the participants to achieve the goal. All of these components interact for the purpose of meaning-making and problem solving. While learning and language are means to concrete ends, they are also ends in themselves. When leaning and language are ends, learners become more aware of how they learn and how language functions which enhances their ability to apply them to solving new problems.

CHAT is a theory of learning that can be used to examine all human activities. As we turn our attention to how learning is organized in schools, and in particular for second language learners, it is important to consider the contrast in *object, mediation, rules, division of labor,* and *community* in school vs. out-of-school activities. We will take you through a CHAT analysis of an everyday activity where learning is unfolding in a culturally situated manner. Then we will look at how the same activity might look when organized in a more discrete manner, often found in schooling. In this activity, a mother is teaching her daughter how to make *Pad Thai,* a traditional South Asian dish. The learning goal is *how to make Pad Thai* and we have illustrated the other components through an activity triangle (Figure 10.2).

In this scenario, the principal subjects are the mother and her daughter. The community is the family that will be eating the *Pad Thai,* who all mediate the activity because the mother and daughter consider their preferences, tastes, and perhaps allergies. The mother could determine some explicit rules such as safety

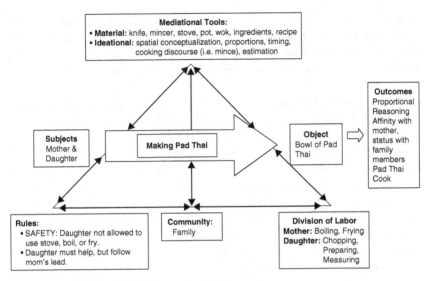

FIGURE 10.2 Making Pad Thai as an Activity System

rules (i.e., the daughter is not allowed to use the stove, boil, or fry), and if she wants to help she must follow her mother's lead. The mother organizes how the work will be accomplished (*division of labor*) by dividing tasks according to the rules of safety: the mother will instruct the daughter and will do the boiling and frying, but the daughter must do all the chopping, preparing, and measuring. In order for the daughter to learn, she needs to move from being a novice cook to becoming proficient in the making of *Pad Thai*. She will be joining the community of *Pad Thai* makers. This movement occurs through mediation, and the process is complex and multifaceted. There are the material tools such as a knife, a mincer, a stove, a pot, a wok, and the ingredients. There is also the recipe, which the mother has memorized, and the mother needs to use language to call out the recipe as she boils the water and fries the chicken. Additionally, there are ideational tools like spatial conceptualization, proportional reasoning, time keeping, specialized cooking discourse (i.e., mince), estimation, and so forth. The mother knows that for every jar of *Pad Thai* sauce, she will need two eggs, two garlic cloves, one-and-a-half packages of noodles, one onion, half a cabbage, and two chicken breasts. As she calls out the ingredients, the girl learns the proportional relationship between the items. She has to estimate half of the cabbage as well as learn skills like chopping (maybe just measuring) onions. The finished product is a *Pad Thai* meal, which is the immediate object of the activity; however, the outcomes can be extended further.

The daughter has been apprenticed into the community of *Pad Thai* cooks. Over time, we could imagine the nature of the mediation, in terms of mother's assistance, changing. As the daughter moves through the *zone of proximal development* (ZPD), she makes the tools her own and is able to make the dish independently.

Through the process she has engaged in advanced problem-solving strategies such as proportional reasoning in order to combine ingredients to make a bowl that would be enough to serve her family. In this activity, proportional reasoning is learning not as an object but a mediational tool necessary to successfully negotiate the task.

Let us reorganize the above activity using a more traditional schooling approach where discrete learning takes place (Figure 10.3).

One of the key differences is the object and mediational tools in the activity system. After the teacher delivers a lecture on the fundamentals of proportional reasoning and fractions, she hands the students worksheets where they perform basic computational tasks, adding and multiplying fractions. The activity is largely text based, and students work individually. The object or immediate goal of the activity is proportional reasoning. The community does not extend beyond the classroom and students do not verbally participate unless they are responding to teacher-initiated questions. There is little opportunity for peer assistance or differentiated instruction. The division of labor is whole class instruction where the teacher does the teaching and the students respond on the discrete worksheets. The mediational tools are pencil and paper, reading, writing, and maybe teacher assistance (mostly procedural and evaluation).

The difference between the two activities is night and day, especially in terms of how learners are positioned. In this activity, the daughter, who is now just another student, is rendered invisible with little responsibility. Since proportional reasoning is now the object of the activity, it is no longer presented as a culturally purposeful tool for solving concrete problems. In contrast, the

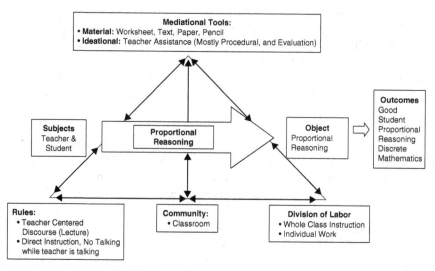

FIGURE 10.3 Making Pad Thai as an Activity System (in School)

home based activity of making Pad Thai provides for more dynamic learner identities for the daughter. Proportional reasoning is a necessary tool for successful negotiation of the activity. Technically, we should not say the schooling activity is "decontextualized" rather it is a new context of learning where children are socialized into the institutional culture of school valued practices. Rather than learning mathematical tools in more culturally relevant ways, the tools become ends for the purpose of successfully "doing school." Schooling, in this sense, could be considered a specific type of performative ritual, a cultural system of its own. In reality, school subjects are presented in ways that don't mirror how members of those cultural systems actually do mathematics, science, biology, or English.

Look at these two activity systems again. What does it tell you about the community? What is learned? What is valued as competence? What do the outcomes suggest about larger issues of identity, ideology, ethics, society, and humanity?

Funds of Knowledge

One of the key mediational tools that teachers can leverage to promote learning is the knowledge and expertise learners possess grounded in their homes and communities. In homes and in communities, students engage a wide range of complex semiotic practices. They have a special affinity with people, places, and historically developed tools. The historically and culturally accumulated knowledge that students share are called *funds of knowledge* (Moll, 2005; Moll, Amanti, Neff, & González, 1992; Moll & Greenberg, 1990). Funds of knowledge are those primarily out-of-school *epistemologies* (knowledge and ways of knowing) that students possess. The family unit and the shared knowledge of parents, children, and siblings are more than background or prior knowledge. Funds of knowledge are central to their development, and they should be foregrounded and "valued" the way "funds" are valued in activity design.

The professional identities of parents, the entertainment discourses they engage in, crafts and hobbies, food and sports are amongst the common household epistemologies that students participate in on a daily basis. These funds of knowledge are discourses that students know and use. For example, a father may work as a land surveyor and much of the dinner-table talk may be about his job. On the weekends, he may even perform tasks that utilize his technical skills while apprenticing his sons or daughters in measurement, geometric mapping, and construction techniques. The children may even learn how to use specific surveyor and engineering tools and read cryptic signs and symbols on the sidewalks. Some children may even understand complex piping systems for water, storm sewers, and sewage that run throughout the city blocks. This type of expertise and discourse was gained through schooling. Another example may be a young girl who has learned how to braid her sister's hair, passing down a culturally and historically developed tool that involves complex steps and symmetrical imaging. Caring for younger siblings, gardening, and food preparation are all funds of knowledge in which students engage outside of school. While these knowledges are outside of school, they contain school-like practices and domains of knowledge. These funds of knowledge are primary discourses that, as pointed out already, can be leveraged in schools. Funds of knowledge may also involve secondary discourses like law, medicine, and formal mathematics. In some cases, the student's funds of knowledge may actually mirror that which is privileged in traditional schooling.

Funds of knowledge addresses the need for educators to recognize that students do not come into schools as "blank slates" to be filled with information. Students engage in problem-solving activities in their homes, often to help their families in times of economic hardship (Moll et al., 1992). This is particularly true of bilingual children who often act as cultural brokers and translators on adult tasks such as accounting and filling out government applications (Faulstich Orellana, 2009). Another type of fund of knowledge is moral and ethical knowledge gained in non-school institutions like temples, churches, and mosques. Religious affiliations and sports teams have their own moral and ethical values that mediate the children's identity outside of school.

Another source of funds of knowledge is digital literacies, including video games (Gee, 2007). According to Gee (2007), one of the key principles of learning is that a learner's knowledge is "*distributed* across the learner, objects, tools, symbols, technologies, and the environment" (p. 227). He has shown how some of the video games youth engage in are in many ways more rigorous and consistent with the principles of learning and literacy we aspire to in schools. Video games actually provide an intense space for students to experiment with different problem-solving skills. Sometimes a child's ethical and ideological perspectives or technological literacies may be in alignment or in conflict with school learning goals. Nevertheless, we will in the next section discuss the idea of *third space* and how these potential tensions are actually valuable learning opportunities from a CHAT perspective. In a context where curricular practices exclude funds of knowledge, it is important to remember how we can organize activities that leverage these tensions in productive ways.

Teachers, often because of the curricular requirements, may not typically engage students on this level. They may not know the vast amounts of knowledge students are bringing into school, and are using to make sense of school activities. In many instances, homes of working class families, immigrant families, low socioeconomic status families, and so forth seem disorganized and are stereotyped as inferior and un- or undereducated (Moll et al., 1992). In fact, however, the lives of students' homes are certainly organized within a cultural framework. Teachers can engage in finding out about students' lives in order to educate the whole child.

Developing a curriculum that incorporates funds of knowledge requires teachers to fundamentally reorganize the classroom's activity system. The object of the system may be to solve a problem where one or more students could provide expertise and mediation to accomplish this object. For example, if the activity was to plan, plant, and care for a garden, students could draw upon household and community epistemologies to accomplish this activity. Traditional curricular goals can also be achieved in the process. While the traditional classroom may use mediational tools, including abstract tools, physical items like pencils, paper, books, and ideational tools like meta-level understandings of language and culture, the funds of knowledge curriculum may also include the content area skills and knowledge as well as home and community funds of knowledge because they would need to be used to plant and care for the garden. The division of labor becomes more distributed and the teacher is no longer carrying the burden of omniscient expert. The rules change as well, though many rules, typical of classrooms and schools, remain the same. The community changes in theory, if not in practice.

Remember the activity system of the classroom above, where the community involved classmates and perhaps other school-wide communities? In a funds of knowledge curriculum, that community is expanded to the families of students and even other community relationships as they are involved in the activity system through the historically and culturally accumulated knowledges and practices. Parents could be invited to participate in activities and expand the cultural and linguistic repertoires the children could use to engage in content area activities such as probability and fractions (e.g., Razfar, 2012d).

Third Space

One of the challenges of implementing a curriculum like a funds of knowledge curriculum is that the academic knowledge and the students funds of knowledge don't always "match." In other words, sometimes the cultural knowledge of the student is not the types of cultural knowledge privileged in schools. This may happen to be moral and ethical knowledge or it may be concepts of mathematics or science embedded in household and community activities. Either way, bringing in students' funds of knowledge into the classroom may create tension.

From a CHAT perspective, these tensions are expected and strategically designed. We design for tensions and learn through the tensions. This presents opportunities for expansive learning (Engeström, 1987) when tension arises between the learning of an individual and groups across contexts. When a student's learning (i.e., through funds of knowledge) comes into tension with classroom learning goals (i.e., other funds of knowledge, or standard curriculum), it may create the possibility of new activities to resolve these tensions and produce new tensions which in turn need to be resolved. Overall, these are productive meaning-making spaces that lead the development of all participants (children, parents, and teachers). This space which is opened by the tension is called *third space* (Gutiérrez, 2008; Razfar, 2012b).

The third space is a metaphor for social interactions that contain both formal and informal interactions, epistemologies, identities, and ideologies (Razfar,

2012a). Third spaces are borne out of a tension between the learning goals of two activity systems:

1. the official activity; and
2. the unofficial activity.

In classrooms, official activities and social spaces consist of a learning goal that is primarily orchestrated by the teacher. Unofficial activities and social spaces are initiated by students. It is important to note that we are emphasizing those unofficial meaning-making practices that are still related to the official learning goals, not "off-task" and unrelated activities. For example, the teacher is talking about fractions and the children begin talking amongst themselves about how it reminds them of how a pizza was divided at a party. Another example could be the teacher is talking about *Brown v. Board of Education* and the students begin talking about James Brown the singer (Gutiérrez, Rymes, & Larson, 1995).

A third space emerges when the activity system is consciously designed to mediate new, shared understandings amongst the participants. Student challenges and tensions in meaning-making are valued assets that are essential for learning and development. From a CHAT perspective the zone of proximal development can be thought of as movement through the third space. Scientific and formalized concepts are developed from and through the tensions children have with their concrete experiences from outside of school (Vygotsky, 1978). When the third space becomes an intentional instructional tool, then teachers find ways to identify content within households that are typically marginalized and ultimately reposition learners in non-deficit ways.

Outside of specific interactions, the concept of third space could be applied more broadly as the tension between mandated curricula that restrict languages used with activities that are more open-ended and include a broad range of linguistic and cultural mediational tools. Teachers have to negotiate these fundamental tensions especially if they wish to organize learning through a CHAT lens. Educational policies mandate homogenous, "one size fits all" activities into the classroom; however, variation is the rule in human learning. All students bring diverse experiences, expertise, and perspectives to those activities. Children from immigrant and multilingual homes also bring additional sets of potential tools, communities, rules that may further conflict with the stated objects of mandated activity systems. Thus, the classroom should be viewed as a space of competing activity systems where meaning-making is fundamentally contested. Through contestation, new possibilities and spaces of meaning emerge. In many classrooms, teacher-centered interactions follow a strict Initiate-Respond-Evaluate/Follow-up (IRE/F) discourse style. Often this would show that the teacher is in control of the classroom knowledge, evaluating students' responses to her questions (Nystrand, 1997; Wells, 1993). However, this teacher-centeredness can be challenged by reorganizing learning to follow a more symmetric participation structure, one that values the cultural and historical context of both curricular knowledge and students' funds of knowledge.

Reorganizing Content Learning: Mathematics as Cultural Practice

Recalling Gee's (2008) notion of primary and secondary discourses, school-based mathematics could be considered a specialized, secondary discourse that is organized in purposeful ways. Funds of knowledge that draw on mathematics in implicit ways can be considered primary discourses. From a CHAT perspective, secondary discourses are developed through primary discourses. Remember our earlier discussion in Chapter 9 about one way to assess learning from a sociocultural point of view: the shift in action/object to meaning ratio. Vygotsky examined how children developed abstract meaning in play activities, moving from concrete experiences and actions to abstract ideas. Abstract in the sociocultural sense does not mean "detached," since abstract and symbolic language are developed through embodied meaning-making. Secondary discourses, such as formal mathematics, represent such a shift in the ratio of actions/objects to meaning, since they are more abstract, generalizable, and capable of being used in novel situations (Sfard, 2002).

The tension between school-based and non-school-based mathematical practices has been the subject of much study. Semiotic practices that involve quantification, spatial relationships, and deductive logical reasoning are the general domain of mathematics. Whether it is number sense, basic arithmetic computations, geometric relations, algebraic equations, integrals and derivatives, mathematics educators have also made the social turn to understand how mathematics is developed culturally, especially in non-school settings. They have also focused on how this type of funds of knowledge could be leveraged to develop formal mathematical problem-solving strategies. While not strictly a sociocultural point of view, the field of *ethnomathematics* provides a valuable body of work that speaks to the alternative cultural models for doing mathematics (Ascher, 1991).

One place where ethnomathematics has helped us think about mathematics as a situated, cultural practice is the use of non-decimal number systems by indigenous communities around the world. For most of us who have been raised in the decimal system, and counting in units of 10 is as natural as breathing, this may come as a "language" shock; however, our most fundamental ideas about numbers are like other systems of meaning-making, grounded in culturally organized activities. Of course, even within the uses of the decimal system there is variation in orthography. For example, the Arabic numeral system is the most common decimal system; however, there is variation in how some of the numbers are represented (e.g., English "7" and Arabic "V"). While the numbers have a different symbol their values are exactly the same because they are decimal systems. The meaning changes, however, when we go to a base system other than the

TABLE 10.1 Non-Decimal Number Systems (www.storyofmathematics.com, 2012)

Modern American	Ancient Mayan	Ancient Sumerian
0		
1	0 1 2 3 4	1 11 21 31 41 51
2		2 12 22 32 42 52
3	5 6 7 8 9	3 13 23 33 43 53
4		4 14 24 34 44 54
5		5 15 25 35 45 55
6	10 11 12 13 14	6 16 26 36 46 56
7		7 17 27 37 47 57
8	15 16 17 18 19	8 18 28 38 48 58
9		9 19 29 39 49 59
		10 20 30 40 50

decimal system. The Chinese abacus, for example, is a combination of binary, or base 2 and base 5. The ancient Sumerians used a base 60 system, and the Mayans used a base 20. A base is how many options there are in writing the number. In a base 10 system there are nine unique symbols, and possibly a placeholder like zero. After the 9th symbol, they start to repeat. In a base 20 system there are 19 unique symbols, which in the Mayan orthography are really combinations of ones (the dots) and fives (the bars). The Mayan system does include a zero as well. Ancient Cuneiform, the Sumerian writing system, does not include a zero, though it does have 59 unique symbols, created from combinations of two symbols (ones and tens). See Table 10.1 to compare the different systems.

Each system is unique in terms of function, purpose, and what is valued by its users. The Mayan numbering system is very efficient for doing quick arithmetic and computation of large numbers. Because they have bars and dots, representing ones and fives, they can quickly subtract and add in the same place value. Additionally, the numbers are stacked, so that 1–19 is at the bottom. The next number up would be used for all multiples of 20 up to 380. Once another 20 is added, the Mayans stacked a third number. The third level was used for all multiples of 400 up to 7600, and so on. This is not too different from the decimal numerical system we use, except we have the numbers line horizontally. We have included several links to online content where you can appreciate how the calculations were performed.

The Sumerian system was base 60, and was aligned horizontally like the modern decimal numerals. However, rather than 111 equaling 100+10+1, the Sumerians would have their symbol for "1" and would equal $(60*60)+60+1$. However, the Sumerian system did not have a zero. Thus, 1 and 60 and 3600 must be differentiated by context alone. Zero, then, is not an absolute number, but rather a culturally developed tool that perhaps was developed to differentiate smaller base systems. It would be much more difficult to get the numbers in a base 60 system confused for everyday business or accounting purposes, for instance (see www. storyofmathematics.com).

While many of the examples cited above might seem like ancient history, there have been many ethnographic studies of urban, rural, and indigenous communities who continue to engage in mathematical meaning-making in non-decimal systems. The "Candy Sellers" study done by Geoffrey Saxe with children in Brazil is amongst the pioneering work in sociocultural mathematics. This ethnographic study showed the contrast between mathematics done in daily life and the mathematics used in schools (Saxe, 1988). Children, aged between five and 15, were often found selling candy on the streets. They built a complex social situation because they have to buy candy from a supplier, and sell it to a customer. As they sold candy, the children had to manipulate currency, as well as orthographic numbers posted in stores. Additionally, the children often developed selling schemes that involved computation of ratios. For example, the child may sell two candy bars for CR$500 or five for CR$1000.[1] This ratio system is often seen in stores, but is used by children. These children were performing complex mathematical functions without the benefit of formal schoolwork.

When the Brazilian candy-selling children were compared with peers in urban and rural areas who did not sell candy, the candy-selling children outperformed their non-candy-selling peers in adding, subtracting currency, as well as using fractions and ratios. They did initially have some difficulty with standard orthography, but this improved greatly over time. With more schooling, they developed more formalized mathematical problem-solving strategies based on their concrete commercial interactions. While they had expertise in mathematical functions, they were novice in the symbolic representation of numbers. They evidently relied on alternative means to identify bills (i.e., colors, shapes, and images) and comparing currencies. In the context of their work, the orthography was not needed, and if they needed help, they could ask for it from more capable peers or shop owners. These daily mathematical practices that were part of the children's funds of knowledge and primary discourse practices were leveraged in schools to develop more formalized, secondary discourses of mathematics. This led to greater performance in the mathematics domains of fractions, ratios, and general numeracy.

Another example of culturally embedded mathematics practices comes from the work of Jerry Lipka and his colleagues with the Yup'ik Eskimos (Lipka, Wildfeuer, Wahlberg, George, & Ezran, 2001). Yup'ik mathematics is part of a broader cultural activity of story-telling. The Yup'ik use images to construct narratives. They often draw scenes in the mud with a knife. These scenes require the use of spatial and directional elements of geometry and mapmaking. For example, a scene of a home could be drawn in the mud, and two people in the home may be indicated by two-dimensional figures. However, unlike typical geometry which is concerned

---

1. CR$ refers to the *cruzeiro real*, the monetary value in Brazil during the time of the research.

with shapes, spaces, and other measurable features, the Yup'ik Eskimos are concerned their story scenes follow the topographic qualities of the pictures. In other words, the scenes incorporate concepts of connectedness and proximity, not necessarily directly quantifiable measurements. The story scenes of the Yup'iks were used to pass down everyday life experiences, not direct mathematical concepts; however, the process challenged young girls to transform three-dimensional objects into two-dimensional images. Later, girls would use these concepts in making clothing and understanding how to make and decorate boots and other clothes. Girls would be required, in the activity of story-knifing, to manipulate images and move them, flip them, and rotate them, without changing the size and shape.

This may sound like a mathematics domain, and it certainly is! In geometry classes, students may learn how to "translate," "rotate," and "reflect" (or "flip"). These transformations take place in Euclidian space, on a Cartesian plane. These are learned as a secondary discourse in schools. They are carried out in worksheets and assessments, not in daily life situations. Unlike the Yup'ik, these transformations are the explicit target of instruction. Also, unlike the Yup'ik, these transformations take place in the idealized space of 3rd Century B.C. philosophical, political, and mathematical assumptions. Euclid's premises were recorded and used for the next two millennia as the foundational text for Western geometry. His laws were culturally and historically developed, as are the Yup'ik's. So, the primary discourse of mathematics, specifically geometry, Yup'ik girls learn through story-knifing are cultural tools used to perform daily tasks and rituals. The translation, reflection, or rotation of figures, is not carried out on a Cartesian plane, but rather on the mud. The translation, reflection, or rotation do not need to maintain the quantifiable Euclidian qualities, but rather may be stretched or pulled to tell a story of elastic change.

This type of thinking could be illustrated in a classroom by drawing shapes and pictures on a balloon and then blowing it up. As it expands the shape changes, but what about the shape does not change? When the balloon is deflated and stretched in different ways, what shapes can be made? Lipka et al. explain how this could be a useful exercise for children, to learn how shapes can be manipulated on stretchable surfaces. Think of a rubber band. Many middle school students have used these to write secret messages. If you stretch the rubber band enough, and write on it, when it returns to its original state the words will be squeezed together. This geometric thinking is more embodied than the geometry typically taught in schools.

Story-knifing for the Yup'iks and some other mathematical games children play (even in preschool and kindergarten, for example) are in many ways embodied forms of thinking about mathematical concepts, although the goal of the activities may not be explicitly solving arithmetic, geometric, or algebraic problems. Another type of embodied mathematics activity, which is intended for calculation, is the abacus. The abacus is a calculation system using beads to perform complex arithmetic. Unlike the school mathematics which includes a lot of writing and reading numbers to record calculations, the abacus involves shifting beads to represent numbers. The relationship of the beads is a different way to conceptualize mathematical relationships than writing discrete numbers. When one knows the abacus well, they can feel or visualize the numbers as beads and adding as movement. Furthermore, dwellings and villages for entire communities are built on complex mathematical concepts, though they may not be formalized as they are in schools.

As can be seen from the examples above, the mathematics being used outside of schools are quite complex. How might these mathematical practices be leveraged in schools? As we have already discussed, when activities are designed on the basis of heterogeneity and multiple mediational tools, then one should expect meaning-making tensions to arise. The key is to provide the mediational means to generate new spaces of meaning-making that build on children's complete linguistic and cultural toolkit. The examples provided above, while mathematical, are generally less effective in new problem-solving situations without a formalized, secondary mathematical language. In general, people with this type of mathematical skills struggle with problems that are not identical to the situations they have experienced. Scribner's study (1997) of dairy warehouse workers showed how they outperformed children on volume computation tasks when it was related to their work. While the dairy warehouse workers were more efficient, they avoided any type of numerical or algorithmic symbols or procedures. They relied on their understanding of the context and visual images to solve problems. In contrast, the children with formal schooling selected an optimal mathematical strategy and would not have been able to even approach the problem without it since they had no concrete experience with trucks and milk cartons.

While mathematics practices embedded in everyday life are more concrete and less symbolic, they are less generalizable problem-solving strategies because the concrete dominates meaning. There are clear advantages to developing the formal, secondary discourse of mathematics such as metacognition and universal application. It is like having a toolbox that one can carry anywhere. This transition from informal to formal, from primary to secondary discourse does not occur spontaneously and must be consciously designed. Given this transition occurs by mediating through third spaces, it is important to provide quality mediation. This is particularly important for second language learners who might have difficulty communicating their mathematical thinking and strategies in a second language.

The following example illustrates how alternative mediational tools can foster dynamic learning environments for second language learners who seemingly are not ready for advanced linguistic production (i.e., speaking and writing). Contrary to conventional SLA theories of acquisition, where basic interpersonal skills (BICS) precede cognitively advanced proficiency (CALP), this case illustrates CHAT's contrarian view of development where learner identities fluctuate between novice and expert roles dependent on the learning goal and the quality of the mediation (Razfar et al., 2011).

Keystrokes as Mediation

In this example, taken from Razfar et al. (2011), we will illustrate learning from a CHAT model. As opposed to individual acquisition of skills and knowledge,

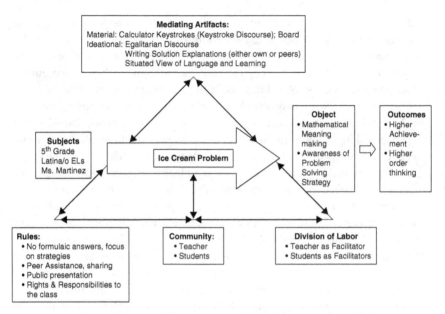

FIGURE 10.4 The Ice Cream Problem Activity (adapted from Razfar et al., 2011)

which we saw in Chapter 9 in second language learning as SLA, learning from an SCT view is always mediated by communication, talk, and discourse. Ms. Martinez was a teacher who explicitly established these norms in her classroom activities even though some of the students were considered to be limited in their English abilities. In Ms. Martinez's fifth grade classroom students had studied geometry and measurement all year long. Calculators were a common tool in the classroom and used in all mathematical lessons. Interestingly, Ms. Martinez redefined the keystrokes of the calculator to mediate in a different way: communication. Since students were expected to communicate their problem-solving strategies publicly, orally, and in written form, this proved to be a challenge for some. As a result, Ms. Martinez asked students to show their thinking using the keystrokes of the calculator as symbols to show the steps they had taken. Above is an activity triangle depicting how Ms. Martinez organized learning for figuring out the dimensions of an ice-cream cone (Figure 10.4).

Students discussed in groups and explained how they solved problems with each other, as well as wrote out their solutions. Students were to calculate the area of this two-dimensional figure representing the ice-cream (Figure 10.5).

Ms. Martinez and the students negotiated how much information they needed to solve the problem, and the students opted for a more challenging problem. This negotiation allowed students to use the language of mathematics using words like "altitude," "radius," and "hypotenuse." Ms. Martinez rarely discussed numbers and procedures, preferring to focus on mathematical meaning-making in English.

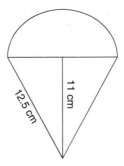

FIGURE 10.5 The Ice-cream Problem (Razfar et al., 2011)

The problem above is rather complex for fifth graders let alone English leanrers. As you can see from the activity triangle, one of Ms. Martinez's learning goals was to talk mathematics rather than simply find an answer. Clearly, the discourse rules demanded a collective orientation rather than individualized work. Students were positioned as experts and expected to perform the higher-order functions demanded of formal mathematics. Ms. Martinez practically accomplished this by redirecting students to ask peers when they came to her as an expert. She might say something like "compare with your team members and if they agree ... maybe you should talk about it with them." Instead of answers she asks questions, "What would you do?"

Ms. Martinez made it clear that students were expected to publicly present their problem-solving strategies. However, she also mediated this in a variety of ways: small group interactions, going to the board, or speaking to the whole class. The egalitarian discourse structure has to be modeled and made explicit. Students may be passive otherwise and defer to the teacher to initiate conversation. In contrast, Ms. Martinez expected students to initiate discourse and in particular they needed to comment on their classmates' strategies. Being scrutinized or making errors in public was normal. This allowed learners to be risk takers without fear of consequence. They were free to clarify, correct, or challenge one another. The expectation of public presentation would not have been sufficient without providing a full range of mediational tools. If students were not comfortable in English, they could use Spanish. If that didn't work they could use images—like the keystrokes on the calculator.

Ms. Martinez repositioned learners to be agents of meaning-making and assume greater responsibility. One way this was evident in this activity was to assume a posture of uncertainty when claims were put forth by students, and students assumed a posture of certainty. The posture of certainty of participants, or *modality*, is a key mediational tool in interactions between experts and novices. For example, one of the students wrote her strategy on the board using "keystroke" symbols and another student buildt upon what had already been written using different color ink. As the students discussed the strategy, she stood back and facilitated

the discussion at times narrating in words what had been written in "keystrokes."
Here she prompted the class to reflect on the strategy presented on the board:[2]

01 S1: Finding the area of the uh:::
02 S2: Finding the area of the quarter circles
03 S3: Quarter circles
04 MS. M: There is no quarter circle
05 SS: No the semi-circle
06 MS. M: The **semi**-circle↑ She (pause)
07 S: [forgot a keystroke]

In lines 1–7, it is clear that Ms. Martinez was on equal footing with the students. She made a claim but they disagreed with her (line 4), others chimed in, and Ms. Martinez continued to maintain her modality in order to encourage more discussion. Students were positioned to do the correcting. This discourse style is not as efficient as teacher-centered, IRE style; however, it is effective mediation of learning and English development in the content areas. Notice how the term "keystroke" (line 7) had become part of the classroom culture. Students were being corrected without fear of stigma and the "keystrokes discourse" was a critical mediator of this. Ms. Martinez followed up the error in strategy identified in line 7 by asking the student to once again explain her thinking. She then prompted her to look at what one of the newcomer English learners had written. This selection was deliberate as this student had been silent throughout. Figure 10.6 shows how this student had written using the keystrokes discourse.

It is interesting to note that this student struggled with oral English but was very proficient in writing, something contrary to Cummin's notion of BICS

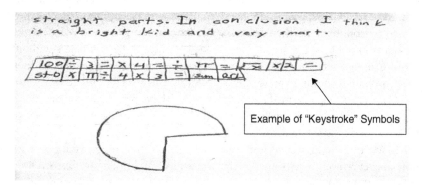

Example of "Keystroke" Symbols

FIGURE 10.6 The Keystrokes

and CALP. More importantly, the activity design positioned him to participate in modalities he was adept at Ms. Martinez even gave this student the floor to present what he had written, "look at your keystrokes and listen to Mauricio again." Through peer mediation, students developed multiple skills beyond the mathematics involved. They learned to persist and struggle with solutions. They expressed themselves in multiple modalities: writing, public speaking, writing on the board, and using invented language like keystrokes to communicate their thoughts. Thus, they developed metacognition. When we consider that this classroom we a heterogeneous group of ELs in terms of length of residency in the United States and English proficiency (at least by standard measures), the outcomes are quite remarkable (Razfar et al., 2011).

The keystrokes provide a concrete object and actions for ELs to develop their thinking. This allows them to develop greater *self-regulation*. Self-regulation occurs as learners appropriate meaning and deeper levels of conceptual understanding. This is how the ratio of object/action to meaning shifts—through mediation with concrete means toward concrete ends. A seemingly inaccessible and abstract question, such as the ice-cream problem, becomes accessible through the keystrokes.

Conclusion

As can be seen from the examples above, social organization can be changed to enhance learning opportunities. All activities are goal oriented, but often the activities in schools are viewed to be autonomous skills that must be acquired. The skills become the assumed goal of an activity. However, as indicated in this chapter, learning takes place in a social context, and activities involve complex social relationships. Activities in schools and classrooms can be reorganized to provide and the mediation needed to accomplish goals. Activities in our lives, like cooking for example, have a goal, and the mediation needed to accomplish that goal may include concepts that are traditionally taught in schools, like science, mathematics, and literacy. Ironically, in schools, mathematics, science, and literacy are often the object of activities, and the learning of these concepts needs to be mediated. Teachers working in classrooms can provide mediation for student learning. As we saw in this chapter, Ms. Martinez used the discourse of keystrokes in her classroom to mediate activities so that students could learn the more formalized systems of mathematics and writing.

From this perspective of mathematics as a discourse, we can begin to analyze how it is used in students' homes through primary mathematics discourses. By drawing on home knowledge, or students' funds of knowledge, we could develop highly sophisticated teaching and learning practices. Ethnomathematics helps us dispel some of our reductive views of mathematics as independent of language and culture. Mathematics is a cultural practice of meaning-making, rather than a universal truth free from variation. Cultural Historical Activity Theory is a learning theory that helps us merge language, learning, and content. More importantly, it helps us see language, learning, and content not as autonomous entities to be taught discretely, but part of purposeful cultural activities that are historical and essential tools for solving human problems—especially the problem of making sense.

TEACHER CASE STUDIES

Anita: Home Visits

Anita, a fourth grade teacher serving a high EL student population, decided she wanted to learn more about her students, specifically by learning their funds of knowledge. She saw that she was having difficulty connecting with her students in her school curriculum, but also recognized that she didn't understand her students that well. They came from a vastly different background. Most of the students were of Asian descent, she was African-American. Most of them had parents who had immigrated, or they themselves were part of the family immigration. She had grown up in the southern part of the United States. Once, during a classroom discussion she was talking about food, and the students said they ate a lot of rice. Anita started to ask them questions:

What do you eat for breakfast?
Rice.
What about lunch on days there is no school?
Rice.
What about dinner?
Rice.
Why are you always eating rice?
We don't know.

Anita watched as the kids often threw away the school-provided lunches and decided to investigate in more depth how the students lived at home. She told the students she would visit their homes, and see their families. She scheduled a visit to each home. On the day of each visit she arrived at the student's home, was greeted by the family, who often did not speak English, and was showed to the common living area where they gave her small portions of food and drink. She began to have more of a sense of who her students were. How their families lived, and even what the students ate. She was introduced to new types of chicken and shrimp dishes. Also, she found out that many of the students' families worked at or owned restaurants in the community, and often the students would help out with small tasks. She took pictures, observed the home set-ups, and asked about activities that the family engaged in. She thought about how she could use this knowledge in class. She decided she would implement a health unit, because she was sure that the students' eating habits were not up to standards, her standards.

In the first lesson of the unit, Anita asked students to record all of the calories they ate over a weekend. This required students to carefully log what foods they ate and approximate portions. In class on Monday, she introduced a computer tool to look up the calorie counts of the foods and had the students calculate how many calories they consumed per meal, per day, and the weekend total. As she compared the totals, she was very intrigued to find out that the calorie count was quite similar to the "official" recommendations by the Food and Drug Administration. She was a little surprised because she didn't recognize a lot of the foods they had listed. So Anita had the students use the food pyramid to analyze their diets. She gave them a food pyramid that was outdated and one of the students pointed out that the food pyramid in the back of their daily planner was different. So Anita went in search of a new pyramid, just to find out that the food pyramids or plans endorsed by the USFDA (United States Food & Drug Administration) were different than other countries. She began to realize that, perhaps, her standard approach to the health unit was not going to work.

Anita began to give her students a bigger role in the unit, culminating with an advertisement to promote healthy eating. But first, they would have to find out what the attitudes toward food consumption and health were in the community. The students created a survey to administer to parents and friends in the community about healthy eating. Students analyzed and charted the results. She took the liberty to show them the different kitchen appliances, like a *George Foreman Grill*, and all of the grease and fat that comes from cheeseburgers and other foods. She was able to draw on students' funds of knowledge to teach her mathematics curriculum (adding and subtracting fractions and proportions) as well as some components of her science curriculum (which included earth science and conservation). Through writing persuasive essays, discussing questions development for the surveys, and writing in food journals, the students worked on literacy development. She found a curriculum developed to go along with hers that included student inquiry and critical thinking (with a computer component that she was unable to complete because the administration didn't allow the computers to be used for "games"). Additionally, students had to learn how to communicate the complex ideas to community members in Chinese, many words and phrases they did not know but had to learn in the process.

Students took up expert roles as they explained cooking processes. At one point a student was talking about fried shrimp, so Anita took over and explained how shrimp was cooked. A student told her she was wrong. She was taken aback, because coming from the south, and spending time in Louisiana, she was sure she knew about fried shrimp. But the student continued to explain how they fry the shrimp, with the shell on, and don't use batter. At first Anita didn't believe him until the Chinese bilingual teacher, who happened to be in the classroom at the time, confirmed it. Anita also learned about *bok choy*, and other foods she had never heard of.

The health unit served to shift the students into roles of expertise as they brought in their funds of knowledge. It also allowed Anita to teach the rest of the curricula, as students sought to solve problems from their daily life (i.e., food related activities, survey of family and friends, and even planning for a public service ad).

Cindy: Smoking Pollution

Cindy's first grade class was learning about pollution and the environment. She read a book to her students about pollution and decided that for the school-wide science fair her class would look at the air pollution in and around her school. They took small caps of petroleum jelly, pollution catchers, and let them sit in different parts of the school and outside. They would gather particulates from the air, as dust, ash, and other tiny particles landed on them. She talked about how there were a lot of trucks and factories so there was a lot of pollution in the air.

Every day the students would look at the different pollution catchers and make observations about what they saw. On the final day they talked about which one had been in the most polluted area. They decided, quite obviously, that it was outside. So Cindy continued to push the students into reasoning about why there was more pollution outside. Expecting them to answer because of the trucks and factories, she was surprised when they answered it was because so many people in their community smoked. Cindy thought about this, and was quite impressed that they had reasoned this, but didn't understand why that was on their mind. This led to an entire unit on smoking.

Students surveyed and interviewed parents and family members about smoking and came back to the class to report. They studied the effects and dangers of smoking, causing tense situations in which values of the homes clearly contradicted the values Cindy was trying to get across. Students evaluated information and struggled with questions of why people would smoke if it harmful to one's health. They drew on funds of knowledge that normally would be marginalized in standard school curricula, and were able to learn about graphing, charting, writing, and even public speaking. They talked about science, including the earth science curriculum, but extending to biology as well. Cindy saw this as a way to educate the whole child, not just to teach unrelated mathematics and science skills.

This opened up more opportunities for group work where Cindy was faced with questions about gender (why girls and boys didn't really talk to each other), family (who the students saw as in the family unit), and other sociocultural issues that arose from a curriculum that valued the students' identities and funds of knowledge.

QUESTIONS/ACTIVITIES

1. Using the concept of the activity triangle, analyze two different social interactions that involve learning. Make a triangle for a classroom activity and then make one for an informal learning activity like a child learning to play baseball. What are the different subjects, tools, objects, communities, rules, divisions of labor, and outcomes?

2. Make a list of all of the funds of knowledge you can think of in your classroom. Think about your students. What do they do outside of school? What do their parents do? What types of activities do they engage in? Now, looking at some of these funds of knowledge, where is the mathematics? Where is the science? What domains of mathematics and science do your students engage in outside of the classroom?

Additional Resources (multimedia)

http://easycalculation.com/funny/numerals/sumerian.php [Calculating in Non-Decimal Systems]

http://homepages.rpi.edu/~eglash/isgem.dir/links.htm [Ethnomathematics]

http://www.mandarintools.com/abacus.html [Online Chinese Abacus]

http://www.prel.org/products/paced/apr03/ed_ethnomath.htm [Ethnomathematics]

http://www.storyofmathematics.com/images2/babylonian_numerals.gif [Babylonian/Sumerian Number System]

http://www.ted.com/talks/ron_eglash_on_african_fractals.html [African Fractals]

http://web.archive.org/web/20060714025120/http://www.saxakali.com/historymam2.htm [Number Systems]

11

FUNCTIONS OF LANGUAGE

Using Language around the World

LEARNING GOALS

1. Understand the functional approach to language study.
2. Explain and exemplify different functions of language.
3. Understand the importance of language in relationship building.
4. Analyze cultural differences in the building of relationships through language use.
5. Develop student inquiry through cultural analysis.

KEY TERMS/IDEAS: functions of language, languaculture, speech act, speech event

Introduction

Throughout this book, we have shown how language is used to accomplish specific purposes in a wide range of contexts and culturally organized activities. Again, we revisit the discussion of what constitutes the stability of language across time and space, and how does it vary from one activity to another. While we have provided many examples of various language functions, in this chapter we will discuss some viable candidates for common language functions shared between the world's languages. In structural linguistics, common features of phonology, morphology, and syntax are described as *linguistic universals*. Similarly, we ask, "What are some functional and cultural universals of language?" Cultural universals, or *functional universals*, are different from linguistic universals in that they are not biological traits contained within the individual. Instead, the idea of functional universals is based on the idea that people from around the world have similar needs, problems, and purposes. As a result they organize similar activity systems and semiotic practices. These shared meaning-making systems from around the world have shared language functions.

Early in this book we examined linguistic universals from a cognitive and linguistic point of view. Ideas like Chomsky's *Language Acquisition Device (LAD)* and Pinker's *language instinct* sought to account for the nature, function, and purpose of human grammar. This nativist account of language and its universal properties was assumed to be generalizable to all human beings. An assumption based, not on empirical evidence and actual human uses, but on deduction and an axiomatic truth (a fact accepted without evidence). However, in a functional approach to linguistics, and "linguistic universals," we note that these "universals" are inductively discovered through case studies and empirical evidence of human *langua*cultures. The inductive, as opposed to deductive, approach means that we don't presume that every language, or every human being for that matter, must utilize a particular language function. We can, however, say that based on the languages we have studied, we find a specific language function present. The possibility of a language not having that feature remains an open proposition. For example, if we claim that "every language has nouns," then this claim is subject to scientific and empirical investigation. This statement should be viewed as an inductive generalization based on every language observed which has a category of words for people, places, things, and ideas. While this claim may be true, the proposition is falsifiable and open to further empirical studies. Thus, the functional approach to questions of the nature, function, and purpose of language is fundamentally a scientific one, always open to investigation.

So, why do all languages appear to have nouns? The nativist would tell us that "nouns" are part of our genetic endowment, innate. A functional approach suggests an alternative explanation not grounded in genetics, but the social world. So, the reason all observed languages have nouns is likely because humans have seen the need to use language to reference things in the world. In order to talk about or refer to things, we would need to have named persons, places, things, and ideas in the world. Thus, the "universal" that all languages have nouns, likely arises from the need to refer to things in the world.

The functions of language are as numerous as the culturally organized activities human beings partake in. In this chapter, we will review several of them and show how these functions are performed through language and across cultures and languages (*languacultures*). While our list is not exhaustive, it does provide a glimpse into some of the more typical language functions that students can immediately connect with and discuss. Recall the "linguistic ladder" from Chapter 1. The sixth level of the ladder is called *pragmatics* and is focused, in a large part, with the way we use language to perform cultural functions and fulfill personal needs.

Speech Acts

One pragmatic level of language is the assumption that when we use language, we are not only "saying something," but, in fact, we are "doing something." Think about all the ways you use language. On the most basic level, we perform actions such as asking questions, giving information, and directing others in purposeful ways. Each of these could be described as a *speech act* (Austin, 1962). The grammatical construction of a sentence is often of little help in what a sentence means. *Supralinguistic* cues like tone, pitch, gestures, and so forth are also very important, as we understand what someone is doing through language. Most importantly, the context of the speech act is required if we are to understand what one means.

Consider multiple scenarios where a basic question like "Who are you?" is used. The form is a basic "WH" question with typical English question syntax. However, this form can be used to perform a variety of functions. It is used to elicit certain types of information related to identity. We could imagine using it to identify a stranger on the phone, the park, or on public transportation. Think, however, of a teenager yelling at his mother, and the mother responds, "Who are you?" This is no longer a request for information, but rather could be taken as either a command to stop the yelling, or a demand for respect. While it looks like a question in form, it is not a question in function.

Some common speech acts are listed in Table 11.1. Searle (1975) developed this taxonomy to explain different ways we use language to accomplish goals. Searle categorized speech acts, whether direct or indirect, in terms of what they accomplish, not how they are grammatically constructed (Table 11.1).

Some speech acts are quite direct and explicit, and we can detect them more readily through their form. For example, in English, questions have particular stems (five "'W's," How?) and rising intonation marked by "?" However, other speech acts are *indirect* and implicit. Like the response the mother gave to her yelling son above, the actual intention of the speech act was indirect, or it did not match the grammatical construction. In fact, it is interesting to note that Searle did not have a category for questions. Searle suggested that all questions are actually directives, since they are attempts to get the hearer to do something.

TABLE 11.1 Searle's Speech Acts

Speech act	What it accomplishes	Example	Explanation
Representatives (or assertions)	Commits speaker to the truth.	The grass is green.	The speaker asserts what he or she believes to be true.
Directives	Speaker attempts to get the hearer to do something.	Can you close the window?	The speaker is attempting to get the hearer to close the window.
Commissives	Commits the speaker to some future action.	I promise to love and cherish you...	The speaker is committing to a future action.
Expressives	Speaker expresses a psychological state.	Thank you for your time. Greetings	The speaker expresses thankfulness, but does not make an assertion of truth.
Declarations	The world conforms to what the speaker says.	I now pronounce you husband and wife.	The marriage (in the world) is declared to be valid (what was said).

It is important to attend to these functional uses of language, especially with second language learners. Grammar based approaches to language learning and instruction emphasize form not the function. Thus, in schools an explicit focus on the function of language should accompany the focus on form. The power of using a question to achieve a command could be the culturally appropriate way of being polite. For example, we would not say at a dinner table in a nice restaurant "Give me the salt and pepper." We might say "Pass the salt and pepper, please." But more than likely, we would soften the command by saying "Would you mind passing the salt and pepper?" or "Can you please pass the salt and pepper." These second two are formally questions, but they are not functionally used to request information. They are the polite forms of an order or command. Thus, understanding the way we use language, and the functions of language are very important for the sociocultural competency of our students.

Speech Events

In any cultural activity, there are norms and rules that tell us how to speak in a given situation. In the example of the dinner table above, there are rules of politeness and formality, though these rules vary in different groups and contexts. It may be terribly inappropriate to say "can you please pass the salt and pepper?" in the context of an informal picnic. Different rules govern these activities, and thus, we perform accordingly with our speech. These activities can be called *speech events*, a term defined by Dell Hymes as:

> "The term speech event will be restricted to activities, or aspects of activities, that are directly governed by rules or norms for the use of speech. An event may consist of a single speech act, but will often comprise several."
>
> (Hymes, 1972, p. 56)

Thus, in an activity, when there are specific norms, we can identify that activity as a genre of speech, or most specifically, as the event of speech. This may consist of a single act, like asking a question, or it may involve several speech acts as in a conversation (which, by the way, may be made up of smaller speech events), or a joke. The *knock knock* joke template, for example, learned by children at a young age, is governed by particular rules. And, often, while children may not have fully been socialized into the dominant discourses of humor, they understand the formal pattern of the joke. This is evidenced by them following the template of the joke, but it isn't funny. Below you find a humorous joke (1) followed by one that follows the template but isn't funny (2):

1. Knock Knock. Who's there? Lionel! Lionel who? Lionel roar if you don't feed him!
2. Knock Knock. Who's there? Jacob! Jacob who? Jacob drinks milk.

Speech events can extend to greetings, business meetings ("I second that!") and other goal-oriented norm-governed activities. As social and cultural beings, we draw on tools that have been developed over time to mediate activities. Thus, in society, as we use language to perform different functions, we can identify these speech events.

For example, take the following situation of a customer at a diner ordering from the waiter, analyzed with Searle's taxonomy (Table 11.2).

In this situation, the speech event could be described as "ordering a meal." However, it consists of several speech acts. This is a common way of ordering food at a diner in the United States. First, the waitress greets the customer, but often this greeting is only customary and actually is not responded to. In fact, the main point of the second utterance is a directive, intended to elicit a response from the customer. The customer, at the diner for food, makes his request. It is important to note that in this situation this is a directive because he is trying to get the waitress to bring him a breakfast special. The directives continue on as the waitress and customer try to elicit responses from each other until, finally, the customer expresses some sort of contentment. In the eighth speech act, the expressive "thanks" is an affirmation that the customer is content with the order. The waitress responds with a promise of food. This is a normative transaction designed to perform the function of ordering food. Thus, we can categorize this type of interaction a speech event. If you walk into diners all over the United States you will likely see a similar interaction of waitresses and customers using directives to negotiate an agreement, which is verified by an expression of affirmation or contentment, and followed by a promise. The rules of ordering can vary between different types of restaurants. For example, in a fast food restaurant, the speech event doesn't follow the diner pattern for ordering food. There are no waiters or waitresses, but cashiers, and the customer serves himself or herself. When the relationships are different, so are the speech events.

The range of language functions is considerable, and naming them helps second language learners better understand how speech events are organized. While certain language functions appear to be universal because they arise out of common needs and purposes, there is variation in how they are performed. If a student has difficulty performing a language function, then the teacher must consider how he/she performs an equivalent function in their primary language.

TABLE 11.2 Searle's Taxonomy

Speech event: waiter–customer	Speech acts
Waiter: Good evening, sir. What can I get you today?	(1) Expressive (2) Directive
Customer: I would like the breakfast special.	(3) Directive
Waiter: How would you like your eggs?	(4) Directive
Customer: Scrambled.	(5) Directive
Waiter: Can I get you anything to drink with that?	(6) Directive
Customer: No, that's all. Thanks.	(7) Representative (8) Expressive
Waiter: OK, that'll be right up.	(9) Commissive

Functions of Language

Scholars from various language-related fields and disciplines have attempted to understand how language works. Table 11.3 outlines some common language functions that we will discuss.

TABLE 11.3 Language Functions

Function	Definition	Example
Referential	Language is used to talk about something else.	General use of nouns standing for people, places, or things.
Negation	Language is used to express the absence of something	No, not, neither/nor, prefixing and suffixing of negative markers.
Counting/ quantifying	Language is used to talk about numbers and quantities.	Metric system versus American system. Base 10 number system versus base 20.
Greetings	Language is used to welcome or acknowledge someone.	Hello as a general greeting versus Salaam with religious ties.
Terms of address	Languages may be used to index social status or solidarity when addressing someone.	Tu/vous in French non-grammatical versus titles.
Honorifics	Some languages have special forms for polite language, and language used to speak to someone of a higher status.	Javanese *Krama Madya* and *Ngoko* forms versus non-grammatical respect registers.
Reproduction	Narratives and cultural ideas of reproduction are expressed through language.	Religiously tabooed discussions of sex versus early sex education.
Affective	Language is used to express emotions.	Expressions of remorse, happiness, sadness.
Ontology	Language is used to talk about the world as it really is.	Religious dogmas versus post-modern relativism.
Epistemology	Language is used to talk about knowledge.	Pirahã empirical morphemes versus formal methodologies for scientific validity.
Climate	Language is used to talk about the weather or environment.	Four seasons (spring, summer, autumn, winter) versus two seasons (wet and dry season).
Time	Language is used to tell and talk about times, dates, and/or historical events.	Lunar calendar versus Gregorian Calendar; 12-hour analog watch versus 24-hour "military time."
Narration	Language is used to tell stories that reveal social identities and cultural values.	Labovian structured narratives versus Ochs and Capps narratives we live by (see Chapter 13).
Transactions	Language can be used to perform transactions.	Monetary system versus bartering system.
Aesthetics	Language can be used to talk about art and beauty.	Iconic figures of beauty.

In this section we will outline some of the most common language functions like *referential, negation, counting/quantifying, greetings, terms of address, honorifics, and metaphysical uses.*

Referential

The *referential* function of language is used to identify objects in the world. It is one of the primary uses of language. It can be verbal or non-verbal, and is used to establish the presence of something within social interaction. For example we use gestures to point to an object that we want. An infant usually does this before developing speech. When human beings interact they point to material and non-material objects in the world. Nouns and noun phrases are metalinguistic categories used to describe person, places, things, and ideas. They shouldn't be confused with the actual function, which is more focused on meaning and purpose. In everyday vernacular, we assume words to be a natural part of the objects they refer to. We don't separate the label (signifier) from the object (the signified). However, there is not an inherent connection and the signifiers are arbitrary. When we refer to a physical object called "chair" it could easily be referred to in some other way.

Negation

Another common language function is *negation*. Negation is the act of rejecting a proposition, taking an opposite stance, or falsifying a claim. While languages negate in different ways, the act of negation is common to all languages. In English, sentences are negated with the common negations like "no, "not," neither/nor," and so forth. However, English, as you may remember from elementary school, never uses more than one negative to make a point. Arabic on the other hand has three different words for negation in the past, present, and future. Some languages, like Spanish, use double negatives for making the negation more unequivocal. However, in Standard English, the use of double negatives is considered incorrect because of the influence of philosophy and how double negatives function mathematically and logically. The mathematical and logical function of two negatives ultimately makes a positive statement. Consider the following sentences:

> ★No one never goes to the store. (Logical fallacy: This would mean "Everyone goes to the store.")

> No one ever goes to the store. (Negative)
> Someone never goes to the store. (Negative)
> Everyone goes to the store.

> ★I don't have no money. (Logical fallacy: This would mean "I have money.")

> I don't have any money. (Negative)
> I have no money. (Negative)
> I have money.

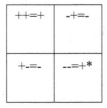

FIGURE 11.1 Logical and Mathematical Properties

In these two situations, the negative word logically cancels out the negative, resulting in the positive formation, which would be acceptable. The matrix in Figure 11.1 reflects the Standard logical and mathematical properties indexed by the Standard English form.

   This final square, with the asterisk, is not possible in Standard English. Generally, it can be seen as logically confusing, so it is avoided. However, for languages not based on this technical logic, double negatives can perform an emphatic function. They can, perhaps, emphasize the negative aspect or some languages may require it as a form of agreement within the sentence. Consider the following interaction between an African-American child speaking AAE and a teacher of "Standard" English:

CHILD: She ain't make **NO::: sense**
TEACHER: You mean, "She **doesn't** make any sense"
CHILD: Yeah, **but,** She ain't make **NO::: sense**

In this example, the teacher corrects the child because she/he assumes that the use of double negatives is incorrect based on her perception of what counts as correct in Standard English. However, the child's response shows that she is using the function differently to emphasize the degree of "not making sense." So, grammatically, the double negative is not "wrong" in the structural sense of grammar, nor is it logically wrong when we look at its uses across activities. The double negative in many languages does not fit the model in the figure above. In fact, many regional dialects of English, like African-American English shown above, use double negatives.

   Whereas prescriptive grammar, that which is taught as "Standard" in schools, is assumed to be normal, even the most renowned masters of the English language use double negatives. Philosophy, logic, mathematics, and science has influenced how we view language rules. However, the human mind can't be reduced to "machine-like" meaning-making. Human language is very capable of going beyond binary-based values like 1 or 0, TRUE or FALSE. Language is much more complicated. There is a large gray area in meaning-making. The use of multiple negatives to express emphasis is evident in Shakespeare's plays. For example, consider the lines of Viola in "*Twelfth night*":

> By innocence I swear, and by my youth I have one heart, one bosom and one truth, And that no woman has; *nor never none*
>   Shall mistress be of it, save I alone. And so adieu, good madam: never more Will I my master's tears to you deplore.
> (Shakespeare, Twelfth night, Act 3, Scene 1)

Likewise, John Rickford, in a pamphlet put out by the *Linguistic Society of America*, noted that double negatives in African-American English may have been derived from non-standard Englishes of indentured servants who interacted with African slaves (Rickford, LSA Pamphlet). Other varieties of English have also been noted to use the double negative for emphasis. Some languages, by their very logic, do not allow double negatives, as with the case of Standardized English varieties. However, many other languages, by their logic, allow the double-negative construction for emphasis or possibly by necessity. For example, compare the logic of Standard English above, with the logic of many languages that utilize double negation for emphasis (Figure 11.2).

In this logical scheme, there is no confusion on the use of double negatives. It is still negative, unlike the formalized logic of standardized varieties.

Negation is used worldwide, however, it operates on a variety of logics. Negation, itself, is a logic that seems to be a universal function of language. While the use of single or double negatives can have different meanings, the use of the initial negative serves to reject a proposition, take an opposite stance, or falsify a claim. For children negation is one of the fundamental ways in which they discover meaning through experience. It is fundamental to the process of inductive learning. When a child wants something but doesn't have the words to refer to it, he or she can use a negation and a gesture to say what they don't want or what they don't mean. When negation is combined with the referential function, you have a system that affirms and negates. This is a system of trial and error to make meaning. Students of any second language, no doubt, have an understanding of negation, if even the ability to say "no." However, their underlying logical scheme may be different, hence the use of constructions like double negatives.

++=+	-+=-
+-=-	--=-

FIGURE 11.2 Logic of Double Negatives

Counting and Quantifying Functions

While all languages of the world have some type of quantifying system, or *numeracy* practices, there is variation in how systems represent number and perform quantitative functions. Like words, numbers are not a natural part of the objects in the world. They are systems used by people to categorize, group, and analyze ideas. While counting seems so natural and common sense, even innate, the variety of systems is evidence that they are socially constructed. Like all categories, numeracy is socially constructed to solve problems and accomplish concrete goals. Some languages, especially in cultures that have traditional counting systems like the base 10 system (e.g., the Arabic numeral system), base 60 (e.g., ancient Sumerian), or base 20 (e.g., Mayan) put an emphasis on the ability to accurately quantify things into discrete numerical categories that account for "countable" objects in the world. From these categories, more elaborate mathematical functions can be developed. However, these number systems, and counting itself, are representations of a universal quantifying function. While the underlying purpose of quantification can be considered universal, the symbolic system is local. Even if the system is pervasive, like the decimal system, it still should be understood as a situated and relative system of representation.

According to Daniel Everett, the Pirahã, a people group in the Amazon jungle, do not have a conventional counting system and they don't perform quantifying functions in standard ways. In fact, they do not have words for numerals, and thus grammatically do not have a way to count or account for numbers. There are no words or grammatical forms for quantifying either. Portuguese-speaking traders frequently exploit this vulnerability. While they do make comparisons (e.g., between a big fish and two small fish), no system of numeracy seems to exist (Everett, 2009).

Despite claims that the Pirahã do have a *one*, *two* and *many* counting system like many languages, Everett (2005) argues that the interpretation of the language in this way only comes from decontextualized experiments. In fact, after long attempts to train the Pirahã to count, they have difficulty with numeracy. Everett also states that this does not mean that the Pirahã do not have some way of quantifying. For example, the Pirahã regularly quantify distances in the jungle, measurements for building homes, and making textiles; however, it has been a challenge to fully predict a coherent system of quantification in Pirahã.

With respect to the universality of quantification functions and numeracy, Pirahã is an anomaly. Among the world's languages it is perhaps the only known language where the existence of quantification and numeracy practices is contested. Another unique feature found in Pirahã is how it morphologically codes empirical knowledge. Each verb contains a morpheme that indicates how a speaker came to knows a particular set of information. Thus, Pirahã has a grammatically built-in citation system. Everett (2009) attributes many of these fascinating structural features of Pirahã to their worldview or *ideologies* (ideas about the world).

One of the core values that inform Pirahã ideologies through language form is the *immediacy of experience principle*. This posits that the Pirahã are concerned only with that which is in their immediate context, and hence do not have a need for counting. Counting and quantifying allows for comparison across time and space, yet the Pirahã don't seem to do this because they don't perceive a need to (Frank, Everett, Fedorenko, & Gibson, 2008).

The underlying value and purpose for quantifying functions is precision. The need for precision in numeracy is found in systems of measurement. Sometimes, however, languages do not need to speak with such specificity, and in fact, sometimes that is counterproductive. Think about the ability to quantify sugar, for example. Sugar is generally considered a mass noun. Mass nouns are not counted as individual units or pieces, but rather are quantified in block measurements. Sugar, for example, is only talked about in terms of *a cup of sugar* or *a pound of sugar* or *a lot of sugar*. It doesn't make sesnse to speak of *one sugar or *two sugars*. In fact, the plural "sugars" is considered awkward and is never used formally. It is not customary to speak of individual grains or crystals of sugar. In English, there is a distinction made between count nouns and mass nouns. The following table shows the two different categories (Table 11.4).

Looking at Table 11.4, we can see that mass nouns are never plural. They need to be measured as in "a handful of rice" where "the handful" is a count noun. Syntactically, "of rice" is a prepositional phrase, which belongs to the noun phrase "a handful of rice." Thus, mass nouns must be measured and cannot be counted individually which is why they do not have plurals. Liquids, grains, and similar types of words are all in the category of mass nouns. Count nouns, on the other hand, can be counted individually. Discrete nouns that can be counted can be pluralized. Linguists and anthropologists have long distinguished the two categories of mass nouns and count nouns. Whorf (1956) was among the first to note this type of distinction, which was taken up in his theory that language shapes our cultures and even determines our thoughts. Whorf supposed that because of these grammatical distinctions made in the language, it required different grammatical

TABLE 11.4 Count and Mass Nouns

COUNT NOUNS: *Stone, person, handful, book, cat, tree, shoe, chair*		MASS NOUNS: *Sugar, rice, water, milk, furniture*	
Number or quantifier word	Example	Number or quantifier word	Example
(plurality)	"books"	Cup	"a cup of water"
Couple	"a couple handfuls"	Some	"some milk"
Few	"a few stones"	Little	"a little rice"
A	"a stone"		
Five	"five trees"		
Multiple	"multiple chairs"		

structures. Notice how the distinction above does not allow us to say ★"five waters" or ★"a few milks."

Actually, mass nouns, like sugar, are not always mass nouns. Language functions in such a way that new terms and uses are appropriated. Coffee and tea (most likely coffee) drinkers in New England may very well talk about *one sugar* or *two sugars*. This is because the unit of measurement would be a sugar cube, and, since it is a common cultural experience to add cubes to your coffee, one could talk about them as *sugars*, thereby dropping the measurement word "cube." It is also very possible that in a science lab there would be much talk about sugars. In fact, there are very specific types of sugars like *glucose, fructose*, and *sucrose*. These are only three sugars that are very common. Likewise, a baker may talk about sugars as well. In fact, it is very important to know which sugar you use. Brown, white, and confectioners (or powdered) sugars are some of the more common in amateur baking. Thus, the mass nouns and count nouns are not simply discrete categories of nouns, but rather help us to culturally talk about significant amounts of objects that need to be measured. Rice, meat, and several other words fall into this category in English. In more general uses, they are not counted, but measured. However, in some contexts, they may become a count noun, where they can be counted.

Mandarin, requires classifier words before almost all of its nouns, though this is not to say that languages with classifiers like Mandarin do not have count and mass nouns like English (Yi, 2009). The classifier system is quite complex. The most general would be "gè." So when referring to one object, it would be "yī gè ___." In Mandarin yīshítou (literal translation: "one stone") is considered incorrect since a classifier is needed. Table 11.5 lists several common Mandarin classifier words.

There are many ways languages count or quantify. Sometimes this is based on mass and count nouns, and many linguists argue all languages have this distinction, and even Pirahã seems to have this distinction (Everett, 2005). Sometimes there are classifier systems (which may include count and mass nouns). Sometimes there are not even specific numbers, but rather proportional relationships. However, all languages have numeracy practices of some type for the purpose of quantification.

Greetings

Greetings are a normative language function found in all observed languages of the world. Human beings have devised greetings in order to accomplish initial contact with each other. While the greetings function is universal, there is tremendous variation in how it is performed. Depending on the relationships and situation, the greetings function has a wide range of implicit and explicit rules. For example, greeting relatives and friends would be considerably different from formal greetings found in the workplace. Even if greetings across contexts appear to share a common form, the affective dimensions can vary significantly. Technology can also mediate

TABLE 11.5 Chinese Classifiers

Classifier	Approximate English translation*	Example
Shape or noun category (similar to English count nouns)		
个 *Gè*	General classifier, for people, time, and abstract nouns	一 个 人 *yī gè rén* "one person" 一 个 月 *yī gè yuè* "one month" 一 个 问题 *yī gè wèntí* "one question"
支 *Zhī*	Something that is long and thin	一 支 笔 *yī zhī bǐ* "one pen"
块 *Kuài*	Lump	一 块 石头 *yī kuài shítou* "one stone"
张 *Zhāng*	Sheet	一 张 纸 *yī zhāng zhǐ* "one sheet of paper"
Container or weight of a noun (similar to mass nouns)		
杯 *Bēi*	Cup	一 杯 水 *yī bēi shuǐ* "one cup of water"
瓶 *Píng*	Bottle	一 瓶 水 *yī píng shuǐ* "one bottle of water"
碗 *Wǎn*	Bowl	一 碗 饭 *yī wǎn fàn* "one bowl of rice"
包 *Bāo*	Bag	一 包 饭 *yī bāo fàn* "one bag of rice"
斤 *Jīn*	Pound (approximate)	一 斤 饭 *yī jīn fàn* "one pound of rice"
Number of nouns		
双 *Shuāng*	Pair	一 双 鞋子 *yī shuāng xiézi* "one pair of shoes"
套 *Tào*	Set	一 套 衣服 *yī tào yīfu* "one set of clothes
些 *Xiē*	Several	一 些 衣服 *yī xiē wèntí* "several questions"

the nature, function, and purpose of greetings. For example, greetings through a phone, instant messenger, or e-mail are different depending on the relationships and situation. Gender norms also impact greetings in terms of physical contact, space, and what is considered appropriate practice. Other norms that inevitably impact greetings are age, status, and honorifics.

Consider the first time you meet a stranger, or even someone you've had minimal contact with. What do you do? Do you shake hands? Do you hug? Do you kiss on the cheek? Do you bow? These are some common greeting conventions found around the world. For example, in Korea, sometimes a slight (or deep) bow is important depending on the status and age difference of the participants. When two people are greeting each other, the younger person is expected to initiate the greeting as a sign of respect toward the elder. It should be evident that the underlying relationship plays a significant role in how the greeting is accomplished. However, different cultures weigh different factors when it comes to the appropriateness of the greetings. For example, standing up when an elder enters the room may be considered as a sign of respect in one culture or a sign of disrespect in another. The same can be applied to gender. In many orthodox religious communities, there is virtually no physical contact when members of the opposite sex greet each other. If a male initiates a handshake it may be considered disrespectful, and vice versa.

These differences can be seen not only transnationally but also between urban and rural settings. For example, it is common in rural communities to greet everyone who passes by. One might nod, wave, or offer a simple "hello." In many countryside areas of the United States, these are not considered token greetings and could even be followed up with a small conversation beginning with "Hey there! How are you?" In the countryside, this requires a response. The greeter asked a question, and a response is needed (often with another question) to complete the greeting. In more metropolitan urban areas, however, "How are you?" is often not a question, but a standard greeting to a passerby. Many country-folk, who move to the city, or even visit, might be surprised or even offended by the seemingly distant and impersonal greeting. The greeter might think, "How come there was no chance for a response to the question?" So, the simplest of greetings, seemingly so normal, can vary within a region. Thousands of languages have words and phrases similar to "hello," and though they may not be direct translations, they serve the same greeting function (Runner, 2012).

Like all language functions, greetings index worldviews and histories of the communities who use them. For example, many greetings from around the world are rooted in sacred invocations of blessing and/or peace. In many Spanish-speaking cultures, it is appropriate, often necessary, to greet someone with *benedicion* or *Dios te bendiga*. This may be found in English-speaking cultures only in religious contexts, like churches when one would say "Blessings" or "God bless you." Peace is extended in much of the Arabic-speaking cultures, and in Islamic communities as well with *as-salamu alaykum* (السلام عليكم) and the response *wa alaikum assalaam* (و عليكم السلام) meaning "peace and blessings be upon you" and "upon you be peace." The Hebrew greeting *shalom* (שלום) or the extended version *shalom aleikhem* (שלום עליכם), which is similar to Arabic, is also regularly used. While greetings are a universal language function, they are executed in a variety of ways depending on local customs and values. It is important to explicitly discuss this variation with second language learners in order to help them appropriate the greeting function in their new community.

Terms of Address

The variation in greetings was determined by the situation as well as the closeness or distance in the social relationship. Language functions typically carry with them implicit and/or explicit markers of social status. There are numerous factors that could mark social status and this impacts another closely related language function: *terms of address*, or how we address another person. In many languages this is encoded morphosyntactically, and in other languages it is marked lexically through the use of titles.

One of the most pervasive ways terms of address differentiate status is through the variations in the second person pronoun: *you*. This used to be a feature of Old English where it marked "thee" and "thou." Many Indo-European and Romance languages (e.g., Spanish, French, and Farsi) distinguish between formal and informal uses of "you." One example of terms of address is the Spanish use of *tu*. In informal talk amongst peers, the *tu* form can be used to address the other. This also impacts how one conjugates verbs with the informal *tu* being different from the formal *usted*. The following list of verbs shows the difference in the way different verbs would be conjugated, depending on who is being addressed (Table 11.6).

Likewise, French has a respect form very similar to that explained above where *tu* is similar to the Spanish *tu* and *vous* is similar to the *usted* form. The use of formal language or informal language can be used to mark difference or build solidarity in status. In French social interactions, there is significantly more complexity than simply *tu* (T) being informal and *vous* (V) being a formal term of address. Brown and Gilman (1960) have noted the complex social organization created by the uses of *tu* and *vous* forms in French. Whereas, intuitively, we would assume that informal T forms would be used when speaking to an inferior or in building solidarity with peers and V forms would be used to address superiors and in distancing from peers, Brown and Gilman noted an interesting complication in French. In Table 11.7, they describe the uses of T and V forms in French.

As seen in this table, T and V forms can be used for many different relationships; however, there is a complication that emerges. Namely, if there is a superior, with whom one is comfortable with, and therefore building a close relationship based on solidarity (top left box), then one has to decide whether the T form is used (since there is solidarity) or the V form is to be used (since the person is of a higher

TABLE 11.6 Spanish "You"

Infinitive	Usted form (formal)	Tu form (informal among peers)
estar "to be"	¿Como esta usted?	¿Como estas?

TABLE 11.7 T and V Form Tensions in French

Position/Solidarity	Solidary	No Solidary
Superior position	Conflict between T and V forms.	Use the V form.
Equal position	Use the T form.	Use the V form.
Inferior position	Use the T form.	Conflict between T and V forms.

status). The opposite is also true (bottom left corner) where a superior must decide whether to use the T form to show that he is a superior talking to an inferior, or the V form because there is distance in the relationship. Examples of the first relationship would be a son talking to a father. There is a clear status difference, yet the relationship is very close and it changes over time. In addition, the situation may dictate which form to use. For example, if the father is in a disciplinarian stance or a more brotherly posture. An officer speaking to a soldier where there is a hierarchical, distanced relationship is another example. Brown and Gilman indicate that in standard French usage, these decisions are made based on solidarity, not status, a change from earlier assumptions. Thus, the two complications would be resolved based on solidarity rather than status, so using the T form likely resolves the father–son relationship and the officer–soldier relationship is resolved by using the V form. Thus, in Table 11.8, the forms are resolved, as solidarity trumps status.

This has clear implications for teacher–student relations, especially language learners. When coming from a framework like this, where forms of address are highly important, students and teachers must reconcile a relationship that is either based on status or solidarity, with status being the dominant form. In English, we can use formal titles such as Mr., Miss, Ms., Mrs., Dr., or some other title marker to establish a more formal, yet distant, relationship. Teachers rarely speak this way to students; however, it is normative for students to use these titles when addressing teachers. Perhaps, this dynamic shifts during graduate school when students begin to address their mentors on a first name basis. Nevertheless, this transition is not universal and sometimes unpredictable.

The decision to use a formal title or a first name is based on a convergence of interpersonal factors and societal expectations. Beyond the terms of address, it impacts one's speech style and word choice throughout the conversations. These are decisions we consciously or subconsciously make all the time. How do we begin an e-mail to a professor? How about our boss? A customer? These different relationships change over time as well. If you become closer to your boss you may address him or her by the first name. In Spanish and French, and many other languages, however, the difference is made at the morphological level, changing the form of the words. Thus, within these languages, the ideas of solidarity and status are made apparent through linguistic structure. When working with second language learners from these frames of reference, understanding how language functions as a marker of solidarity and status is critical to English learning.

TABLE 11.8 T and V Forms in Modern French (Brown & Gilman, 1960)

Position/Solidarity	Solidary	Not Solidary
Superior position	Use the T form.	Use the V form.
Equal position	Use the T form.	Use the V form.
Inferior position	Use the T form.	Use the V form.

The same issues are present even though they are accomplished differently and with varying norms. Terms of address serve as significant indicators of social relations. The complexities of human relations are linguistically marked in both static and dynamic forms. While a language like French has six different relationship forms, other languages are even more complicated in how they mark relationships through language.

Honorifics

In examining *greetings* and *terms of address* functions across languages, we noticed that issues of status and solidarity were prominent. Another key ingredient in this equation was how language functions mark status and solidarity through *honorifics*. Honorific language is a specialized group of words, or lexicon, that is used for the sole purpose of marking social difference (e.g., economic class, education level, political hierarchy). For example, the Javanese language has six different honorific levels. Irvine (1998, p. 53) draws from Errington (1988, pp. 90–91) to describe how the same sentence is constructed based on the difference of the social status of the speaker and addressee. In the following example, the different levels are not solely linguistic levels. Rather, they are socially and ideologically constructed categories that are grammatically expressed on the sentence level. Note that in Javanese, the whole sentence is affected by these forms. Ngoko is the informal register, with Madya in the middle, and Krama as the polite and formal register.

Errington (1988) used the sentence "Did you take that much rice?" to illustrate the honorific structure in Javanese. The sentence in the formal and polite, Krama, honorific level would be as follows:

English:	Question word	"you"	"take"	"rice"	"that much"
Krama 1:	*menapa*	*nandalem*	*mundhut*	*sekul*	*semanten*
Krama 2:	*menapa*	*panjenengan*	*mendhet*	*sekul*	*semanten*

In these two levels, there are substantial differences, even though the "meaning" is the same. As one moves into the Madya, or the middle register, the "meaning" again stays the same, but the social distance is different. It is not as formal and polite.

Madya 3:	*napa*	*sampeyan*	*mendhet*	*sekul*	*semonten*
Madya 4:	*napa*	*sampeyan*	*njupuk*	*sega*	*semonten*

Finally, in the Ngoko register, the social situation is quite informal. The same sentence would be spoken very differently. The two utterances classified as Ngoko are:

Ngoko 5:	*apa*	*sliramu*	*mundhut*	*sega*	*semono*
Ngoko 6:	*apa*	*kowe*	*njupuk*	*sega*	*semono*

As can be seen, the same sentence can be said six different ways to mark different levels of social formality and politeness. Like Javanese, Japanese and Korean also have very highly developed honorific systems.

While it seems that language functions to indicate respect and politeness are universal, only some languages have an honorific system at the structural level. Nonetheless, people use language functions to index, or point to, their collective ideas, values, and *ideologies* of respect and honor.

Metaphysical

Human beings throughout history and across the world have universally pondered and philosophized about worlds beyond reach. From the ancient Egyptians, Sumerians, and Greek philosophers to the indigenous populations of the Americas, language has been developed to address people's fundamental need to make sense of metaphysical experiences. The ability to *pray* to unseen (or sometimes seen) deities is a major function in the world's languages. In English we even have the word "pray" to designate a particular type of talk, namely that which addresses a metaphysical being that we call "God." People seek to relate to beings, or higher powers, or ultimate realities in many different ways. For example, in monotheistic religions with a God, like Judaism, Islam, and Christianity, prayer is the central way to communicate with the metaphysical being, God. Talk addressed to God is functionally different than talk addressed to human beings. This may be marked by rituals (e.g., facing Mecca or closing one's eyes), respect registers (e.g., "Most Holy God, Lord of Heaven"), special language (e.g., glossolalia, or "speaking in tongues," Arabic, or Hebrew), pattern prayers (e.g., the Lord's Prayer, the Rosary, patterned morning prayers for *Fajr*), and so forth. Formal creeds like the *Apostles' Creed*, testimonies, or the *Shahada* are also uses of language that differ greatly from other forms of speech.

There are many other religious and spiritual systems around the world as well. There is tremendous variation within religions, across religions, and other metaphysical discourses for solving esoteric questions that are beyond the five senses. One of the most common language functions is how it is used to communicate with the afterlife, other worlds, and other dimensions. For example, studies of *near-death experiences* and narratives suggest the impact of these discourses in contemporary cultures. It is possible to analyze these communicative events and unpack the rules and goals that constitute the activity. For example, the experiences of the Yanomamo Shaman, the Sufi mystic, the whirling Dervish, and the Hindu mystic are undoubtedly different qualitatively speaking; however, they are all communicating through some type of language with the metaphysical world. Furthermore, their "visions" and "commuiques" become artifacts that organize the cultural practices of later generations. Additionally, registers of people in trances, in heightened spiritual states, and séances are also markedly different practices. The sustainability of these language practices across time and space is a constant feature of human cultures. While there are some who deny the fundamental premise of metaphysics and its derivations (e.g., soul or "heart of language"), they cannot deny the existence of metaphysical discourses across the human experience. This categorical rejection of metaphysical language functions is in part due to the domination of modern science or *positivistic* philosophical approaches to the study of human development, cognition, language, and identity.

Metaphysical language functions may also include the use of scriptures, attributed to coming from a deity as *inspired* text (e.g., Quran, Bible, Torah). Prophets, shamans, fortunetellers, and so forth may claim to have words from the metaphysical world or entities, and thus use language to communicate from another world or another experience. The function to interact with the metaphysical world is a common, if not universal, function of language, though the actual speech events vary drastically.

Conclusion

There are many other functions of language that seem to be universal. This is not because language itself or some cognitive mechanism requires language to work in some particular way. Languages have these functions because they arise from people's need to solve authentic problems and answer deep identity questions about who they are, where they've been, and where they are going. People organize cultural activities and refer to objects in the physical world. Language is used to mediate these activities. Language is used to show respect. Language is used to greet people. Language is used to count or quantify material objects. Language is used to negate claims and propositions. We can call these "universal" functions because they share common purposes and goals across human societies. While the functions are stable and constant, there is much variation in how the goals are accomplished and how language mediates those goals.

The universal, itself, is not within the language. This has been a significant debate in linguistics. Linguistic determinism and strong forms of linguistic relativism suppose that culture is shaped, or defined, by language. Thus, language determines how people operate in culture. One alternative is that language arises from people's needs and the cultural system they construct to address them. So, the need to greet people requires that a language has a system of greeting.

This is sort of a chicken-or-egg situation. Which comes first, language or culture? This type of ontological question is perhaps the wrong question. Language and culture should not be viewed separately to begin with, hence Agar's term *languaculture*. This term complicates language and makes it less of a scientific phenomenon to study. This is only true if we reduce science to the material world and we only count knowledge that can be determined in a laboratory. This epistemological fallacy puts us in an awkward position when it comes to how language works and how human beings really use language. It prevents us from asking questions about meaning and values as it pertains to language use.

Language is not a static entity and our analysis of it should be dynamic, even if it is messy. When we move beyond the "flesh" of language (i.e., structure and form) and include its "heart" (i.e., meaning, function, and ideologies), then it becomes clear that language emerges through ALL of our needs, physical and metaphysical. Since questions of meaning and values are fundamentally non-physical, they require different kinds of tools for answering them. This is the domain of narratives, aesthetic prose, and poetry. These are language functions that are generally ignored by those assuming a narrow view of language. We will explore these functions in the coming chapters in order to reclaim both the flesh and heart of language as a single entity that resides not in the individual, but in the collective interactions of people with all their worlds.

TEACHER CASE STUDIES

Sam: Reproduction

Sam was a teacher in a predominantly Mexican-American school in a large urban city. She had been born in the city to a recent immigrant family from Palestine. She grew up in a tight-knit, traditional Palestinian-Muslim household. One day she overheard some of her middle school students talking about sex, a topic that was very uncomfortable for her. She decided to investigate how sex was typically talked about in her students' community, and then compared it with how she and her community had talked about the topic.

After talking with some of the teachers who were from the community as well as other community members she found out that it was quite normal for students to have had some sex education in school, but it was likely a taboo topic at home.

Sam learned that many of the families in her school practiced Catholicism. Because of the moral statutes within Catholicism regarding sex, the topic was generally a taboo. It was not discussed openly in the home, nor was it discussed in school. Many of the students had never had a formal explanation of sex, and thus were learning the "unofficial" version from the media and their peers. Many of her colleagues recounted euphemisms and sayings their parents told them when they were young like: *Date por valer,* or "Make yourself worthy"; *Date a respetar,* or "Give yourself respect"; or *Tu domingo siete,* which means "Don't come home pregnant." These sayings, along with others, displayed a high moral expectation, especially of the girls in the community, to avoid sex.

This taboo was all too familiar to Sam. She remembered the day when she first heard about sex in school from peers. She came home screaming! Her mother sat her down and explained, quite vaguely, about the clearly sensitive topic. Sam also knew, however, that this was a much different story than her cousins back in Palestine had. The taboo was so strong that in many Muslim countries schools were segregated between boys and girls. In fact, it was not until high school (sometimes middle school) that female instructors would teach the girls about changes to their bodies while male teachers would attempt to guide young men through puberty. Like her students, Sam noted that this taboo was largely religious, as Islam, like Catholicism, took a strong moral stance that girls should remain virgins until they were married.

In the senior year of some students in Muslim countries, there was finally a discussion of sex. In school, students would learn about the way a baby is formed in a mother's womb as well as some other sensitive information pertaining to sexuality. However, sexual intercourse would likely not be discussed directly. At this time, in the senior year of high school, many students would be engaged to marry. They would discuss the topic of sex in informal spaces. For men, it was likely among friends. They would learn about ways to ensure pregnancy, though this was clearly not the most reliable information. Most of Sam's cousins, as she later found out, were never told about sex, until they were married and it was discussed with their husbands. In fact, the extent of their sex education was about how to please their husbands with cooking, cleaning, and so forth.

Sam analyzed these taboos in her culture and in her students' cultures and recognized that there were many similarities in the underlying moral structure of sexual restrictivism. Besides the lack of sex education at home, there was no discussion of contraceptives. Again, the religious morality of Catholicism and Islam created a taboo around the use of contraceptives. While in some Muslim and Catholic-dominant societies the taboo against sex is more pronounced, in the United States, the topic of sex was more freely discussed in public settings such as the classroom. This challenged Sam to think about how the students, like herself, stand at a clash of cultures. The language function of talking about sex and reproduction in the American context was much more open than in her parents' home country. A taboo was formed regarding sex, and therefore it was rarely, if ever, explicitly talked about.

Cindy: Respect

Cindy was also a teacher in a predominantly Mexican-American community. She, herself, however, was part of the Assyrian diaspora. She knew much about her heritage, though only spoke a few words of Assyrian, which was largely used for religious and heritage purposes. While her parents spoke it occasionally with elders in the Assyrian community, she rarely spoke it with them. In fact, she noticed that much of the time her parents and other members of the Assyrian community would use English for the nouns in a sentence, but may use Assyrian prepositions and other grammatical words. She thought this was because Assyrian was quite an old language and therefore may not have needed particular words. It was easiest to borrow the words from English.

One very interesting thing she knew about Assyrian was that there were few time words. In Assyrian there were not words to fit the calendar her family used in the United States. English words were needed for "week" and "month" as well as the names of days of the week and months. Assyrian, however, did have names for relational time words like "today," "tomorrow," and "yesterday," as well as the times of the day. Still, the Assyrian community had to adopt the new English time words to fit into the culture.

After spending time in her school community she began to notice some interesting similarities and differences between her students and her own culture. Many of the students' families would be late to report card pick-ups, parent–teacher conferences, school meetings, and other community events. In fact, she noticed once, while attending a church mass in the community as per a friend's request, that the mass didn't start on time and that many members of the congregation were standing talking in the foyer, even once it was clear that mass should be beginning. This had always been one point of tension Cindy faced in the school community. She thought people were always late! Yet, she reflected on her own time growing up. She would always be on time for church, especially, but to appointments and other meetings as well. Her family never rushed out of church, but they would stick around and talk to other people. Cindy thought it was ironic that in the Assyrian community, though they lacked some time words, they had a high value on punctuality.

She also recognized that many of the Mexican-American families at her school were late not because they didn't value punctuality, but rather because they valued relationships and quality time spent with others. Another emphasis she saw in the community in which she worked was that the families seemed to be much more invested in their families, community, and religion than work. Work seemed to take a back seat sometimes so that these other obligations could be taken care of. These different functions of time were very fascinating to Cindy. She learned a lot by analyzing how time is seen differently in different communities. Ideas like punctuality and tardiness are often defined by the values of an institution (e.g., school) rather than the values of the community. Cindy saw that this may have some implications for her parent–teacher conferences and school meetings. Namely, that punctuality could not be defined by looking at a clock, but rather in terms of relationship building.

QUESTIONS/ACTIVITIES

1. Have students in your classroom gather data about different types of greetings, or some other function of language. For example, first have your students write about how they greet someone. How do they greet their mother? How do they greet their friends? How do

they greet a stranger? Students should attempt to describe different types of greetings and reflect on why they greet people the way they do. Next, ask students to investigate how someone from a different culture greets people. What do the students notice?

2.   Talk with a group about how you describe emotions. How would you describe "anger"? What synonyms are there for "anger"? What is the difference between these synonyms? How about sadness? How about happiness? Rank the following in terms of severity compared to others:

Angry
Irritated
Irate
Enraged
Mad
Furious
Upset
Livid

Compare with others. What differences were there? Can you rank terms for sadness?

12

NARRATIVES

Living a Narrated Life

LEARNING GOALS

1. Understand the role of narratives in our daily lives.
2. Analyze narrative structures using two different frameworks.
3. Analyze grand narratives to understand cultural values.
4. Use narrative analysis to study classroom narratives.
5. Use narrative inquiry to create opportunities to learn about students' funds of knowledge.

KEY TERMS/IDEAS: verisimilitude, moral stance, embeddedness, linearity, tellership, tellability, narrative

> *"The planet does not need more 'successful' people. The planet desperately needs more peacemakers, healers, restorers, storytellers and lovers of all kinds. It needs people to live well in their places. It needs people with moral courage willing to join the struggle to make the world habitable and humane and these qualities have little to do with success as our culture has set."*
>
> Dalai Lama

Introduction

Of all the language functions, narratives are arguably the most comprehensive practices that provide insight into local cultural expectations and norms. Narratives are a window into tacit, hidden, and "common sense" cultural practices. While narratives vary significantly with respect to content and genre, the process of narrative across human cultures is less varied. The range of narratives falls between two categories:

1. narrative as *emergent*; and
2. narrative as *performance*.

In terms of identity development, interpersonal affiliation, and ideological solidarity, narratives are the preeminent cultural tools. It is through narratives that we develop, break, and fix relationships. Whether narratives are micro or macro, our lives a continuous biographical sketch that is constantly reviewed, revised, and retold. In organizing learning in the classroom, narratives are the single most important way to get to know students, develop sociocultural language proficiency, and uncover hidden cultural resources to mediate second language learning.

Narrative is a forum for giving structure and coherence to the uncertainties, tensions, and challenges of everyday life. We use narrative to examine and re-examine surprising, disturbing, and unexpected events. Through narrative we show what we care about, what we collectively aspire to, and what we count as legitimate or illegitimate (Razfar, 2012c). The moral and ideological stances are practiced and lived through narratives (Ochs, 2004). As we navigate and position ourselves in the social world, we constantly make decisions loaded with affect, attachments, and ideological commitments. These decisions induce us to take positions vis-à-vis authority or authoritative voices. We must decide to either claim or disavow authority and to align or disalign with others in social interaction (Gee, 2008). We call these decisions *stances* defined simply as the smallest unit of social action (be it verbal or non-verbal) through which social actors simultaneously evaluate objects, position subjects (themselves and others), and align with other subjects, with respect to any salient dimension of the sociocultural field (Du Bois, 2007). More critically, stances involve the explicit or implicit invoking of a system of values that create relations of equivalence or difference (Fairclough, 2003; Kress, 1995).

Think about the wide range of narratives we use in our daily lives. From the moment we wake up until bedtime, our lives are a continuous sequence of events filled with moral decisions and dilemmas. For the most part, we are unaware of these decisions, but we are aware of the dilemmas. When it comes to most of the mundane decisions of our lives they are rarely newsworthy or *tellable*. However, the unexpected turns and dilemmas are different. We share these stories at the dinner table, the playground, or around camp-fires. Often the stories are selected or embellished to garner a particular effect or teach a lesson. Whether the stories are more fact or more fiction is irrelevant. Narratives are always a story of what the author(s) intend to accomplish in relation to others: status, solidarity, and difference.

Different types of narratives serve varying functions and purposes depending on the goals of people. These *genres* of narrative consist of different goals, styles, and literary conventions such fiction, non-fiction, aesthetics, dramatic arts, and other types of performances. Each of these genres are bound by local cultural practices and mediated by situated goals, rules, and structures. For example, the genre of bedtime stories is distinct from the middle-class, dinner-table genre. Bedtime stories are often not about one's daily experiences whereas dinner-table narratives are geared toward personal issues of the day. In our professional lives, we often occupy multiple positions of authority and responsibility. Sometimes we are expected to present or report our work to those who are in a position to evaluate it. Other times we use narrative to manage those who we wield power over. In each case we employ narratives and embark on a co-authorship of a story with the respective audiences. Bedtime stories, novels, and testimonies are other examples of common narrative genres we engage in.

Similar to other language functions, narratives are cultural productions that serve multiple purposes. One of the key purposes of narratives is to codify collective perspectives, moral values, ideological stances, and shared information regarding events. Sometimes these narratives are organized through prose, poetry, oral, or written mediums. It serves as a bridge to the past and connects future generations. With each passing of the torch, each generation, each individual has an opportunity to insert themselves into the narrative. This process is a dialectical process whereby each rendition is a re-invention of the self but not totally free from the constraints of the past. When we look across the world, we notice a wide variety of grand narratives. For example, some of the grand Russian narratives are written in large volumes such as *Anna Karenina* or *The brothers Karamazov* by Leo Tolstoy and Fyodor Dostoevsky respectively. The Russian grand narratives are markedly different from the novels of Charles Dickens, or even more different from the short stories of John Steinbeck in terms of style and length. The *One thousand and one nights*, also known as the Arabian Nights, is a contrasting example where multiple folk tales from the Islamic Golden Age begin with an initial frame story of a king (شهريار, meaning ruler or king) and his wife (شهرزاد, of noble lineage) who the king suspects of infidelity. The remaining tales are embedded within this original frame and range from one to ten lines and consist of poetry, hymns, melancholic verse, and riddles that carry moral lessons for each generation to contemplate and consider.

In modern journalistic practices, mass media and social media sites serve similar purposes of organizing our collective consciousness and choosing which events deserve attention. Each news agency, for example, paints a unique stance on shared experiences. Whether one gets news from CNN, Fox News, the Huffington Post, the Drudge Report or lesser known blogs and tabloids, the readers of these different outlets will interpret similar events with divergent ideological stances. In more indigenous communities that are detached from the trappings of electronic media, collective narratives are transmitted through oral histories, gossip lines, and personal testimonies. Whether it is gossip lines found in Central Africa or personal accounts of a shaman or medicine man meeting spirits in the Amazon jungle, oral traditions have endured and been sustained for thousands of years without the benefit of print or electronic recordings. Instead, these narratives have been sustained by the hearts of people who invested themselves in the style and message of their collective life story.

What is Narrative?

No matter what the form, type, or purpose of the narrative, all narratives are defined by a sequence of events, ideological stances, and evaluation of moral positions. The most basic criteria for what counts as a narrative is *a sequence* of events. This means that a narrative must minimally include a least two sequenced clauses. It is easiest to think of this as two chronological events that took place in the past. Even a very simple construction like the following would qualify:

The Little Red Hen baked a pie. Then she ate the pie.

The example above represents the most basic type of construction that could qualify as narrative. While sequence of events provides a good starting point for what counts as narrative, this minimal definition has been expanded to include ideological stances and moral evaluations. Some argue that all narratives, including minimal ones, have these moral evaluations, while others argue that only elaborate narratives contain moral evaluations.

We may refer to stories and narratives as having a "moral of the story." For example, think of the children's story of the *Little red hen*. It is told to children all over the United States, England, and many other places in the world. The story privileges hard work, and undoubtedly is used to teach this moral lesson. Likewise, all narratives have some type of moral evaluation and ideological stance. It is important to define what we mean by an ideological stance or moral evaluation. The stance or evaluation may be moral in the ethical sense of good or bad, but it doesn't need to be. It could very well be the part that tells us why the narrative is worthy of telling, or a narrative's *tellablity*.

All narratives, short or long, fiction or non-fiction, are used by people as symbolic resources that give coherence to their lived experiences. Through narrative activity, human beings solve their moral dilemmas, seek answers to everyday questions, and create social networks across time and space. People see themselves through the lens of narrative. Whether it is a fable like *Little red hen*, or a narrative about eating dinner yesterday, multiple narratives converge to tell a bigger story of self, community, and nation. We live to tell a story and we live through the co-construction of narrative. Every telling of a story requires the self in relation to another. Thus, narratives are not truly autobiographical as there is always a teller and an audience that is compelled to listen. Narratives display some of the foundational functions of the human language use. As we noted earlier in Chapter 5 on syntax, the assumption that grammar contained recursion was foundational to Chomskyan thought, but that was found to be untrue of at least one language, Pirahã. While

Everett claims that recursion is not found in the grammatical structure of the language, we do see narratives in Pirahã embedding ideas within other ideas. The inherent syntax of narratives function to organize ideas in the same way grammar hierarchically organizes dependent clauses in relation to independent ones. How narratives are told, when and where they are told, who they are told to, are all as relevant as the explicit storyline. We can see narratives, then, as cultural ways to communicate ideas and express thoughts. Presently, all known human cultures have been observed to have the language function of narrative, including Pirahã (Everett, 2009). Therefore, we can safely say that narrative is a universal language function.

In this chapter, we will provide a way to use narrative inquiry in the classroom to better understand students' funds of knowledge and also to more clearly understand the inextricable link between language, culture, and mind. The study of narrative helps us understand the human mind as more than organic flesh contained within the relative frame of an individual body. Instead, the mind and human cognition is principally located in the interpersonal networks of affinity, affiliation, and historical connections that transcend immediate time and space.

Narrative Inquiry

Since narratives are such an important way in which we draw upon symbolic resources to organize our life worlds, it has been the subject of interdisciplinary study including psychology (Wertsch, Bruner), sociology (Goffman), anthropology (Geertz), literature (Barthes), history (Wertsch), and education (Connelly & Clanidinin, Noddings & Withrell). Each of these disciplines have different purposes and ways of studying narratives, but they all recognize the centrality of narrative in all scales of human development: the individual, the society, and civilization.

Narrative inquiry is a form of research that is concerned with how people construct reality through culturally organized narrative activity. It is less concerned with authenticity in the "true-to-life" absolute sense. However, narrative inquiry is more concerned with the process of narrative events. Narrative inquiry is not an exact science in the sense of seeking and identifying an autonomous, absolute Truth. As Jerome Bruner (1991) states:

> Unlike the constructions generated by logical and scientific procedures that can be weeded out by falsification, narrative constructions can only achieve "verisimilitude." Narratives, then, are a version of reality whose acceptability is governed by convention and "narrative necessity" rather than by empirical verification and logical requirement, although ironically we have no compunction about calling stories true or false.
>
> (pp. 4–5)

The conventions of narrative telling are essential, and when we study them, we look for *verisimilitude*, or believability. We may call a narrative true or false, and people often do, but the burden of truth is not on the narrative itself. We assume that its telling is a version of subjective reality, rather than an absolute objective reality independent of the goals and intentions of its author(s). In this way, narratives, whether it is a first grader recounting a soccer game, a witness giving testimony in a courtroom under oath, or a paranoid schizophrenic telling seemingly disjointed and incoherent stories, are all evaluated on the basis of verisimilitude, or whether they make accounts that resemble reality, not whether or not they can be independently verified. A focus on verisimilitude, a concept similar to "believability," allows researchers to look at how each narrative resembles a reality rather than mirrors *the* reality of the researcher (thus evaluating truth and falsehood).

As Bruner noted, narratives adhere to conventions and are bound by cultural rules. This allows us to recognize different genres of narrative. It allows us to differentiate between the courtroom testimony and the first grader's story. These cultural conventions provide a way for us to understand the speaker's mastery of the narrative form, but it also provides people access to project their subjective reality through narrative. While the conventions of narrative vary from situation to situation, a good narrator will achieve verisimilitude employing and even manipulating these conventions to achieve his/her goals. Narrative is simultaneously science and art. Powerful narratives require precision of flesh (physical science), while swaying the heart of their audience. They invite people into a new subjective reality through the telling to foster a more shared and "objective" reality, or greater *intersubjectivity*.

We see the power of narrative in courtrooms when the prosecution and defense build their stories through the same evidence. Even if the objective evidence is frail or strong, a skilled attorney can rearrange the evidence through a plausible narrative that makes an impression on the hearts and minds of an indecisive jury. The attorney goes through every piece of evidence to construct a possible reality of what happened to "prove" the case in his/her client's interest. The defense attorney then gets up and builds an alternative story, using the same evidence. Remember Johnny Cochran at the end of the OJ Simpson Trial when he held up the glove and tried to put it on then dramatically declared, "If the glove doesn't fit, you must acquit!" The jury chooses between multiple narratives including their own narratives with believability trumping any sense of independently verifiable objective truth.

Much of narrative inquiry is concerned with stories that are about the self and construction of identity within social contexts. There are many areas of narrative inquiry such as autobiography, autoethnography, testimony, case studies, biography, personal narrative, life history, oral history, memoir, and literary journalism to name a few. With social media and digital literacies, this list continues to expand. In all these genres and narrative styles, the self is a principal protagonist in the journey of life. Narrative analysis, by far, is one of the richest places to look for one's subjective understanding of self in the world. The goal is not to uncover the Truth, but to understand the projected and subjective truth (small 't') of narrators.

Narrative Analysis

Narrative inquiry is both science and art. It must account for the stable and objective features of stories while maintaining the subjective variation of the narrator. This balance may seem difficult, but we do this all the time, albeit subconsciously. The unit of analysis (data) is the content and syntax of the narrative and a researcher must manage his/her subjectivity vis-à-vis the narrator's. A researcher's claims about the data are subject to verisimilitude, not verification of an objective, detached Truth. This really is a paradigmatic point. Narrative inquiry, as a qualitative methodology, grounded in the philosophy of phenomenology, does not see the social world as "True or False," "Black or White," but rather as a continuum of relative truths and falses and the shades of gray that is meaning-making. As researchers and teachers attending to the language use of students, we seek to understand our students in these spaces of tension and open-ended questions knowing that we are interested in not only who our students are but who and how they are becoming through lived narrative. We may ask "What are the narratives they live by and what are the the narratives they die by?" This question points to the core of narrative in identity construction.

Collecting Narratives

There are a variety of methods for collecting narratives for research purposes. They are recorded in field-notes, elicited through interviews, and found in written archival data. Teachers are in a unique position to be "researchers" and ethnographers of their students' lived narratives. Literally, everyone has a story and everyone is a narrative. More accurately, everyone is multiple open narratives that are in the process of being written and re-written. There are many modes in the classroom through which these narratives emerge. For example, journals allow privacy and time to write and construct accounts. Think-out-louds and show-and-tells allow students to tell stories in the public space of the classrooms. High school students can write plays, or even make videos and music videos. Freestyle raps and spoken word poetry are becoming even more popular to be used to express the self in both schools and out-of-school contexts. These are only a few ways in which artistic and expressive classroom activities could be created to elicit personal narratives, with each bound by its own style, rules, and conventions.

As students master these forms and techniques, they are provided with new ways to construct their realities, and teachers can collect these to learn about the ways these students live, and the realities in which they construct. If a student lives in a reality constructed by narratives in hip-hop culture, and structures his or her reality in a similar manner, we as teachers need to understand this reality. This is not to say in our literature classes we ignore classical or "old school" narrative genres. We need to learn the affordances of the stories by which our students live and leverage them into different learning goals and new genres of expression. The analysis of narratives helps build such bridges.

Analyzing Narratives

We have throughout this book shown that language and culture are inseparable, hence the *languaculture* (you must be getting used to this word by now). We know that languacultures are stable and varied at the same time. Cultural variation is the rule and the expectation from a sociocultural view of language. Even grammatical structures are bound by cultural activities (Everett, 2009). Therefore we can look at narratives as a cultural tool that also has structural constraints. Understanding these boundaries helps us understand the category of "narrative" across all cultures. It is a universal of human function, yet its form varies depending on local goals, purposes, and needs. While all ELs in classrooms tell narratives, they often draw on divergent cultural and ideological frames.

The analysis of narrative provides insight into the implicit and subconscious aspects of culture that participants are not aware of until they engage in narrative activity, but even more so when they are analyzed (Bell, 2002). Over the years, narrative analysis has helped counter deficit views of non-dominant populations and their narrative practices that are often dismissed in school settings. Shirley Heath's pioneering ethnography of Trackton and Roadville (1983) noted the different literacy practices of the White and Black families in two mining communities. She meticulously showed how the aesthetic and competitive narrative styles of the Black children in her study were cognitively advanced and displayed the type of abstract thinking typical of academic settings. In addition, it combined rich aesthetic and performative style, which was not valued in school literacy practices.

Throughout this book we have emphasized the semiotic aspect of language (question #3 and the issue of meaning). Since all narratives are a selection of possible renditions, the choices we make also have meaning. The what, where, when, why, and how of a narrative depends on what the narrator is trying to accomplish. On the surface, the content of a narrative might be the same, but the situation and delivery is not. These choices impact the moral stances present in the narrative. The use of passive and active voice in English is one of the common ways moral evaluations and ideological stances are made within simple and elaborate narratives. In English, if a narrative is told almost completely in passive voice, the agency of people is obfuscated and the focus turns to impersonal events. Take for example a simple narrative such as "The ball was hit by Jim," and its content equivalent, "Jim hit the ball." In both cases the sequence of events and the objective information appear to be the same in that a ball was hit and Jim did the hitting. However, in a story, likely the latter would be used if the emphasis was on Jim. If Jim was the protagonist, we would make sure we highlight the fact that he did the hitting. However, if, perhaps, the ball hit a window and broke it, maybe the passive voice would be used to acknowledge that Jim hit the ball, but it wasn't intentional. Through the use of a passive voice, Jim's culpability is blunted. These choices are important to understand meaning in a narrative.

One of the keys to narrative analysis is to treat the narrative as a whole. While we typically think of a narrative as a self-contained unit with internal coherence (*intratextual*) in order to properly analyze the "whole" narrative, it is important to make connections to external texts as well (*extratextual*). Both the intratextual and the extratextual combine to create a fuller account of the narrative and analyst aim to bring cohesion to both dimensions (Halliday & Hasan, 1976). The analysis needs to account for the ideological contexts of the narratives by asking, "What are the underlying and historic values of the narratives?" This question can be asked of both fiction and non-fiction narratives. In more *performative* narratives the moral and ideological stances tend to be more singular, while in more *emergent* and *embedded* narratives these stances are often multiple and even contradictory. This is a normal part of emergent story-telling as human beings try to give coherence to moral dilemmas, ideological tensions, and unsettled conflicts.

G.K. Chesterton, the renowned literary critic and journalist, in his essay "The ethics of elfland," in *Orthodoxy* (1908), wrote that works of fiction were superior, in many ways, to the world in which we live. Fairytales give us a base of morals and values that we continue to live by. We live these stories in our daily lives, in our minds, and in our hearts. Many of the fairytales, myths, fables, and so forth that we learn as children are to teach moral lessons and ideological frames. Sometimes the lessons are meant to be universal; however, most of the time they have a specific context. For example, we may teach the fable of the *Boy who cried wolf* in order to teach the universal moral lesson of always telling the truth. However, we rarely complicate the moral dilemma. We rarely, while reading to children, makes distinctions between small lies, big lies, or even times when telling the truth could be harmful to an individual or the collective. If someone asks, "Do I look ugly?" How does one respond? Fairytales, as a fictional genre, are not constrained by the material reality of life, and allow for projection into other timescales, spaces, metaphysical realities, and idealistic possibilities. Chesterton notes that the limits of fairytales are the limits of our imagination. He notes that the breaking of some mathematical concepts is an example of our finite imagination. While the boundaries of imagination are arguable, it is difficult to argue that the symbolic representations of "unlimited thoughts" are bound in cultural systems.

Understanding the cultural activity systems through which narratives are constructed requires participatory ethnographic methods. These methods rely on deep interpersonal relationships built with communities over long periods of time. Like all meaningful relationships, it is built through mutual trust and more importantly solidarity building. These relationships extend beyond the individuals and include the often tension-filled histories of the communities from which the individuals come from. This type of contact challenges the ideologies, worldviews, and assumptions of each individual participant. Given that variation is the rule, we should assume each student will have a unique stance and a different narrative than the teacher. It is often helpful to start with a common narrative that all students can connect with, then move into the variation. It is through engaging the variations that intersubjectivity, shared understanding, and ultimately solidarity is achieved. This variation will be both in terms of narrative content and style. For example, commons modes of classroom narrative delivery in U.S. schools such as reading out loud in a circle, author's chair, or book reports may feel strange to non-U.S. students. In contrast, we often find a distinct performative style in telling and sharing narratives. This is an important point of consideration in narrative analysis.

When a story is told to different audiences, how does it differ? For example, how does one tell a story at a family gathering versus on public television? What do these differences say about the values of the speaker(s) and audience(s)? What values are being emphasized? Why might these values be emphasized in certain situations?

In the analysis of narratives, a close study of linguistic and paralinguistic devices such as tone, word choice, pauses, and so forth is important. In terms of moral evaluations and ideological stances, examining multiple narratives and establishing the similarities and differences helps reveal the contradictions and attempts to achieve cohesion. This further shows how identity is constructed as well as issues of status, solidarity, and difference.

Narrative Structure

As we have seen earlier in this book, we can study the structure of language to help understand function and meaning. First, we must account for *the code* and *performative* qualities: the FLESH and SKIN of language (Questions 1 and 2 from Chapter 1). Second, we must account for the *semiotic* and *ideological* dimensions (Questions 3 and 4 from Chapter 1). In order to do this, we have located these questions within the broader research paradigms related to narrative.

While there is quite a bit of variation in how narrative analysis is used in the social sciences, most of it can be divided into two broad categories that in practice exist along a continuum. It is typical of the broader approaches to language:

1. those who emphasize structure, form, and the flesh of language;
2. those who emphasize meaning, relationships, and the heart of language.

Exclusively structural approaches to narrative, which we will call "Type 1" for now, was championed by the early sociolinguistic community emerging from the social turn and the reaction to Chomsky's generative grammar approach to language, which was an approach that never looked at human narrative activity (e.g., William Labov). The second type, "Type 2" narrative, has emerged from more anthropological and ethnographic approaches to narrative (e.g., Elinor Ochs, Bambi Schieffelin, and Lisa Capps). We will present both types of narrative analysis here, and show the benefits and limitations of each through model narratives illustrating both.

The Type 1 Narrative Syntax

Type 1 narrative analysis is exclusively focused on the structural components, especially the *syntax* of the narrative. When Labov set out to study narratives in the early 1970s, he was trying to see how young African-American males told stories. Of course, this was located within a broader sociopolitical context that viewed the language of African-Americans as lower status and illegitimate. As was typical of most early sociolinguistic work, Labov (and others) elicited the narratives within the walls of the Ivy League ivory tower. They asked Black children to respond to prompts in order to get a specific kind of narrative, namely *the performative* narrative. The context of the elicitation was obviously not the naturalistic environment through which narratives typically emerge. They were elicited in laboratory or office settings that for the most part were unfamiliar and strange places for the children who were asked to provide the narratives. This would be followed by an analysis of content and structure. This methodology was later critiqued for lack of authenticity and in some cases unethical treatment of subjects. Nevertheless, historically and politically, the early sociolinguists brought attention to an understudied phenomenon and non-dominant linguistic varieties.

Labov examined narratives according to six elements: *abstract, orientation, complication, evaluation, results,* and *coda* (Labov, 1972). Labov's theory searches for these six elements, though not every narrative must contain each one of these elements. To illustrate this method of studying narrative, we will use a story a teacher told about home visits she had conducted as a part of one of our action research projects that included the gathering of funds of knowledge to teach English though content integration with mathematics and science. Lisa had visited the homes of students in her classroom and was reflecting on that experience. We asked her to tell us about a specific example and how the example affected her and her students. The full text of her narrative is in the appendix.

When prompted to tell a story, with a little bit of preparation, the usual result would begin with some type of abstract, or explaining what the story is about. It doesn't have to necessarily be an explicit statement of "I'm going to tell you a story about …" but the narrative will usually have a type of summary statement. In this narrative the abstract would be in lines 1–4. Here Lisa tells us that the story is going to be about visiting a student's home and a change that happened to her and the student. The *abstract* tells us what the story is about.

The second feature of narratives is an *orientation*. This element provides additional background information about whom, what, where, and when the story takes place. It is the setting of the story. Without the orientation, the audience wouldn't know where the story fits or what the context of the story is. Often, because stories may be told in the middle of a larger conversation, these questions may already be answered. For example, if two brothers were reliving stories about growing up on a farm, they likely would not begin the story specifying a particular place since they are both oriented to that place in the conversation.

The brothers might, however, need to specify time, who was involved, and so forth. This feature, in the sample narrative, is displayed in lines 5–7. In these lines, Lisa oriented the interviewer by telling about the student and why that student was important for her to talk about. She also tells the interviewer "like the girl I told you," which is another way she oriented the narrative.

In this model of narrative analysis, all stories have some type of *complication*. A complication represents something unexpected, straying from the norm, and makes the story worthy of telling (*tellablility*). One could imagine a really "boring" and mundane story, perhaps a student rambling about what she or he did the previous day after school. To the listeners, there seems to be no point. It may seem like there is no "complication" in the sense of plot building, but something did, in fact, happen. You wouldn't have a narrative if there were not at least two sequential events. One is not enough, it needs to be complicated by a second, thus producing the narrative. In the example narrative, lines 7–16 are the complicating action. In this section the events are sequentially ordered and causally arranged. One event leads to another, which leads to another. Each consequence and its antecedent is a complicating action in the narrative.

While Labov focused his analysis on the structure and content of the narrative, the *evaluation* allows for understanding the viewpoint and stance of the speaker. The evaluation provides the speaker's rationale for telling the narrative and includes his/her moral judgments, the "moral" of the story. This is the narrator's take on the constructed set of events. The evaluation is not always explicit, and the audience may have to infer it from other non-verbal and paralinguistic cues such as a cringing face, a sigh, or a cryptic smile. Without an explicit or implicit evaluation, the purpose of telling the narrative is unclear. For example, Lisa makes evaluation statements about what she did (lines 16–19). She takes a sort of moral highroad (opposing both the mean aunt and the poverty she sees in her student) and she explains the benefits of the visit (that the student did well). Really, "I think it's both" is perhaps the best example of evaluation in this story, as it answers the topic at hand. Lisa even says, "I think," indicating her own moral stance toward the story. These would be evaluations, which tell us the reason for telling the story.

Most performative narratives contain some type of resolution to the complication. Given Labov's elicitation method in the university, the children already had a predetermined ending. The children wanted to put on a show in order to generate the maximum theatric effect and give the professor what he was looking for. The resolution is categorical, clear, and compelling for not only Labov but also anybody who will hear it far and wide. In Lisa's story we have been analyzing, the student's transformation is the resolution and the "so what" for the telling. She now greets the teacher as opposed to giving dirty looks, and she improved academically.

The final element in a narrative is the *coda*. The coda either explicitly or implicitly lets the audience know that the story has concluded. At the conclusion of a *Loony Tunes* cartoon, the curtain falls and a voice sings, "That's all folks!" and the signature "The End" flashes on the screen. This is one way we know the story has ended. Most of the time narrators begin with an abstract summarizing the story, and conclude it with a summary. Other times the narrator simply stops speaking after the point has been made. Lisa's coda was to say "So, I think it's both. Is that ok?" and the interview is complete.

Type 2: Naturalistic and Emergent Narratives

The Type 2 narrative, in contrast to Type 1, is open-ended, non-linear, emergent, and co-authored sets of events. Ochs and Capps (2001) provide a model for narrative analysis that includes both Type 1 and Type 2 forms of narrative. Most narratives in human activity are of the Type 2 variety. These are the lived narratives of our life and the framework through which we organize our thoughts, values, and position in the world. They emerge through interaction with others in the context of organized cultural activities. Narratives serve as tools to project future possibilities and identities as well. There are five dimensions that we should consider when analyzing all narratives. For each dimension, the narrative lies on a continuum.

The five dimensions of narrative presented in Table 12.1 emphasize the context of a narrative. Even Type 1 narratives are produced in a context even though Labov doesn't consider the context in his analysis. Generally, if a narrative is on the 1–2 part of the scale on all five dimensions it is a Type 1 performative narrative. That said, we still must consider the context of the narrative in our analysis. This is a fundamental difference in how language and, in this case, narrative, is viewed. The first dimension is *tellership*, which analyzes how many tellers or authors are involved in the narrative. Elicited narratives, like Type 1 narratives, have one principal author who tells the entire narrative independently. Upon closer analysis,

TABLE 12.1 Dimensions of Type 2 Narrative Analysis

Dimension	Narrative Continuum				
1. Tellership	1	2	3	4	5
	One teller			Many tellers	
2. Tellability	High tellability			Low tellability	
3. Embededness	Detached from context			Embedded in the situation	
4. Moral stance	Single message			Conflicted messages	
5. Linearity	Temporal and causal			Open and spatial	

even in the strictest interview situations, the interviewer plays some role in the telling of the story. Every narrative needs an audience; thus, all narratives are necessarily a co-construction of teller and audience, no matter how passive or active, how immediate or distant the audience. This could be by nodding, asking questions, guiding, and so forth. However, in these situations, there is still one primary teller, relatively speaking. These types of narratives are not typical and emerge in highly controlled circumstances. Emergent and naturalistic narratives always have multiple tellers/authors. Multiple people may recount an event together and co-author the narrative. Each teller contributes his/her own evaluation and stances that sometimes corroborate or contradict other tellers within an interaction. A collective narrative is the product of multiple tellers negotiating the authenticity and accuracy of their shared experience.

The second dimension is the *tellability* of a story, which roughly corresponds to the range of the audience. How many people hear or should hear the story? It is the difference between a private and public narrative. A story with high tellability is generally heard or could be heard by anybody, whereas a story with low tellability is intended for a restricted audience. Highly tellable narratives may interest many people and be widely understood by a cultural group. Grand narratives such as national holidays or institutional narratives such as corporations, schools, or community organizations are examples of highly tellable narratives. Narratives that have low tellability are more personal and a larger audience would need a lot of mediation to even understand what is transpiring. Think about a narrative with a lot of "inside jokes." They are funny to those within the circle and corny to those who might overhear. These narratives are contextually bound and cannot be easily told in new situations. A dinner-time story about a hard day at work may have high tellability in the context of the home where the family members understand. However, the same story on national television is less compelling and difficult to understand. Therefore, this narrative has low tellability. Tellability cannot be reduced to number of people hearing it, per se, but the degree to which others can participate without help as well as their level of interest. Understanding the underlying relationships and social context of the narrative is even more critical toward analyzing Type 2 narratives.

The third dimension, *embeddedness*, refers to how detached or embedded the narrative is to the context of the teller, the events being described, and the nature of the problem being addressed. Type 1 narratives, for example, were far removed from the situation in which the events occurred. These narratives were scripted and detached, whereby they were elicited outside the social conditions that produced it. An embedded narrative emerges spontaneously in the context of naturally unfolding events. The tellers are part of a continuous conversation, debate, and/or relative similar events. One way to tell whether a narrative is embedded or detached is to gauge whether it can be told in multiple situations. In other words, *"you don't have to be there."* A story that is highly performative is generally detached, while one that involves a lot of backtracking and stumbling to be told is probably embedded.

Type 1 narratives, as Labov demonstrated, have a singular evaluation by the speaker. Type 2 analysis allows for variation within evaluation, thereby describing multiple moral evaluations and ideological stances. These stances can be divergent, but they can also converge. Take, for example, a fable or the story of an angry complaint directed at a bad waitress. There is a singular moral lesson such as the virtue of hard work. On the other side of the continuum there may be conflicting accounts and alternative stances. Perhaps the waitress and the angry complainer had a prior relationship and conflict that was outside the customer–waitress interaction. These alternative stances may emerge from multiple tellers of the same events; however, it is possible that the same variation occurs within a single author who is trying to make sense of events using multiple lenses and sources of information. If one were recounting a recent break-up, there might be many different stances about right and wrong in the story. As the person tells the story there may not be a coherent moral evaluation, but it may be shifting and changing because the issue present is open and unresolved. Through narrative activity people work out their issues and make sense of events in relation to their ideals, values, and pragmatic considerations. It is a continuous process and, in some ways, all narratives remain open to revision and new insights since they are never "figured out" completely. In the midst of traumatic experiences, it is normal to feel unsettled about the meaning of events in our lives. We talk it through with trusted friends or distant strangers where the consequences of judgment can be suspended.

The final dimension is *linearity* and *temporality*, which refers to the way the events in a story are ordered. If a narrative is on the far left end of the continuum (1–2) then it is closed and linear in terms of time and the causal flow of events. If a narrative is on the far right of the continuum (4–5) then it is open and non-linear in terms of time and space. This would be like a movie that goes in and out of different time frames when it shows flashbacks or imaginations of the future. Thus, stories can follow a linear or circular logic temporally and spatially. Poetry is a genre that organizes narratives with a more circular logic.

In a Type 2 analysis, the goal is not to have a predictable linear plot line of beginning, middle, and end. The goal is to describe the narrative on the continuum of the five dimensions outlined above. Most narratives that are elicited for analysis, like Labov's, tend to yield narratives that settle on the far left of the continuum (1–2). There would be the assumption of one teller, high tellability, detached from the context of where the events were experienced, a singular moral evaluation following a linear chain of events.

To imagine a narrative on the right side of the continuum, imagine students discussing recent gang violence in their neighborhood. As the events are recounted, a narrative emerges. The tellers are trying to make sense of their shared experience. They argue and dispute about what occurred, assign fault and blame, and even worry about how they will be perceived through the narrative. As different tellers come in and out of the narrative, new information is emerging and the narrative is being re-written. The *tellability* fluctuates from high to low depending on the circle of tellers and hearers. The narrative is not quite ready for wide dissemination. On the other hand, the same set of events could have received some media attention and was the "talk of the town." The classroom version and the community version are in tension with one another. The version that emerged in the classroom is personal and embedded while the community one is detached. The presence of multiple tellers introduces different voices, multiple viewpoints, and ideological stances. Contestation of ideological frames should be expected and the narrative doesn't follow a predictable linear pattern, as there is a lot of back-and-forth, a tug-of-war of perspectives. It doesn't follow the X→Y→Z formulaic pattern.

The purpose of the Type 2 narrative analysis is to understand the social identities of the speakers and those narrated about and to. As we take moral stances by declaring situations right or wrong in narrative, we cling to or distance ourselves from other moral agents. Sometimes we align ourselves with certain groups of people and ideas showing *solidarity*. Other times we do the opposite (*resistance*). Either way, narratives provide valuable insight into the tacit and often hidden processes of our "common sense," a window into our lives and the lives of our students.

Funds of Knowledge and Narration

One of the significant uses of narrative analysis in education is to understand students' lives and to learn about their funds of knowledge. Narratives provide an opportunity for students to talk about who they are and how they understand their worlds. It is critical information for organizing learning and planning curriculum. There are two types of narratives that we will mention as they pertain to funds of knowledge inquiry: *grand narratives* and *personal narratives*.

Grand Narratives

Grand narratives are broader shared narratives that are generally scaled on national and global levels of shared understanding. These would be a type of discourse that is rooted in historical and institutional power relationships. For example, the grand narrative of "The Revolutionary War for American Independence" is one example. This historical grand narrative has an official version in the United States, an official version in Great Britain, and unofficial versions within both nations. As the saying goes, history is written by the victors, and most often grand narratives carry the moral evaluations and ideological stances of those who dominated, not the ones who were subjugated. Of course, the "unofficial" versions of the subjugated persist albeit in much more muffled tones. Take for example the battles over whether or not Native American and indigenous symbols should be used as mascots for sports teams. For the team's fan it is a symbol of affection, and for a number of Native Americans it is a symbol of humiliation, two conflicting narratives evoked by the same symbol (Figure 12.1).

FIGURE 12.1 Chief Osceola and Renegade, Mascot for Florida State University

Narratives about historical figures, holidays, creation accounts, and so forth are all grand narratives. They reveal how we see the world and what groups of people we align with. They have moral evaluations and ideological stances embedded within a widely accessible discourse. Contrastive analysis of grand narratives helps understand scaled-up, institutionalized, and national level differences. Students grow up learning many of these grand narratives and position their personal narratives within the grand narratives in alignment, opposition, or most likely somewhere in between. Many immigrant students are familiar with U.S. grand narratives due to the pervasive reach of Hollywood and mass media. Teachers can use these resources to engage in critical discussions about language, identity, and ideology.

Personal Narratives

Personal narratives are focused in the individual's emergent autobiographical narrative. They include interpersonal and institutional relationships of affinity and marginalization. As teachers we draw on an ethnographic approach to "describe, analyze, and interpret the culture of a group, over time, in terms of the group's shared beliefs, behaviors, and language" (Gay, Mills, & Airasian, 2006, p. 441). This type of analysis in the classroom requires longitudinal commitment to the students and their communities. It would require a close look into how students are constructing narratives within their homes and out-of-school lives. It would seek to find out why narratives are told the way they are, who tells them, when, and how. All of this information could help us understand how students make sense of their daily lives. Of relevance to schooling, it provides insight into the everyday tasks and problems where they use mathematical, scientific, and other literacy tools to develop problem-solving strategies. This knowledge can then be leveraged in the classroom to develop more conventional, school-based literacies. These narratives give us access to students' primary discourses which are then leveraged to develop specialized, secondary discourses.

There are a variety of methods to elicit narratives while always paying attention to the constant flow of emergent narratives. One way to gather these is through picture prompts, telling a personal story to get a story, or video ethnographies of the community. It is important to use a wide range of modalities for generating rich narratives. Non-classroom spaces can also be a valuable context for narrative analysis. While eliciting narratives, either orally or written, it is important to provide ample time and space.

Conclusion

We make sense of our lives through narratives. Narratives can be elicited through purposeful interviews or emergent in the natural flow of life. In this chapter, we looked at how we can use narrative analysis to learn about our students' lives as well as to learn about how our students make sense of the world. Our identities are constructed through narratives of mundane events that sometimes go astray. They emerge through dinner-time conversations, neighborhood encounters, national events, social media, and ceremonial practices. Nation-states and families organize relationships, identities, and ideologies through narrative. Disciplinary knowledge like mathematics, science, and history is constructed and transmitted through narrative. We can analyze all narratives through the continuum of *tellership*, *tellability*, *embeddedness*, *moral stance*, and *linearity*. We narrate our identities and therefore must understand them to understand our students. Therefore, it is important to understand how narratives are formed, what they mean, and how we can leverage them in our classrooms. In the next chapter we will look at other ways in which language relates to identity.

TEACHER CASE STUDIES

Janice: Holidays and Fables

All too often people associate "culture" with heroes, holidays and food. In other words, culture is reduced to only the most visible expressions. Janice, a Korean-American, in a preservice teaching program, noted that the typical American understanding of Korean culture did not really sit well with her. She knew that she was more than the kimchi and elaborate television dramas, but she struggled about how to explain that to her peers. She began to analyze one of the Korean fables she was taught growing up, *The frog's tears*. She noticed there were some major differences in the moral lessons compared to many fables taught to American children. She began to compare *The frog's tears* to *The ant and the grasshopper*, both of which can be found in the online content.

Janice noted that there were some similarities between the fables. Most significantly, they both had a moral lesson or a set of values they were teaching. Janice began to study the morality that was taught through these narratives. One of the common values was the emphasis on hard work. Both of these narratives emphasize hard work. However, whereas the *Ant and the grasshopper* exhibited individualism, the *Frog* taught children about filial piety and respecting elders. Janice reflected on her life growing up in a Korean-American household and how these two stories were taught to her and often provided some dissonance. Janice then thought about how, if she is only teaching fables well known to American students, that might conflict with the students' home values, morality, and knowledge.

She then turned to an example from her student teaching in a school made up of predominantly Mexican-Americans. She had originally associated the Day of the Dead with Halloween, because it was the closest familiar holiday. The festivals happen only days apart, and both seem to celebrate a breakdown between the natural and spiritual worlds. These two holidays can easily be confused because, as Janice pointed out, the symbolism looks on the surface very similar. They both had religious and spiritual connections and were picked up by the Catholic celebrations around All Souls' Day. However, the students challenged Janice that they were not the same. In fact, many of the Mexican-American students did trick-or-treat and a few days later celebrated with masks, sugar skulls, and Pan de Muerto. Janice began to study the underlying narratives to these popular holidays, and realized there were some major differences both in the origins and the teachings. She saw this as important because of the lessons taught through the holidays. The stories live on, and the students live through them.

Halloween began as a Celtic festival called Sahmain and was eventually incorporated as a Roman Catholic celebration of the spiritual realm's influence on the natural world. The Day of the Dead was also incorporated as a Roman Catholic religious holiday, but only as the Aztec Festival of Mictecacihuatl continued to be celebrated in some parts of Mexico. Whereas Halloween celebrated spirits in general, and on the days that followed, patron saints in particular, the Day of the Dead honored deceased family members and ancestors. In the U.S. version of Halloween, Janice noticed that it has become a major commercial holiday, though it still retains some of the spiritual elements, at least symbolically, if not in practice. The Day of the Dead, however, Janice noticed, seemed to be much more of a community and family event, at least for the students she worked with.

Like the fables, Janice saw how these narratives of holidays, history, heroes, and other "surface level" cultural features often may come into a conflicted space in classrooms with diverse populations. She saw that she needed to have a way to understand how to analyze the narratives and values of her students. The students live through these narratives. Whether it is hard work, individualism, or family honor, they are the narratives we live by. Often they compete with one another, and Janice began to reflect how she could help mediate students' learning by using these conflicting cultural narratives.

Rachel: The Man with the Scar

After learning about narratives, Rachel wanted to see how one of her students would construct a narrative. She hoped this would provide helpful insight into how her students understood the world. This provided a dual task of working on sequencing of events and writing conventions for one of her students in particular.

> I took several photographs that I knew would elicit a narrative or story. I had my 18 year old senior Oscar choose the picture which he felt he could write the most about. Out of 35 powerful photos we looked at online, he chose the very first one. This picture shows a Hutu man mutilated by the Hutu "Interahamwe" militia, who suspected him of sympathizing with the Tutsi rebels. I didn't tell him what the photograph was about, so that he could tell me his own narrative of what he sees. Although it is only the image of a man (a black and white photo) Oscar is able to write what he believes happened to this man and how this picture made him feel.

Rachel allowed Oscar to choose the photo, and rather than explaining to him what the picture showed, she allowed him to make meaning with it by constructing a narrative of what had happened to this man.

Rachel found that Oscar was able to look at the picture and develop a narrative about it. This was particularly helpful because it allowed Oscar, an EL, to tell the story in English. When Rachel followed up with him, he said:

> What I can see in this is picture is that the world has a lot injustice, I think it was during a war or a gang fight it looks like the guy maybe suffered torture at a very young age, a lot of physically and mentally abuse, I see sadness, pain. Maybe he lost his family, it seems that this happened in somewhere in Africa or maybe here, I would feel terrible if this happens to me or any member of my family or friends because is very scary to see what a human can do to others, and the type of damage we can cause in other peoples lives.

It is important to note that the narrative Oscar constructs, namely that the man suffered, was abused, and perhaps lost his family is connected to a larger theme of injustice. This embedding of the picture into a larger category of "injustice," Rachel found, was a moral stance which also indicated a stance against wars and gang fights. This was significant, because "we see that it scares [Oscar] to see what other human beings can do to others. He knows that by this man having all the scars on his face he was treated unfairly. Oscar believes it is wrong to commit such acts of violence and treat someone this way."

Rachel also noted that while the picture, for her, invoked the war in Africa between the Tutsi and Hutus (prior to reading the caption), Oscar seemed conflicted where such injustice could happen, it could have been in Africa or here (the United States). She found this to be an interesting point because she saw that she had associated the violence with Africa, but Oscar saw it as a wider human problem.

This activity gave Rachel the ability to see the world through Oscar's eyes. Oscar made sense of the picture by drawing on his own experiences and knowledge. Of course, it should also be noted that Rachel saw the potential dangers in such an activity. She recognized, later, that had Oscar been one of her other students, some refugees from Sudan, this picture may have had severe emotional implications. She saw how Oscar's reaction to it involved strong emotions and empathy, and recognized that if others had experienced something similar to the man in the photograph, it may have had severe implications she would not have been prepared to handle.

Additional Resources (multimedia)

http://www.bitstrips.com/create/comic/ [Create comic strip narratives]

http://www.squiglysplayhouse.com/WritingCorner/StoryBuilder/index.html [Story builder by entering in words]

http://www.aesopfables.com/ [Fables]

http://www.grimmfairytales.com/en/stories [Grimm's tales]

http://electionwatch.enm.bris.ac.uk/US-Elections-2012/index.html#[Political Narrative Pattern Tool (analyze election coverage)]

http://storybird.com/ [Create story books with pictures]

http://www.twitter.com/ [Analysis of social media, constructing narratives in real time: search, hash tags]

Google.com/trends [search online narrative of a topic]

topsy.com (e.g., search Tunisia, election terms, etc.)

Facebook's Timeline [Social Media & Emergent Narratives]

Appendix: Lisa's Home Visit Story

01 I had a more EMPATHY for them and understanding and it was a change in
02 them because they respected the fact that I went to SEE them and they were

03 just so humbled that I came! You know. They were just so glad. I could see
04 they had a better attitude.
05 Like that one girl I told you, you know. I didn't know what was wrong with
06 her she had like a chip on her shoulder and she wouldn't smile at me and
07 would give me a dirty look and stuff. And I read her journal, that her
08 aunt called her stupid. And so when I went to see her, her mom was there
09 and her grandmother and I said "don't."
10 Well I said to her, right in front of her mom and grandma, "Look, don't
11 listen to anything your aunt says you're not stupid you're beautiful,"
12 Because her mother was showing me she used to be a model in China, a China
13 model. So I said "don't listen to your aunt. You are a smart girl and you
14 can amount to something and it's going to be great and you're going to"
15 they live in a one room thing you know with a one bedroom, and so I said
16 "you're going to amount to something."
17 And now everyday she comes to my door and waves and says "hey Ms. G." and
18 she scored high. She did really well in her academics and it was a change
19 in a me and in them you know so I think its both is that OK?

13

LANGUAGE AND IDENTITY

Who We Are and How We Speak

LEARNING GOALS

1. Summarize current trends in identity research.
2. Understand the relationship between language and identity.
3. Use discourse analysis as a tool for identity inquiry in the classroom.
4. Understand the politics of language as it relates to identity formation.
5. Observe and analyze trends of linguistic discrimination.

KEY TERMS/IDEAS: code-switching, linguicism, Nature-identity, Institution-identity, Discourse-identity, Affinity-identity

Introduction

One of the most interesting areas of linguistic research is the connection between language and identity. Almost all areas of linguistics have to deal with this question at some level. Early linguistic theories made a connection between language and society, in that a language represented a cohesive people group most likely in a particular area. Later, during the cognitive revolution, identity would be construed as a natural phenomenon that often corresponded to language. Since language was "natural" and a part of our biological makeup, identity would also be reduced to biology, meaning genetically determined traits and attributes. Constructivist theories view language as essential to identity construction, yet still have a narrow view of the context of development. In sociocultural theories, language is a mediational tool through which identities are assumed and stances are taken to identify ourselves and others in socially organized activity systems.

We have examined various aspects of these ideas throughout this book already. For example, in Chapter 4 we discussed accent, in Chapters 9 and 10 we discussed learning and here we will focus on what we mean by "identity" from a sociocultural perspective. In Chapter 11 we examined how relationships mediated universal language functions, like terms of address, greetings, and honorifics. In Chapter 12, we focused on the role of narratives and identity. Thus, we can see that language and identity are tightly intertwined.

In this chapter we will review different approaches to understanding student identity as it relates to language and learning. First, we will look at how identities in learning contexts shift (i.e., between novice and expert). Then, we will look at four different analytic lenses of identity. Finally, we will look at classroom and pedagogical implications of identity research.

Learner Identity: Novice and Expert

One of the key assessment tools is to closely look at the shift in learner identities. It is very important to understand the term "identity" as it is used by cultural historical approaches to learning and development. In Chapter 11, we discussed CHAT as a situated theory of learning and development that affords special insights into examining learning not only from the top of the class ("the good student's perspective") but also from the margins and non-school spaces of life. When we view learner identities as continuously linked across time and space, we can provide better mediational tools to achieve our learning goals. The activities we design ought to generate shifts in learner identities, specifically between "novice" and "expert" in a particular activity. As teachers, we regularly talk about learners and learning using a wide range of metaphors handed down from the ivory towers. It is not surprising that we sometimes mix and match the metaphors without fully exploring the implications of each. We might not even realize that some of these metaphors may inadvertently cloud our vision about learners and learning.

One of the dominant metaphors of learning that persists in the public discourse regarding learning is Howard Gardner's notion of "learning styles." Often, the learning styles metaphor frames learners and learning in static terms. We have all heard people, or perhaps even ourselves, say things like, "I'm a kinesthetic learner," "I'm a visual learner," or "I'm an auditory learner." The problem that arises is that we typecast ourselves, others, and sometimes entire populations with these statements. Stereotypical statements such as "our people are kinesthetic" or that group is "more logical" or "we are not mathematical" can be and often are debilitating. More significantly, it is quite contrary to what research shows about learning and human development.

If there is one lesson we can take from a cultural historical view of human development and learner identities it is that human beings are never *one kind* of learner. The roles of learners are continuously shifting based on how they orient themselves within activity systems. Through social mediation, the roles of participants in an activity are constantly shifting through changes in mediation. The identity of the learner moves from one of novice to a more competent person in the moment-to-moment instances of activities. According to Razfar and Yang (2010):

> Through semiotic mediation, children participate, negotiate, and interact in cultural and social practices. They constantly act on and interact with the world through semiotic tools. As they engage in meaning-making, they become increasingly adept at using the tools, and eventually they achieve greater independence or "self-regulation" in using the tools in novel situations without assistance. This is different from dominant views of "transfer," in that the novel situations in which semiotic mediational tools are used have a continuous relationship with previous and historical contexts of use.
>
> (p. 115)

Funds of Knowledge and Expert Learner Identities

We have previously discussed the concept of funds of knowledge as a mediational tool for learning, especially in the contestation of third spaces (Chapter 10). We also highlighted the importance of making connections with students through the use of personal and cultural narratives (Chapter 12). Leveraging student knowledge and positioning them according to expert learner identities requires a deeper connection with their funds of knowledge. Entering a learner's home and their non-school expertise is not always about physically going to their house and interviewing and/or conducting observations of specific activities outside of school. While these actions are often necessary, they are not sufficient for building a relationship based on solidarity and sacrifice that enables one to gain profound insight into the nuances of meaning-making outside of school. How is this solidarity achieved? This is the question that is fundamental to our approach to language and learning. The intersections of language, learning, and learner identities converge in the relationships between peers, teachers, and the communities of each. These are the bonds of solidarity that are critical to learning and development. We will now examine the different dimensions of identity using a sociocultural and *sociocritical* framework (Gutiérrez, 2008; Razfar, 2011).

The NIDALS Approach to Identity

As teachers, we see students learn in-the-moment, during a unit, over a school year, and sometimes even beyond that. Our students might only see us in the context of the classroom. Recall the first time you saw your teacher in the supermarket and how strange that seemed. It was a moment when we realized the teacher is also a mother, a regular person. To move from a stereotypically static to a more dynamic and fluid perspective of social identities, we need to regularly challenge the boundaries that mark each identity. This is particularly true of the learner identity(s) that are ascribed to students within the classroom milieu. We see them shift between novices and experts, as explained above, and see learner identities change as they take on different roles within activities. When we analyze interactions on a microgenetic level we can see how students change and transition through their struggles to solve problems, make meaning, and use language. In these moments, it is critical, or should we say *sociocritical*, to have an articulated theory of identity that helps us reflect on more macro-level implications of what we are observing. Thus, what are the different types of discursive identities that we may look for?

We provide a broad spectrum and typology of how to begin answering the questions raised above drawing on Gee's (2000) model of situated and discursive identity. We call this model the *Natural, Institutional, Discursive, Affinity, Learner, and Solidarity (NIDALS)* approach to identity. This model is useful in that it combines sociocultural principles of learning with critical understandings of language. We have already discussed "Learner" (L) identities in the previous section and chapters. Now we will take into consideration four questions that have been discussed throughout this book and examine five more types of identities: identity as nature (N-identity); identity as institutional (I-identity); identity as discursive (D-identity); and finally, identity as affinity (A-identity), and solidarity (S-identity). In Figure 13.1, the five views of identity are summarized according to where their sources of power are derived from. When we talk about identity, especially the identity of our students, it is important to understand what we mean, and how those identities are ascribed by us, inscribed by peers, and described to the outside world (representation by researcher).

Natural, N-identities

Our primordial identities that are the basis of how we present ourselves to the world are grounded in nature, biology, and our physical characteristics. These are the traits we generally consider to be unchangeable, determined, and out of our control. Often we are viewed as simply a set of genes and environmental factors that are outside of our control. In schools and society, this becomes most noticeable when we talk about students as having "disorders," like Attention Deficit Hyperactivity Disorder (ADHD), autism, speech pathologies, or even linguistic deficits (Limited English Proficient, semi-lingual, a-lingual). These "disorders" are reduced to immutable biological irregularities.

Discussions and debates of nature vs. nurture at all levels are really ideological stances of N-identities. Leaving the epigenetic insights aside, if one is born a particular way, or if one has developed due to outside environmental factors, there virtually is no individual or collective agency in descriptions of N-identities. You are who you are, and "natural" traits/abilities are "normally" distributed according

Learning through Identities

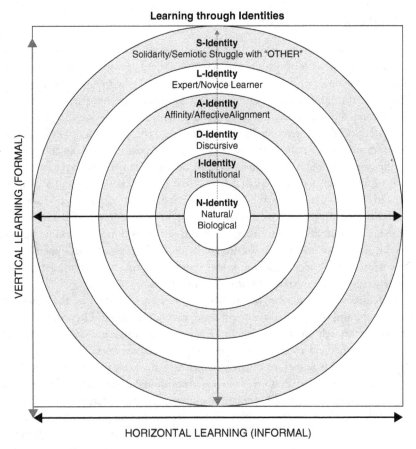

FIGURE 13.1 Learning through Identities

to a *Bell Curve*. Whether genetics, some higher power, or the environment shapes the human being, the focus here is on static categories of identity that are beyond one's control. In schools, many of the assumptions regarding ability, assessment, achievement, learning styles, learning disorders, and disabilities are couched in an N-identity frame. For example, we often talk about race, ethnicity, or gender as inherent traits borne out of biological functions. When it comes to race, terms such as Black, Brown, Red, White, and Yellow are grounded in eugenic ideologies of race that reduce it to phenotype and not a sociopolitical construction. Similarly, our ideas of gender, beauty, intelligence, and physical disabilities are also due to natural forces. A good classroom activity would be to have students, individually then in small groups, list and discuss the various N-identities that shape their life. It is also important to explore questions of agency and sociocultural factors as they impact their interpretations within society.

Institutional, I-identities

In our day-to-day life, many of the functions we perform and identities we display are situated within institutional activities. These activities even shape what seems like "natural" or common-sense identities. Naturally, one may be a male or female based on the presence of XX or XY chromosomes, but the dichotomous distinction is also shaped by institutional designations and practices. Segregated or integrated social arrangements based on gender are clear examples of how natural identities are socially constituted. Whether it is the separation of males and females in religious ceremonies, separate bathrooms, athletic teams, or work environment, institutional practices are mediated by explicit dichotomous ideologies of gender. This becomes more apparent when we consider the erasure or exclusion of "OTHER" identities such as transgender and/or hermaphrodite identities. This is further complicated when other N-identities such as skin complexion, height, weight, hair color mediate institutionalized norms, practices, and expectations. This is very visible in the entertainment industry. As an activity, consider gender norms across a wide variety of institutional contexts.

I-identities make us who we are because they are governed by the power of social and political legitimacy that precedes individual agency. They authorize or stigmatize through sanctioned labeling systems. Institutions and institutionalized practices go beyond formal businesses and/or social services. They are part of broader, cultural practices, or discourses that have the power to include based on alignment, or exclude based on resistance. Institutional practices of inclusion and exclusion, domination or subordination, equivalence and difference all mark status within socially organized activities based on ideological preferences. Thus, the students mentioned above as having ADHD or being LEP are marked with an innate biological "disorder" that is formally diagnosed and marks the student as different or OTHER than the norm. This difference is usually a lower status as well. Because these labels are institutionally authorized, a student who is said to have ADHD or be LEP in a school setting actually gains the I-identity of ADHD and LEP both within and beyond the institution. Unlike the N-identity, whether the student has the quality of ADHD/LEP or not, the declaration of that identity is what makes the student who he or she is within the cultural milieu of the school.

Race, ethnicity, and gender are all social constructs that have been institutionalized. There is a definition of who is and who is not African-American or Black. Every decade, the U.S. government elicits this type of information through census forms and research is based on these categories and figures. Throughout U.S. and Western European history, race has largely been treated as a biologically determined trait that was assumed to be natural. Furthermore, this notion has been reproduced and reified by institutionalized practices that give race its sociopolitical meaning. We can look, then, at a category such as "African-American" as both something that is natural, based on biological heritage, as well as an institutional term determined by government agencies. This can be seen in the "one-drop" rule that was used to enforce Jim Crow laws. Any biological heritage that was African-American or Black, despite appearance or phenotype, led to the institutional labeling of one as African-American/Black. Under this system of racial segregation, the "normative" race, which was White Anglo-Saxon, was not labeled. Only the "OTHER" or the different are labeled. Until the Civil Rights era of the 1960s, the United States largely based its official identification on assumed biological identities. It was an identification system that differentiated and ascribed unequal status on the basis of eugenic understandings of race. Critical race scholars argue that while the explicit demarcations of race have largely disappeared, the United States is far from a "COLOR BLIND" society in terms of institutionalized cultural practices. They primarily cite evidence from segregated housing practices, urban–suburban disparities, school achievement gaps, and disproportionate referrals of non-White students to special services, economic disparities, and incarceration rates.

In schools, these issues are complicated further by political considerations when it comes to ethnic/racial identification. Students in Chicago, born to Mexican parents, for example, are naturally defined as being "of Latin American descent." However, institutionally the identities become more complex and contested. This is further complicated by issues of immigration and documentation status. U.S. policy makers are regularly hotly debating the labels with each one carrying ideological valences: are they Americans? US citizens? Mexicans? Mexican-American? Hispanic? Latino/a? All of the labels and names have different institutional affiliations and ideological implications. In U.S. education this has become a critical issue, especially for the thousands of students who were either born in or immigrated to the United States early in life. If they or their parents are not "institutionally" recognized as U.S. citizens, how will they receive social services and education? The rhetoric surrounding policies like the *DREAM Act* (S. 1291, 2001) and immigration laws focus only on the "nature" of the person, identifying them as biologically un-American because of birthplace or parents' immigration status. Thus, in practice, the I-identity of a person is often tightly linked to the N-identity.

Discursive, D-identities

The third view of identity is the *discursive identity*. In this view, someone is who they are because of how they are positioned with others in talk and face-to-face interactions. Unlike the N-identity, where characteristics do not change, D-identities vary greatly. A student could be a "smart" student, but undoubtedly was not born this way, and their "smartness" depends on the situation. This could be thought of in the colloquial terms of "street smarts" vs. "book smarts." However, if rational people have a reason to treat the student as "smart," say because he or she is high performing on academic tasks, then the student will be discursively positioned as such.

From this perspective, a bank teller is not a bank teller because of the institutional affiliation alone, but precisely because people talk to him/her like a bank teller.

Likewise, students who are "ADHD" or "LEP" are not necessarily diagnosed formally, but they are positioned as such through discursive practices. For example, an LEP student may be seen as not initiating talk or not being recruited to solve a problem within a peer group.

Likewise, one is an African-American or Black because, in talk, he or she is recruited to that identity. This could occur through the use of *Black English* which includes White students, in the N-identity sense, who use Black English. Think of "White" rappers like *Eminem* who regularly draw on Black English features in his songs. From this perspective, identity is largely studied in social interactions. We would not be so concerned with genetics, nor would the institutions be the only way we understood identity. While these are important because they often play into how we respond to each other, largely those who study from a D-identity point of view look at how talk is structured to position others.

Affinity, A-identity

The fourth layer of identity analysis is the *affinity identity*. Affinity suggests an affective and/or ideological connection that binds the participants with common immediate goals, practices, and larger purposes. Affinity is found with the other people who engage in those same goals and practices. Our allegiance to the practices and experiences of affinity groups can be multifaceted and change over time. Affinity is generally developed on four, not necessarily hierarchical, levels: intrapersonal, interpersonal, institutional, and ideological alignments. Affinity is on the outer portion of the circles of identity because it draws on N-identity, I-identity, and D-identity. When alignment is achieved on all four levels, then we can say there is a powerful sense of *solidarity*. Through mutual sharing, engagement, and profound semiotic struggle to make sense of the "OTHER" we achieve intersubjectivity and ideological solidarity. One possible discursive manifestation of this process is the transformation from using pronouns of separation (I, you, and they) to using pronouns of inclusion ("we" and "us"). We, in a sense, choose whether or not we want to struggle and make the actual and symbolic sacrifices necessary to build relations of affinity that become connections of solidarity.

The student with ADHD or LEP may very well find affinity with OTHERS who share the same labels and experiences. This becomes a new affinity group: The ADHD or LEP students. In addition, both groups may develop solidarity with one another based on their common difference. One who is perhaps energetic and doesn't pay attention well in class may identify as "ADHD" or "LEP" though there is not natural or even institutional precedent to do so. Sometimes a person may inscribe themselves into these popularized deficit notions. We may loosely use such terms when we can't pay attention or are distracted. The affinity can come from how the student feels in a classroom, or from reading about ADHD or LEP, or simply by being unofficially associated with similar students. Many Latina/o students, while not officially labeled LEP, may share an affinity with other Latina/o LEP students because they share a common struggle and/ or sense of being different. This commitment to the identity makes it affinity that leads to solidarity of linguistic and cultural actions. Another way this is manifested is through commitments to the use of "non-standard," or "non-White, middle-class" varieties of English.

A-identities are somewhat tricky to understand because they are often contrary to the way we see identity in daily life. What it means to be African-American/ Black is to have a shared experience with and allegiance to a social practice. This means that one could have no phenotypical or stereotypical attributes of being an African-American/Black, nor does any institution validate him or her as an African-American/Black person. Further, even in most social interactions people do not respond to him or her as African-American/Black. However, in some way, he or she finds allegiance with social practices that African-Americans/Black are known to engage in. We could easily imagine this scenario with any of the A-identities (e.g., White-American, Latina/o, Asian). While engaged in those practices, and only while engaged, the A-identity can be invoked and displayed for others to see. With social media and virtual spaces, people can find affinities with groups in new ways. Since these mediums have the potential to obscure phenotypical attributes and privilege the symbolic, such cross-boundary interactions are more feasible. Since N-identities and I-identities can be more readily masked in virtual spaces, people can find affinity with new groups. Gender, race, and ethnicity, and religion in these spaces, can be viewed as an A-identity, joining in practices people have allegiance and access to.

Classroom Implications: Building Solidarity (S-identity)

In classrooms, we think about our students and ourselves all the time. Who they are and who we are. Who they are not and who we are not. We can now ask these questions through the models described above, not to make static judgments of identity, but to build solidarity for the purposes of learning and mutual development. If we are thinking about them with the NIDALS identity approach, then we consider the full context of our student's development. This is diametrically opposed to how our identities are typically constructed. The labels we give them, the names we call them, all of these have specific assumptions and values attached to them. We need to understand more, ourselves, the basis and implications of the labels we use to ascribe and describe OTHER people's children. We must critically unpack our assumptions and examine how we know what we know. It is more convenient to ascribe institutional identification of students, but at the same time we must consider the longitudinal impact of classifications. Through the centrality of their funds of knowledge, we recognize that students identify and position themselves differently, so as teachers we must continuously ask who are we, who are they, how do we know, and how do we become "we" and "us"? This requires struggle and sacrifice of self and time in order to engage these questions.

Language, Identity, and Indexing

Language plays an integral role in identity development and representation. In many communities where "minority" or *non-dominant* populations seem to clash with "majority" dominant populations there is a sense of *in-betweenness* for those who live in multiple, contentious linguistic and symbolic worlds (Sarroub, 2002). Language is tightly connected to ALL of our NIDALS identities through a process called *indexicalization*. We even find affinities with linguistic systems that arise from the experience of in-betweenness. W.E.B. Du Bois referred to this double bind as a dual consciousness that non-dominant people adopt in order to navigate and negotiate contested linguistic, cultural, and symbolic territories (Du Bois, 1994).

Through indexicality, we announce our identities and ideologies through the spoken and/or written word. When we answer a phone and hear someone speak on the other end, their sounds immediately cause us to ascribe various identities along the NIDALS spectrum. We probably make judgments about where they are from, are they "from here" or are they "like me?" One reason this happens is because language has an indexical relationship to identity. By indexical, we mean that the structure of language "points to" particular speakers of the language and their communities. When we hear someone from the Southern United States speak, we are "pointed to" the South. This also happens with race as language in the flesh has "skin colors" as well. If someone pronounces the word "ask" as "ax" we often judge the speaker to be African-American, at least linguistically speaking. The language form actually "stands in" for the perception of a language ideological viewpoint, which we will explore more fully in the next chapter.

There is an example from the Bible where the Gileadites and the Ephriamites were in a conflict. The Ephriamites were banned from crossing over a particular bridge. The Gileadites set up a code word to differentiate who can gain access to the bridge. When someone came to the bridge, the Gileadites would ask if the person was from Ephriam. If the person said no, then the Gileadites would tell them to say "Shibboleth." If the person pronounced it correctly they would be permitted to cross. If, however, they said "Sibboleth," like all Ephriamites would pronounce it, they would be stopped and thrown over the bridge. Some 42,000 Ephriamites were killed in this way. The different way of pronouncing "Shibboleth" "pointed to" or "indexed" Ephriamite identity. Now, the "Shibboleth" has become an icon of linguistic differentiation and boundary drawing.

This story, recorded over 3000 years ago, still echoes in the present context where certain language structures point to certain identities and have implications for access to social goods and services. While this may be seen on different levels (think back to the butterflies in Chapter 1, accents in Chapter 4, and other discourses in Chapter 10), it can clearly be seen in the context of American race discussions. As Wolfenstein (1993) says:

> Languages have skin colors. There are white nouns and verbs, white grammar and white syntax. In the absence of challenges to linguistic hegemony,

indeed language is white. If you don't speak white you will not be heard, just as when you don't look white you will not be seen.

(Wolfenstein, 1993, p. 331)

When a neutral, non-ideological, and non-critical perspective of language prevails (i.e., language is free from values, interests, and historical relations of power, etc.), then language becomes the "safe" and allowable public arena to mask or erase historical grievances, disparities, and the roots of educational equity. *Language ideologies* are the ways we view and use language structure to index larger sociopolitical and historical relations. This has been a powerful organizing theme throughout this book and in the next chapter will provide ways for educators to think about how language ideologies mediate their practices. One significant way is by examining our corrective practices, especially *other repair*.

Depending on how we use it, the act of correction can target various aspects of language such as word choice, grammar, situational appropriateness, or even ideological stances (Razfar, 2005). The following narrative is an example of one teacher becoming critically conscious of the intersection of race and language use, by reflecting on the practice of repair (Razfar, 2010):

"Eh, Ms. Nasir!" shouts David from across the classroom, "You finna' give us our ice cream party on Friday?" My students are promised a monthly party as a solution towards rewarding and promoting students who exhibit positive behaviour in the classroom. I turn towards David and respond, "You mean are we going to have our ice cream party on Friday?" It was a norm in my classroom to answer to my students in Standard English and to have them respond back using Standard English as a form of correction. Hence, I became alarmed when David challenged this norm by standing out of his chair, throwing his hands up in the air, and exclaiming, "Why you be always tryin' to make me into a white duu [dude]?!" My eye brows raised up perplexed, and my mouth dropped speechless and bewildered at his words. I wasn't always trying to make him be white. What did he even mean by this statement? Was he associating Standard English to being white? I'm an Asian-American, who speaks Standard English, yet I don't think I'm white, and David's skin colour is black, so how can he possibly think I would want him to be white or that I even had a choice in the matter? The question of race confused me, you can't change your skin colour, and so what does it even mean to be a white dude? To imply that I always do this made me reflect on my own everyday language practices in the classroom. What am I always doing to reinforce David's interpretation of whiteness? What bothered me the most out of his sentence was him phrasing that I'm making him into something that he is not: white. [e-mail received from teacher taking Linguistics for Teachers course, Spring 2009].

(Razfar, 2010, pp. 14–15)

In this example, the teacher became aware in the moment that her correction of the student's language actually had a much deeper connection than simply correcting a language form. Here, she realizes that language not only has "SKIN" but it also indexes powerful ideological stances and affinity identities. This narrative was a movement from a language ideology based on "flesh," to a language ideology based on "heart." "Language" as a construct is not, alone, comprehensive enough to understand the deep-rooted connections between language and identity. In New York, for example, Zentella (1997) studied the language use of a community, *el bloque*, of New York Puerto Ricans (NYPR or Nuyorican). Both Spanish and English were used in this community, which marked them as a community. It wasn't the Spanish alone, nor the ability to speak English, but rather the language practice of code switching, or *translanguaging* (García, 2009). In a chapter entitled "Hablamos los Dos, *We Speak Both*," Zentella records over a decade of language practices, which mark the people of *el bloque*. The *Nuyorican* community was an identity that required a unique blend of Spanish and English, used for different purposes, in different ways. Thus, the emphasis was not only on being bilingual, but "*doing* being bilingual" in a particular way. As opposed to much research on Spanish and English bilingualism in the United States, where one is a public language, and the other reserved for home, the NYPR community did not make a distinction of one being distancing or the other being more intimate. In fact, being NYPR depended on being able to co-author and co-interpret conversations that took place in one or more of several dialects including non-standard Puerto Rican Spanish, African-American English, Hispanicized English, Puerto Rican English, and New York City English. These different dialectal boundaries needed to be manipulated and crossed to engage in the NYPR community. Thus, language and identity are related not simply by being able to speak a certain way, but rather by being able to *do* language a certain way (Zentella, 1997).

As can be seen from these examples, the way we use language has a very particular relationship to all of our NIDALS identities and through idexicality they are invoked within interactions. This is another reminder that language is not an object in the outside world, which we can obtain; rather language is something we do through social practice. We use it to negotiate particular identities. We use it to navigate and negotiate borders and contested territories that are historically and ideologically shaped and, through our collective agency, *re-shaped*.

In-betweenness

People do not engage in a single, monolithic culture free from variation and diversity. Geertz (1973) explained that culture "denotes an historically transmitted pattern of meanings embodied in symbols, a system of inherited conceptions expressed symbolic forms by means of which [people] communicate, perpetuate, and develop their knowledge about attitudes toward life" (p. 89). Therefore, culture is not static, but rather is dynamic and changing. This leaves us always interacting in a complex social world in which we are *in-between,* as Sarroub (2002) describes it, adapting symbols to new contexts. It is from the margins of in-between spaces that we best understand the page of life. Sarroub used the term to understand how a group of Yemeni-American teenagers used a wide variety of texts and languages to pave new symbolic territory.

In this ethnographic study, Sarroub described how a group of Yemeni girls drew upon religious texts such as the *Qur'an* to delineate school practices into two categories: *haram* and *halal.* Haram actions are those that were explicitly deemed undesirable and "forbidden." These are analogous to the Old Testament commandments that follow the formula "Thou shall NOT . . ." All other actions were *halal,* or allowable. As Sarroub points out, this includes things like literacy and learning. The *haram and halal* classification is obviously more categorical and black and white. However, there is a whole range of actions that can be considered more in the gray area and subject to multiple perspectives. The range of actions within this area are generally classified as *mustahab* (that which is better) or *makru* (disliked, but technically allowed). These actions are less explicit edicts from the Quran or the recorded traditions of Prophet Muhammad. These are the perspectives of the girls within their cultural frame of references and their local interpretation of Islam. The girls appropriated these terms with their own purposes and goals, not using them necessarily in an academic or legal sense, instead using them to navigate their life-worlds, especially around issues of gender identity and modesty. Thus, as Sarroub points out, they were appropriating signs from their religious texts into the school context, even if they did not map on exactly.

Sarroub discussed another sort of text that mediated their life-worlds: the texts of music at parties. The Yemeni girls in her study participated in parties with other Yemeni girls and sometimes would remove their headscarves and loose-fitting dresses, donning the fashion of the dominant culture and styling their hair accordingly. They would dance and listen to music, which some classified as *haram* because of the explicit lyrics. In these spaces, the girls brought the dominant texts of secular music into Yemeni homes, though they would never allow the adults to find out about this. Other examples were given regarding wedding invitations, Arabic schools, and school literacy practices. These in-between practices resonate in the context of schooling and language use. People shift in and out of these contexts, seeking to make it in dominant society while maintaining non-dominant practices from the non-formal part of their lives. Students feel these in-between practices, and their sense of the whole, is shaped from this position.

English learners (ELs) in schools often come from communities with different values and different literacy and language practices from dominant society. Thus, when they come into school, to a different culture, they somehow fit in the in-between space, where symbols are adapted for the new context. This in-between space shouldn't be viewed as a marginal space, but rather, a space of creativity and innovation. Nuyorican and the Yemeni girls above are case studies of linguistic trailblazers. Sometimes these multiple literacy and identity practices are based on religious texts, as Sarroub demonstrated, or with other texts such as the celebration of holidays or sacred days and sacraments. In the lives of many students, religion plays a major role, and finds its way into the classroom. Around third or fourth grade, for example, Catholic students go through their first communion. This is usually accompanied by Catechism,[1] to prepare the students. In tight-knit communities, many students in a classroom may go through these experiences together, and it brings another text into the classroom. Students may very well be in-between conflicting narratives (e.g., about the creation or evolution of the world), moralities (e.g., as Sarroub demonstrated with *haram* and *halal*), languages (e.g., some uses of code switching or translanguaging), and so forth. Through these semiotic struggles, these students develop a double consciousness that allows them to successfully negotiate the tensions. This in-betweenness is yet another way students are identified in schools. The question becomes is in-betweenness constructed as an asset or a deficit by institutional actors? They are on the one hand "Americans," in the dominant, mainstream sense of the word because they engage in practices common to all Americans. Yet, they are simultaneously able to represent themselves in alternative ways and in novel situations. In educational settings, we should always assume that variation, diversity, heterogeneity is the rule for ALL of our students. Homogeneity and standard learning is actually an exception. This is a fundamental shift in how we see our students using the NIDALS model. We learn to center and foreground the "in-betweeness" of our students, especially those who are closer to the boundaries of various socially constructed identities.

Conclusion

In moving from N-identities to a position of Solidarity (S-identities), teachers must purposefully and consciously embark on a journey of learning about their students. This is necessary so that they can build learning environments that are grounded in students' funds of knowledge and the "in-between" epistemologies that they undoubtedly possess. This must be done with students from the dominant culture as well as those from the non-dominant cultures. As teachers, we need to understand that schools become a space in which symbols are appropriated from homes, communities, synagogues, churches, mosques and international spaces, as with those in the "borderlands." When we struggle with students to make sense of these borders and tensions, it will often lead them to saying, "She/he didn't have to do that." When we see our whole SELF in the OTHER then we are ready to teach and embark on a collective journey of mind, body, and heart. The following poem captures the essence of this chapter:

---

1. Catechism is a type of religious education that focuses on theology and religious practice.

The Secret of Solidarity

The sacrifice of self, seems a high price to pay
Only if the HEART is darkened in disarray
To Put the OTHER before the self, is the question to ask
To build SOLIDARITY, need to remove the mask
The mask that veils relational vision
And sow the seeds of envious division
So unmask the HEART with the trappings of FLESH
With service to OTHER, the HEARTS refresh
Don't crave the attention of self that's inherently blind
Push the OTHER to the front, and lead from behind
If rage overcomes you to strike with a fist
Take a deep breath and extend with your wrist
When you feel the need to speak down to the OTHER
Withhold your tongue and listen like a BR-OTHER
If you feel like standing up, to look down on your M-OTHER
Then kneel down on your knees, and propose like a father

TEACHER CASE STUDIES:

Enrique: "Feeling In-between"

Enrique entered his college class on Bilingualism in Society. He was a college sophomore but still had not declared his major. Currently he was taking education courses because he thought he might be able to help kids like him in the future. He was born in Mexico but was raised for most of his life in a large city in the Northern United States. His parents spoke mostly Spanish, but, for some reason, decided not to live in a predominantly Spanish-speaking community. They told him it was to give him a better life. Thus, as Enrique went to school, most of his classmates were White and spoke only English.

Enrique struggled in school. He had difficulty with assignments, like the other kids, but when he took the assignments home he got little help from his parents. Actually, his parents both worked long hours and rarely were home until late. Enrique did have a few friends, some even who spoke Spanish like he did, but for the most part, he just felt out of place.

On Sundays the family went to Catholic mass at Enrique's tia's (aunt's) church. She lived in a predominantly Mexican-American neighborhood and mass was always in Spanish. Actually, if Enrique's family was not at their own home, they were in this community. Enrique had several cousins, all of whom spoke Spanish with each other. Enrique also spoke Spanish with them, but it was a little difficult growing up because it seemed like he only used Spanish on special occasions or with his family. Most of the time he spoke English. He did not write Spanish either, since the opportunity never came up.

Now that Enrique was in college, he didn't really feel like he fit in with everyone. He didn't quite feel like he fit in with the "Hispanic group" either. Most of them had been much more recent immigrants, and they always spoke Spanish with each other, something he did not feel as comfortable with. He was starting to feel like he did not belong here, at college. Truth be told, he didn't know anywhere else he would feel more comfortable though.

In class one day, the professor asked the class to write the first thing that came to their minds about their "linguistic identity," a concept that had been a theme throughout the class. Enrique wrote one word: "in-between." The class was asked to volunteer to share, and many students seemed to have eloquent responses. Enrique was quiet, until the professor called on him, that is. Enrique hated to be called on in class, it made him uncomfortable. However, at least this time he could just read off of his paper. "I feel in-between." "In-between?" the professor asked. "Yes, in-between," Enrique said. "I feel neither English nor Spanish. With my family I speak Spanish. Everywhere else I speak English. When I am with family I want to speak English. When I am everywhere else I want to speak Spanish. I feel in-between." The professor thought about this and began to ask questions. Enrique didn't feel socialized into either community. He felt as if he existed in the middle, somewhere. Slowly a couple of other students spoke up too, they also felt like that described them. They were in the middle, somewhere in-between too.

Manuel: Friends and Linguicism

For a linguistics class in college, Maria was tasked with trying to find out how judgments were made on the way people speak. Being a Spanish speaker herself, she knew that sometimes if people picked up on her accent, people might think she was uneducated or a recent immigrant. In fact, she had been born and raised in the United States. She decided to interview one of her adult ESL students, who, unlike herself, had moved to the United States during his school years.

Early in 1989, Manuel received the shocking news that he was moving to Chicago with his mom. He attended elementary school where he was taught in English and received ESL instruction as well. Manuel had a negative experience because he felt like he was being dumped into the English language. He did not feel like he was in a comfortable environment. Luckily, he received a few hours of ESL instruction where he was taught math and reading on an individual basis. He remembers his ESL teacher as the only person that provided key moments in learning English for him. This teacher used Spanglish, which Manuel saw as a helpful tool. The teacher would say things like, "Go get the puerta" so students would make the connection that it meant "Abre la puerta."

Manuel then went on to high school, where during his freshman year, he was taught for half the day in Spanish and half the day in English. His English classes consisted of U.S. history, English, gym, and automotive mechanics. His Spanish classes consisted of Spanish, mathematics, world history, and biology. I thought it was ironic that he was taking Spanish when this was his native language and there were other languages being offered at school. He said his teacher placed him in Spanish without giving him any other option. Why shouldn't he have the opportunity to learn in the "World's languages" department too? Looking back, however, he thought this may have been the best decision since adding another language to his academic load would have been very difficult when he was still not fluent in English.

At this point Maria noted the assumption that Manuel should automatically be placed in the Spanish class. However, he wasn't given a choice like his peers. Of course, learning the formalized Spanish would be helpful, but she pondered why he wasn't able to choose for himself while the English speakers were.

Manuel's schedule of classes during his sophomore year of high school was pretty similar to his freshman year. Halfway through his sophomore year he finally felt a little more confident speaking English. He still felt like he needed to improve his reading and writing skills, however. His junior year of high school was another key moment in learning English. Aside from his general education courses he chose art and automotive mechanics as his electives. During his mechanics tests he remembers his teacher noticing that he could not express himself very well in writing when providing step-by-step instructions to his answers. He said this was especially difficult for him since he found a lot of the terminology in mechanics to be similar, which confused him. He is grateful to that teacher who, instead of giving him a failing grade on his tests, gave him a chance to prove his knowledge using an alternative method. The teacher would seek verbal answers from Manuel to explain his answers to him as he took down notes. Manuel felt a sense of relief when he was receiving this culturally sensitive instruction.

Unlike many ELs in high schools, Manuel actually felt like his teachers understood some of his language needs. Unfortunately, in many cases, even in mechanics classes, ELs are evaluated on language, not whether they can recount the step-by-step instructions, fix a car engine, or build a motor.

Senior year for Manuel was another key moment in learning English. He decided to take art as one of his electives. He says he did not have the most positive learning experience while expressing himself in English but got through it with the help of a classmate. In art students worked in groups where together they shared ideas as they collaborated on their group projects. At this point, Manuel was speaking English but could not keep up with his peers. When they went around to share their thoughts, Manuel tried very hard to express himself but everyone would look over at another bilingual student and ask, "OK, what is he saying?" The fact that Manuel's peers did not understand him despite his effort to express himself really depressed him, but he was thankful to the student that would take her time to translate for him.

Again, Maria noticed that in high school, even in art class, Manuel had difficulty communicating in English. This inhibited his experience in art class. Maria identified that sometimes students are left out because of their language. She identified this as similar to racialized and racist attitudes in society in general, but here it was specifically regarding language.

Overall, Manuel's experience in learning English was somewhat like being forcefully dumped into a new language. His steps to acquire his second language began with his non-voluntary immersion followed by summer camp and a girl who spoke English. About halfway through his freshman year he became interested in a girl who was from India. She became his girlfriend for a few weeks despite the fact that he was not fluent in English yet. His best friend was his translator and with his help he successfully took her out on a date to the movies. This was definitely a motivation for him to learn the new language. Finally, aside from all of his experiences with learning English, he says he mostly followed the curriculum, which helped him tremendously.

Today Manuel is still fluent in Spanish: speaking, reading, and writing it. Although, he feels that because of learning English it created a mix-up of languages, which caused him to not be able to express himself as well in either language. He works at an exclusive Golf Course and because of his Mexican accent he feels he is sometimes the target of linguicism. He has noticed that some people look at him differently but having experienced this throughout his high school years he remains strong and positive about any type of stereotypes. He is a confident individual that has strong oral, reading, and writing skills in his native language and is working on improving his English oral, reading, and writing skills everyday. He loves to be up-to-date with current events in his community and the world through reading the newspaper. At the same time he knows he is strengthening his skills in his second language.

As Maria pointed out here, Manuel was a "target" of linguicism. He was treated differently because of his language use. People identified him as inferior, incapable of making choices, doing mechanics, talking about art, and working. His language was tied so closely to his identity that is caused severe social consequences.

QUESTIONS/ACTIVITIES

1. Reflect on what it means to be a speaker of the language or languages you speak. What does speaking that language mean to you? Many of us rarely take the time to actually think about language and how it relates to our identity. Do you use "text-language"? Why or why not? What groups of people do you feel most comfortable speaking around? How about less comfortable? The goal of this exercise is to stop and reflect on our own language practices and what they mean about who we are.

2. Use the different views of identity to analyze your students. From a nature perspective, who are they? From a discursive perspective, in your class, who are they? From an affinity perspective, what groups are they a part of? How do you know? Finally, from an institutional perspective, who do institutions (and what institutions) say they are?

14

LANGUAGE IDEOLOGIES

LEARNING GOALS

1. Understand contexts of language change on a global level.
2. Understand contexts of language change on a local level.
3. Analyze language variation in local contexts.
4. Teach students to understand and analyze language change in their own community.
5. Study students' language use in formal and informal spaces.
6. Critically assess goals of bilingual programs.

KEY TERMS/IDEAS: language ideologies, repair, plurilingualism, multilingualism, bilingualism, diglossia, language death, language shift, pidgin, creole

Introduction

Over the course of this book, we have been looking at different levels of language. From the very smallest parts of language, the sounds (phonetics), we moved to how those sounds were organized (phonology). As we worked our way up the ladder, we studied morphosyntax, or the way words and sentences are built. Finally, we found ourselves looking at how language is meaningful through semantics and semiotics. In this, the concluding chapter, we conclude our journey from *phonology* to *ideology*. This is the fourth question of language analysis that we started with: the question of values, worldviews, and our ideas about the nature, function, and purpose of language. Language ideologies bring together the micro and macro dimensions of language. It is where form and function, practice and theory, FLESH and HEART coalesce into a single critical juncture of how language envelops our lives. According to Razfar (2012b), "Language ideologies makes an explicit connection between language use and the interests of the nation-state power structure, including educational policies advocating 'English-Only' or other 'standard' varieties" (p. 132). Furthermore, language ideologies help us understand the power relations between dialects and the standard language, language change and revitalization, as well as language death. In the United States, this is encapsulated by the status of African-American English. In this chapter we will also examine how corrective practices and repair can serve as an ideal context to facilitate teacher discussions about language. Thus, through discussion of repair and corrective practices, teachers can become more aware of their own language ideologies.

Over the last two decades, we have witnessed the rise of linguistic and curricular restrictivism in the United States (Razfar, 2012b). Most of the English learners are in the southwestern part of the United States with California having the highest number of ELs. National educational policies like No Child Left Behind (NCLB) and now Race to the Top have created a climate of accountability that favors uniformity over heterogeneity and frames variation as the outlier and not the rule when it comes to learning and development. These policies have not only not improved academic success for ELs and non-dominant populations, they have been disastrous for them, their teachers, and teacher education programs throughout the United States (Gandara & Contreras, 2009).

The demographic shifts, especially of the Latina/o population, throughout the United States, accompanied by the rise of anti-immigration, anti-bilingualism, and English-only movements, suggests a strong correlation between language policies and the discriminatory policies targeting Latina/o and other non-White populations. There is a tremendous disconnect between language research, policy, and practice. Most of these policies emphasize linguistic code and ignore the last three questions related to what language actually is: performance, semiotic, and ideology. It is as if when it comes to language, the earth is still flat. Why does language remain flat in these policy, curricular, and broader societal perspectives on the nature, function, and purpose of language? One way we can address this question is by assuming an ideological approach to language and literacy in schools.

Language Ideologies

If we argue that language is critical to learning and development then it follows that a restrictive language policy will impact learning within all domains. Ultimately, it will impact ALL learners. *Language ideologies* are beliefs about language that users articulate in order to provide the rationale for how they use language in particular situations. In addition, speakers often assume their ideas about language to be self-evident, natural, common sense, and they are loaded with moral and political interests (Irvine, 1989; Silverstein, 1996a). Most importantly, language ideologies are "not confined merely to ideas or beliefs, but rather is extended to include the very *language practices* through which our ideas or notions are enacted"

(Razfar, 2005; emphasis added). In English learner classrooms a typology of practices that one can look at to examine how language ideologies mediate learning and instruction is as follows:

1. Voicing (Iconization, Fractal Recursivity, Erasure) (Razfar, 2003)
2. Repair (Razfar, 2005)
3. Affective Alignment (Razfar, 2010)
4. Metadiscourse (Razfar & Leavitt, 2011)
5. Social Organization of Learning (Razfar & Rumenapp, 2011)
6. Student Challenges (Razfar, 2011)
7. Narrative and Teacher Beliefs (Razfar, 2012c)
8. Awareness (Razfar & Rumenapp, 2012)
9. Numeracy Practices (Razfar, 2012d).

In each of these practices, the question of what is the nature, function, and purpose of language and its relation to learning is generally addressed through the analysis of discourse. The answers to this question can be made explicit through the named practices. Some have argued that linguistic restrictive trends, like English-only, are equivalent to other exclusionary discourses, especially race (i.e., "Colored-only"). Given the inextricable link between language and racial identity, this argument has some traction; however, not all exclusionary discourses are equivalent ideologically and morally, at least that's not what our discursive practices indicate. Certainly, the nuances of such a conversation are worth exploring with educators and society at large. The main message and purpose of this book is to know how to foster critical conversations about language, learning, identity, and ideology. It is our view that the development of a critical consciousness of language is an essential professional responsibility, especially engaging in the *metadiscourse* of language with both non-dominant and dominant populations.

At the heart of language AND learning debates is the ideological tension between the polyglot standard and the monoglot standard (Silverstein, 1996b). The problem is not "standards" per se, it is what standard? When we consider the issues of identity, ideology, and language together, the struggle between dominant and non-dominant discourses and languages is really an issue of linguistic sovereignty. Imagine a language ideology based on the "Mom and Pop" model of language. It is the "Main Street" of basic economics, a "bottom up" approach. This model gives local communities greater authority, privileges variation, empowers more people with sovereignty, and fosters more symmetrical distribution of the modes of production and capital. However, prices will generally be higher, there is less regulation and quality control, and perhaps less security. The converse of a "Mom and Pop" model is a large corporate structure like WalMart. We will call this the "WalMart" approach to language and learning. We can imagine greater standardization, better economy of scale, efficiency, and lower prices for more. However, capital becomes concentrated in the hands of a few, there is asymmetrical distribution of power, greater regulation, and even exploitation of domestic and international labor markets. Regardless of which model we, as a society, choose, it is certain that the choice is an ethical, moral, and ideological one.

Formal and cognitive linguists, those who have taken a narrow and so-called "scientific" approach to language, tend to seek utilitarian or scientific reasons for their opposition to English-only and/or advocacy for bilingual education. The limitation of scientific approaches is that they can only describe a small portion of the nature, function, and purpose of language in human life. Therefore, language ideological debates cannot be limited to the scientific study of language. This will only produce the FLESH of language (questions 1 and 2). It must also include the aesthetic, the ethnographic, and the HEART of language: meaning and values which are beyond the five senses of science.

The "formalist/cognitive linguists" typically argue that multilingualism is good for the economy or bilinguals have "cognitive advantages" as compared to their "monolingual" peers. They might even remind us that immigrant populations "want to learn English" without ever addressing the linguistic and cultural responsibilities of the dominant population. The problem with these ideological maneuvers is that they are disingenuous in that they don't present a complete portrait of what language is, how it functions, and its centrality to our collective identity and ethical well-being. When the *Linguistic Society of America* (LSA) issued a statement in opposition to English-only legislation, they principally argued from a deficit view of immigrant populations that still reinforced the monoglot standard rather than advocate for a more principled stance which aligns more closely with the four questions of language. They did not assume the ethical imperative of moving the whole society toward a polyglot norm and an asset view of the linguistic and cultural repertoires of non-dominant populations. Michael Silverstein's response to the weak LSA resolution tells the story:

> Such wide-eyed innocence—perhaps coming from the referentialist/structuralist dogma—about what is really at stake for the groups concerned with language in relation to a culture of monoglot standardization embarrasses me and makes me realize that perhaps my high-school math teacher was right when he said that language is too important to be left to the linguists.
> (1996b, p. 301)

Language Change

In the last chapter, about the relationship between language and identity, we saw that language is deeply personal. Language also brings cohesion among social groups across generations. These are connections filled with hopes, dreams, ideals, and ideas about how to solve seemingly mundane and dramatic existential problems. Languages are rarely isolated, and even those that are relatively isolated are susceptible to change because human beings are dynamic. This is who we are as an inspired species. Languages are universally cultural tools used by groups of people to accomplish individual and collective, immediate and transcendent goals, needs, and relationships.

Languages change over time, but not because of time. They change because each individual speaker brings a distinctly unique subjectivity and transforms the voices that preceded him or her into their own. In some ways, this transformation is restrained by the inertia of convention, tradition, and history, but change eventually comes at a collective level. Each new word, each new sentence, each new story, each new attempt to make sense of ourselves and each other is a micro-step in the direction of greater collective intersubjectivity. An ideological approach to language allows us to appreciate these seemingly small yet grand changes in the journey of humanity. These changes begin at the phonological level with subtle shifts in pronunciation. These changes continue through the lexical level with the "borrowing" of words, or in some cases, the dying of words. In this chapter we will discuss some of the different ways in which languages may change on the broader macro-scale, and what the implications may be for us and our students.

Usually changes occur because one language comes into contact with another. This contact can be due to commerce, conflict, or even companionship. Sometimes this may result in changes of one language, but could eventually result in the replacing of one language by the other. Regardless, there is always a trace, no matter how discrete, even seemingly invisible. Sometimes languages change in their phonology, which is a little more difficult to explain by language contact alone. In English, some time around the 1400s and the 1700s, there was a major shift in English phonology, often called the "Great Vowel Shift." Many English words retain spellings from Old or Middle English, even though the vowels have shifted. One example would be the word "peak," which most likely would have been pronounced with a short "e" sound [ɛ] and later like the "ea" in "steak" before becoming the [I] sound. No one knows why this shift occurred, though there are theories from historical linguists. Another example would be the alleged Spanish king with a lisp, who, not wanting to be made fun of, required all Spaniards to say the "s" sound as a "th." Thus, to this day, according to the legend, all Spaniards speak with a lisp. Even if it wasn't overt force, he was the king after all and emulation is the greatest form of flattery!

Language Contact

Language contact happens when speakers of two languages come into frequent contact with each other. In many places in the world, several languages are spoken in the same region. Often, in these situations, people from one language will borrow words from the other. Borrowing can be due to either implicit or explicit forms of coercion. By the same token, borrowing could be the effect of deep-rooted efforts to establish solidarity and common understanding. We have to consider the ideological positioning of the inter-linguistic contact. For example, think about the dominant, Anglo-American forms of English. When English speakers invaded and colonized the Americas they were exposed to new produce, objects, and places for which they had no words. In situations like this, either existing English words would have to be used, a new word would have to be developed, or the "foreign" word adapted in some way. The most efficient and economical way to solve this dilemma would be to import the word from the "other's" language. So, in American English, there are many words and names that were originally used by various Native American and indigenous languages. For example, canoe, teepee, avocado, and chocolate are just a few. It is interesting to take this last one, chocolate, which originally came from Nahuatl, a language in Mexico, and see how other languages have borrowed it as well. In Hebrew, for example, it is שׁוקולד, pronounced "sho-ko-LAHD." And we thought chocolate was Swiss!

While much of language borrowing comes in friendly circumstances, other times it emerges through conflict and confrontation. In these conditions, policies are made to explicitly prevent loan words from coming into the language. This is how identity and ideology is protected through language policy. Hebrew, for example, once it was revitalized, after thousands of years out of common use, attempted to use ancient Hebrew words or words from other Semitic languages, languages similar to Hebrew, as much as possible, rather than borrow words from European languages. Even the use of Yiddish, which was a hybrid of Germanic and Semitic languages, was frowned upon. France is another example of a country that prefers its language to remain "pure" and to borrow as few words from other languages as possible. The French recently banned the use of the word *Hashtag*, the 2012 American Dialect Society's "Word of the Year." These examples show the mutual interdependence of "language" as a national entity and the nation-state superstructure that upholds it. Truly, as the old linguistic saying goes, the only difference between a "language" and a "dialect" is a language is a dialect with an army.

In addition to loan words, there is also a process by which *calques* are made. A calque is similar to a loan word in that it has been imported from a different language; however, unlike loan words, the calque is made up of words already present in the original language. Often calques are phrases or compound words. A common example would be "blue-blood" from the Spanish sangre azul. "Blue blood," or to be of noble ancestry, was not originally an English expression. It was taken from Spanish, but the words were translated to English.

Language Shift

Another type of language change is called *language shift*. This is when a group of people, over generations, begin to shift from primarily using one language to primarily using another. In the United States, both of these types of shifts have happened. Consider the first type, how English, the most widely spoken language in the United

States, became English. Despite the dominance of English, many other languages continued to be spoken in the Americas. Due to different sociopolitical reasons, however, many of these other languages ceased to be used by the majority of the speakers after living in the United States. For example, German immigrants ceased to use German in public during the world wars because of social repercussions. Thus, within one or two generations German immigrant families no longer spoke German. In less than a decade, the number of German speakers in the Midwestern part of the United States plummeted from 25% to 1%. Spanish-speaking cities throughout the Southwestern part of the United States, on the other hand, have maintained Spanish to a larger degree across generations and in some places it even functions as a *lingua franca*. In addition, hybrid forms such as *Spanglish* and *Chicano English* have also emerged.

In more pronounced ethnic enclaves similar language shifts have also occurred. For example, in "Chinatowns" throughout North America, Mandarin is supplanting Cantonese as the language of the community. What is the language ideological story here? After all there are more than two dialects of Chinese. The word "Mandarin" is not actually used by its speakers and is a strange word with no meaning, at least to Chinese speakers. The speakers of the official dialect in mainland China call it "Pu Tong Hua," which literally means "common or standard language." While some try to explain that the English word "MANDARIN" is a reference to the officials of the Qing Dynasty (Man Da Ren), this is an urban legend meant for foreign consumption. Cantonese refers to a dialect spoken in the Guangdong province and also in Hong Kong. Since most of the earliest contact with the West originated from this region, their dialect became known as "Cantonese." Now there is greater variation of immigrants from different parts of China into the United States, hence the language shift. Now there is a shift in our perception of the tremendous linguistic and cultural variation within mainland China.

Language Death

Language death occurs when a language ceases to be used in everyday practice. Occasionally a language may continue to be used for a specific purpose, as Latin is used for ceremonial purposes, but is not used for oral everyday communicative purposes. These would still be considered, usually, a "dead" or "extinct" language. The imagery invoked by "dead" and "extinct" draws attention to the fact that something living was lost. *The Hans Rausing Endangered Languages Project*, a major funding source for documenting endangered languages, states that "today, there are about 6,500 languages. Half of them are under threat of extinction within 50 to 100 years" (HRELP, 2012).

Concern or lack of concern regarding the death of languages comes from one's language ideological position. If we ascribe to a more sociocultural language ideology where language is synonymous with identity, history, and values as we saw in the last chapter, then we would approach the issue of language death with a greater sense of urgency. From this position, linguistic genocide becomes equivalent to physical genocide (Skutnabb-Kangas, 2008). The death of language is generally correlated to a deeper dysfunctional relationship between cultural groups. To lose a language is to lose an identity. While this does not mean that if the language dies, the people cease to exist at least in flesh, they do however suffer a more heart-wrenching death, the death of their collective memory and history.

If we subscribe to an autonomous language ideology, and language is reduced to questions 1 and 2, a random collection of physical sounds and algorithmic rules, then only WalMart languages shall remain in a Darwinian world where only the fittest languages survive and Mom and Pop languages die. We have tried to repeatedly show that language is more than just bits of information, it is identity and historically built epistemologies of how to solve relational, physical, and communal problems. This is what is lost when a language dies. To care or not to care is an ethical and philosophical question. A question whose answer reveals us, and our relationship to others. Do we see ourselves in the plight of others? Should we fight for the rights of oppressed ethnolinguistic communities? These are tough questions with conflicting points of interests. They are necessary questions though as we think of the implications for educating "other people's children" (Ballenger, 1998; Delpit, 2006).

Language Revitalization

Many people and groups of people have seen that the loss of languages is a loss of human culture, knowledge, and even humanity itself. Therefore, large grants, universities, and other organizations have sought to support reviving some of the languages that have died, or to protect those that are endangered. Usually this cannot be done without the movement of speakers of these languages at the grassroots.

Some of the major projects, which have been more or less successful over the years, have been Hebrew, Hawaiian, and Irish Gaelic. Hebrew, as mentioned before, had ceased to be spoken in common practice after the ancient Israelites were conquered by the Babylonians roughly some 600 years B.C. Many theories exist as to the prevalence of the use of Hebrew after this, though most claim that Aramaic took over as the *lingua franca* of the Israelites while in captivity. Sometime the Hebrew/Aramaic language changed due to contact with European languages, creating hybrid languages like Yiddish. Hebrew, however, was not regularly spoken on a large scale again until Jews began moving back to Palestine in the 19th and 20th Centuries. Then, the religious Hebrew began to be used for everyday talk and literary writing. With the establishment of the modern nation-state of Israel, the Hebrew revitalization efforts gained significant momentum and Hebrew once again became a "language" with national status and support. However, it is important to note that the language could only be revived in written form since there was a millennial break in the oral tradition. The communicative and cultural contexts of ancient Hebrew could not be reinvented in the modern context. Despite the break, we can see the powerful ethos and connection of Hebrew as a language to modern Jewish identity. Without such a connection, the revival of Hebrew, at any level, would be less likely.

Another recent, somewhat successful, language revitalization effort took place in the state of Hawaii to revive indigenous Hawaiian. After the United States colonized Hawaii in 1898, legislation was introduced that facilitated the erasure of the Hawaiian language from common usage. English-only policies established English as the primary medium of communication in official spaces such as schools and government. In the middle of the 20th Century, however, some people began to take note of the Hawaiian language's decline and initiated the first dictionary project. In the 1980s, immersion programs for students to learn Hawaiian were established. While the percentage of people in Hawaii speaking Hawaiian is minuscule, Hawaiian now does enjoy the status of an official language along with English. There are Hawaiian newspapers, radio stations, and school/university programs.

A third example of state-sponsored language revitalization is the Gaelic language in Ireland. For a time, there were relatively few speakers of Gaelic in Ireland, and there remain only a few places in Ireland where it is spoken as a first language. However, though a minority language, it is privileged as the first official language of Ireland, with English being second. While it is common practice to use English more frequently, even for government business, there are presently nearly five times as many Irish Gaelic speakers as there were in the early part of the 20th Century.

While the three examples above have enjoyed major nation-state support, this macro-support would have likely failed without the micro-level, grassroots participation. We might even argue that the state support followed populist demands and advocacy. The struggle against language death is organic and continuous as the cases of Hawaiian and Gaelic illustrate; they are not off the endangered list yet. Macro-level policies and language revitilization programs are necessary but not sufficient to prevent language death.

From Bilingual to Heteroglossia

Languages do not exist in a vacuum apart from other languages. Although there are attempts to build fortified physical and metaphorical walls of separation, ultimately human beings through agency make cracks and connect through the walls. Languages are markers of human relationships, so often they are in competition with one another. Sometimes there is conflict of interests and other times points of convergence. Political pluralism and language ideological pluralism are like identical twins. It is difficult to live with one and not the other. How do we sustain a culture with a polyglot standard and plurilingual reality? Each language has specific functions and purposes. Not surprisingly, where there is territorial overlap, there is contestation and when the functions are distinct there is harmonious coordination. Either way a polyglot society must be comfortable turning contestation into harmonious coordination all the time.

While the term bilingualism is used to describe individuals who speak two languages, the term *diglossia* speaks to the complex interactions and communal ways in which at least two languages are used. Diglossia focuses on the community, context, and contestations that emerge through the use of two languages. In diglossic communities, languages are ascribed different levels of status and the speakers are aware of these differentiated uses and the accompanying status markers. Many communities are not only diglossic but *heteroglossic* (Bakhtin, 1981, 1986), meaning multiple languages are used in the ways described above. Multiple languages are not separate within the individual, but exist as a continuous interrelated melody made by the speakers. It may appear to be voices of cacophony to outsiders with monolingual expectations. However, on the inside, speakers systematically arrange to give these voices linguistic cohesion. This cohesion is mediated through language ideologies that are polyglot, sociocultural, and ideological (Razfar & Rumenapp, 2011). While in multilingual situations the term plurilingual is becoming more in vogue, we believe heteroglossia not only captures the plurality of languages but also the contestation that inevitably arises from sometimes conflicting functions, goals, and divergent language ideologies.

Pidgins and Creoles

One of the most fascinating phenomena of language contact is when new languages emerge on the boundaries of discourses between groups of people who otherwise don't have a common language. These languages, also known as pidgins and creoles, arise as the need for communication between the ethnolinguistic groups increases. They develop through boundary objects that mediate cross-group relations. These reasons are often due to globalization and changing market relations. These languages may be referred to as "trade languages" because they originally are used for commercial purposes. Every language constitutes a type of social capital that has a currency in the marketplace of ideas as well as the marketplace of commercial exchanges. As languages that have benefited from high status, English or French come with an in-built economic power. For other groups to engage with this new economic force certain aspects of the commercial language must be used. This could be the lexicon and/or morphosyntactic features. In Tok Pisin, a pidgin in Papua New Guinea, for example, the words were primarily drawn from English, though the lexicon contains words from other languages as well, but the grammar doesn't have tense markers. The language serves only one major purpose, for inter-group communication regarding trade. Hawaiian Pidgin is another example and is widely used in the state of Hawaii for similar purposes.

Sometimes a pidgin is needed for more than just trade. If children begin to learn pidgins as a first language, the pidgin may develop into a *creole* so it can be used to meet many more needs. Currently there are several languages undergoing creolization in the world. Tok Pisin and Hawaiian Pidgin both have achieved creole status according to many linguists. This is evidenced, in part, by the translation of vast materials, including religious texts like the Bible, into the language. Tok Pisin is also one of the official languages of Papua New Guinea. The most important feature of these languages, however, is that some youth are growing up with the creole as the primary, and sometimes only, language. In Hawaii, this is bringing about an interesting sociolinguistic landscape. While the revitalization of Hawaiian is taking place, as mentioned above, many of the youth find more affinity to the creole than Hawaiian or English. Some educational programs have recently begun to recognize Hawaiian Pidgin (or Hawaiian Creole) as its own language, and therefore teach as though it is a bilingual context (which it is!). This, often, is to the dismay of older Hawaiians who still see it as only a pidgin, and often as a broken form of English, a colonial language. Thus, there are generational differences in language ideologies.

Dialects and Vernaculars: The Case of African-American English

Like all non-standard varieties, pidgins and creoles have sometimes been constructed through the prism of deficit and purist language ideologies. They are given pejorative status markers like "slang," "broken," or other types of degraded categories. Hawaiian Creole, for example, is sometimes called "bad English" rather than be recognized as a legitimate language. Thus far, we have attempted to expand the concept of "language" so as to not only mean national languages backed by nation-states (e.g., Arabic, Chinese, English, German, Spanish, etc.). Rather, we speak of "language" in a broader sense, a sign system that is used to communicate and accomplish situated goals.

Variations from the standard language are often called dialects, and we have already mentioned the old critical linguistic saying when it comes to the difference between a dialect and a language. However, the more conventional and neutral linguistic definition is "a variety of language defined by both geographical factors and social factors, such as class, religion, and ethnicity" (Tserdanelis & Wong, 2004, p. 521). Usually related dialects are all considered one language, but vary in significant ways, according to more structural linguistic criterion. They may have different phonology, morphology, and even syntax. Their speech styles, conventions, and sometimes orthographies may also be different. This definition is limited in that it ignores the semiotic, historical, and ideological differences. The same words have different meanings, sometimes even opposite, because of the etymological and ideological differences. Where and when the term gets used depends on the language ideologies of the speakers.

One of the best case studies of this issue within the United States is the story of African-American English or Black English. Even the name is a controversial topic. What's in name we may ask? Each naming invokes a different language ideological stance. When people refer to African American English (AAE) as a dialect, they are recognizing it as a variety of some version of Standard English. It is exclusively derived from English, but it falls short of being an independent, sovereign "language" in the strict sense of the word. After all, where is its army? Where is its official dictionary? AAE is often judged as sub-standard, or non-standard, when compared to its parent language, "standard" English. With this framing, what we call "standard American English" or "SAE" is the big brother or father of AAE, a patriarchal relationship. Like Hawaiian Creole, it is often viewed as a "broken" form of English.

AAE is generally defined as the language that is spoken by roughly 80% of African-Americans. There is, of course, much variation within AAE. AAE has also been called "African-American Vernacular English," or "Black English Vernacular," which underscores that it is the common speech, or vernacular, of English-speaking African-Americans. This, again, reinforces the idea that AAE is a derivative of Standard English, thus erasing its sovereign history.

These names and the issue of linguistic sovereignty have made the name of the AAE phenomenon a highly contested debate. In fact, not all linguists consider AAE a dialect of English (Morgan, 1993). Instead of being exclusively a derivative of an earlier version of Standard English, African-American English is a hybrid variety that combines multiple historical strands from Africa, the Americas, Asia, the Caribbean, and Western European worlds. It represents the nexus of broader historical struggles for identity that bring together the painful legacy of enslavement, the counter-narratives of resilience, and the emergence of new possibilities in the face of seemingly insurmountable odds. Thus, AAE developed as a creole during the slave trade. Similar to the pidgins we looked at above, English would have served as sort of a base for a pidgin so that the speakers of many different African languages could speak with each other and the slave traders. A creole developed into the full-fledged language that further split into AAE, Jamaican creoles, and Gullah (Tserdanelis & Wong, 2004).

From the transatlantic slave ships to the presidency of the United States, the African-American story is inextricably linked to the language. AAE is a highly racialized discourse that, when discussed, re-opens narratives of pain and guilt from seemingly distant places that we thought we had no role in. It is not just about one group of people but ALL those who have had contact with it from multiple positions of domination, subjugation, and solidarity. AAE is not just a local phenomenon but a global one as evidenced by its influence on hip-hop with its literacy implications (Alim, Ibrahim, & Pennycook, 2009). In addition to the historical and ideological issues, some challenge the dialect view on the basis of structure, form, and style.

The most interesting name for AAE that captures many of the issues outlined above is the term *Ebonics*. The term was originally coined in the early 1970s by the social psychologist Robert Williams. It was derived from the words "ebony" and "phonics" or "Black Sounds" in order to distinguish it from the emerging linguistic and popular definitions that aimed to frame it as a dialect of SAE. The name was popularized in 1996 as a result of the controversies surrounding the Oakland School Board's attempts to formalize recognition of Ebonics in an effort to give it equal status with other languages. This would allow districts with predominant AAE users to qualify for English learner support services. African-American Language (or Black Language) is another term used to identify AAE, and this is a declaration of complete autonomy from the legacy of SAE.

The status distinctions we ascribe to dialects and languages are a function of our tacit and explicit language ideologies. When comparing so-called dialects with their parent language(s), especially in terms of form, it is important to remember that one is not inherently better or worse, more or less grammatically correct. Yet, we hear these types of stances all the time. Structurally speaking, linguists have extensively described the distinct formal properties of SAE and AAE. The differences are not random, nor are they trivial. For example, in SAE verbs have different forms, but in AAE, the third person singular form is actually different. This seems to make more logical sense, as the SAE morphological addition of "-s" seems out of place.

It is not the structural difference that makes them superior dialects or inferior. The rationale of "better" or "worse" lies in the sociolinguistic and ideological field. Nothing inherently is better about saying or writing "He *wants* us to come to the park" rather than "He *want* us to come to the park." It is a systematic convention of language that is developed differently by SAE and AAE.

Repair: Building Language Ideological Consciousness

One of the practices that helps facilitate discussions about the nature, function, and purpose of language with teachers is the practice of *repair* and other forms of corrective feedback. In the last chapter, we presented a narrative from Ms. Nasir discussing her repair practices of African-American English (Razfar, 2010). Over the last decade, Razfar and colleagues have provided an ideological view of *repair* practices in order to better understand how language ideologies mediate instruction in English learner contexts (Razfar, 2003, 2005, 2010; Razfar & Leavitt, 2011; Razfar & Rumenapp, 2011). This work has spanned multiple ages (elementary and secondary) as well as disciplinary domains (language arts and mathematics). It has also been a prominent feature in teacher education courses. The work has moved from its early renditions that were more critically descriptive (Razfar, 2003, 2005) to more transformative and critical examinations of the context of repair and corrective feedback (Razfar, 2010).

In addition, Razfar and Leavitt (2011) have examined an activity called *Math Pathways and Pitfalls* (MPP) which was designed to foster mathematical problem solving through expanded discussion mediated by discussion stems that would encourage conceptual thinking. Of significance is how this activity explicitly reframed errors in a more positive and non-threatening way. Thus, the activity engendered a culture of risk-taking whereby errors or "Pitfalls" became normative and all learners could openly discuss errors in problem-solving strategy or language. The MPP activity provided a *metadiscourse*, a language about language that fostered metalinguistic awareness, enhanced metacognitive practices, and led to greater self-regulation for ELs and other non-dominant speakers. All practices that are indicative of learning through the zone of proximal development (Vygotsky, 1978). Finally, the students in this study were a heterogeneous group based on race, ethnicity, English learner status, gender, ability, and even non-EL students.

The discussion of what, where, when, and how teachers correct student language practices is one of the best indexes of how language ideologies are practiced. Other methods used to elicit language ideologies or language attitudes such as focus groups and/or interviews reveal how teachers reflect ABOUT language outside the natural context of instruction (e.g., Razfar, 2012b).

In the context of classroom discourse, we might see teachers engaged in repair practices that are not about meaning or even the use of "correct form," instead they are about regulating normative classroom interaction patterns and reinforcing the purist notion of a singular, correct English free from alternative variations (Razfar, 2005). Razfar (2005) provides a vivid example of a teacher posing a question about an author's age to which several students respond incorrectly. The teacher then proceeds to ask one student to answer the question correctly to which she responded, "This *ain't* a math class." The teacher then proceeded to pick out the word "ain't" and asked "what class is this?" and urged the student to speak English "in the correct way." This example is cited as a clear illustration that repair is not always about meaning but can be mediated by purist and assimilationist language ideologies.

Generally, discussions of repair and corrective practices can be very evocative and sometimes lead to feelings of guilt as Ms. Nasir's narrative illustrated. It may even lead to questions of whether one should correct, or not correct. Not surprisingly, this is typically how the questions have been framed in the broader second language acquisition (SLA) literature. It formed the basis of the *Whole Language* vs. *Phonics* debates discussed earlier in the book. In another study, Razfar (2010) argues that the question itself draws our attention to individual practices rather than considering the overall context and relational factors that mediate such practices. Through Ms. Martinez's practices over a year of language arts activities, he shows an alternative approach to doing repair with ELs (Razfar, 2010). Furthermore, he showed that establishing *confianza* with students required a range of practices and an ethnographic sense of who each student is. In this study, Ms. Martinez established solidarity with students in a number of ways in order to provide effective feedback. For example, she employed *terms of endearment* in Spanish to foster a homely classroom environment and engender affective solidarity, or *confianza*, with them. She redirected corrective feedback to peers and asked questions that led toward more conceptual thinking rather than simply providing the "correct" answer. Finally, with some students she spoke very directly about their writing in private ways. The case of Ms. Martinez, who by all measures was one of the best teachers in the school, confirms that correction, whether explicit or implicit, is more about the relationship one builds with students rather than the potential cognitive benefits or harm of isolated acts of repair.

In a course designed for pre-service teachers, we regularly ask teachers to read such work and critically examine their own repair and corrective practices. The discussions are often evocative, heated, and sometimes even lead to critical evaluations of the instructor. Both professor and student have to be prepared to share, take risks, in order to engage in authentic and critical discussions about language use. In one memorable exchange that lasted six weeks, a teacher noticed that an African-American student insisted on saying "We is" instead of the "correct" form of "We are." Other students had similar queries such as "aks" vs. "ask" or "finna" vs. "gonna" vs. "going to" and we even read about mathematical examples such as Eleanor Wilson Orr's "Twice as less" vs. "Twice as much." In each case, I (Aria) urged the student to find the reasons for such uses and asked, "How does this make sense?" The teacher, who resisted, continued to insist on the basis of a singular notion of correctness and the fact that "how are these kids going to get jobs?" While the appeal to utilitarian ideology is common, it is a convenient escape from grappling with the underlying issues of identity and ideology.

After weeks of struggle, this pre-service teacher got her answer when the African-American student explained why he says "we is": "*cuz 'we one'* ... "*we family*'." So, it turns out, he did make sense on a number of levels: structural and ideological. He is structurally correct because if he sees "we" as singular then the correct verb should be "is" based on agreement in number, a syntactic rule of SAE. There is also an ideological stance borne out of a collective ethos vs. rugged individualism. He even provided the collective noun "family" as an equivalent. This story was confirmation for us that discussions about language are more than cognitive, metalinguistic activities. They are moments that build solidarity and a sense of being "with them." It reminded us of the Buddhist term *mettā* referring to "an active interest in the other," which is the perfect metaphor to show that **mettā** discourse, instead of the usual "metadiscourse," encompasses the cognitive, affective, and solidarity functions of language.

Ode to Ms. C or Mr. G

> I said ain't
> You said isn't
> I said we is
> You said we are
> I said aks
> You said ask
> I said you trippin Ms. C
> You said "tripp-ing"
> I said "No!"
> Tripping is for the body
> But trippin's for the mind
> Trippin's for the soul

Don't worry Ms. C
It'll all make sense
If you ask me more
I am my language
Don't need fix'n anymore!
(Razfar, 2012e)

Conclusion: NOT "THE END"

We have journeyed together from phonology to ideology, from linguistic form to sociocultural function, and from the embodied perspectives of language and cognition to the inspirited perspectives of meaning and collaborative learning. Our goal throughout has been to provide the teachers and students in ALL of us with a small but significant tool that will facilitate and *mediate* an equivalent but not equal journey in teacher education courses and beyond. With this work, we hope to move beyond spaces of "cultural and linguistic sensitivity" and land in a destination of engaged struggle and ultimately solidarity: in words, deeds, and most importantly in HEART.

TEACHER CASE STUDIES

Tanavia: Growing up with AAE

Tanavia is a veteran teacher returning to get an endorsement to teach English learners. She has been teaching third grade in an urban school with a large Chinese-American population. As she was teaching her ELs, she began to reflect on her language learning experiences from high school, where she studied Spanish. She said it wasn't a good experience, though, because it never seemed like an authentic context. However, as she was reliving her Spanish learning experiences, attempting to identify with her students, she realized that she had gone through a very interesting language learning experience when she left for college.

Tanavia grew up in a predominantly African-American community in a large city. She did well academically and was well involved in the community and her school. She applied and was accepted to an Historically Black College (HBC). Her years at college were rigorous, and heavily concentrated on writing and spoken communication—she was in a teacher education program. Soon after graduation she began to work at a school that was primarily made up of White students.

As she reflected on these experiences, she noted:

> I've kind of struggled with different dialects, because growing up I think, just around the neighborhood, it was more Ebonics spoken and then when we were in school we had to speak Standard English. When I went away

to college, and I went to a historically black college, they spoke Standard English.

As a professional in the schools she worked in, she was also expected to speak what she identified as Standard English. However, when she returned home for visits, and eventually to live and work, she said, "Then I came back here, and it was almost like I started to offend the people back in the old community. They would say 'you don't need to talk to me like that.'"

Because she lived near her old community and worked in a predominantly Chinese-American school, she saw herself as having to switch the way she spoke in different communities:

> They don't want to hear me speak Standard English to them. In that environment it's like you have to switch, and sometimes when you switch between the two they kind of run together on you in different situations. So that's my struggle now because now that I'm back and I have to go from one community and then work or school. Then you have to switch it. You have to keep switching.

Like her Chinese-American students, she saw her own struggle as oscillating between two different language communities. The different languages could both be used, and indeed, both needed to be used in different contexts for different reasons. As she noted, sometimes they would "run together," another indication of language contact and plurilingualism. The rules needed to be negotiated. She needed to be able to interact in different spaces and with different people in different ways.

She saw her students in much the same way. They were switching between English in the classroom and Chinese at home, much like she did as a child. She knew that when they went to college they would speak English almost exclusively. Then she thought about the students coming home. What would their Chinese be like? Most of them wouldn't be able to read or write in Chinese, although most of them would be able to carry on some type of conversation. She began to ask herself, "How would those parents feel?" "Would their community be offended like mine was?"

She also noticed that during her time teaching at the school, speaking almost exclusively Standard English, and living with her old community, speaking almost exclusively AAE, she was forgetting some of her academic school talk. When she talks with friends in law school or recent graduates from Harvard, she said she struggled to keep up with the talk because:

> The fact that I teach third grade has really limited my vocabulary. I don't use it as much. Now that we started this Master's program I see how important it is, I've been trying to go back and grab pieces of it. Even the teachers who teach first and second grade don't use a lot of that vocabulary over the years, this is like year nine for me teaching third grade.

So, she was struggling to hold on to the academic talk she learned in college, and be able to speak the Standard English in school, all while she still needed to communicate with her family and community at home. This plurilingual situation is very similar to what many people encounter on a daily basis. They have to speak different languages in different situations.

Finally, Tanavia recalled recent encounters with her daughter. When she took her six-year-old daughter to visit some of the elders, her daughter noticed the way they spoke. Tanavia was a little unsure how to respond, though, because like the Chinese parents, she saw the Standard English as necessary for social advancement, but she also knew that, like Chinese, it was important to understand monolingual elders and keep the social relationships in the community:

> My daughter speaks more Standard English now than some adults I know. So it's just its weird because they say "Oh my goodness how proper!" She kind of notices certain things to and she starts to correct people and I tell her "No it's ok." Then she says "What? They didn't—" I'm like "that's ok." I start to speak it she notices it too and so depending on how I feel I don't speak it because I can't teach her something that's incorrect based on the feelings of someone else because my first obligation is to her. I want her to be able to succeed academically, even if it hurts the elders' feelings.

Tanavia had to consider the different relationships, status, and power of the languages she spoke and her daughter spoke. Interestingly, while she was able to manage the switching, and grew up switching, she had a sense of hope that her daughter would speak just "correct" or Standard English. She saw this as nearly the same as her students' parents, who all wanted their children to speak English "perfectly" and not necessarily Chinese.

Juan: Abuelita's Story

Juan was in a teacher education program, taking a class about bilingualism in society. For an assignment that included an interview with a bilingual person, Juan decided to interview his ailing grandmother, Abuelita. She had moved to the United States from Honduras after her husband died nearly 20 years ago to be with her children and grandchildren. She spoke very little English because she lived in a Spanish-speaking neighborhood and her family all spoke Spanish. Over the past five years, however, she began to show signs of Alzheimer's. Slowly, Juan noticed that she occasionally slipped into talking in another language. Juan knew it wasn't Spanish or English and so he began to ask questions about her childhood. He had never learned much about her childhood, but knew that she had grown up in the capital of Honduras, Tegucigalpa.

As Juan began to ask his family members about Abuelita, he learned that she actually had been taken as a young girl from a small village in the south of Honduras to the capital city. Since there would be more opportunities for her in the capital, her parents had sent her away, never to see her again. She had spoken an Indian language, *Lenca*, in the village. Once she had come to the capital, though, she was forced to speak only in Spanish, so as to appear "less Indian." She grew up, married, and had several children, all of whom moved to the United States.

Juan never knew these things about his grandmother, but decided to ask her. Because of her ailing health, and the Alzheimer's, she wasn't able to answer many questions, but did tell a story to Juan. She was, of course, young when the story happened, but recalled it very well, as it followed the death of her mother. One of her brothers, who had been away for work, driving a truck, returned to the village after hearing that his mother had passed away from a violent illness. After the funeral, the traditional *novena*, a prayer ritual for the departed soul. On the last day of this ritual, people often ate and drank. Abuelita's brothers both became intoxicated. An argument broke out and one brother hit the other with a machete. The other pulled a gun and shot at the other, hitting him in the arm. Abuelita rushed into the room shouting at them to stop, which they did. She bandaged up the wounds. Not too long after she was sent (though some family members contended that she was forcibly taken) to Tegucigalpa. Ending the story, however, Abuelita turned to Juan and said some words he could not understand. They were clearly from another language. Juan asked her what that meant, and she said "you know exactly what that means." She slowly drifted back off and Juan turned to his father and uncle who were in the room. Neither knew what she had meant, but they suggested it was probably *Lenca*.

Lenca is a language that is in danger of extinction. There are only a handful of speakers in Honduras and El Salvador, though nearly 140,000 people claim Lencan heritage in these countries (Lewis, 2009). So few people understand the language that Juan never did find out what his grandmother had said. It was an example of an endangered language, almost literally, going to the grave with its speakers. Abuelita had rarely used the language since she was young and was taken from her family. It is likely that she may not have spoken the language in decades, if ever since her young years. Yet the language was tied up with her identity, an identity that was covered up to obtain access to education and job opportunities. On her deathbed, and in her fragile state, with her memory degradation (possibly why she used the language in the first place, mistaking Juan for someone from her youth), the language surfaced. How long had she used that language to make meaning in the world? How long had it been a part of her identity she was conscious of?

Juan was so grateful to have had this experience with his grandmother. It was perhaps the last opportunity he would have to ever hear that language, and very few people in the world would ever have this chance. It reminded him of his heritage, a heritage that is fading. It is possible that in only a generation or two, the language would no longer exist, but at least Juan had the oral story of the language's existence.

REFERENCES

Agar, M. (1994). *Language shock: Understanding the culture of conversation* (2nd ed.). New York, NY: Perennial.

Alim, H.S., Ibrahim, A., & Pennycook, A. (Eds.). (2009). *Global linguistic flows: Hip hop cultures, youth identities, and the politics of language*. New York, NY: Routledge.

Ascher, M. (1991). *Ethnomathematics: A multicultural view of mathematical ideas*. Pacific Grove, CA: Brooks/Cole.

Austin, J.L. (1962). *How to do things with words* (2nd ed.). Oxford: Oxford University Press.

Baker, C. (2006). *Foundations of bilingual education and bilingualism*. Bristol, CT: Multilingual Matters.

Bakhtin, M.M. (1981). *The dialogic imagination: Four essays*. Austin: University of Texas Press.

Bakhtin, M.M. (1986). *Speech genres and other late essays*. Austin: University of Texas Press.

Ballenger, C. (1998). *Teaching other people's children: Literacy and learning in a bilingual classroom (practitioner inquiry series)*. New York, NY: Teachers College Press.

Bandler, R., & Grinder, J. (1979). *Frogs into princes: Neuro linguistic programming*. Moab, UT: Real People Press.

Bandura, A. (1986). *Social foundations of thought and action: A social cognitive theory*. Englewood Cliffs, NJ: Prentice Hall.

Bell, J. (2002). Narrative inquiry: More than just telling stories. *TESOL Quarterly, 36*(2), 207–213.

Berlin, B., & Kay, P. (1969). *Basic color terms: Their universality and evolution*. Berkeley, CA: University of California Press.

Bickford, J.A. (1998). *Tools for analyzing the world's languages: Morphology and syntax*. Dallas: Summer Institute of Linguistics.

Boers, F., & Demecheleer, M. (2001). Measuring the impact of cross-cultural differences on learners' comprehension of imageable idioms. *ELT Journal, 55*(3), 255–262.

Brown, R., & Gilman, A. (1960). The pronouns of power and solidarity. In T.A. Sebeok (Ed.), *Style in language* (pp. 253–276). Cambridge, MA: MIT Press.

Brumberger, E. (2003). The rhetoric of typography: The persona of typeface and text. *Technical Communication, 50*(2), 206–223.

Bruner, J. (1991). The narrative construction of reality. *Critical Inquiry, 18*(1), 1–21.

Bundgaard, P.F., & Stjernfelt, F. (Eds.). (2010). *Semiotics.* New York, NY: Routledge.

Chandler-Olcott, K., & Mahar, D. (2003). "Tech-savviness" meets multiliteracies: Exploring adolescence girl's technology-mediated literacy practices. *Reading Research Quarterly, 38*(3), 366–385.

Chesterton, G.K. (1908). *Orthodoxy.* New York, NY: Doubleday.

Chomsky, N. (1957). *Syntactic structures.* The Hague/Paris: Mouton.

Cole, M. (1996). *Cultural psychology.* Cambridge, MA: Belknap.

Crawford, J. (1995). *Bilingual education: History, politics, theory and practice* (rev. ed.). Los Angeles: Crane.

Cummins, J. (2000). *Language, power, and pedagogy: Bilingual children in the crossfire.* New York, NY: Multilingual Matters.

Cummins, J. (2008). BICS and CALP: Empirical and theoretical status of the distinction. In B. Street & N.H. Hornberger (Eds.), *Encyclopedia of language and education,* 2nd Edition, Volume 2: Literacy (pp. 71–83). New York, NY: Springer Science & Business Media LLC.

de la Zerda, N., & Hopper, R. (1979). Employment interviewers' reactions to Mexican American speech. *Communication Monographs, 46*(2), 126–134.

Delpit, L. (2006). *Other people's children: Cultural conflict in the classroom* (2nd ed.). New York, NY: The New Press.

Dewey, J. (1916). *Democracy and education: An introduction to the philosophy of education.* New York, NY: Macmillan Company.

Du Bois, J.W. (2007). The stance triangle. In Robert Englebretson (Ed.), *Stancetaking in discourse: Subjectivity, evaluation, interaction* (pp. 139–182). Amsterdam: Benjamins.

Du Bois, W.E.B. (1994). *The souls of black folk.* New York, NY: Gramercy Books.

Duranti, A. (1997). *Linguistic anthropology.* Cambridge, MA: Cambridge University Press.

Eisenbach, M., & Eisenbach, A. (2003). *phpSyntaxTree,* http://ironcreek.net/phpsyntaxtree/ (accessed September 24, 2012)

Ellis, R., Loewen, S., Erlam, R., Philp, J., Elder, C., & Reinders, H. (2009). *Implicit and explicit knowledge in second language learning, testing and teaching.* Tonawanda, NY: Multilingual Matters.

Engeström, Y. (1987). *Learning by expanding: An activity-theoretical approach to developmental research.* Helsinki: Orienta-Konsultit.

Engeström, Y. (1999). Activity theory and individual and social transformation. In Y. Engeström, R. Miettinen, & R.-L. Punamaki (Eds.), *Perspectives on activity theory* (pp. 19–39). New York, NY: Cambridge University Press.

Erikson, E.H. (1950). *Childhood and society.* New York, NY: Norton.

Errington, J.J. (1988). *Structure and style in Javanese.* Philadelphia, PA: University of Pennsylvania Press.

Everett, D.L. (2005). Cultural constraints on grammar and cognition in Pirahã: Another look at the design features of human language. *Current Anthropology, 46*(4), 621–646.

Everett, D.L. (2009). *Don't sleep, there are snakes: Life and language in the Amazon jungle.* New York, NY: Vintage.

Fairclough, N. (2003). *Analysing discourse: Textual analysis for social research.* New York, NY: Routledge.

Faulstich Orellana, M. (2009). *Translating childhoods: Immigrant youth, language, and culture.* New Brunswick, NJ: Rutgers University Press.

Foreign Policy (2005, October 14). The Prospect/FP top 100 intellectuals, http://www.foreignpolicy.com/articles/2005/10/13/the_prospectfp_top_100_public_intellectuals.

Frank, M.C., Everett, D.L., Fedorenko, E., & Gibson, E. (2008). Number as a cognitive technology: Evidence from Pirahã language and cognition. *Cognition, 108*(3), 819–824.

Freedberg D., & Gallese V. (2007). Motion, emotion and empathy in esthetic experience. *Trends in Cognitive Sciences, 11*(5), 197–203.

Gallese, V. (2006). Intentional attunement: A neurophysiological perspective on social cognition and its disruption in autism. *Brain Res. Cog. Brain Res., 1079*(1), 15–24.

Gandara, P., & Contreras, P. (2009). *The Latino educational crisis: The consequences of failed social policies.* Boston: Harvard University Press.

García, O. (2009). Education, multilingualism and translanguaging in the 21st century. In Ajit Mohanty, Minati Panda, Robert Phillipson, & Tove Skutnabb-Kangas (Eds.), *Multilingual education for social justice: Globalising the local* (pp. 128–145) New Delhi: Orient Blackswan (former Orient Longman).

Gardner, H. (2011). *Frames of mind, the theory of multiple intelligences* (3rd ed.). New York, NY: Basic Books.

Gay, L.R., Mills, G.E., & Airasian, P. (2006). *Educational research: Competencies for analysis and application* (8th ed.). Upper Saddle River, NJ: Prentice Hall.

Gee, J.P. (2000). Identity as an analytic lens for research in education. *Review of Research in Education, 25*, 99–125.

Gee, J.P. (2003). *What video games have to teach us about learning and literacy.* New York, NY: Palgrave Macmillan.

Gee, J.P. (2007). *What video games have to teach us about learning and literacy* (2nd ed.). New York, NY: Palgrave Macmillan.

Gee, J.P. (2008). *Social linguistics and literacies: Ideology in discourses* (3rd ed.). New York, NY: Routledge.

Geertz, C. (1973). *The interpretation of cultures: Selected essays.* New York, NY: Basic Books.

Goffman, E. (1974). *Frame analysis: An essay on the organization of experience.* London: Harper & Row.

Goody, J., & Watt, I. (1963). The consequences of literacy. *Comparative Studies in Society and History, 5*(3), 304–345.

Grosjean, F. (1989). Neurolinguists, beware! The bilingual is not two monolinguals in one person. *Brain and Language, 36*(1), 3–15.

Gumperz, J., & Hymes, D. (1972). Directions in sociolinguistics: *The Ethnography of Communication.* New York: Holt, Rinehart and Winston.

Gutiérrez, K. (2008). Developing a sociocritical literacy in the third space. *Reading Research Quarterly, 43*(2), 148–164.

Gutiérrez, K., Rymes, B., & Larson, J. (1995). Script, counterscript, and underlife in the classroom: James Brown versus Brown V. Board of Education. *Harvard Education Review, 65*(3), 445–471.

Hall, A. (2009, November). "I screamed, but there was nothing to hear": Man trapped in 23-year "coma" reveals horror of being unable to tell doctors he was conscious, http://www.dailymail.co.uk/news/article-1230092/Rom-Houben-Patient-trapped-23-year-coma-conscious-along.html.

Halliday, M.A.K. (1978). *Language as social semiotic: The social interpretation of language and meaning.* College Park, MD: University Park Press.

Halliday, M.A.K. (1993). Towards a language-based theory of learning. *Linguistics and Education, 5*(2), 93–116.

Halliday, M.A.K., & Hasan, R. (1976). *Cohesion in English.* London: Longman.

Halliday, M.A.K., & Hasan, R. (1985). *Language, context, and text: Aspects of language in a social-semiotic perspective.* Geelong, Victoria: Deakin University Press.

Hatano, G., & Wertsch, J.V. (2001). Sociocultural approaches to cognitive development: The constitutions of culture in mind. *Human Development, 44*(2/3), 77–83.

Hauk, O., Johnsrude, I., & Pulvermüller, F. (2004). Somatotopic representation of action words in human motor and premotor cortex. *Neuron, 41*(2), 301–307.

Heath, S.B. (1983). *Ways with words: Language, life, and work in communities and classrooms.* Cambridge, MA: Cambridge University Press.

Holm, J., & Michealis, S. (Eds.). (2008). *Contact languages.* New York, NY: Routledge.

Holquist, M. (1990). *Dialogism: Bakhtin and his world.* New York, NY: Routledge.

Howard, E.R., Christian, D., & Genesee, F. (2003). *The development of bilingualism and biliteracy from grade 3 to 5: A summary of findings from the CAL/CREDE study of two-way immersion education (Research Report 13).* Santa Cruz, CA and Washington, DC: Center for Research on Education, Diversity & Excellence.

HRELP (2012). *The Hans Rausing Endangered Languages Project, http://www.hrelp.org/* (accessed December 16, 2012).

Hymes, D. (1964). *Language in culture and society.* New York, NY: Harper & Row.

Hymes, D. (1972). Models of the interaction of language and social life. In J. Gumperz & D. Hymes (Eds.), *Directions in sociolinguistics: The ethnography of communication* (pp. 35–71). New York, NY: Holt, Rhinehart & Winston.

Irvine, J.T. (1989). When talk isn't cheap: Language and political economy. *American Ethnologist, 16*(2), 248–267.

Irvine, J. (1998). Ideologies of honorific language. In B.B. Schieffelin, K.A. Woolard, & P.V. Kroskrity (Eds.), *Language ideologies: Practice and theory* (pp. 51–67). New York, NY and Oxford: Oxford University Press.

Kay, P., & McDaniel, K. (1978). The linguistic significance of the meanings of basic color terms. *Language, 54*(3), 610–646.

Krashen, S. (1985). *The input hypothesis: Issues and implications.* New York, NY: Longman.

Krashen, S., & Terrell, T. (1983). *The natural approach: Language acquisition in the classroom.* Oxford: Pergamon.

Kremer-Sadlik, T. (2005). In J. Cohen, K.T. McAlister, K. Rolstad, & J. MacSwan (Eds.), To be or not to be bilingual: Autistic children from multilingual families. *ISB4: Proceedings of the 4th International Symposium on Bilingualism* (pp. 1225–1234). Somerville, MA: Cascadilla Press.

Kress, G. (1995). The social production of language: History and structures of domination. In P.H. Fries & M. Gregory (Eds.), *Discourse in society: Systemic functional perspectives. Meaning and choice in language: Studies for Michael Halliday* (pp. 115–140). Westport, CT: Ablex Publishing.

Kress, G. (2000). Design and transformation: New theories of meaning. In B. Cope & M. Kalantzis (Eds.), *Multiliteracies: Literacy learning and the design of social futures* (pp. 153–161). London: Routledge.

Kress, G. (2004). *Literacy in the new media age.* London: Routledge.

Labov, W. (1972). The transformation of experience in narrative syntax. In W. Labov, *Language in the inner city* (pp. 354–396). Philadelphia, PA: University of Pennsylvania.

LaFrance, J. (July, 2007). *Evaluation of CEMELA School 2007: University of Illinois at Chicago.* Tucson, AZ: LeCroy & Milligan Associates, Inc.

Lähteenmäki, M. (2004). Between relativism and absolutism: Towards an emergentist definition of meaning potential. In F. Bostad, C. Brandist, L.S. Evensen, & H.C. Faber (Eds.), *Bakhtinian perspectives on language and culture: Meaning in language, art and new media* (pp. 91–113). Houndmills: Palgrave Macmillan.

Lai, C.S.L., Fisher, S.E., Hurst, J.A., Vargha-Khadem, F., & Monaco, A.P. (2001). A forkhead-domain gene is mutated in a severe speech and language disorder. *Nature, 413*(6855), 519–523.

Lakoff, G., & Johnson, M. (1999). *Philosophy in the flesh, the embodied mind and its challenge to western thought.* New York, NY: Basic Books.

Lambert, W.E., & Tucker, G.R. (1972). *The bilingual education of children. The St. Lambert experiment.* Rowley, MA: Newbury House.

Lantolf, J.P., & Thorne, S.L. (2006). *Sociocultural theory and the genesis of second language development.* New York, NY: Oxford University Press.

Lau v. Nichols, 414 U.S. 563 (1974).

Lave, J. (1988). *Cognition in practice.* Cambridge, MA: Cambridge University Press.

Lawley, J., & Tompkins, P. (2001). *Metaphors in mind, transformation through symbolic modelling.* London: The Developing Company Press.

Levinson, S.C. (2000). Yélî Dnye and the theory of basic color terms. *Journal of Linguistic Anthropology, 10*(1), 3–55.

Lewis, H. (2011). *Baseball as a second language.* lulu.com.

Lewis, M.P. (Ed.) (2009). *Ethnologue: Languages of the world* (16th ed.). Dallas, TX: SIL International. Online version: http://www.ethnologue.com/.

Lindholm-Leary, K. (2001). *Dual language education.* Clevedon, England: Multilingual Matters.

Lipka, J., Wildfeuer, S., Wahlberg, N., George, M., & Ezran, D.R. (2001). Elastic geometry and storyknifing: A Yup'ik Eskimo example. *Teaching Children Mathematics, 7*(6), 337–343.

Luke, A. (1996). Text and discourse in education: An introduction to critical discourse analysis. In M.W. Apple (Ed.), *Review of Research in Education* (pp. 3–48). Washington, DC: Washington DC, AERA.

Mayo Clinic (2011). Positron emission tomography (PET) scan. *Mayo Clinic,* http://www.mayoclinic.com/health/pet-scan/MY00238 (accessed October 13, 2012).

McCafferty, S.G., Jacobs, G., & Iddings, D. (Eds.). (2006). *Cooperative learning and second language teaching.* Cambridge: Cambridge University Press.

Medearis, A.F. (1995). *Poppa's new pants.* New York: Holiday House.

MIT News (1992). *Chomsky is citation champ,* April 15, http://web.mit.edu/newsoffice/1992/citation--0415.html.

Moje, E. (2000). "To be part of the story": The literacy practices of gangsta adolescents. *Teachers College Record, 102*(3), 651–691.

Moll, L.C. (2005). Reflection and possibilities. In N. González, L. Moll, & C. Amanti (Eds.), *Funds of knowledge: Theorizing practices in households, communities and classrooms* (pp. 275–287). Mahwah, NJ: Erlbaum.

Moll, L.C., Amanti, C., Neff, D., & González, N. (1992). Funds of knowledge for teaching: Using a qualitative approach to connect homes and classrooms. *Theory into Practice, 31*(2), 132–141.

Moll, L.C., & Greenberg, J.B. (1990). Creating zones of possibilities: Combining social contexts for instruction. In L.C. Moll (Ed.), *Vygotsky and education: Instructional implications and applications of sociohistorical psychology* (pp. 319–348). New York, NY: Cambridge University Press.

Morgan, C. (1998). *Writing mathematically: The discourse of investigation.* London: Falmer.

Morgan, M. (1993). The Africanness of counterlanguage among Afro-Americans. In S. Mufwene (Ed.), *Africanisms in Afro-American language varieties* (pp. 423–435). Athens, GA: The University of Georgia Press.

My Fair Lady (1964). Warner Bros.

Noll, D.C. (2001). http://web.eecs.umich.edu/~dnoll/primer2.pdf.

Nystrand, M. (1997). *Open dialogue: Understanding the dynamics of language and learning in English classrooms*. New York, NY: Teachers College Press.

Ochs, E. (1986). Introduction. In B.B. Schieffelin & E. Ochs (Eds.), *Language socialization across cultures* (pp. 1–13). New York, NY: Cambridge University Press.

Ochs, E. (2004). Narrative lessons. In A. Duranti (Ed.), *A companion to linguistic anthropology* (pp. 269–289). Oxford: Blackwell.

Ochs, E., & Capps, L. (2001). *Living narrative: Creating lives in everyday storytelling*. Cambridge, MA: Harvard University Press.

Olson, D.R. (1991). Literacy as metalinguistic activity. In D.R. Olson & N. Torrance (Eds.), *Literacy and orality* (pp. 251–270). Cambridge, MA: Cambridge University Press.

Ong, W. (2002) *Orality and literacy: The technologizing of the word* (2nd ed.). New York, NY: Routledge.

Padilla, A.M., & Gonzalez, R. (2001). Academic performance of immigrant and U.S.-born Mexican heritage students: Effects of schooling in Mexico and bilingual/English language instruction. *American Educational Research Journal, 38*(3), 727–742.

Parmentier, R.J. (1994). *Signs in society: Studies in semiotic anthropology*. Bloomington, IN: Indiana University Press.

Pease-Alvarez, L., Samway, K.D., & Cifka-Herrera, C. (2010). Working within the system: Teachers of English learners negotiating a literacy instruction mandate. *Language Policy, 9*(4), 313–334.

Piaget, J. (1952). *The origins of intelligence in children* (M. Cook, Trans. 2nd ed.). New York, NY: International Universities Press. (Original work published 1936.)

Pimm, D. (1987). *Speaking mathematically*. New York, NY: Routledge.

Pimm, D. (1995). *Symbols and meanings in school mathematics*. New York, NY: Routledge.

Pinker, S. (1994). *The language instinct*. New York, NY: Harper Perennial Modern Classics.

Pirurvik Centre (2012). *Inuktitut Tusaalanga*, http://www.tusaalanga.ca/ (accessed September 27, 2012).

Pun of the Day (2011). www.punoftheday.com/cgi-bin/disppuns.pl?ord=S&cat=11&sub=1101&page=1 (accessed September 20, 2012).

Raposo, A., Moss, H.E., Stamatakis, E.A., & Tyler, L.K. (2009). Modulation of motor and premotor cortices by actions, action words and action sentences. *Neuropsychologia, 47*(2), 388–396.

Rauch, I., & Carr, G.F. (Eds.). (1994). *Semiotics around the world: Synthesis in diversity (Volume 1)*. Proceedings of the 5th Congress of International Association of Semiotic Studies. Berkeley, CA: University of California.

Razfar, A. (2003). Language ideologies in ELL contexts: Implications for Latinos and higher education. *Journal of Hispanic Higher Education, 2*(3), 241–268.

Razfar, A. (2005). Language ideologies in practice: Repair & classroom discourse. *Linguistics and Education, 16*(4), 404–424.

Razfar, A. (2010). Repair with *confianza*: Rethinking the context of feedback for English learners (ELs). *English Teaching: Practice and Critique, 9*(2), 11–31.

Razfar, A. (2011). Ideological challenges in classroom discourse: A sociocritical perspective of English learning in an urban school. *Critical Inquiry in Language Studies, 8*(4), 344–377.

Razfar, A. (2012a). Discoursing mathematically: Using discourse analysis to develop a sociocritical perspective of mathematics education. *The Mathematics Educator, 22*(1), 39–62.

Razfar, A. (2012b). Language ideologies and curriculum studies: An empirical approach to "worthwhile questions." *Journal of Curriculum Theorizing, 28*(1), 127–140.

Razfar, A. (2012c). Narrating beliefs: A language ideologies approach to teacher beliefs. *Anthropology of Education, 43*(1), 61–81.

Razfar, A. (2012d). ¡*Vamos a jugar* counters! Learning probability through bilingual discourse and play. *Bilingual Research Journal, 35*(1), 53–75.

Razfar, A. (2012e). *Talking repair: Metalinguistic awareness and the reframing of errors in life-long and life-wide language learning.* Invited presentation by the Graduate School of Education, University of California, Berkeley, March 2, 2012, Berkeley, CA.

Razfar, A. (2013). Dewey and Vygotsky: Incommensurability, intersections, and the empirical possibilities of metaphysical consciousness. *Human Development, 56*(2), 128–133.

Razfar, A., & Leavitt, D. (2011). Developing metadiscourse: Building mathematical discussions in an urban elementary classroom. *The Canadian Journal of Science, Mathematics and Technology Education, 11*(2), 180–197.

Razfar, A., Licón Khisty, L., & Chval, K. (2011). Re-mediating second language acquisition: A sociocultural perspective for language development. *Mind, Culture, and Activity, 18*(3), 195–215.

Razfar, A., & Rumenapp, J.C. (2011). Developmental context(s): Mediating learning through language ideologies. *Human Development, 54*(4), 241–269.

Razfar, A., & Rumenapp, J.C. (2012). Language ideologies in English learner classrooms: Critical reflections and the role of explicit awareness. Language Awareness, 21(4), 347–368.

Razfar, A., & Yang, E. (2010). Sociocultural theory and early literacy development: Hybrid language practices in the digital age. *Language Arts, 88*(2), 114–124.

Rogoff, B. (2003). *The cultural nature of human development.* New York, NY: Oxford University Press.

Runner, J. (2012). *Jennifer's language pages: Greetings in more than 2,400 languages,* http://users.elite.net/runner/jennifers/index.htm (accessed October 1, 2012).

Sampson, G. (2005). *The "language instinct" debate.* New York, NY: Continuum.

Sarroub, L.K. (2002). In-betweenness: Religion and conflicting visions of literacy. *Reading Research Quarterly, 37*(2), 130–148.

Saxe, S.B. (1988). Candy selling and math learning. *Educational Researcher, 17*(6), 14–21.

Schieffelin, B., & Ochs, E. (Eds.). (1986) *Language socialization across cultures.* Cambridge, MA: Cambridge University Press.

Scribner, S. (1997). Mind in action: A functional approach to thinking. In M. Cole, Y. Engstrom, & O. Vasquez (Eds.), *Mind, culture, and activity: Seminal papers from the Laboratory of Comparative Human Cognition* (pp. 354–368). Cambridge, MA: Cambridge University Press.

Scribner, S., & Cole, M. (1981). *The psychology of literacy.* Cambridge, MA: Cambridge University Press.

Searchinger, G., Chomsky, N., Newmeyer, F.J., Gleitman, L.R., Miller, G.A, Thomas, L., South Carolina Educational Television Network., Equinox Films Inc., & Ways of Knowing, Inc. (1995). *Discovering the human language: Colorless green ideas.* New York, NY: Ways of Knowing, Inc.

Searle, J. (1975). *Indirect speech acts.* In P. Cole and J. Morgan (Eds.), *Syntax and semantics,* vol. 3: *Speech acts* (pp. 59–82). New York, NY: Academic Press.

Sebba, M. (2012). *Spelling and society: The culture and politics of orthography around the world.* New York, NY: Cambridge University Press.

Selinker, L. (1972). Interlanguage. *International Review of Applied Linguistics, 10*(3), 209–241.

Sfard, A. (2002). Learning mathematics as developing a discourse. In R. Speiser, C. Maher, & C. Walter (Eds.), *Proceedings of 21st Conference of PME-NA* (pp. 23–44). Columbus, OH: Clearing House for Science, Mathematics, and Environmental Education.

Shanahan, T. (2005). *The National Reading Panel Report: Practical advice for teachers.* Naperville, IL: Learning Point Associates.

Shannon, S.M. (1995). The hegemony of English: A case study of one bilingual classroom as a site of resistance. *Linguistics and Education, 7*(3), 177–202.

Shillock, R.C., & Monaghan, P. (2003). An anatomical perspective on sublexical units: The influence of the split fovea, http://www.westminster.edu/staff/nak/courses/documents/WordsAnatomy.pdf (accessed October 15, 2012).

Silverstein, M. (1996a). Encountering language and languages of encounter in North American ethnohistory. *Journal of Linguistic Anthropology, 6*(2), 126–144.

Silverstein, M. (1996b). Monoglot "standard" in America: Standardization and metaphors of linguistic hegemony. In D. Brenneis & R. Macaulay (Eds.), *The matrix of language: Contemporary linguistic anthropology* (pp. 284–306). Boulder, CO: Westview Press.

Sinha, C. (2006). Epigenetics, semiotics, and the mysteries of the organism. *Biological Theory, 1*(2), 112–115.

Skinner, B.F. (1957). *Verbal behavior.* Acton, MA: Copley Publishing Group.

Skutnabb-Kangas, T. (2008). *Linguistic genocide in education – or worldwide diversity and human rights?* New Delhi: Orient Longman.

Smitherman, G. (1977). *Talkin' and testifyin': The language of Black America.* Boston, MA: Houghton Mifflin.

Spolsky, B. (1970). Navajo language maintenance: six year olds in 1969. *Language Sciences, 13*, 19–24.

Stephens, M. (1998). *The rise of the image the fall of the word.* New York, NY: Oxford University Press.

Street, B. (1985). *Literacy in theory and practice.* Cambridge, MA: Cambridge University Press.

Street, B. (2003). What's "new" in new literacy studies? Critical approaches to literacy in theory and practice. *Current Issues in Comparative Education, 5*(2), 77–91.

Stuart, M. (1999). Getting ready for reading: early phoneme awareness and phonics teaching improves reading and spelling in inner-city second language learners. *British Journal of Educational Psychology, 69*, 587–605.

The Office (2005–2012). NBC Universal.

Trumbo, D. (1939). *Johnny got his gun.* New York, NY: Citadel Press Books.

Tserdanelis, G., & Wong, W.Y.P. (2004) *Language files: Materials for an introduction to language and linguistics.* Columbus: Department of Linguistics, Ohio State University.

Valdés, G. (2001). Learning and not learning English: Latino students in American schools. New York, NY: Teachers College Press.

Vygotsky, L. (1978). *Mind in society: The development of higher psychological processes.* Cambridge, MA: Harvard University Press.

Vygotsky, L.S. (1987). *Thought and language* (A. Kozulin, Trans.). Cambridge, MA: Cambridge University Press.

Wells, G. (1993). Reevaluating the IRF sequence: A proposal for the articulation of theories of activity and discourse for the analysis of teaching and learning in the classroom. *Linguistics and Education, 5*(1), 1–37.

Wertsch, J.V. (1981). *The concept of activity in Soviet psychology.* Armonk, NY: M.E. Sharpe.

Wertsch, J.V. (1998). *Mind as action.* New York, NY: Oxford University Press.

Wertsch, J.V. (2008). From social interaction to higher psychological processes. *Human Development, 51*(1), 66–79.

Whorf, B.L. (1956). *Language, thought, and reality: Selected writings of Benjamin Lee Whorf.* J.B. Carroll (Ed.). Cambridge, MA: MIT Press.

Wolfenstein, E.V. (1993). *Psychoanalytic-Marxism: Groundwork*. New York, NY and London: The Guilford Press.

Wolfram, W. (1969). *A linguistic description of Detroit Negro speech*. Washington, DC: Center for Applied Linguistics.

Wortham, S. (2003). Accomplishing identity in participant-denoting discourse. Journal of Linguistic Anthropology, *13*(2), 189–210.

Yavuzer, G. (2012). Aphasia. In J.H. Stone & M. Blouin (Eds.), *International encyclopedia of rehabilitation*, http://cirrie.buffalo.edu/encyclopedia/en/article/9/ (accessed October 13, 2012).

Yi, B. (2009). Chinese classifiers and count nouns. *Journal of Cognitive Science, 10*(2), 209–225.

Zantella, A.C. (1997). *Growing up bilingual*. Malden, MA: Blackwell.

Zhao, B., Ondrich, J., & Yinger, J. (2006). Why do real estate brokers continue to discriminate? Evidence from the 2000 Housing Discrimination Study. *Journal of Urban Economics, 59*(3), 394–419.

INDEX